"In this eclectic collection of sho... Michael Casey brings surprise, challenge, comfort, and encourag... to the reader who wonders at the workings of God in everyday life. His usual sharp wit, profound insight into the very heart of the human condition and the scriptural text, along with his uncanny ability to make the quirkiest of connections with all manner of sources, make this work an apt companion to one who desires a word of wisdom as they journey through a year of seeking God."

—Carmel Posa, SGS
Co-editor of *Tjurunga: An Australasian Benedictine Review*

"*Balaam's Donkey* is the work of a creative genius. Who else but Michael Casey could take the leftovers of 50 years of homilies, and serve up a splendid meal? The table of contents is comprised of 366 words, giving us one word leading into a reflection for each day of the year. Who else but Michael Casey could take words such as 'and' or 'cold water' and let them lead us into a meaningful meditation for the day?

"As these words find an echo in your heart you begin to feel, more than see, the interconnectedness of the book. Casey calls it 'random ruminations' but I noticed after reading the meditation for the day and putting the book down, I felt better about the coming day. Hope and encouragement is the golden string binding these reflections together like the 'bundle of myrrh' so dear to the lover in the Song of Songs 1:13."

—Abbot Brendan Freeman
Mellifont Abbey, Ireland

"Casey's 'repurposed' homilies are the best fruit of *lectio divina*. Wherever you stick your thumb in, you pull out a spiritually wise and theologically thought-provoking plum. Engaging turns of phrase and energetic prose promote reflection that is both sweet and sustaining."

—Bonnie Thurston
Author of *Maverick Mark: The Untamed First Gospel*

"You ("God") set
your love on me . . ."
— Ps. 91 —
3rd Week Evening
Prayer on Thursday

Balaam's Donkey

Random Ruminations

For Every Day of the Year

Michael Casey, OCSO

LITURGICAL PRESS
Collegeville, Minnesota

www.litpress.org

Imprimi potest.
Abbot Steele Hartmann OCSO
Tarrawarra Abbey
April 11, 2018.

Cover design by Tara Wiese. Cover photo provided by the author. Used with permission.

Excerpts from the English translation of *The Roman Missal* © 2010, International Commission on English in the Liturgy Corporation (ICEL); excerpts from the English translation of *Rite of Baptism for Children* © 1969, ICEL. All rights reserved.

Philip Larkin, "Faith Healing" from *The Whitsun Weddings. Collected Poems* (Farrar Straus and Giroux, 2001). Copyright © Estate of Philip Larkin. Reprinted by permission of Faber and Faber, Ltd.

Helder Camara, "Put Your Ear to the Ground" from *The Desert Is Fertile.* © 1974 by Orbis Books. Reprinted by permission.

© 2019 by Michael Casey
Published by Liturgical Press, Collegeville, Minnesota. All rights reserved. No part of this book may be used or reproduced in any manner whatsoever, except brief quotations in reviews, without written permission of Liturgical Press, Saint John's Abbey, PO Box 7500, Collegeville, MN 56321-7500. Printed in the United States of America.

1   2   3   4   5   6   7   8   9

Library of Congress Control Number: 2018952991

ISBN 978-0-8146-8463-4   ISBN 978-0-8146-8488-7 (e-book)

Dedicated to those who
during the last half century
have had the magnanimity
to think up nice things to say
about these homilies.

"Then the LORD opened the mouth of the donkey."
Numbers 22:28

"God will not abandon any who wholeheartedly seek to know God's will in truth. In all things God shows them the way according to his will. For those who turn their heart to his will God enlightens a little child to speak his will."
Dorotheos of Gaza, *Instruction* 5, #68

Contents

Introduction

In this year leading up to the golden jubilee of my priestly ordination I have whimsically decided to relive some of the homilies I have preached during the last half century. They were delivered in different places around the world and to different kinds of congregations. Mercifully, some of them, especially those delivered during the 1970s, have gone the way of other hot air emissions. Nevertheless, evidence of many remained. Mostly I never wrote out a complete text but, after spending a week or more pondering the liturgical readings, simply jotted down a few points on a 3 × 5 inch card and used this as a blasting-off point for my words. Usually these sprang fairly directly from whatever space I was in at the time and drew their content from whatever happened to be occupying my mind. Afterward I filed the cards away and forgot about them. Until recently.

In tracing my own journey, it became clear to me that it might be useful to translate these outlines into brief reflections and make them available to those whose lives have been marred by the tragedy of not hearing me preach. This meant trying to decipher my handwriting, filling in the gaps, and working out the significance of topical allusions whose relevance is now unclear. Inevitably the refashioning of the previous texts has been seasoned by whatever is going on in my life at this moment; that adds another level of meaning. Above all, in the process of converting them into brief daily reflections, I have modified the language of past decades to meet contemporary expectations. I have reduced the content of the original homilies to about a third of their former length, pruning away much of what was specific to the original time and place of delivery. It is like taking the meat out of a sandwich and throwing away the rest. Sometimes the reflection summarizes the whole content of the original; in others, I have concentrated on one part and expanded it. As a result, the end product probably has a sharper focus and a bit less padding, although some suggestions of a broader horizon may have had to be clipped.

In decontextualizing the reflections, I have usually detached them from the biblical readings of the day, the feast being celebrated, and whatever events happened to be current at the time they were delivered. Just for fun I have retained a few local references. Each of these pieces has, therefore, three contexts. First there is the original liturgical context in which they were developed; the dates may give some indication of this. Then there is the 2017–2018 context in which I recast in the form of short reflections whatever I had retained of the original homily. The third context is that in which you are reading them—your context, with all its particularities. To my mind, this last is the most important of the three. In the intervening years people have sometimes asked me for a copy of my homilies. Habitually no copy existed. What I always said to them was, "What you hear is more important than what I say." The same holds true of these written pieces. Whatever echo you may hear in your own heart is much more significant than anything I have written. It is living and active and worth attention.

I have decided to present these reflections under the rubric of systematic randomness. I have picked out cards randomly, mixing up the years and the liturgical seasons of both the original and its later recycling. I have sorted them in alphabetical order according to the keyword that I habitually give to every homily and then assigned them to one day each for the course of a year. I choose randomness deliberately, as a ploy to help the reader think outside the liturgical box and so leave the making of life connections to the Holy Spirit. You will notice that the keywords are not always indicative of the content. Sometimes they were meant simply to trigger a train of thought or to act as some kind of counterpoint.

As I reread the various outlines and attempted to recast them into usable essays I have become aware that there are many themes that recur. This is not surprising since they were originally composed to respond to a limited sequence of liturgical readings and liturgical feasts. I suggest that you read the pieces one at a time; resist the temptation to binge. Take a moment after you have read the text to reflect on your own experience to see whether the reading has sparked any echo in your heart. You may find that prayer flows freely from a few moments of silence. Otherwise I have provided a formula of prayer, following standard liturgical models, that you may (or may not) find useful. The important point is that I see these essays as a starting point for your own reflections and not as the final expression of my own.

Do I practice what I preach? Of course not. Preaching is proclamation, not autobiography. But I have occasionally presumed on the reader's indulgence to include a few personal reminiscences that serve to illustrate a point. As usual, not all first-person statements are totally true; some are merely rhetorical flourishes. And, from time to time, whatever I happened to be reading while the homily was in process makes an appearance in the text.

Mostly it has been an interesting journey for me, and I hope that you, the reader, enjoy at least parts of this book. I have often thought that time spent listening to homilies should be deducted from that spent in purgatory, so maybe reading this collection will have the same benefit. I have eliminated the duds and the duplicates, as far as possible, but I recognize that some of the pieces are better than others. That's the price to be paid for trying to find 366 homilies that could survive a second airing. Despite the fact that my reflections stem from the same cycle of liturgical readings, regularly repeated, I have noticed a fair amount of variety in how a topic is approached. That is probably a good thing. I hope there are not too many repetitions, though it sometimes seems that I have been singing from the same few pages most of my life. Nor am I disturbed by the fact that there are a few examples of what may appear to be contradictions;

these are more likely different emphases. This is inevitable over a fifty-year period. Father Malachy Mara, one of our veterans and a dramatic preacher, used to claim that you were permitted one, and only one, heresy in each sermon. In that case, if there is heresy in any one of these reflections, you will probably find the opposite heresy in another. In this way, I hope, everything balances out in the end.

The eighth-century Palestinian monk Dorotheos of Gaza makes the point that God can use any channel to communicate a message—and this includes Balaam's donkey. I have always thought that the donkey-prophet is the perfect image for preachers of homilies, for they often unknowingly transmit a word that transcends their own competence and understanding. May that happen here!

Michael Casey
Monk of Tarrawarra Abbey
June 15, 2018

January 1   ✠   *Abask*

Today we are abask, not only in the brilliant light of high summer, but also in the warm glow of a newborn year. You will remember the question mooted at the birth of John the Baptist, "What will this child be?" The same wonderment attaches itself to every newborn infant. Each is complete, intelligent and unique, yet so little, so dependent, so vulnerable. Whatever potential the child has is all in the future.

All parents have a dream for their child, perhaps embedded in the name they give, but for the moment the urgent task is nurturance, bringing the unique gifts of the child to a high level of fulfillment. That task will continue for years, if not for decades: helping and encouraging the child to realize its destiny, to endure and overcome setbacks, to be a source of blessing for others.

We are the proud parents of a newborn year. We may not neglect it. We may not leave it to work out its own future. If we do nothing, then decline will set in and the year will die unfulfilled. We wonder what the future of this year will be, but our immediate task is to engage in positive nurturing to ensure favorable outcomes. This requires attention and intelligence, and some degree of self-forgetfulness.

I don't know whether others take New Year's resolutions seriously; I must admit I don't. But it would not be a bad idea to go beyond narcissistic goals of self-improvement to think creatively about what we or I could do in the immediate future to make the world and the church a better place. What could I be doing to enhance goodness and restrain evil? Probably not much, objectively speaking. But if I start small, I may well find momentum growing and something substantial resulting. Give it time to grow.

Abask in the joy of new birth, Mary, the mother of Jesus, kept pondering in her heart all that had happened: wondering, dreaming, hoping, but also nurturing. We too are to join her in this role

1

of doing what we can to build up the Body of Christ—both locally and universally—looking beyond our own advantage: wondering, dreaming, hoping, nurturing. (January 1, 2017.)

God of all ages, look upon your church at the beginning of this new year, and grant that the days ahead may be for us a time of growth in faith and hope and charity. May we work with greater zest to cooperate with the coming of your kingdom, redeeming the times and basking in the light of your love. We ask this through Christ our Lord. Amen.

January 2   ✠   *Abandonment*

Jean Pierre de Caussade, an eighteenth-century spiritual writer, is known for his emphasis on the role of abandonment in the spiritual life. By this he meant giving oneself into the hands of the God who can write straight on crooked lines, trusting in the planning of Divine Providence. Abandonment is not the same thing as resignation. It is not a lethal fatalism that withdraws from active involvement and allows one's natural optimism to plummet. Abandonment is a deliberate act of trust, giving greater priority to what we know by faith of God's benevolence in our regard over what appears to be a looming or present disaster.

It is probably true that the response to hard times is the best indicator of character. We are all happy when we win the lottery or meet an old friend. It is not difficult to find joy in such circumstances. But how do we respond when we are treated badly, or when we fall ill, or when trouble strikes our family? Theoretically we accept that bad things sometimes happen to good people, but in practice it is not so easy to deal positively with such situations. Remember what Friedrich Nietzsche wrote: "What does not kill you will make you stronger." Only the stoutest saplings survive the rigors of winter. They alone experience the surging energies of spring and the full flowering of summer. If we struggle too much against our difficulties, they may not accomplish in us the work they were intended to do.

The first component of genuine abandonment is humility. This involves the avowal that I do not always know what is good for me. I am certainly able to discern what is pleasant and what is painful at this moment, but I really do not have the capacity to know what is to my ultimate advantage. Especially, I might add, if I am not in the habit of stepping back and reflecting on past experience. For every door that seems to close, the possibility emerges of my going through a different door—and that may well open up for me a glorious and unanticipated future.

The second necessary component of abandonment is the willingness to express our pain to God in prayer. Abandonment is not simply stoic indifference. It is active rather than passive. It impels us to use our hardship as a springboard to project ourselves into the ambit of God. Just as human relations are often initiated or improved by our asking for help, so our prayer often becomes more heartfelt in times of trouble. We will often find that things are better between us and God if we allow ourselves quietly to relinquish control over our own lives and confidently place them in the hands of God. (August 5, 2013.)

Loving Father, give us the faith to see your providence at work in all that happens to us and around us. Give us the courage to respond boldly to the challenges we meet. Give us the wisdom to learn from our own difficulties the art of coming to the aid of others. We ask this in the name of Jesus our Lord. Amen.

January 3 ✠ *Abbreviation*

The Western fathers of the church loved to ponder a text from Isaiah, later quoted in the Epistle to the Romans, which, in the Latin translation, makes reference to "an abbreviated word." They saw in this little phrase a compendium of the theology of the incarnation. The Word becomes human; the fullness of divinity takes up residence in a body like ours. The eternal Word, in no way contained in space and time, undergoes self-emptying and accepts to be limited in time and place and culture, in the same way that we are.

When we think of the reality of Jesus' early life, we may be inclined to move away from the eloquent and imaginative speculations of preachers and prefer instead the Gospel of Mark. The evangelist makes the point that, in the eyes of his contemporaries at Nazareth, there was nothing special about Jesus. His life was ordinary, obscure and laborious, like theirs. Like ours. We know that his genealogy was not a litany of saints; he had his fair share of scoundrels lurking in the background. He could not be in two places at once, there were only twenty-four hours in his day, he had to navigate through a labyrinth of assets and liabilities just like us. Quite definitely he was not the gnostic savior of future centuries, an androgynous epiphany whose feet barely touched the ground.

The abbreviated Word demonstrates to us that those elements that we most want to excise from our biographies are not necessarily obstacles to the realization of God's plan in us. In our fantasies we may dream about being not only perfect in character but also endowed with all kinds of gifts and talents. And greatly loved. That is fantasy, not reality. Human life is necessarily abbreviated; we will come to the fullness of life only when, by God's gift, we reach that glorious day when God is all in all. Meanwhile we have to endure a very abbreviated form of human existence. But God doesn't seem to care. This is because God's attitude to us is based not on a momentary snapshot, but on the whole story of our life from beginning to end. Even though we pass through some pretty ugly patches, God still boasts about us, "I was able to bring safely home even someone in as bad a mess as this one." Abbreviated existence may seem like a problem to us; but it is not so for God. (December 28, 2008.)

Father, you so loved the world that you sent your only Son to be like us in all things but sin. Help us to accept and love our earthly reality, with all its limitations and failures, and to place all our confidence in your power to bring us to the

destiny for which you have fashioned us. We ask this through
Christ our Lord. Amen.

January 4 ⨯ **Abide**

The Greek verb *menein* appears very often in the Saint John's
gospel and epistles (about sixty-five times in all). Its usual meaning is simply to remain, to stay, to dwell, to persist. Yet, because
it assumes a more solemn note, perhaps it is better rendered as
"abide." In the Fourth Gospel it connotes an enduring relationship, such as what exists between Father, Son, and Holy Spirit.
Surprisingly it is also used to indicate the mutual presence of the
believer and God. Those who believe in Christ and follow him
enter into the life of God and abide there. They are no longer
casual visitors or even servants, but friends who receive from
Jesus all that he received from his Father. The branches derive
enduring life from the vine-stock; grace for grace; it is the source
of their vitality and fruitfulness.

There is a behavioral component to this theme. We are exhorted to abide, to remain constant, to be stable in our discipleship. We are to commit ourselves to the struggle of perseverance,
knowing that it is not enough to begin a journey; we have to
follow it through to the end. Sometimes remaining on the vine
is a happy experience, watching the new leaves spring forth and
the fruit slowly ripen. But sometimes we pass through winter,
when the branches are bare and the future seems bleak. During
such inevitable spells of dormancy, the act of abiding takes the
form of enduring, doggedness, patience. The land must quietly
lie fallow until the time for plowing and sowing arrives.

In particular, Christ calls us to abide in his love. This means
that we don't allow urgent and important concerns to cause us
to drift away from an awareness of God's love, made visible in
Christ. It means fidelity to the practice of prayer and *lectio divina*, despite pressing alternatives and inertia. We are not to pull
down the blinds and remain enclosed in hermetic self-sufficiency,

but to allow ourselves to be irradiated by divine love. If we receive love, we will return love, and we will have the capacity to share love. If we do not receive, nothing will follow.

Abiding in love is abiding in Christ's word. We easily lapse into forgetfulness, beset by anxieties, ambitions, enthusiasms, hobbies. We are called to remember. To make a positive, proactive effort to give the words of Jesus a home in our thoughts, both to influence our choices and to solace our troubles.

Our prayer must be, in the words of the Emmaus disciples, "Abide with us, Lord, for it is evening, and the day is nearly done." (May 17, 2009.)

Lord Jesus Christ, you are the source and sustainer of our life. Help us to open ourselves fully to your gifts and give us the courage to remain steadfast in times of temptation and trial. For you are our Lord for ever and ever. Amen.

January 5 ✠ *Abomination*

One of the least quoted verses in the Gospel tradition is Luke 16:15: "That which is highly esteemed by human beings is an abomination in the sight of God." It was spoken by Jesus to the Pharisees in a particular situation, but its gnomic formulation makes it suitable as a general principle. Sometimes what people esteem and pursue is in opposition to what God intends. The divergence begins with the human will, not with God.

The word *bdelugma*, used for "abomination," is sometimes used to indicate idols. Idolatry, in the literal sense, is not a problem for most of us. But Saint Paul understands avarice as its equivalent. "Money is the root of all evil," and those who set its acquisition as their highest goal are, in his mind, idolaters.

The consumerist society encourages unprincipled ameliorism; we are always trying to make what we have into something bigger, better, flashier. And every day wants disguised as needs cry out for our attention: money, things, food, sex, status, reputation, knowledge, security, revenge. The list could go on forever. There is always something that we don't have that we want. And what we want we sometimes pursue with single-minded unconcern for the price that we or others have to pay.

Jesus places before us a stark moral choice: God or mammon. We cannot serve both. The key word is *serve*; we are not to let material benefits enslave us. We cannot do without all these things, but we have to use them in a way that does not distort our outlook on life or our attitudes to things of permanent value. We are not gymnosophists—philosophers who renounce everything and walk about naked—it is far too cold for that. We have to make use of material things; we have even to make friends with them, as Jesus says. But we don't want to become addicted to endless acquisition. Like the ancient Israelites on the point of the exodus, we are admonished to "pillage the Egyptians." We are to take from our technocratic world all that can serve our fundamental purpose, but insulate ourselves against becoming its slaves. (September 22, 2013.)

> *Creator God, all that you have made is good, and all creation proclaims your glory. Help us to coexist with the things of this world in a way which is of mutual benefit, so that every creature, each with its own voice, may sing your praise forever. We ask this through Christ our Lord. Amen.*

January 6　✠　*Absence*

Sometimes the best evidence is the absence of evidence. One of the skills of G. K. Chesterton's Father Brown was an ability to look at what was not there, which was sometimes more eloquent that what was. The fact that the dog did not bark is an important component in the solution of the crime.

At Easter it is the emptiness of the tomb that is most striking. The angels could be delusions, but you can't fake nothing. Nothing has nothing to offer the senses, but it shouts loudly to faith. The beloved disciple looked in, saw nothing, and believed.

So we are talking about an absence or emptiness that contains more meaning than a presence. This meaningfulness seems hidden because it is not accessible via the senses and, therefore, cannot be part of our normal rational processes. The chief priests were puzzled and perturbed by the emptiness of the tomb; to them it was absurd, a surd with no meaning. They had no understanding. Their response was action that was both frantic and ineffectual.

How do we access the hidden meaning of what seems to be absurd? The answer is faith. Faith is not darkness, as some seem to assert. Faith is a superior form of experience and illumination. It allows us to be impacted by realities which have no audible or visible footprint in the world of space and time. The fact that faith is not a part of ordinary experience is a pointer to its relative superiority, not to its unreality. Faith is a means of penetrating the fog that results from the interplay of conflicting data. You can argue a case about almost anything by cherry-picking the evidence. As a result, we become distrustful of our capacity to discern the truth and prefer to live in a maelstrom of unsubstantiated possibilities and probabilities. We are used to not being certain about anything. Faith gives us certainty by endowing us with a superior vision.

Sometimes in our own life nothing makes sense. Sometimes, at least, the nonsense is a call to go deeper, to find meaning beneath and beyond the fatuous interplay of events. In fact, this strident absence may be an important signal for us to look elsewhere. It is time to stir up the gift of faith we have received, to recognize that "in God alone does my soul find rest." (March 24, 2008.)

Loving Lord, you have made us your children and have placed before us the prospect of eternal life. Stir up our faith to embrace the way that Christ set forth, and to show by our lives the reality of the hope by which we live. We ask this in the name of Jesus our Lord. Amen.

January 7 ✠ *Adhesive*

Our human experience is often scarred by the anguish caused by separation—being away from those we love, being in conflict, our own inner division. Sometimes even the sense that in our spiritual endeavors we are getting nowhere. Even without such problems our lives are fragmented, broken into bits. Once a moment has passed it is beyond recovery. Our childhood is far behind us, and those who enriched it have long since departed.

When we think of the work of the Holy Spirit, perhaps it is worthwhile to see it as adhesive. The spirit begins the task of integrating all the elements of our life-experience in a single, harmonious whole. What now we sometimes sense is that we are on a journey to wholeness. A journey that will have its culmination only in eternal life, where nothing will be lost, nothing left out, and every moment of our existence will sing in the choir. Theologians define eternity as being "the total, simultaneous and perfect possession of life."

The adhesive role of the Holy Spirit is to bring our broken lives together through what Saint Bernard termed the "glue of love": *gluten amoris*. This happens in four complementary ways.

- By helping us to remember, the Spirit brings Jesus into our lives as present and active; a dear friend, a wise counselor, and a strong helper.
- The Spirit progressively brings us to an interior harmony by supporting us in the struggle between good and evil: inspiring us, prompting us, sustaining us in difficult times.
- As the civil war within us loses its ferocity, the Spirit enables us to live in harmony with others, as members of Christ's Body. The Spirit is the source of unity that enables us corporately to proclaim the Good News to a waiting world.
- As our advocate and intercessor with the Father, the Spirit is the enabler of our prayer, bridging the infinite gulf between us and God, negating our sins, making us members

of God's household and sharers in the divine nature. It is the Holy Spirit who gives us the boldness to pray, "Abba."

To open ourselves to the Spirit is to begin the process of transformation that will have its culmination in eternal life. It is a journey to holiness, but it is also a journey to wholeness—one that will benefit not only ourselves but also serve as a grace to all whom we encounter. (June 4, 2017.)

Come, Holy Spirit, fill the lives of the faithful with your abundant grace. Take away the stony hearts within us and give us hearts that are open and responsive so that, guided by your inspirations, we may play our part in bringing all people to salvation and to the loving knowledge of the truth. For you are the source of our hope for ever and ever. Amen.

January 8   ✝   *Adulthood*

I recently heard of a child who did not speak for several years. Eventually, after puzzling many physicians and other experts, he began to speak clearly and then made rapid progress. A year or so later he was asked why he had remained mute. He replied that it was because he did not want to speak. He preferred to remain a baby.

The process of growing up is no fun. It involves our being dragged out of our comfort zone and compelled to accept new obligations and shoulder new responsibilities. In large measure, it is moving out of a period of passivity into activity, with the ever-present possibility that our actions are ill chosen, badly executed, or frustrated. It is easier to do nothing.

Some of us are reluctant to move beyond infancy in our attitudes to religion. We tend to rely too much on the grace of God, forgetting that the effect of grace is to get us moving. Grace gives us the desire to improve matters, the energy to make a start, and the perseverance to keep going even when the novelty has worn off. One of the fantasies that fuels our procrastination is that somehow God will suddenly sweep us off our feet and fill our lives, so that we do not have to make hard choices or live with the results of them.

Reality is a bit more grinding. As adults, we are called on to conduct an assessment of our situation, to make conscientious choices and to implement them, even though these initiatives cost us a lot of effort. Our faith has to grapple with the fact that, although it is the source of a certain light and guidance, there is still much darkness to overcome and a long, hard journey to endure.

Adult faith clings to God in the subdued light of hope and love. It does not avoid labor and learns to deal with hardship. It seeks and finds God in the undramatic challenges of every day. And it is willing to be delighted when, unpredictably, Christ comes through the closed door and lights up our life. (August 9, 1987.)

Loving Father, help us to grow into the full maturity of Christ. With Christ may we be tireless in doing good and avoiding evil, striving with Christ to show your love to all those around us. We ask this in the name of Jesus our Lord. Amen.

January 9 ✠ Adventure

We don't hear many exhortations to develop in ourselves the spirit of adventure. Most of us are seriously risk averse. When Jesus invites Simon Peter to come to him over the water, we think him crazy to attempt it and titter at his foolishness. We pay attention to the announcement, "Please remain seated until the boat docks at the jetty." We sit tight, singing to ourselves, "Rock of ages set on high, keep us always safe and dry." What did Peter get from his act of daring? He got wet and cold. We congratulate ourselves that our prudence saved us from that.

Yet Peter is rebuked not for his brashness, but for his doubt and hesitation. Not for having a dream and pursuing it with enthusiasm, but for paying too much attention to the negative data coming from "reality." For every good action we envisage, there will probably be a thousand difficulties and obstacles. Impetuosity is probably the least of our vices. Our problem is that we try to play it too safe. We don't want to do anything that does not have a positive outcome guaranteed.

Apart from getting wet and cold, Peter probably gained a new sense of his own limitations and a correspondingly stronger recognition of his need to depend on Christ. That works out at a net gain. On one level he failed, but his failure brought precious insights that those sitting safely in the boat never received. Peter failed often; the reason for this is that he often stuck out his neck while the others held back. Peter dared to live dangerously. And this is also our vocation. Perhaps we underestimate the seriousness of the vice of timidity.

In the Acts of the Apostles, the disciples of Jesus are described as having received from the Holy Spirit the gift of boldness, and these lukewarm, lily-livered followers became ardent leaders, unafraid to appear before kings and governors to speak the Good News that had been entrusted to them. Our faith derives from theirs. If, after Pentecost, they had remained closeted in the upper room, saying their prayers and being nice to one another, we would never have had the fire of new life kindled within us. They ventured everything, and we are the beneficiaries. Perhaps we too should risk praying that the Spirit infuse into our stale discipleship a stronger sense of adventure. (August 11, 1996.)

> *Come, Holy Spirit, stir up in us that boldness with which you filled the apostles. Give us the courage to give ourselves to the task which the Father has entrusted to us, confident that we also will receive power from on high. We ask this in the name of Jesus our Lord. Amen.*

January 10   ✝   *Affinity*

I have heard it said that the most effective police forces are those that draw the majority of their members from the same background and class as the criminals with whom they deal. Such officers already know much of what cannot easily be learned. They start with an advantage. This is the kind of knowledge that flows from affinity. As the ancient Latin poet Terence wrote, "I am a human being and nothing that is human is foreign to me." That Jesus was fully human as well as fully divine is the ultimate source of his ability to read the hearts of those he encountered. The first disciples were an unpromising bunch, yet he saw beyond and beneath their obvious liabilities. Like the well at Sychar, the Samaritan woman was deeper than she seemed. To the scribe who responded thoughtfully he said, "You are not far from the kingdom of God."

Jesus' ability to go beyond surface indicators tells us that he was not blocked by the usual impediments to a deep relationship: the radical otherness of each individual, the social restraints resulting from cultural norms, the barriers erected by racial or religious differences, and the rejection attached to an irregular morality. Jesus brings people to a better state not because he is different, but because of his shared humanity. By communicating a sense of affinity to those in trouble, he mirrors their own nature and makes visible to them their deepest desire. Jesus is a catalyst to the kind of self-knowledge that draws to conversion.

As Jesus was, so are we called to become. Just as we desire to be recognized and loved for our intrinsic worth—notwithstanding our visible failings—so part of our outreach to others must be to help them to own their personal giftedness and to make use of the talents they have received. We will discover that it is often by animating others that we make our small contribution to the betterment of the world. (March 7, 1999.)

Heavenly Father of us all, help us to recognize all people as our brothers and sisters, sharing the same nature, called to the same high destiny and bedeviled by similar weaknesses. Help us to grow stronger by helping others to grow stronger. We ask this through Christ our Lord. Amen.

January 11   ✠   *Ambiguity*

The visitations of Jesus after his resurrection always carried an element of ambiguity. Not only the puzzle of the empty tomb but also his sudden appearances. The witnesses experienced initial uncertainty and hesitation. It was not so obvious that this was Jesus; something had changed. This should be something of a consolation for us who are among those blessed because they do not see with their eyes.

The lesson we can take from this is that we should not be too hard on ourselves if we are not 100 percent sure of the truths of the faith. There is darkness, uncertainty, and doubt in the assent of faith, initially and continually. In the wake of the Second Vatican Council an interview was published with Father Karl Rahner, one of its luminaries. In the course of the conversation he often said that something or other was "self-evident." I remember thinking at the time that what was self-evident to Karl Rahner was not necessarily self-evident to Michael Casey.

We need to remember that faith is essentially an act of the will. It is the giving of assent much more than it is a moment of insight. There is always a risk involved in what has been called the "leap" of faith. We commit ourselves to something we do not understand or fully agree with. Temptations to faith come disguised as common sense and rationality. "Wait a little until things become clearer, wait until you are sure." We don't deny what we have glimpsed, but we postpone taking a stand on it. Maybe tomorrow, when it might be easier; perhaps I should consult someone, read something. Anything but respond to the grace of the moment.

Faith is a commitment made and kept on the basis of incomplete, ambiguous, and maybe conflicting data. It is not unreasonable, but it is beyond the power of reason to deliver a verdict. Faith is a work of the will, a work of love. By it our lives can change from being head-centered to heart-centered. As Blaise Pascal once wrote in *Pensées*, "The heart has its reasons of which reason knows nothing. . . . We know the truth not only by means of the reason but also by means of the heart." (April 22, 2007.)

Revealing God, we thank you for our moments of light. Give us the simplicity to respond to them calmly and gratefully. Help us to live in the light of faith and, by our deeds, to carry it to others. We ask this through Christ our Lord. Amen.

January 12 ✠ Ambition

Saint Bernard wrote somewhere that the vice that catches most people unawares springs up only when we have managed to rid our lives of the most disreputable failings: sexual sins, drunkenness, anger, violence, and the like. What he has in mind is ambition, which wends its invisible way through our motivations and renders toxic even our most virtuous actions. The passion that previously powered our overt vices is sublimated and, instead, provides the underground thrust that makes us want to be number one, whatever the cost. Not only at the top of the political heap, but even to achieve preeminence in the sphere of holiness. To be famous for our humility.

Ambition is not the same as the will to achieve or a sense of purpose. There is a snide element in ambition which is obvious to others but hidden from ourselves. At its center is the placing of self above every other concern. In the pursuit of self-advancement it is exploitative of others. They can be used and thrown away. It brings in its train extreme individualism, competition, rivalry, hostility, and envy. It is the very opposite of communion.

The way to offset any tendency to ambition is to cultivate the art of conversation. Being ready to take time to be with others, to listen to them, to laugh and play with them without any ulterior motive. Not mere chatter to fill the time nor a smokescreen to avoid confronting real issues. Conversation is a celebration of trust, expressed in the ability to relax with others, to be oneself, to feel free to lay aside roles and expectations. In it we express our sense of interdependence. Each one contributes something to the finishing of the jigsaw. No one person has, or claims to have, all the answers to all the questions. Our conversation mirrors the rest of our life.

To engage in equitable conversation demands of us a measure of self-dispossession. We have to learn to set aside some of our own concerns in order to allow others to express theirs. We make room for them by pulling back. We discard our repetitive monologues. If we talk more than 30 percent of the time, we need to shut up. We avoid bombast. A theologian wrote recently that the Christian church is meant to be a school of conversation. This is a comment worth pondering. It makes us collaborators instead of competitors. (September 24, 2000.)

Heavenly Father, you have called us all to a more abundant life and, in your providence, you have mapped out our path. Help us to avoid rewriting the script of our life to suit ourselves and, instead, teach us the joy that comes from sharing with others. We make our prayer through Christ our Lord. Amen.

January 13 ✠ *And*

Saint Thomas Aquinas once stated that the whole of morality was contained in a single verse from one of the psalms, "Turn away from evil and do good." It is a simple enough text; is it strong enough to bear the weight of such gravity as he assigned to it?

The first summons is to turn away from evil. Once I was with my sister when suddenly she called out to my two-year-old nephew, "Stephen, stop it!" A minute later he poked his head around the corner, quite confused as to how she could have seen him. She said to me, "Whenever he's quiet, I know he is up to some mischief." In a sense the same is true of most of us; we are always up to some kind of mischief. If we are not aware of this, it is probably because our conscience is either dead or dormant. Most of us are a little too happy with ourselves; a reality check would do us no harm. We will often find that we are blind to inconsistencies in our behavior, blind spots, rationalizations. A more searching regard will reveal no shortage of things from which we must eventually turn aside. Then we must also do good. The possibilities of doing good are almost infinite; the great danger is that we don't engage with any of them, simply because we fail to notice what is going on around us. We walk along the other side of the road. Sometimes the church's fervent preaching against sin seems to be more important than the task of inducing congregations to see possibilities for doing good and to act upon them.

The most important word in the text is *and*. People who spend their lives avoiding evil find that it is pretty much a full-time occupation. They are so busy avoiding wickedness that their energies are used up. The possibilities for doing good are allowed to slide past unheeded. On the other hand, people who are zealous in doing good do not always see the collateral damage they do—the mother who always ties the child's shoelaces prevents the child from learning how to do it for oneself. Beyond this is the perennial question of motivation. To do the right deed for the wrong reason is not good enough.

A small verse contains a giant program for life: "Turn aside from evil *and* do good." (January 23, 2005.)

Loving Father, you have called us to live in this world as reflections of your goodness. Help us to turn away from all that is evil and to find our joy in being good, in doing good, and in creating opportunities for goodness to grow. We ask this in the name of Jesus the Lord. Amen.

January 14 ✝ *Angels*

An angel appeared to me on a street in Shanghai. I was enjoying a leisurely morning stroll, taking in the unfamiliar environment, when suddenly the angel appeared. What did the angel look like? A middle-aged woman with a shopping bag in one hand as with the other she gestured toward my feet, and she was sternly admonishing me. I looked down and immediately understood what she was saying. She was warning me not to keep walking with my head in the clouds, but to pay attention to the cobbled pavement, which was extremely irregular. It would be very easy for anybody who was not concentrating to trip and do oneself serious damage. Even thinking about it sends shivers down my spine. Emergency ward, language difficulties, bureaucratic paperwork, insurance hassles, interrupted itinerary—all this on top of whatever harm I would have done myself. From all this the angel delivered me.

I must admit that my journey through life has often been facilitated by strangers who were inspired to intervene either to prevent some disaster or to point me in a better direction. It has often been the source of some wonderment that these angels materialize out of nowhere and then disappear, never again to cross my path. It is as though pieces on a chessboard are being moved by the Grandmaster to achieve the desired result. Neither they nor I am aware of it, but our interaction is all part of the master plan.

For this reason, it is probably no surprise that I am a firm believer in the ongoing effectiveness of God's providence. God does not usually move mountains just to suit us, or bring rain on a summer's day. Sometimes, perhaps. Mostly, God seems to work by inspiring other human beings to step in and do something practical. They themselves may not know why they acted in such a way; the thought came, and they followed it.

To believe that our lives are in God's hands is a comforting thought. But we also need to be challenged by the workings of Providence that may, out of a cloudless sky, urge us to do something entirely uncharacteristic for the benefit of others. If others can be angels to us, we also can be angels to them.

As for the woman on the street in Shanghai, sometimes I think of her. And I often pray that, if she is ever in need, God will inspire someone to step in and help her, as she did for me. (March 12, 2018.)

Heavenly Father, even the sparrows in the sky are the objects of your care and concern. Watch over us as we continue our journey. Protect us from whatever could harm us and inspire us to exploit every opportunity to do good to others. We ask this through Christ our Lord. Amen.

January 15 ✠ Anxiety

It sometimes seems to me that the commandment most often broken is that contained in the words of Jesus, "Do not be anxious." The theme is resurgent throughout the New Testament: "You worry and are anxious about so many things, yet only one is necessary." "Seek first the kingdom of God and all else will be added to you besides." "Cast your care upon the Lord." "When you stand before kings and governors . . ."

Again and again the New Testament insists that anxiety is a denial of our faith in the God who loves us and in the Providence that arranges all things for our ultimate benefit. Jesus promised a hundredfold to those who made sacrifices to follow him, even though, inevitably, there would be some form of collateral persecution.

It is hard to continue believing in a loving God when bad things happen to good people. Jesus himself recognized that the scandalous behavior of some could cause others to fall away—and we ourselves see this more often than we should. It simply means that it is of the nature of faith that it has to grapple with apparent contradictions when events run counter to our expectations.

The thing we have to do when hard times roll over us is to hold fast to what we have experienced as true, meanwhile battening down the hatches as we are tossed about by the storm. God writes straight on crooked lines and, as long as God is in control, eventually all will be well.

As a child, the Downyflake restaurant, with its automated donut-making machine in the window, seemed to me about as close to heaven as you could get. Lots of sugary treats and no vegetables. I remember that it had a poem on its menu: "As you ramble on through life, brother, whatever be your goal, keep your eye upon the donut, and not upon the hole." In other words: think positive. Troubles of various kinds afflict everyone. When they strike, we need to look beyond immediate hardship and refresh our memories of the firm promises of God. "My grace is sufficient for you." It is still hard going, but, in eternity, we will look back on these slight momentary afflictions in a spirit of wonderment, saying with Saint Paul, "In all these things we have overcome, because of him who has loved us," for nothing can separate us from the love of God. (February 27, 2011.)

Lord God, we come to you by way of many difficulties and temptations. Give us courage to face these difficulties and not be downcast. And when we fail, give us the grace of resilience so that we may come to you boldly for cleansing and healing and liberation. We make this prayer through Christ our Lord. Amen.

January 16   ✠   *Apartheid*

Whenever Queen Elizabeth meets commoners and shakes hands with them, she always wears gloves. No contact. Australian Prime Minister Paul Keating was once lambasted by the British tabloids because he dared to redirect Her Majesty (apparently) by placing his hand on her back. This is a trivial incident, but it illustrates the importance that separation plays in protecting the distinctions that society likes to impose on different classes of people. Our society is riven by distinctions based on color, race, age, religion, education, employment, rank, money, sexual orientation, manner of speaking, and as many other categories as we can dream up.

When I entered the monastery in 1960 there were, in one monastery, an abbot, priests, solemnly professed, temporarily professed, novices, postulants, solemnly professed lay brothers, temporarily professed lay brothers, lay brother novices, lay brother postulants. Each level signaled by a distinctive garb. Ten different ranks—more than are found in the angelic choirs! Yes, we love making distinctions between people.

Perhaps we ought to take a more determined stand against setting the scene for class warfare. It is high time that we came to the realization that superficial distinctions between persons exist mainly in the mind and not in reality. Give a beggar a haircut and a swanky suit and any toffee-nosed doorman would admit him into his domain. We make judgments on such superficial things. Lord and Lady Codswallop may have a title and a big car, but this doesn't make them better people. Come the revolution, all that distinguishes them will soon be swept away.

The clear message of the gospels is that the separations we try to impose are artificial and mostly unjust. Part of our discipleship must be the willingness to learn from Jesus that there must be no distance between us and others. Jesus received sinners and touched lepers. This was not a man who kept apart.

We fear to come close because we think we may be contaminated. We are afraid because we are insecure about ourselves, and so we have to create some means of trumpeting our uniqueness. A man who is insecure about his height—or lack of it—may secretly add a couple of extra inches to his shoes. In a similar way, we are always trying to add some distinction to our life, to manifest that we really are worthwhile. We would save ourselves the bother if we just learned to accept ourselves as we are. As God does. (Undated.)

Creator God, with you there is no distinction of persons. You created us all in your own image to share in your life, each of us uniquely. Help us to regard others as you do and, seeing them as precious, want to draw close to them and be with them. We make this prayer through Christ our Lord. Amen.

January 17 ✙ *Appearances*

A lesson that nearly all philosophies and religions attempt to teach their adherents is that there is a difference between appearances and reality. Things are not always what they seem. Apparently, the Earth is not flat, although it looks that way. And the sun does not circle the Earth, although we continue to speak of sunrise and sunset. The same misperceptions occur in our judgments about people. Often what we see to be reprehensible in them is really only the mirror image of the blemishes we refuse to admit in ourselves. We project onto others what we fail to accept in ourselves.

Perhaps it would be good to be less self-assured about our judgments, recognizing that there is a limit to how much we can see. There is no need for me to insist that I know everything. The fact that I have immediate experience and understanding of some things does not mean that I am able to comprehend the full truth about anything. A snapshot reveals the external details of a single moment, but inner realities are hidden, as are the events that preceded the moment and what came afterward. To judge I need to know the whole story.

This is why faith is not unreasonable. There is much in the universe that is beyond our knowledge and beyond our capability to know. It is faith that gives us some access to this unseen world of spiritual reality. That is precisely the role of faith. It transcends appearances. It is the experience in the depths of our being of a reality beyond space and time. A spark that kindles a glimmering flame deep within us and is gone. A moment's enlightenment. A door opening that invites us to enter. If we are to become even a little more spiritual, we must first recognize that there is more to human existence than what meets the eyes. Beyond appearances there is a subtler and deeper and dearer reality. (May 28, 1978.)

Unseen God, Creator of all things, open our eyes to discover what is now hidden from our sight. Teach us how to seek the things that are above, where Christ is, seated at your right hand. And we ask this in his name. Amen.

January 18   ✝   *Approachability*

Have you ever found yourself in a strange city, completely lost and completely bewildered? When I have found myself in that situation I try to work out for myself where I am and how to get to where I want to be. If that fails, as it often does, I have to think of asking for guidance from someone. I am looking for someone who is both knowledgeable and approachable—and with whom I share a common language.

What is it that makes a person approachable? In the first place, they need to be persons who are not so caught up in their own plans that they do not welcome any deviation. Usually I look for someone possessed of an air of leisure, a certain openness to uncontrolled experience. A kind face; I would never approach one whose face has been marked by years of surliness and bad temper.

What started me out thinking along these lines was the picture that the gospels paint of Jesus as one to whom so many were attracted, even to the point of being emboldened to cross social boundaries to make contact. He must have generated a strong sense of common humanity. People would say to themselves, "He is one of us, not one of them."

This common humanity was, however, suffused with a subtle sense of what the gospels term *authority*. He gave the impression that he was not only willing but also able to help. That he had answers to the questions they dared not pose.

If we are genuine disciples of Jesus, our commitment will eventually stamp itself on our whole being. It may well happen that others approach us seeking a word that will be life-giving. We may feel our inadequacy, but we need to be bold and allow the grace of the moment to inspire us.

Once, in Paris, I was completely lost. I approached a woman and asked her how to arrive at my destination. I have always remembered her reply. "Oh, it is far too complicated for me to describe it. But walk down this street until you come to that statue. Turn up that street and then ask somebody else for the next stage."

We may not be able to supply ultimate answers, but often, by God's grace, we can help people progress a little along the way. We can point out how to get to the next stage, and then somebody else can help them to go farther. (September 12, 2005.)

Loving Father, you are always working to bring us home to you. Do not allow us to wander too far off the track. Send us prophets and guides who may point us in the right direction so that we do not become lost in the labyrinths of life. We ask this through Jesus, your Son, who is our way for ever and ever. Amen.

January 19 ✠ As

Sometimes good things come in small parcels. After all, an ounce of gold or saffron is worth more than a ton of plastic. And the converse is true. Big words can sometimes be no more than a smokescreen, lacking all substance. Which I suppose is why people with nothing worthwhile to say often use them.

I would like to spend a few moments on one of the smallest words in the New Testament. The word is *as*. We are commanded not just to be perfect—which, I suppose is easy enough, though I have never tried it—but to be as perfect *as* our Father in heaven, as holy *as* the all-holy God. That takes self-improvement to an impossible level.

On the understanding that the measure we use for others is the measure that is used for us, we are instructed to pray, "Forgive us *as* we forgive." For many of us this is to ask for a very meager measure of forgiveness—we are condemned by our own words.

Most difficult of all is Jesus' command, "Love one another *as* I have loved you." This involves loving one's enemies and being prepared to give one's life for them. This is love taken to extremes, giving and forgiving, going out to others and forgoing one's own rights and privileges, seeing them as they really are and foreseeing what they might become if they know themselves loved. Such a love holds all persons close and withholds nothing from them. It is a love that is not exploitative. It is not subject to seasonal variation. It is unconditional.

Such a love is clearly impossible, so that we cannot interpret Jesus' words as a command but as a promise, a gift. The little word *as* is not comparative, but participative. We are invited to share Christ's love. Since all that he was by nature we can become by grace, if we allow ourselves to be filled with Christ, we will also be filled with Christ's love—reaching out, reviving, restoring, redeeming. Just as Christ has loved us back into life, so he gives us the power of life-giving love to be shared not just with our nearest and dearest, but with everyone we encounter, friend or foe. (May 9, 2004.)

> *Lord Jesus Christ, you have offered us the gift of sharing in your love and the challenge of putting it into practice, as the saints have done throughout the ages. Give us the courage to say yes to love so that by our lives this world may become a little more loving. For you are our Lord for ever and ever. Amen.*

January 20 ✝ *Ascension*

It was Saint Mark who first came up with the idea, later developed by Saint Luke, of portraying the life of Jesus as a journey from Galilee up to Jerusalem. This conception stamped the life of Jesus with a certain purposefulness that could serve as a dynamic model for Christians to imitate: to follow Jesus from the first beginnings of discipleship through death to resurrection and eternal life.

A generation later, the Fourth Gospel developed the idea anew. Jesus' life was seen as a descent from Father to the earth and then, when the time was right, an ascent back to the Father. "I have come down," Jesus says in that gospel, and "I return to the Father." If we look at the prepositions used we find *down* and *up, from* and *to, out of* and *into*. A double movement.

Jesus' time on earth was more than a visit. It was to gather together the scattered children of God into unity. Jesus proclaimed himself the road by which we can arrive at eternal life, following him as he returns to the Father. Like all the mysteries of Christ, the Ascension is "for our sake and for our salvation";

it is not just his own glorification but an invitation for us to follow and an indication of how we must travel.

The primary task of Christians is to ascend. Lift up your eyes! Lift up your hearts! "If for this life only we have hope in Christ Jesus, then, of all people, we are the most to be pitied."

Here are five channels that will provide us with the energy needed for the ascent.

- First, we accept our identity as citizens of heaven: that means we become strangers to the standards of behavior that are contrary to the gospel.
- Second, we consciously direct our hope and aspiration to the future life. Seek the things that are above!
- Third, by prayer we open the windows of our soul to the fresh air of eternity.
- Fourth, by acting in a Christlike way we begin to be formed by his values.
- Fifth, by an attitude of humility we make ourselves ready to be lifted up: God lifts up the lowly and the last.

By the grace of God we can begin to live a heavenly life now. By opening our hearts and lives to spiritual reality we profit not only ourselves but, mysteriously, we make the world a slightly better place. (June 5, 2011.)

Heavenly Father, help us to keep our hearts fixed on Jesus, your Son. In his earthly life he showed us how to live, and now, seated at your right hand, he calls us to share the joyous gift promised to those who stand fast in his love. Help us to rise with him who came down for us, Jesus Christ our Lord. Amen.

January 21   ✠   *Aurora Leigh*

Some lines from a poem by Elizabeth Barret Browning: "Earth's crammed with heaven / and every common bush afire with God.

/ But only he who sees takes off his shoes, / the rest sit around and pick blackberries." These words speak to the relation between heaven and earth, time and eternity, the spiritual world and the world of ordinary experience. The differentiation is to be found in the observer, not in the reality. Some people are more able to perceive the union of heaven and earth than others. The others are too concerned with picking blackberries to be bothered even to pose the question.

Earth is not an autonomous zone, even though we are unable easily to perceive upon what ultimate reality earth depends. The whole of salvation history, as portrayed in the Bible, is one in which there are interventions from beyond the confines of space and time. They begin with creation. Thence there is an uninterrupted conversation between heaven and earth: God was involved with Adam and Eve, Noah's flood, Abraham's covenant, the law of Moses, the missions given to the prophets, right up to the time that God so loved the world that he gave his only Son. The Bible presents us with the picture of an earth in constant dialogue with its Creator and Sustainer.

Heaven is present on earth. The inverse is also true. Christ has opened a door to give us access to the spiritual world. He is the door through which we may pass. Where Christ himself has entered, we are invited to follow. We are to set our hearts and minds on realities that are above. We are invited to the feast; it is not permissible to allege alternative obligations: I have a wife, a farm, I cannot come. Even now the invitation comes: enter into the joy of your Lord.

Our degree of contact with the spiritual world is the measure of our humanity. Only thus do we realize our full potential; otherwise we are leading lives that are merely drowsy, inert, and reactive. Walt Whitman, like Saint Paul, allowed himself to be drawn into the third heaven; later he wrote in *Leaves of Grass*, "I cannot be awake, for nothing looks to me as it did before, / Or else I am awake for the first time, and all before has been a mean sleep." He was not filling his day picking blackberries. To be thus drawn beyond the mundane is to cross—be it ever so briefly—the threshold of eternity. It seems, after all, that heaven and earth are not so far apart. (August 15, 1996.)

Lord Jesus Christ, our Immanuel, you have promised to be present with us until the end of this age. Give us the grace also to be present to you, not allowing our hearts and minds to wander, but to keep them fixed on realities that endure forever. For you are our Lord for ever and ever. Amen.

January 22   ✟   *Autonomy?*

One of our strongest misapprehensions is that if only we were free to decide everything for ourselves, instead of living at the behest of others, we would be much happier. Perhaps we have tried to live like this but quickly discovered that the cloudless happiness we were seeking was still beyond our grasp. If only we had listened to ancient philosophers like Aristotle, we would have been led to accept that we human beings are "social animals." We are not made to live a self-enclosed life, but our coming to maturity is a matter of growing in voluntary union with others. This means learning to live in interdependence; we depend on others and allow them to depend on us.

Beyond human maturity there is a further possibility. As beings endowed with a spiritual nature, we have the potential to live in the context of the invisible world which is the sphere of God. We are called to establish a connection with our Creator and to live our lives in relationship with the One who has reached out to make contact with us. This means learning to live in dependence on God.

This dependence means, first of all, living in accord with the nature that we have received from God. We have been given the gifts of intelligence and free will so that we may choose our own paths and so safeguard the life that has been given us and bring to full development the gifts that are our birthright.

But there is more. God has spoken to us, through the words of revelation, to make even clearer to us what is to be pursued as life-giving and what is to be avoided. And to bring all things to completion, God has sent his Son as one of us, to be our way and our truth and to lead us to life.

A cold, autonomous life is not fully human. Not only are we made to live with others, we are also called to live in a warm, dynamic union with God, to take delight in the unseen mystery of God's love, and to be sustained and renewed by the boundless mercy of God. Just as we have direct experience of how our lives are enhanced by our relationships with others, so, if we allow ourselves to venture into a more intense relationship with God, we will certainly find that, despite the added demands, our lives are greatly enriched. Letting God and others into our lives is the only way in which we can mature. But we have to make a choice and follow through with it. (July 21, 2016.)

God of love, let your face shine on us and we shall be saved. Give us ears to hear, eyes to see, and a heart to understand what you continue to reveal to your faithful people. And help us to live always mindful of your loving attention. We ask this in the name of Jesus our Lord. Amen.

January 23 ✠ *Awake*

In several of the parables of Jesus the message is clear: wake up, and stay awake. We are not asleep, so we have to take the words as metaphors. What is Jesus saying to us by this image?

In the first instance, wakefulness is more than not being asleep. It involves living in a state of greater mindfulness. We recognize that our brains are limited; the only way for us to cope with the huge welter of data streaming into us is to make a selection. We deliberately dismiss as irrelevant to our particular purposes perhaps 90 percent of what we sense. If we are driving in heavy traffic, we don't pay attention to the beauty of the leaves on the trees by the roadside. We consciously choose to keep our eyes fixed on the road. We do the same thing in everyday life, often unconsciously. We allow ourselves to be 90 percent unaware.

Living mindfully means taking each moment seriously. When Jesus said that offering a cup of water to one in need would not go unrewarded, he was saying that the smallest action can be the carrier of the widest meanings. Provided that we invest ourselves in what we are doing, rather than act with a minimum of thought or care. If I believe that every choice that I make or fail to make can have ultimate significance, then I will probably take a little more time to choose wisely.

The opposite of mindful living is bad faith, when I refuse to see emerging patterns. The fact is that individual choices are not isolated events, but each has an impact on others. We are all serial sinners. Addictions and bad habits are formed because I don't see the connectedness between repeated actions. I was not alert to the overt significance of each step in the sequence and the fact that it was leading me to a place to which I did not want to go.

Staying awake is to make the transition from deeds done in the fog of darkness into a life lived in sunlight; it is to be aware of the quality of my actions. Only thus will I become aware that some of my split-off behavior is inconsistent with the avowed priorities by which I claim to live. Not being awake is not morally neutral. It is a kind of lethal forgetfulness that leads to a paralysis of my spiritual faculties.

Beyond morality there is a mystical aspect of wakefulness. When my inner eye is trained to see beyond the world of space and time, sometimes I will catch a glimpse of God. When my inner ear is alert, I may well hear the angels sing. And then the inner self becomes ever more fully alive, tasting and seeing for itself that God is good. (December 2, 2007.)

Loving Father, each day you speak to us and call us to yourself. Train our inner ears to hear your voice. Open our hearts to your message. And give us the confidence to respond boldly to your summons. We make this prayer through Christ our Lord. Amen.

January 24 ✢ **Backup**

In the 1980s there was a saying that two kinds of people use computers: those who have experienced a major data loss and those who are about to. The lesson constantly underlined was: back up everything. It is very simple, isn't it? It is similar to what we are told about possible electricity outages: have a generator, keep spare batteries on hand. Also very simple. For some reason, like the girls who missed out on the wedding because they did not bring oil with their lamps, we don't do it. It is too inconvenient. Too much bother. And so often the smallest things that are left undone result in a major disaster. More often than not, prudence is defeated by procrastination.

It is important to distinguish between tasks that are important and tasks that are urgent. When something has to be done urgently, it conveys its own energy. A fire alarm sounds, and we spring into action. When the telephone rings, we stand up immediately and answer it. Important things that are not urgent we tend to postpone from hour to hour and from year to year.

In a similar vein, we know that learning languages, acquiring skills, and building up expertise are all important, but too often we fail to include them among our priorities. This is because the rewards they offer are delayed, sometimes for years. We are victims of the instant gratification syndrome. Looking far into the future is beyond us.

Obviously, this means that lifting our attention from this everyday world to the afterlife is a colossal challenge. We will do it if it becomes urgent; if we have five minutes before the plane crashes we will willingly beef out the act of contrition and really mean it. But for the time being we tend to concentrate on what is visible and tangible. Whether there is life beyond the grave is never going to be known with absolute certainty in this life. What is possible, however, is that we make a choice to accept this proposition as real. On the basis of the promises of Christ, we live now as we would five minutes before the end: with a sense of what is truly important and what is merely transitory.

This is a minimalist position, a kind of backup in case there is a judgment and there is an afterlife. Nevertheless, it may well be the foundation on which a sturdier faith is built, a faith lit up by occasional glimmers that lead to intimations of immortality. And it is better than nothing. (November 6, 2011.)

Lord Jesus Christ, you have planted in our hearts the desire for eternal life, and you have promised to lead to it those who follow you. Protect us from the cynicism and doubt that surround us and help us to run with growing hope toward the goal you have set before us. For you are our Lord for ever and ever. Amen.

January 25   ✝   **Balance**

I often think that the value of balance is overestimated. When we say that someone is "balanced" or "unbalanced," we are clearly presupposing that balance is a good thing. Yet walking is a succession of moments of imbalance. There is not a single stage of a simple stroll that we could maintain for very long. Police interrogators know this and, in some countries, there are stories about people being forced to stand—sometimes on one leg—for hours on end, until they keel over and fall. The only way we can achieve physical balance is prone on the floor and preferably dead. We might even define life as a celebration of ongoing imbalance.

Sometimes people seem to think that what God expects of us is that we march from one end of the narrow road to the other not only without deviation but even without a sidelong glance. I can scarcely credit this of a God "who knows the dust of which we are made." Does God really anticipate that for a whole lifetime we will observe a steely middle course between opposite extremes? Preachers may praise such a life, but it just doesn't happen. We wobble from one side of the road to the other. Sometimes we go off the track altogether and hare off madly in the wrong directions. Then we have to backtrack and find our way again. Perhaps we get tired and sit down for a while and then forget which direction were we following. Life is very complicated, but it is not less beautiful because of that.

It is crazy to think that each moment of our life has to balance out. Perhaps at the very end of our life, say in the last ten minutes, we will see in retrospect that somehow a balance has been achieved. But it will have been achieved over the course of a lifetime. If we are organized enough we may be able to partially balance our accounts on a weekly basis, using the weekend to attend to matters neglected on workdays. But for many of us even this is impossible, even though we try. We have to take for granted that life will see to its own balance; if we lean over too far in one direction, it will urge us to lean back. If we ignore the warning, we will fall over.

God accompanies us on our journey, not as a nagging elder, but, as was the case with the Emmaus disciples, as a companionable fellow-traveler, firing up our hearts and bolstering our flagging energies. With God's help we will get there in the end. (March 10, 1985.)

Loving Father, you call us to yourself, and you give us the means to respond. Never let us lose hope because of our wandering hearts. Help us to be more concerned with living in love than with measuring our own progress. We ask this in the name of Jesus our Lord. Amen.

January 26 ✠ **Baptist**

What can we know about John the Baptist? From the twin testimony of the Gospel tradition and Josephus, we know that he was an austere eschatological prophet who preached a baptism of repentance and who was murdered by Herod Antipas. The pious back story composed by Luke about his conception and birth gives us little in the way of history. However, what the gospels tell us about the relationship of John and Jesus seems likely in its general outline. It has been suggested that Jesus was originally a disciple of the Baptist but then went his own way, changing the emphasis of his preaching from fiery retribution to the good news of God's love.

Although the Baptist achieved a certain level of fame and attracted many disciples, most of them never stayed with him. They went back to their own lives. He was primarily a herald of the Last Times and felt no need to back up his proclamation either with biblical precedents or with the kind of arguments used by the rabbis. Both Josephus and Luke agree that there was a moral strand to his preaching, but this was wholly in service of the need to amend before the coming of the end.

Rereading the various gospel passages in which the Baptist appears, I am struck by how much of his life seemed to have passed in darkness. His own mission was eclipsed by that of Jesus, who did not fit his expectations of a fiery messiah who would bring definitive judgment on the wicked and about whom John remained doubtful. Twice the Fourth Gospel has him say, "I did not know him." And there is a poignant episode when, in prison, suffering and near death, he sent disciples to inquire of Jesus whether he was the One.

In many ways, what began as a brilliant career seems to end in an antiheroic death. Without crediting all the details contained in Mark's account, it is reasonable to assume that the Baptist's last days were squalid and his death dismal. Whatever the precise reasons for Herod's antipathy, we can be certain that John was murdered because he spoke out, because of the message that he proclaimed.

We can revere the Baptist as a man of constancy and courage, who kept faith with his vocation and mission. One who served God all through a lifetime of darkness and unknowing, a life of progressive diminishment as he stepped back into the shadows to make room for Jesus. To some extent the words attributed to him must find an echo in our own hearts: "He must increase; I must decrease." (June 24, 2008.)

Loving Father, you called John to witness in the wilderness.
Give us the courage to maintain our commitment to the truth

*and to endure the hostility that such fidelity engenders. And
keep us faithful until the end. We ask this through Christ our
Lord. Amen.*

January 27 ✠ *Bargain*

Sometimes we grumble against God on the grounds that too
much is asked of us and too little given; we feel that the rewards
of the future scarcely compensate for the labors of the present,
especially when we are liable to be definitively doomed for a
momentary weakness. Perhaps we congratulate the Emperor
Constantine for his cleverness in postponing baptism until his
deathbed, thus reaping the rewards and avoiding the efforts.

This attitude derives from our loss of contact with the promise
of heaven. How rarely we hear sermons on this topic. It is difficult to preach about because "eye has not seen, nor ear heard,
nor can the human heart imagine what has been prepared for
those who love God." The crass popular images of heaven serve
as a further deterrent. So, we don't speak much about heaven.
We much prefer long moral monologues and vague metaphysical
discussions. And then we wonder why people are not motivated.

It seems different in Islam. When young men and women put
their lives on the line in *jihad*, or volunteer as suicide bombers,
it is because they see these actions as providing immediate access
to paradise. Even for those of less radical inclination, the demands
of Islam (the *shahadah*, daily prayer, almsgiving, fasting, and the
haj) are practiced because they guarantee entry into heaven. There
is a linkage between present obligations and future rewards.

In Christianity the connection between good living and eternal
life has become fuzzy. We are conscious of all sorts of obligations
and we struggle to meet some of them, but we are far too preoccupied with the price we pay. We have forgotten what a great
bargain we are being offered. For this slight momentary affliction,
we are being offered an eternal weight of glory. We overvalue what
we do and undervalue the gift that God has prepared for us.

Whenever we feel the burden of the day and its heat and find ourselves wondering whether it is worthwhile, we need to remember that we are not the firstcomers. We are the lastcomers, arriving well past the eleventh hour. The denarius we receive is worth far more than we can earn in a thousand lifetimes. Those who are saved will be certain for all eternity that what they are receiving is a very good bargain indeed. (September 19, 1999.)

Lord Jesus Christ, you have promised eternal life to those who take up the cross to follow you. Help us to fix our gaze on things that are above, and from the hope you have enkindled let us draw much confidence and joy. For you are our Lord for ever and ever. Amen.

January 28   ✛   *Beasts*

Saint Mark concludes his narrative of Jesus' time in the desert with a curious sentence that finds no echo in the later gospels. "He was with the wild beasts and the angels were ministering to him." There is no definitive termination of the time of temptation; it is as if the tension was lifelong, as seems to be the idea in the Fourth Gospel. Jesus experienced, as we do, the tug-of-war between the spiritual and material.

Here, it seems to me, the wild beasts are not only the feral animals that prowl the wilderness far from human habitation, but also the untrammeled desires that inhabit the human heart: the instinctual passions that pull us in directions that are inconsistent with the form which we want to give to our lives. The contrary imaginations and desires that sometimes make it difficult to act in the way our better self approves.

In the mid-fourth-century *Life* of Antony of Egypt we are presented with a symbolic picture of the saint keeping vigil while surrounded by a throng of wild beasts sent by the devil. What is surprising in this vignette is the calmness with which Antony confronts the threats. The servant of Christ, he avers, has no need to be afraid of anything the demons can do.

Jesus was sustained by the ministry of angels, according to the verse of the psalm, "God has given the angels charge over you." So, too, will we be sustained in our struggle with our own deviant tendencies to the extent that we maintain our contact with the spiritual world and open our hearts to God's loving ministration, whether directly or through angels.

There is no need for us to be ashamed of the duality of our experience or to deny the existence of forces trying to divert us from our following of Christ. Like Saint Antony we can confront these with equanimity, knowing that those who are for us are greater than those who are against us. Angels are stronger than wild beasts any day! (August 25, 2014.)

Loving Father, you gave your Son into the care of angels as he walked our earth. Watch over us amid the many dangers that beset our path and protect us from all that would diminish our loving service of you and our neighbor. We ask this in the name of Jesus the Lord. Amen.

January 29   ✠   *Beatitudes*

Thirty-eight years ago, in 1971, I heard a sermon that I still remember. The gospel of the day was the Sermon on the Mount and, in particular, the Beatitudes. The point that really stayed in my mind was that the preacher repeated the refrain, "Oh, if only we were hearing these words for the first time!" He spoke about the poetic beauty of the text, which has earned for it a place in many anthologies of world literature. Then he paused to lament that, sadly, familiarity does breed contempt. As soon as we hear the opening bars of the overture we stop listening. We know what is to follow. We have heard it many times before. Blessed are the poor in spirit and all that! And our thoughts go off to graze on something more interesting.

To say that the philosophy of life propounded in this short text is revolutionary is an understatement. It completely overturns many of our most dearly held beliefs. We don't really think that poverty, grief, and meekness will make us happy. We may accept that mercy and purity and peacemaking are good things, but they don't figure greatly in the choices we make about our daily behavior. As for hungering after righteousness and hoping for persecution, that is a bit out of our league.

We have to remind ourselves that these few verses are not intended merely as an aesthetic banquet but as a spur to changing our whole way of thinking about life. This text invites us to see the way of the Gospel as putting a question mark alongside some of the complacent assumptions that rule our culture. What seems to be present advantage may not be so if it reduces our desire for the world to come, if it cuts off our sense of dependence on God. "We have all that we want; we don't need God."

What is unexpected is that those disasters which crack open the comfortable world we have built for ourselves often open us up to the mercy of God. When all else fails, there is only God. Once contact has been made, hope is born. The future, however bleak it seemed, becomes merely the darkness before a radiant dawn. And so we too may start to find an inner happiness even in poverty and persecution. In such a scenario, the Beatitudes begin to make sense. (November 1, 2009.)

Lord Jesus Christ, you call us all to change our way of thinking and to seek first the kingdom of God. Help us to take your words seriously and to allow ourselves to be drawn into the deep joy that will follow our wholehearted commitment to the law of the Gospel. For you are our Lord for ever and ever. Amen.

January 30   ✝   *Being Saved*

I don't know if it is still regarded as valid, but it used to be said that if you were trying to save persons from drowning, it would sometimes be necessary to knock them out. The idea was that in struggling to regain control of the situation, they may well endanger the lives of those who were coming to save them. Most of us do not want to be saved and are prepared to fight to retain our delusional autonomy.

This is certainly true in the spiritual life. One of our greatest liabilities is our determination to be fully self-sufficient, so that we do not need to be saved. We think that we can manage nicely on our own. For us to maintain this belief we have to turn our backs on the truth and mentally repackage our life until it conforms to our delusional self-image. This vision of self depends on a defective memory, an inability to distinguish fantasy from reality, and the sincere conviction that anything untoward that has happened in our lives is to be blamed on others. Its effects are usually invisible to ourselves; others bear the brunt of them: self-righteousness, harshness toward perceived "sinners," and an absence of any healthy sense of our own sinfulness.

Christ came to save us, and sometimes the only way for him to overcome our unhelpful resistance is to knock us out, to puncture our hyperinflated self-esteem, to bring to nothing the grand designs that allowed us to think more highly of ourselves than we should. In the aftermath of such an intervention we begin to come to the realization that we cannot save ourselves. Our integrity is spotty. Our virtue is precarious. Our self-reliance is delusional. If we have even a glimmer of intelligence, we will reluctantly conclude that we need to draw on resources outside ourselves. The grace of Christ certainly. But also the guidance and support of the Christian community. With this insight, we are well on the way to being saved. (September 1, 2013.)

Lord Jesus Christ, you came to save sinners. Help us to recognize our need for your help and overcome our resistance to grace and our reluctance to abandon the false self. Help us to live in the truth of your loving mercy. For you are our Lord for ever and ever. Amen.

January 31 ✢ *Being-Toward-Death*

"Being-toward-death." This is how the philosopher Martin Heidegger described human reality. Since Karl Rahner once used it as the theme of a beautiful Lenten sermon, perhaps we also may be permitted to spend a few moments reflecting on this theme.

Mostly we don't want to talk about death, even though we acknowledge its inevitability. Hundreds are killed in road accidents every year, thousands destroyed by war and violence, tens of thousands through the mismanagement of Earth's resources. All of us know that even we will eventually succumb to its lethal embrace.

Our view of human life is incomplete unless we take into account the reality of death. The way we live is largely determined by what we believe takes place after we die. If we are convinced that we will vanish in a wisp of smoke issuing from a crematorium's chimney, then we will live trying to cram into our lives every possible pleasure and indulgence. If we accept the reality of an afterlife patterned on the way we live now, we will probably try to pass our days ready to accept inconveniences and troubles in the hope of making ourselves ready to receive God's ultimate gift. Wisdom can be understood simply as trying to live as we would like to be when we cross that final threshold.

Pleasure, possessions, and power are the alternative attractions. Whoever we are, we are all drawn to them: babies, children, adolescents, people who work in fish-and-chip shops, bishops, bank-managers, politicians. Maybe we seek them in different ways; maybe we successfully disguise our lust for them. But we are all tempted to make the most of the moment, forgetting eternity. "Vanity of vanities and all is vanity, says the Preacher." Sometimes not only vanity but also insanity. We destroy our health, ruin our families, poison the environment, and cut ourselves off from eternal life, all for the sake of some temporal and temporary advantage.

Belief in an afterlife is the keystone of our faith, as Saint Paul reminds us. "If for this life only we have hope in Christ Jesus, then, of all people, we are the most to be pitied." It is also the foundation a life well lived, attentive to God and solicitous for the welfare of our neighbor. (August 3, 1980.)

God of infinite compassion, you have sent your Son into our world so that we might come to the feast of eternal life. Give us a strong faith that you will complete the good work begun in us by baptism and sustain our hope that we too might become children of the resurrection. We ask this in the name of Jesus our Lord. Amen.

February 1   ✠   **Blessed**

We have a problem in English: two words are spelled the same but have different meanings and, so, are often confused. The word is *blessed*. Pronounced as a monosyllable, "blest" is a past participle and means spoken well of or praised. Pronounced in two syllables, "blessèd" is an adjective and means happy. In Latin the two words are *benedictus* and *beatus*. Two quite different words.

When we speak of the Blessed Trinity, in what sense do we use the word? The Latin is clear. O *beata Trinitas*. Certainly, the triune God is to be spoken well of and praised, but that is not what the title is conveying. It is speaking of the happy Trinity. The essential nature of the triune God is an eternal ecstasy of joy. In more mundane terms we might say that God is always in a good mood; our God is not like the capricious and occasionally grumpy gods of the Greek pantheon.

From our own limited experience of happiness, we know that it does not want to betake itself into a corner to be privately happy. It wants to shout its joy abroad. In terms of traditional theology, good is self-diffusive. Something that is really good wants to spread its goodness further afield. That is why God created us. To have intelligent beings capable of finding joy in God. God is a vortex of most profound happiness, drawing us ever deeper into its own deepest center.

Martin Luther's great insight was that the righteousness of God is contagious. It has the effect of making righteous whatever it touches. In the same way, the blessedness of the Blessed Trinity makes blessed all whom it encounters. When we were baptized in the name of Father, Son, and Holy Spirit, we were immersed in a sea of happiness and invited to become one with it. As children of God we could perhaps see our mission in life as allowing ourselves to be more fully possessed by the divine happiness and willing to pass it on to others. Mother Teresa of Calcutta once said that whenever we say goodbye to someone we should aim at leaving them a little bit happier than they were when we met. If we do so, then we are acting like God, diffusing happiness. (June 7, 2009.)

Eternal and Blessed Trinity, we have been signed in your name and recognized as your children. Help us to open our hearts to your presence so that we may be agents of happiness to all those around us. We ask this through Christ our Lord. Amen.

February 2   ✠   **Bootless**

Shakespeare used the word *bootless* twenty-eight times. It doesn't mean going without shoes. It is an Old English legal term meaning, among other things, something that is void of profit, unavailing, useless. And this is the sense in which Shakespeare used it. A bootless life is one that is going around in circles, that can't get out of first gear, that is destined to end in frustration.

To live a bootless existence is to have no goal and, therefore, no objectives. Without objectives there is no clear vision of what means need to be taken and no possibility to commit to a persistent course of action. Such a life is a life without seriousness; the days are filled with escapist activities, self-indulgence, and the urgent search for entertainment. The little-used term to describe such an existence is *acedia*, the inability to commit oneself to anything beyond the floating butterfly life of each moment. Such a life is unavailing and absurd, a living death.

So, avoiding bootlessness is not a matter of wearing shoes, but rather of having a clear sense of a goal that will guide the choices that we make. I must ask myself: What is the ultimate purpose not only of human life in general, but of my life in particular? Usually the goal is distant and complex; we have to break it down into several more immediate objectives. This will help us to work out what practical steps we need to take and, more importantly, what good habits we need to develop.

Most of us want to be free, but sometimes we confuse freedom with spontaneity. If I want the freedom to become an opera singer or a brain surgeon, I can't just hang around and wait for the moment that I feel like taking up either profession. To have the freedom to sing like a bird or do surgery like an artist I need a lot of theoretical knowledge and years of practice. Spontaneity won't accomplish this.

For the most part, freedom is not something we have, but something into which we must grow, and this is accomplished only by sustained and purposeful action. Usually this means having a plan that is flexible enough to survive the changes that life brings, realistic enough in its demands to make continuance feasible, and effective enough to make its outcomes proportionate to the effort expended.

In most matters, including spirituality, we need a livable rule of life. (July 11, 2007.)

Creator God, you have called us to travel along the way that leads to eternal life. Give us the good sense to remain on the road your Son has indicated, the strength to keep moving onward, and the hope that fills us with the joyous expectation of arriving. We make our prayer in the name of Jesus our Lord. Amen.

February 3 ✢ *Boundaries*

The fourth chapter of Saint John's gospel contains a long and beautiful narrative about Jesus' interaction with a Samaritan woman. It is a well-told story, and it has a profound theological message. The work of salvation involves the dismantling of the boundaries that we set between ourselves and others, even those apparently sanctioned by long tradition and approved by the religious authorities.

Jews did not use the same drinking vessels as Samaritans; in fact, they did not want to have anything to do with these neighbors, whom they regarded as an aberrant sect. And the feeling was reciprocated. Beyond this division lay the division between genders typical of a heavily patriarchal society. The disciples were surprised to see Jesus talking to a woman—not this particular woman, but any woman. And it was an expansive conversation begun by Jesus humbly requesting a drink, asking a favor not only of a stranger but of an alien.

There is yet another boundary broken in the conversation. As usual, Jesus does not recognize any frontier between himself and the unrighteous. The fact that the woman is fetching water from the well at midday, long after the women of the village have gone home, suggests that she is something of a pariah. No doubt the reason for this can be found in the five husbands and the present non-husband in her life. I don't think you could find anybody so despised by respectable people of that culture as a Samaritan woman living an irregular life.

Yet all this negative evidence seems to have made no impression on Jesus, who engaged freely in conversation, revealing himself to her and leading her to a fuller self-knowledge that, in turn, impelled her to become an evangelist to the townspeople. What an impact he had on her through simply being himself, tired and thirsty and willing to meet her where she was! No boundary existed between them.

If we look into our own lives, we will probably discover many different frontiers that we are reluctant to cross. Most of them we create out of a sense of fragility and fear of the unknown, hoping that they will serve as a bulwark against unpleasant surprises. Salvation is a matter of Christ building bridges; damnation is a matter of us building walls. (March 3, 2002.)

Lord Jesus Christ, help us to recognize the gifts of God present in all people without distinction. Help us to reach out, beyond the divides we create, to proclaim your Good News to all who are thirsting for the waters of life. For you are our Lord for ever and ever. Amen.

February 4   ✠   Bridesmaids

In a perfect world, bridesmaids would not exist. A totally frivolous institution, all aflutter about dresses and hairdos, with no real function except standing around and looking vaguely ornamental. It was no surprise to me that, when Jesus told the parable of the bridesmaids, half of them didn't have enough sense to provide themselves with sufficient oil for their lamps or, at least, to stay awake long enough to discover their default.

I suppose Jesus wanted to emphasize in this parable the seriousness of every human life. We are being warned, here as elsewhere, not to let ourselves be carried away by frivolous concerns so that we fail to do what needs to be done to ensure that we are fit for purpose. We assign too much importance to trivialities and forget to pay attention to what is essential. Like the Pharisees, who strained out gnats and swallowed camels. Like Martha, who was distracted and disturbed about household tasks and failed to attend to the one thing necessary. Like those who gain the whole world but suffer the loss of their soul.

Here we are circling around a virtue that doesn't have much exposure: the virtue of prudence. Prudence concerns itself with choosing the best course of action among several options. Note that it is a choice. One of the vices opposed to prudence is the failure to make choices, to let matters take their course without intervening. If a car is heading toward a precipice, you can either stop it, change direction, or bail out. Arguments can be mounted for each possibility. Doing nothing, due to a failure to decide, is a surefire recipe for disaster.

An important part of prudence is recognizing the situations in which a choice will have the possibility of yielding a better result. Then it is a question of practical judgment between options. This presupposes an openness to as much data as possible. Prudence does not walk a narrow path. It welcomes a second opinion, and a third. We can make a certain judgment in the sphere of logic; concerning such issues as $2 + 2 = 4$, the mind enjoys a measure of infallibility. But concerning practical decisions, the best we can hope for is probability. A sound assessment of probability is based on canvassing as many options as necessary, according to the importance of the matter and the urgency of doing something.

The sensible bridesmaids looked ahead and acted prudently. The silly ones did not take their situation seriously, allowed themselves to forget what they were on about, and so missed the wedding. (November 6, 2005.)

Lord Jesus Christ, you have admonished us to stay awake and to prepare ourselves to enter the banquet of eternal life. Keep our minds and hearts fixed on things that really matter and give us the strength not to be overwhelmed by the prevailing superficiality of the epoch in which we live. For you are our Lord, for ever and ever. Amen.

February 5   ✠   *Buses*

There are currently eight hundred big, red double-decker buses going around London emblazoned with the sign, "There's probably no God. Now stop worrying and enjoy your life." An attempt to hold a similar campaign in Melbourne was effectively blocked.

What we are seeing in such undertakings is an organized campaign by aggressive atheism to peddle its views. In line with current secularist thinking, it attacks, caricatures, and mocks religious belief, religious experience, and religious persons without having to engage in rational discussion or provide an explanation for the ultimate questions with which humanity has to deal.

The campaign seems to be based on the premise that belief in the existence of God is a source of worry that causes us to extract less enjoyment from life. What sort of parody is that? If you read this book, you probably believe in God. Is your life more worrisome and less enjoyable because of that? Just because something is written on a bus—or even on eight hundred buses—it doesn't mean that it makes any sense.

There are three fundamental questions that even the most articulate atheists find difficult to answer.

- Why anything exists, and where it all comes from.
- Why some things are alive and are gifted with the capacity of self-motion.
- Why some living things are self-aware.

We may not be skilled enough to counter their pseudo-philosophical bluster, but the hypothesis of an infinite being outside our sphere, creating and conserving the universe, is not irrational.

It is hard not to be influenced by the propaganda of a secularist culture that has been very successful in eroding the general view on many issues of morality. We need to be aware that we are being bombarded by opinion contrary both to the values of the Gospel and to any demanding option regarding justice or ethics. Is there any issue on which the media campaigns for a stricter personal morality? After a while even we begin to think we are weirdos if we are serious about issues of life and death.

The basis of our alternative worldview is our acceptance of an afterlife and our hope to find our fulfillment in God's gift of eternal life. This sets us apart. We are, as Jesus said, "children of the resurrection," and it should take more than a group of modern-day Sadducees and their eight hundred buses to make us resile from our faith. (November 6, 2010.)

Risen Lord, you have called us to follow you into eternal life. Give us the confidence to resist everything that undermines our faith and trust in your promises, and the courage to reveal the truth of the Gospel by the quality of our lives. For you are our Lord for ever and ever. Amen.

February 6 ✠ **Caesar**

In a press conference, former British Prime Minister Tony Blair was once asked a question about religion. His reply was, "We don't do God." I suppose his purpose was to draw a clear demarcation between politics and religion.

Such was not the approach taken by Pharisees and Herodians when they approached Jesus with a question about the legitimacy of paying tax to Rome. It was a clever pincer move, since it would be almost impossible to give a response that would satisfy both the collaborationist Herodians and the strict Pharisees. In replying, Jesus used a similar approach to Blair's. In effect he said, "We don't do Caesar."

In asking to see the silver denarius, which was a full day's wage and likely to have been only in the purses of the rich, he was asking for the Roman occupation currency that should not have been carried into the temple precincts. He was already driving a wedge between his questioners. Having wrenched from them the admission that the coin belonged to Caesar's sphere of influence, he acknowledged the possibility of an obligation to Caesar but added the rider that they were equally obliged to pay their debts to God.

Jesus stepped back from involving himself in such issues, as he did when he refused to settle a quarrel between two brothers: "Man, who made me an arbiter over you?" As he is reported by the Fourth Evangelist to have said to Pilate, "My kingdom is not of this world."

Some forty years ago the theologian Johannes Baptist Metz wrote *The Theology of the World*. He insisted that the church needs to let go of the medieval notion that it can dictate to science, philosophy, or the state. These have become autonomous entities, governed by their own laws. He pointed out that Vatican

II favored dialogue, based on mutual respect and thus requiring the humility to find common ground. This is the way to go.

It is by the presence, witness, and action of Gospel-driven individuals and communities that the seeds of the Word are sown in the hearts of all. Osmosis is a much better means of evangelization than pontifical decrees. (October 19, 2008.)

> *Lord Jesus Christ, you have taught us to seek first the kingdom of God. Help us to give priority to whatever will speed our journey toward this kingdom without neglecting our role in temporal affairs. For you are our Lord and God for ever and ever. Amen.*

February 7 ✛ Care

The story of Mary and Martha reminds us that the two components of hospitality seem always to be in competition. We all know how difficult it is to reconcile the roles of entertainer and worker. Inevitably we favor one option and face criticism that the other has been neglected. So the story rings a bell with us, but there are two corollaries that are easily overlooked.

The first concerns multitasking. We can do two things at once only when each is based in a different hemisphere of the brain. Otherwise our attention is divided and the quality of both tasks declines. This is even more obvious when we try to juggle several activities. Speaking on the phone has been demonstrated to be more destructive of good driving than elevated alcohol levels. When we attempt several simultaneous activities, the amount of care we give to each is reduced; if an emergency or a surprise occurs, our response time is slower.

The lesson here is that we need to be alert and prudent. To give ourselves to what we are doing without having a contrary soundtrack running through our brain. We can learn something from the Zen practice of mindfulness: to restrict our attention to the narrow corridor of present action, not allowing thoughts and emotions from past or future to intrude.

Having affirmed the value of being careful, we need to remember that what seems to be its opposite is also true. The New Testament often regards care as a vice. Jesus tells us to have no care for tomorrow, and the first letter of Peter advises us to cast all our care on God. Anxiety is not part of Christian discipleship. Quite the contrary, knowing that God is our loving Father, able to write straight on crooked lines, means that we are less prone to the soul-destroying obsessiveness about details that seems to have been typical of the Pharisees. We are called to be carefree. Not careless, but giving due care to each moment and leaving the rest to God. (July 17, 2016.)

> *Loving Father, we recognize that our life is in your hands and that you can supply for all our defects. Increase our sense of trust in your providence so that we are free from anxiety about the future but always attentive to make the most of the opportunities of the present. We ask you this through Christ our Lord. Amen.*

February 8 ✠ *Career Path*

The biographers of famous people are often at pains to demonstrate that those who have made great progress in their chosen fields often began very young. Madame Melba, our local opera diva at the start of the twentieth century, began singing lessons at the age of five. Teilhard de Chardin was already lyricizing over matter at the age of six; at the age of seven, Ronald Knox was writing Greek verse. And most elite athletes begin their way to the top while they are still children.

I suppose we could ask ourselves whether holiness also demands an early start. Certainly, biographers of the saints often attempt to portray their subjects as models of holiness even from the cradle. And while it may be true, as Thomas Aquinas thought, that life-shaping choices are often made as early as the dawn of reason, there are other pathways to holiness. We need to avoid giving the impression that holiness consists primarily in quickly making the right choices and then sticking to them. Of course, our contribution to the process is important, but it is not primary. The fundamental reality in the journey to holiness is the call of God, the invitation to walk this road, the summons to follow Christ. This is the grace that energizes and sustains us through all the twists and turns of the journey. It can come early, or it may wait for the eleventh hour. Sanctity is not mainly our activity, but that of God showing mercy. The initiative in outstanding holiness is God's.

Far from being a matter of choosing early and then systematically following through, holiness often involves a change of direction, a conversion. This is the pattern we see in the calling of the first apostles and in the dramatic turnabout in the life of Saint Paul. God intervenes at a time not of the person's own choosing. A vocation implies being called, and that means being called by another.

Even a positive response to the divine invitation is not the end of the story. Christian discipleship is not without its puzzling interludes; sometimes there are dead ends, blind alleys, and periods of stagnation. We may be compelled to let the soil of our soul lie fallow for a time in the hope that it will recover its potential. The lives of the saints remind us that often there is a second journey to be undertaken, a new adventure in hope and courage. And even a third or a fourth.

This is all a far cry from a clear, straight pathway to the top. Even more mysterious, if our Christian commitment is real, the road will lead inevitably to Calvary—because that is the only doorway through which we can enter into the more abundant life we are seeking. (March 19, 1969.)

Loving Father, you call us to yourself and invite us to leave behind the certainty of earthly security. Help us to be true pilgrims as we journey through life, accepting each day as it comes but with our eyes and our hopes fixed on our journey's end in the kingdom of your love. We make this prayer through Christ our Lord. Amen.

February 9   ✠   *Catholic*

Is God a Catholic? Well, often we seem to think so. We take for granted that God is on our side and listens more attentively to our prayers than to those of others. Such a view is like that of the tribal God of the Old Testament, who fights for us and who dispossesses and slaughters any who are opposed to us. But God is not a Catholic, in the sense of belonging to our sect. God is catholic, in the sense that there are no limits to God's care and compassion.

God's love, as it is presented in the New Testament, has no ethnic preferences (Gentiles are as welcome as Jews) and, seemingly, is not based on ethical divisions. This is stated explicitly in the gospels. Our heavenly Father "makes the sun to shine on the wicked and the good and the rain to fall on the righteous and the unrighteous," and "is kind to the ungrateful and the wicked." It is a love without borders. God wills that all people are to be saved and come to the knowledge of the truth. Not even one of the little ones is to be lost.

If we accept that God's love is non-preferential, then religious wars and controversies are not only stupid, but are getting close to being blasphemous. The problem often begins with our attempts to define God. Creating definitions means putting fences around realities. If I insist on thinking about heaven and earth as distinct, I lose the Semitic idea that heaven and earth constitute a single reality; they belong together. When I attempt to define God, I can necessarily isolate a single aspect of God that, in the process, becomes exaggerated. If I define God as judge, then much of the divine reality is lost. If I emphasize only divine mercy, then something else disappears. The only way to define God is to say that God is beyond definition. God is closer to "everything" than to "something."

Since we are called on to be like God, as holy, as perfect, and as merciful as God, it follows that something of the divine catholicity must be evident in our attitudes. None may be excluded from our care and concern. Nobody may be defined as outsider or opponent. And if we have "principles" that cause us to exclude anyone, then we would be better off ditching those principles than failing to reproduce in our own small way the non-preferential character of God's love for all. (February 25, 2014.)

Loving Father, you cause the sun to rise on the wicked as on the good, and the rain to fall equally on everyone. Help us to be magnanimous in our love, giving to all generously and making no distinction between persons. Help us to love others as you have loved us. We ask this in the name of Jesus the Lord. Amen.

February 10 ✠ *Cause and Effect*

In the kingdom of God nothing is as it seems it should be. Our expectations are constantly frustrated. We know that this was true in the case of Jesus' contemporaries. They hoped for a messiah who would lead them to a period of peace and prosperity, but their hopes yielded nothing. The townspeople of Nazareth rejected Jesus precisely because he was too ordinary. Nothing special could be expected from him.

The visible results to be achieved in the kingdom are not commensurate with the labor we may invest. Jesus takes care to remind his followers that "one sows and another reaps." We cannot immediately see the fruits of our exertions, and yet, when we do seem to have some success, it is usually the result of what others have done to prepare the ground. Saint Paul was aware of this paradox when he wrote, "I planted, Apollos watered, but it is God who gives the increase."

The anticipated shattering of causal certainty invites us to consider that when we do the work of God we are acting as part of a larger whole. We cannot always appreciate what role our small contribution will make toward the final outcome. We do our best but often cannot know what impact our words or actions will have. We try to be unwearied in doing good, confident that God is acting through us to bring all things to completion. Then sower and reaper will rejoice together. The truly selfless love, about which Saint Paul wrote in 1 Corinthians 13, is not so much a virtue achieved by willpower. It is, rather, the overflow that comes from years of doing our best to live according to the Gospel, without expecting dramatic or visible results but quietly trusting in God's power to make something great out of the almost-nothing that we achieve. Somehow living like this changes us and everything else for the better. (January 30, 1977.)

Loving Father, help us to keep working in your vineyard even when there seems to be little to show for our labors. Help us to be satisfied with a discipleship that is ordinary, obscure, and laborious so that in all things you may be glorified. We ask this through Christ our Lord. Amen.

February 11 ✠ *Change Fatigue*

As I get older, life appears to be getting more complicated. The world of my youth seems to have been very simple by comparison. It is not only the exploding world of new technologies, but the many revolutionary changes in the social order as well. And, of course, since Vatican II, the changeless church has changed considerably.

Many of us are beginning to suffer from change fatigue. We have lost faith in the process of acquiring new insights and skills because, it seems, they are outdated as soon as we have acquired some degree of competence. We have become customers for a quick and easy fix. My doctor once remarked that patients are usually happy to take medication; they can be convinced of the need for surgery, but there is no way they will be persuaded to change their lifestyle. We want instant fixes. That is why people often choose package deals for their holidays; all the decisions are made for them. This is why voters generally maintain loyalty to a party line and cast their ballots without examining the issues carefully. This is why fundamentalism is such an easy option for interpreting the Bible; we don't have to go to the trouble of acquainting ourselves with the huge volume of critical work invested in understanding the Scriptures better.

All this has led to a lower level of participation in social and political life. Parish pump politics has almost disappeared; we prefer to be disinterested bystanders, seeing politics as a form of entertainment. Letting others make the running.

Isn't it time for us to stand up and to begin acting like reason-endowed adults, to judge issues for ourselves, acting independently when it is possible? Otherwise we are just reeds buffeted by the wind, changing our intellectual stance to suit ephemeral fashion. To act like this will involve having a personal code of belief and value that is profound enough to reflect our deepest aspirations and flexible enough to respond to a changing world.

For us Christians, our guiding star must be the person of Jesus Christ, as is placed before us in the Gospel tradition. The more we are breathless in trying to keep up with the pace of change, the more important it is for us to stop and step back from the ever-flowing river and take our bearings. Then, perhaps, we can move from being passive victims to becoming influential participants. (January 29, 2006.)

> *Lord Jesus Christ, you have set before us the path that leads to eternal life. Give us the wisdom to follow this way, the courage to persevere when times are tough, and the zeal to share what we have learned with others. For you are our Lord for ever and ever. Amen.*

February 12   ✠   **Cheap Grace**

The phrase "cheap grace" comes from Dietrich Bonhoeffer, who used it in the negative. There is no cheap grace. In his context, it was meant to balance out the Lutheran insistence on the primacy of grace. His point was that lifelong fidelity to grace takes a great deal of effort and may even lead to martyrdom, as it seems to have done in his own case.

This teaching is useful for us in our different context. We live in an age of instancy. We are sometimes reluctant to accept that some things necessarily take a long time and can cost a great deal of effort. A lot of advertising seems to have as its basic premise that we want to do things easily and have the results more speedily: to wash the dishes with the touch of a button, to clean the carpets by dancing over the floor with a Hoover, to play the guitar after twenty minutes of instruction. And any issue, no matter how complex, must submit to be covered in a sound bite or fully explained in a three-minute, in-depth interview.

Albert Einstein was habitually out of his depth in dealing with practical money matters. On one occasion a friend suggested he enter a competition that offered a generous prize for a 1,500-word explanation of the theory of relativity. Einstein's response was, "The theory of relativity cannot be explained in 1,500 words!"

If we are honest, we have to admit that there are many truths that are beyond our present comprehension, there are many worthwhile skills in which we are incompetent, and there are many good and noble deeds from which we hold ourselves aloof. This means that if we are to make progress toward a richer life, then considerable effort will be required of us, and a large measure of perseverance.

Our participation in the kingdom of God is not exempt from this obligation. Jesus reminds his followers that the gate is narrow, the road is hard, and the journey long. There are no backdoor deals. No under-the-counter discounts. To take possession of the treasure we need to sell everything. To be a disciple we need to take up the cross. To rise with Christ we must die with Christ. It would be nice if there were another way, but there isn't one. (August 24, 1986.)

Lord Jesus Christ, prepare our minds to accept the cost of discipleship. Inspire us with the confidence to put our best efforts into everything we do, while accepting that it is your providence that will determine the outcomes. For you are our Lord for ever and ever. Amen.

February 13 ✠ *Cheerfulness*

I love the story about the martyrdom of Saint Laurence being burned alive on a gridiron. Well, not his being burned, but the cheerfulness with which he faced this horrible death. He is reported to have said to the grisly executioners surrounding him, "Turn me over now. I'm cooked on one side." There are other stories of happy martyrs from those days. When Saint Adauctus—so called because no one knows his real name—saw Christians being carted off to execution, he ran after them shouting, "Wait for me; I am also a Christian." So they simply called him Saint Added-On. Or then there is a similar saint about whom nothing is known except that, as the moment of death approached, he or she cried out "Alleluia!" And so we have Saint Alleluia.

By contrast, how many reputedly good Christians are sad sacks. Their favorite psalm is "Hear my voice, O Lord, as I complain." A parish acquaintance of my family was sometimes referred to, behind her back, as "Weeping Willow" because every week, it seemed, she had to endure a new tragedy, the details of which were generously shared.

Saint Paul exhorts us to be cheerful givers, not mournful receivers. This admonition seems to presuppose our taking control of our life and not allowing the small frustrations and disappointments to undermine our fundamental sense of well-being. We are very foolish if we permit our sense of good cheer to be dependent on external factors. That way we will be up and down all our life, like a perpetual yo-yo.

Cheerfulness is a choice that we make. It can coexist with hard times. It is not merely the result of temperament or a philosophy of life that bids us always to look on the bright side. For Christians, cheerfulness comes from faith in the promises of Christ. Despite present reverses, in the end all will be well.

We can go further. The Epistle to the Galatians reminds us that joy is one aspect of the Spirit's indwelling; there is a joy that surpasses human understanding. So well was this understood that some ancient writers went so far as to believe that sadness was the worst of all sins and the source of many evils.

My father often repeated the verse from the psalm: "This is the day the Lord has made; let us rejoice and be glad therein." (August 10, 2012.)

Jesus, joy of our desiring, fill us with confidence that the hundredfold you have promised will be poured into our laps, shaken down and overflowing. Help us to surmount the inevitable difficulties of life with serenity and joy, in the confidence that nothing can separate us from our loving acceptance by God. For you are our Lord for ever and ever. Amen.

February 14 ✠ *Christlike*

When preachers exhort us to be Christlike, we mostly feel frustrated at being asked to do the impossible. It is probably true, as Saint Augustine often said, that whatever Christ was by nature we can become by grace, and yet, for most of us, this represents an impossible ideal.

This is where we need to be clear about what is meant by becoming Christlike. It certainly doesn't mean driving out our demons, curing the sick, raising the dead—or dying on a cross. And it certainly doesn't mean performing such wonders by dint of undeviating willpower. Becoming Christlike means allowing ourselves to receive the same Holy Spirit who descended on Jesus and remained with him.

Receiving the Spirit does not mean that we are about to become clones of Jesus of Nazareth. It means, above all, that we become ourselves; we become the beautiful and unique creatures God has created us to be. Each of us has our own special gifts from God, and it is the work of the Spirit to bring these talents to their full flowering, not only for our sake but for the benefit of all. Our nature and our culture and our history all have a formative effect on how these gifts are expressed, but the gifts themselves are from God and are part of the divine plan for the enhancement of creation.

How can we discern what are God's gifts to us? Jesus gives us a key principle: "By their fruit you shall know them." If this seems to be too vague a criterion, we can find guidance in a text from the Epistle to the Galatians. Saint Paul speaks of the fruit that results from the work of the Spirit. It is many faceted, but he lists its most palpable characteristics: "love, joy, peace, patience, kindness, goodness, faithfulness, meekness and self-control." That is quite a list! But think how different our world—and our immediate surroundings—would be if these qualities, each expressed in our uniquely personal way, marked the way we lived. Whatever the circumstances in which we find ourselves, if we aim to respond to them according to this plan, we are progressively showing ourselves to be genuinely Spirit-led, uniquely Christlike, and fully human. (May 19, 2013.)

Come, Holy Spirit, transform the hearts of all the faithful so that by your inspiration we show forth in our lives the loving kindness of our God, and so begin the work of renewing the face of the earth. Be with us always, now and forever. Amen.

February 15   ✝   *Christos anesti!*

I've been told that, even in its most repressive years, nearly everybody in the Soviet Union knew the date of Easter, even though it was forbidden to make the slightest allusion to the fact in the public media.

Perhaps, in the West, we place disproportionate emphasis on Good Friday and the death by which Christ paid the price for our sins. As a result, Easter can almost seem like an afterthought. We are very eloquent in our portrayal of the sufferings of Jesus but tongue-tied when it comes to celebrating the reality of his risen life. On the one hand, this can lead to religious practice that gives more importance to saying no to the life of this world than to saying yes to the life of the next. Mortification takes precedence over celebration. On the other, as Christians have left aside the celebration of Easter Sunday, the space is left available for Easter bunnies and Easter eggs and football matches.

As you know, the traditional Easter greeting in Greek communities is *Christos anesti* (Christ has risen), to which the reply is given, *Alethos anesti* (He has truly risen). This is a phrase that we should imprint on our hearts and minds, as the counterpoint that keeps pace with everything that happens in our life. Especially deathlike experience. As our journey through life continues it can serve as a kind of litany. The world is in a mess. But Christ has risen! Our leaders have lost the plot. But Christ has risen! The church is besieged on every side. But Christ has risen! Our family has its share of tragedies. But Christ has risen! My life is in the pits. But Christ has risen! We can confront and endure every vicissitude and reversal of fortune because of our faith that Christ has risen. That has changed everything. Nothing is the same again. *Christos anesti. Alethos anesti.*

The other great song of triumph of the Easter season is taken from Psalm 118. "This is the day that the Lord has made; let us rejoice and be glad therein." Perhaps we may come to the point where we say this every day, beginning when we first awake. And if someone asks why this is so, we can reply *Christos anesti*: Christ has risen. (April 1, 2018.)

> *Lord Jesus Christ, risen from the dead, our present source of joy and our confidence in the world to come. As we journey toward your heavenly kingdom, fill our hearts with your burning zeal so that we may become beacons of hope and optimism to all whom we encounter on the way. For you are our risen Lord, now and forever. Amen.*

February 16   ✠   **Cloud**

There are three great symbols of Christ's victory over death and sin. The empty tomb signals that death had no power over him. The mighty wind that accompanied the sending of the Holy Spirit demonstrates that he has power to renew the face of the earth. The cloud that covers him from sight as he returns to the Father is a constant reminder to us that he is not here: we must seek the things that are above.

We live under this luminous cloud. We do not have access to the total radiance of the divine glory, but we are not totally excluded from it. We cannot see God directly, but we are not completely in the dark. We live in the mediated radiance of faith, somewhere between complete unknowing and face-to-face contact.

Too often we describe faith in terms of its being half empty when, in reality, it is half full. We concentrate on what we cannot see, and we fail to celebrate how faith represents a spectacular advance on living by our own lights.

Faith is the light of the glorious Christ shining through the cloud of our mortal existence. Instead of emphasizing its limitations we should be ready to affirm that faith is a greater gift than seeing the physical presence of Christ. "Blessed are those who have not seen and have believed." This is why he said to his disciples, "It is expedient for you that I go." Faith is not the denial of sight but the progressive development of a different mode of seeing.

What do we perceive by faith? Three things. Firstly, through faith we become aware of the personal presence of Christ in our lives and are drawn to communion with him in prayer. Secondly, this encounter inspires a sense of vocation or mission in us; we are moved by a zeal for the kingdom—to be other Christs for a needy world. Thirdly, we are comforted and encouraged by a mysterious hope for the future; faith makes us strong in bearing the inevitable difficulties of life.

The cloud is a symbol of our faith; it is not something that obscures the outshining of eternal light but instead something that moderates it to accommodate it to our weakness so that we are not bereft of its assistance as we journey through life. (May 8, 1986.)

> *Lord Jesus Christ, you have promised to be with us until the end of time. Deepen our perception of your presence so that*

we may find in you a dear friend, a wise counselor, and a
strong helper. For you are our Lord for ever and ever. Amen.

February 17 ✠ Cold Water

The recipe for salvation is simple. Take one cup of cold water and, in the name of Christ, give it to someone who is thirsty. That's all it takes. At least, this is what we may infer from the words of Jesus on this topic. We can achieve high sainthood without being called to spectacularly heroic actions. It is just a question of living in the present moment and acting in a Christ-like way as opportunities present themselves.

We tend to evaluate actions quantitatively; the bigger the splash they make, the more important we consider them. Yet occasionally we experience a sense of delight at some small trifle, an unheralded act of kindness or gratuitous courtesy. We can give others the opportunity to feel a similar surge of energy by a thousand small gestures that do not cost us more than a blink of the eye.

The key to sainthood is to learn to imitate the God whose nature it is to give. For us, unlike God, giving involves giving away. When we give, we have less than we had before. We are voluntarily diminished when we give something to others, even if it is only our time, our attention, our recognition of their talents. We are stepping back to make room for them. We are putting our own needs and desires on hold while we attend to theirs. We are subordinating our own instincts and inclinations to the will.

This is more than self-denial. More often than not it is an exercise in the empowerment of others. Because of our action, they move away from the encounter with a smile on their faces, with more energy to deal creatively with the new challenges that this day will bring. Jesus said that to welcome a prophet is to receive the reward to which the prophet is entitled. When we encourage others to act virtuously, we participate in the good deeds that they perform.

A cup of cold water isn't much, and that is why we undervalue its potential not only to create a little local goodness, but also make the world a slightly better place. Imagine what the world would be like if, on a given day, a billion people gave the equivalent of a cup of cold water to their neighbor. I think the result would be close to heaven on earth. (June 30, 2002.)

> *Our Father in heaven, you so loved the world that you gave us your only Son. Give us the grace to share in your generosity by recognizing the needs of those around us and meeting those needs with the gifts that you have given us. We ask this in the name of Jesus our Lord. Amen.*

February 18   ✠   **Collapse**

To the Galilean followers of Jesus, the temple in Jerusalem was a magnificent spectacle. In Mark's account they are stunned by the size of the stones; in Luke's narrative it is the splendor of the decoration that seizes their admiration. Beyond its visible impact it was also imbued with a mystical significance; the Psalms sang of the sacredness of Mount Zion and promised that it would endure forever. To the country boys from Galilee, seeing this huge structure for the first time, it must have seemed very probable that it would stand firm forever.

In fact, around the time when Mark's gospel was compiled, the temple would be besieged, ransacked, pillaged, burned, and destroyed, almost as Jesus predicted: with scarcely one stone left on another. As the story of the tower of Babel reminds us, there is no permanence for any human undertaking apart from God. "Unless the Lord build the house, in vain do its builders labor."

Using the language of apocalypticism, Jesus reminds his disciples of two basic truths. Trouble is inevitable, and maintaining one's faith in times of trouble is what marks us out as true disciples. Jesus did not preach a prosperity gospel, but bluntly insisted that tragedy and loss are universal elements of human experience. It is faith that helps us come through the times of crisis. I remember speaking with a woman who had just been diagnosed with terminal cancer. Her response? "I am just so grateful to have the gift of faith. Without it this situation would have been intolerable."

If God allowed his glorious temple to be reduced to rubble, we can be reasonably sure that we will not escape the pangs of loss and desolation. We need to be prepared for that and for the mental confusion that follows. Jesus' message to us is quite simple. Do not be frightened. Do not allow yourself to be drawn into resentment and doubt. This is the time for faith to grow into hope. This is not the end, but it is a time when we can demonstrate our trust in the fatherly providence of God, even though we do not understand what is happening. When everything collapses, that is the time to start seeking God. It is more like the end of the beginning than the beginning of the end. (November 18, 2007.)

Father, help us to accept that all that comes from your hand is good and to our benefit. Give us a strong trust in Providence and the fervent belief that all things work together unto good. We ask this through Christ our Lord. Amen.

February 19   ✠   Come as You Are

When the previous cathedral in Los Angeles was condemned after an earthquake, a new one was built. Our Lady of the Angels stands proud, just up the street from the Frank Gehry-designed Walt Disney Concert Hall, with a huge plaza, underground parking lot, and a separate building for hospitality and other services. The whole space exudes a sense of welcome and friendliness.

The strongest memory I have comes from the series of 25 huge tapestries on the north and south walls, depicting no less than 135 identifiable saints, together with a dozen or so anonymous figures, including children. The tapestries are designed to look like frescoes and are woven in muted colors. The figures are in clothing typical of their own period in history and culture;

there are no halos, no white robes, no harps. Each of the 135 is an individual. More recent saints are recognizable from their faces, others by subtle indication of feature or clothing.

The saints are shown as belonging to every race, gender, and age group. A variety of vocations or occupations is indicated. They look just like the people who constitute the congregation: ordinary, down-to-earth folk, relaxed, comfortable in their own skins, but with a serene and subtle dignity. Walking up the central aisle is like joining these saints in a vast procession, heading toward the altar and the great cross window in the east wall.

Yet viewing these tapestries was not like seeing an exhibition of art. It was not the case of an observer and an object. There was a strong sense of continuity between the walls and the pews. People up there are just like those down here. I was reminded of the medieval belief that there was a second choir above the monastic choir, one composed of angels who joined the monks in singing the praise of God, bowing in unison with them at the doxology.

The lesson to be learned from these tapestries is one of catholicity and inclusion. We are not alone in our struggles; a great cloud of witnesses has gone before us, people like us with limitations and difficulties and failures. They have overcome these liabilities through their willingness to receive the love that God offers.

If the saints are not much different from us, then we can come as we are. We don't have to change anything. We don't have to hide from any aspect of our history. We don't have to make ourselves respectable. The vicissitudes of our personal history don't matter; God's love embraces all. Just come. Come as you are. (November 1, 2007.)

Loving Father, with open arms you welcome us all to your house of many mansions. Give us the faith to see ourselves as citizens of heaven and members of your household. Give us the grace to live in this world conscious of our communion with all the saints and mindful of the equal dignity of all. We ask this in the name of Jesus our Lord. Amen.

February 20 ✠ *Comfort*

In 1967 a book appeared by the sociologist C. Y. Glock and others, entitled *To Comfort and to Challenge: A Dilemma of the Contemporary Church*. The point was that it is very difficult to find the right balance between comfort and challenge in proclaiming the Gospel. Too much comfort and people get slack; too much challenge and they lose heart. Bernard of Clairvaux in the twelfth century noticed the same phenomenon.

Perhaps the gospel writers were also aware of it. There are many challenging statements attributed to Jesus, particularly those that insist that his disciples leave everything and follow him, even to the cross.

What a relief it is, then, to find the saying Matthew preserved from an older tradition. "Come to me you who labor and are burdened and I will give you rest. Take my yoke upon you and learn from me that I am meek and humble of heart and you will find rest for your souls. My yoke is easy and my burden light."

First of all, note that it is not an invitation to indolence. There are four active verbs. *Come. Take. Learn. Find.*

Jesus calls us, and if we are to receive comfort, we must respond by coming to him. How do we do this when he is not physically present? We need to go to that space from which his call resounded. We go within to the heart or conscience. We hear the voice, and we say, "Here I am." Our task is to pick up Christ's yoke, the mission by which we become his coworkers. To share his labor and by association to learn about him, to get to know him by working with him. His presence at our side makes the labor light; we discover that even serious toil can become a source of rest rather than an effort.

To experience the comfort of Christ asks of us a trusting gift of ourselves, persevering labor and an openness to interior reality. Giving myself into the hands of Christ means acknowledging that his ways are more loving and life-giving than my own and allowing the sense of well-being that comes with his company to become stronger. To be open to the comfort of Christ is also a challenge. (July 4, 1999.)

Jesus, meek and humble of heart, help us to learn how to act in a way that is both fully human and fully divine. Strengthen us for the challenges of the Gospel so that we may console others with the consolation we ourselves have received. For you are our Lord for ever and ever. Amen.

February 21   ✠   **Commandments**

When Jesus was asked about the greatest commandment, the question was not designed to initiate a serious discussion of morality. It was a game. The rabbis distinguished 613 different commandments found in various places in the Hebrew Scriptures. They loved debating the order of precedence among them. It didn't matter how the respondent answered; there was always occasion for the parry and thrust of intellectual debate: who can attempt to juggle 613 objects without at least one of them dropping to the floor?

Jesus takes the discussion beyond the borders of entertainment and treats the question seriously. He cites two texts that together affirm the vertical and horizontal aspects of morality: we need to have appropriate attitudes both to God and to other human beings. Do this, and all will be well. Some of the rabbis used the same combination.

But, we may ask, can love really be the object of a commandment? It is possible to order children to eat their breakfast cereal, but it is useless to insist that they enjoy it. You can't make others love what they do not. Love is something that is spontaneously drawn from us; we cannot force ourselves to love, no more than we can force ourselves to relax. We can make choices about our behavior, but our feelings dance to a different tune.

Perhaps what Jesus is indicating by his response is that true religion is more than the observance of specific commandments. It is a global attitude of acceptance and attachment to all reality, divine and created. It is communion. Certainly, this communion is expressed and reinforced by particular actions, but the relationship transcends these secondary manifestations. Our primary gift is to live in the context of God and others, which involves basing our choices on the practical opportunities that are offered us every day. Sometimes we will be called to solitary communion with God in prayer, and sometimes we will be drawn forth to practical concern for another. Always our religious zeal must seek to free us from self-concern and self-centeredness so as to allow ourselves to be filled with a greater and infinitely more attractive reality.

Meanwhile, before we scoff at the rabbis for their 613 commandments, it would be well to remember that the current Code of Canon Law for the Latin rite contains no less than 1,752 commandments. Significantly, love of God and love of neighbor are not included among them. (October 29, 2017.)

> *God of Love, teach us to abandon selfishness so that we may be drawn into your mystery and carry away from this experience the desire to build bridges to all who cross our path: to show compassion to those who suffer and to empower those who are oppressed. We ask this in the name of Jesus, the Lord. Amen.*

February 22   ✠   *Communion of Saints*

Every Sunday as we race toward the end of the Nicene Creed we profess our faith in the communion of saints. I suppose most of us don't think much about what this means; we are only too glad to get to the end of the Creed. There is, however, an important point being made. Our Christian commitment is not only—or even not especially—a commitment to a defined set of beliefs and values. It is essentially a joining with other people who are making the same journey toward God that we are.

The dual commandment endorsed by Jesus obliges us not only to love God but also to love our neighbor. We cannot serve God in total isolation. Even hermits draw their faith from others and live in solidarity and charity with the whole church. In an obvious sense our personal faith is given specific context by the group of persons with whom we regularly share our worship and, ideally, in whose company our faith continues to grow. But there is a wider church composed of people of every tribe and race and language. Paramount among these are the great heroes of our faith, those great saints who have truly been lights upon a mountain.

Politicians soon learn that only in the rarest circumstances are they elected for their policies. Mostly it is that mysterious quality called "charisma" that gets them across the line. Most people vote for or against persons rather than for or against policies.

This leads to the conclusion that Christ's faithful people are the most powerful tools of evangelization. It is the example of ordinary people trying to live according to Gospel values that is the most powerful force in helping others to find their way to the church or back to the church. Think of the impact of Pope John XXIII or Mother Teresa. Their obvious goodness served as a signpost to the world.

Our conclusion is twofold. Firstly, if we want to strengthen our own faith then we should look to the great heroes of our faith for inspiration—men and women who, in times past and in the present, have put into practice what many preached. Secondly, we should recognize our own responsibility to hand on what we have received, to evangelize others by our life and good actions. This is how we live our faith in the communion of saints. (August 10, 1980.)

Lord God, you are the light that radiates from the lives of your holy ones. Open our hearts to be touched by the holiness that surrounds us and give us the courage to be for others a living proclamation of the Good News. We ask this through Christ our Lord. Amen.

February 23 ✝ *Community*

Richard Dawkins made a fortune with his 1976 study, *The Selfish Gene*, which provided some scientific backup for the idea that competitiveness is the key to survival and success. To many in our individualistic culture this proposition seems almost self-evident.

In 2011, Martin Nowak advanced a counter proposition. In his book *SuperCooperators*, he argued that the key to survival and success at all levels, from the gene upwards, is not competition but cooperation. Evolution is best served by cooperation. Cancer, for example, is a failure in cooperation: individual cells mutate and work against the common good of the organism. The success of their selfish competitiveness, however, ultimately leads to self-destruction.

From another angle, Nicholas Humphrey reached a supporting conclusion. Species that live a social life are smarter, and so they evolve more quickly. Cooperation increases the breadth of individual insight and achievement.

Primitive societies are totally aware of our common need for one another. We cannot all do everything, and, therefore, we must rely on others to contribute part of what is necessary for our flourishing. Contemporary Western society, on the other hand, seems to espouse the idea that a large portion of our existence can be devoid of any sense of dependence on others. We rely on computers and *algorithms* to give us the information we need. Self-service kiosks mean that we can get what we want without having to say "Good morning" to another human being. Online shopping allows person-to-person interaction to be reduced. For some it seems that virtual reality is more real than reality.

Maybe we should give some thought to the values inherent in doing things together. Of course, it will necessitate my yielding up some of my precious autonomy; but I will gain many advantages, chief among which is a heightened awareness that I am not alone in this world. It may seem obvious, but many who lament the loneliness of their existence feel that way because they have gradually withdrawn from communal or corporate activities in favor of "doing their own thing."

Cooperation demands the willingness to work with people and presupposes a certain restraint in self-assertion. It asks that

I pull back in order to make an inviting space for others. Far from being a celebration of selfishness and competitiveness, cooperation builds community and in so doing makes all of us smarter and happier. (July 3, 2011.)

Lord of all, help us to recognize that we are parts of a glorious whole and that our happiness is to sing in harmony with the rest of creation. Take from us all that would isolate us and make us self-sufficient, and teach us to live happily in mutual dependence and mutual support. We ask this through Christ our Lord. Amen.

February 24 ✝ **Compassion**

We all know that human existence is as much tragedy as it is comedy. Suffering, of one kind or another, is a universal component of our experience, from the day of our birth until we breathe our last. Of our own suffering we are acutely aware. We are much less conscious of or responsive to the suffering of others.

We are all aware that there are admirable philanthropic organizations that do much to alleviate the pain of those who are victims of natural disasters and human malice. Perhaps we are among those who contribute to these organizations to assist their work. This is good. But there is a level of compassion that goes deeper than practical help. That is the feeling of compassion. I am moved by the misfortune of others. There is a certain tightening of the muscles in the solar plexus, a gut reaction to their plight.

This was Jesus' own response to the situation of the crowds that flocked to hear him. The Greek word used, *esplagchnisthe*, has a very anatomical flavor; the *splagchna* are the inward parts, the intestines. There was a felt response to what was perceived. The same is true of the Good Samaritan; the gospel tells us that when he saw the wounded man lying by the roadside, he was moved with compassion. The same word. A deeply compassionate person sees suffering and feels something, and it is this feeling that drives them to action.

A compassionate person is one in whom there is a strong sense of solidarity with all other persons, and even beyond the realm of the human. During the period of the Vietnam war, I was very impressed listening to a conscientious objector, who told me of the spiritual experience that had changed his life. After that moment of cosmic union, any sense of self-preference or competitiveness seemed abhorrent to him. He would accept any penalty rather than become part of the military machine. It was not a political stance, but one inspired by a moment of strong spiritual experience.

True compassion is not condescending, but infinitely embracing. It is not flinching from ugliness, mistakes, or mess, but seeing underneath external appearances the reality of our common humanity. This is how Christ responds to us, and he bids each one of us, "Go and do likewise." (September 13, 2005.)

Lord Jesus, you have shown us how to be fully human by showing compassion to all who suffer. Take away our stony hearts and replace them with hearts of flesh so that we may learn to love and care for all as you love and care for us. For you are our Lord for ever and ever. Amen.

February 25   ✝   Competitiveness

We cannot help being bemused by the incident in the gospel in which, after Jesus has spoken solemnly of his upcoming death and resurrection, two disciples approach him with a view to securing first place for themselves. It is a clear indication of one of the most obvious effects of ambition: it blinkers our vision so we have a concern only with the advancement of our own career path. What does not contribute to that has no importance.

Competitiveness is not a very pleasant vice, even though it is often unnoticed. The only way we can get ahead is by scrambling over the top of everybody else. Who remembers those who came second? Ambition dismisses the claims of others and concentrates solely on getting ahead. We see it in politicians, we see it in bishops, we see it in minor functionaries in all sorts of organizations. It seems as though such people can become convinced of their own value only by downgrading that of others. Obviously, it is a very antisocial attitude to life.

Saint James, in his epistle, is quite explicit about the dangers of ambition. "Wherever you find jealousy and ambition you find disharmony and wicked things of every kind being done." Instead of meeting others where they are, we are inclined to push them down so that they do not seem to rise to our level. This in turn provokes a counterattack that eventually issues in external upheaval. Competitiveness, whether disguised or overt, undermines collaboration and eventually destroys community.

The opposite of ambition is evangelical childlikeness, being content with the last and lowest place. This derives from a sense of security about one's own loveableness, which is understood as independent of any notable achievements. A certain simplicity and honesty, free from any hidden agenda. Such a person is both trusted and trusting.

Adults who are at peace with themselves, who are not clamoring for higher status, also make peace for others, building a healthy contentment and preparing the way for the action of God. A person who is content with little is not for sale, and their integrity is difficult to subvert. On the other hand, someone who is always climbing has eyes only for the future, will do whatever has to be done to achieve their goal, and may not be aware that slowly the quality of their life is being eroded. One is happy, the other not. One grows, the other shrinks. (September 20, 2009.)

Lord Jesus Christ, you taught us that the first will be last and the last first. Teach us to be content with our lot, and inspire us to find your presence wherever we are, mindful that you are most easily found among the poor and simple. For you are our Lord for ever and ever. Amen.

February 26 ✠ *Confession*

Ask any priest, and he will tell you that the demand for the sacrament of reconciliation has fallen off greatly during the past few decades. Perhaps it is because people are sinning less. Do you think so? More likely it is because we have fallen out of the habit of going to confession and so feel that we no longer have the necessary attitudes or skills to profit much from the exercise.

Maybe we should take a step back and consider not so much the sacrament as the daily practice of confession. Saint Benedict advises monks that they should make confession every day to God of the wrong things they have done. Such a practice is simultaneously an exercise in self-knowledge and a recognition of God's indulgent mercy. It is probably not such a bad rehearsal for the sacrament—but that is not its main purpose. For many people the problem with going to confession is that they have no sins. Or rather they have no consciousness of sin. They lead ordinary and imperfect lives, but they never rebel against God or mean to offend. Trying to think up sins to confess involves mental contortions that seem to undermine the sincerity of the confession. Following the teaching of Saint Bernard we may surmise that there are three main obstacles that need to be surmounted.

- Habits of sin create a darkness in our conscience so that we are no longer capable of distinguishing right from wrong and thus habitually give ourselves the benefit of the doubt.
- The residue of sins committed weighs us down like a wet overcoat, and we lack the energy to take practical measures to upgrade our life.
- Concern with trivial activities and entertainment fills our life with distraction so that we cease to be serious about the quality of our life.

To each of these a solution may be proposed.

- For over-distractedness, we need to introduce periods of quiet into our life so that the voice of conscience may be heard.
- For the lack of spiritual energy, we need prayer.
- For the darkness of conscience, we need to engage in confession, recognizing the distance that has grown up between us and God and opening our hearts to the grace of reconciliation with God and with our neighbor.

Our practice of regular confession in prayer to God may well lead us to a more frequent approach to the sacrament, but even if it does not, it will certainly help us to be more sensitive to the prompting of our conscience. (December 23, 1989.)

Loving Father, help us to be more acutely aware of the distance we have allowed to develop between ourselves and you. Turn our hearts back to you so that we may be open to receive the glad welcome that you wish to extend to us. We ask this in the name of Jesus our Lord. Amen.

February 27 ✝ Conflict

According to the Creed, the church is "one, holy, catholic, and apostolic." I think a fifth characteristic should be added to this list. The church is conflicted. The New Testament leaves us in no doubt concerning this. James and John tried to outsmart the rest of the Twelve. Peter and Paul engaged in arm wrestling about how discipleship applied to Gentiles. The Lord's brother James and his followers were out of step with those who attached themselves to Peter. History reveals many more instances of disunity. The great ecumenical councils were mostly necessitated by grave disagreements within the church. The papacy itself has been divided, with two—and sometimes three—claimants to the Petrine office.

The root of this problem is that the church is composed of human beings, and, since the time of Cain and Abel, disagreement has been the hallmark of human history. This is not to say that differences, conflict, violence, and persecution are desirable components of our history, but it does indicate that they are the common starting points for improvement. They are the default state underlying all spiritual growth.

One pathway to the healing of conflict is the affirmation of the transcendent otherness of God. To say that God cannot be comprehended by human concepts or categories is to imply that the full meaning of God's action in creating the world and bringing it to completion cannot be contained within the limits of human expression. This seems like a harmless proposition, but the consequence of it is that no time-bound expression of truth can claim to be the whole truth. No single statement can convey the sum total of human knowledge. We speak by approximations. Yet even these inadequate affirmations can be said to express, inexpressibly, the inexpressible mystery of being. The whole is present in the parts, but not in such a way as to be contained within them.

The practical consequence of all this metaphysics is that, while we may be sure of what we truly know, we cannot dismiss the possibility that others see aspects of the truth that are hidden from us. We are different. We see things differently, but there is no need for conflict. The challenge for Jesus' disciples is to transcend differences. Just about everything contains elements of truth; if we are really seekers of truth, we must open our eyes wider and learn to find it in unlikely places. (August 16, 1992.)

O God, source and origin of all truth, teach us to find your traces in all that comes from your creating hand. Help us to see the limits of our knowing, to appreciate that others see things differently, and to seek to bring to completion Christ's prayer that all may become one. We ask this in the name of Jesus our Lord. Amen.

February 28 ┼ Contagion

As SARS continues to rage in Southern China, we have become acutely conscious of how easily life-threatening viruses can be transmitted from one person to another. It is a good reminder that the quality of our lives is very dependent on the quality of our immediate environment. We are social animals, and we cannot be unaffected by what is happening around us.

Epidemics are examples of the negative consequences of communal living. But there are also positive impacts, as demonstrated by the popular saying "It takes a village to raise a child." We are formed, particularly in our early years, by the nurturing care of our families and of others who take a practical interest in us. Whether helpful or not, this initial period of formation has a lifelong influence on the choices that we make and the sort of persons that we become.

I would like to suggest that holiness is also contagious and that is why it often happens that saints occur in clusters; where there is one, often several others appear. My thinking on this point has been influenced by a text of Bernard of Clairvaux speaking about Mary, the mother of Jesus, sanctified by the presence of God's Son in her womb: "Is it not true that someone who handles apples for half a day will keep the fragrance of apples for the rest of the day? How great an effect, therefore, would the power and tenderness of love have had on the womb in which it had rested for nine months?" Medieval apples seem to have been more luscious than most of today's varieties—that is probably why the fruit in the Garden of Eden was thought to have been an apple. The point, however, is that proximity is a fundamental basis of good influence.

When we talk of evangelization, we often think of foreign missionaries and preachers. I wonder: do we appreciate the evangelizing power of good example? At funerals of simple, good people we often hear stories of how their small, everyday actions touched the hearts of their neighbors far more powerfully than the most eloquent of preachers. Often such persons are thought to have been naturally good and kind and thoughtful. I think this is to diminish the strength of their resolve. In reality, the reason why they practiced goodness and kindness and thoughtfulness was that they made up their minds to do so. And they did so at some cost to themselves. We can repay their goodness by following their example through gratuitous acts of kindness and thoughtfulness. When we are touched by goodness or holiness, we need both to welcome it fully and to pass it on. Let us try to begin an epidemic of kindness and thoughtfulness. (March 19, 2003.)

> *Lord Jesus Christ, in your days on earth you reached out to a variety of people. You drew them to yourself, and you sent them out on a mission to bring your Good News to all people. Help us also to be living gospels to bring light and hope to the world around us. For you are our Lord for ever and ever. Amen.*

February 29   ✠   *Contemplation*

Every leap year gives us this extra day as a bonus. It is a pity that we allow it to be swallowed up by our usual calendar, and so it becomes just another working day. This failing is probably because we have lost any appreciation of time that is not spent working. The sense of the Sabbath has disappeared. We don't want to stop and step back. We keep going, according to that ugly modern shorthand, 24/7.

Sometimes when well-intentioned people talk about contemplation and contemplative prayer, it seems that this is simply a matter of putting into effect the correct techniques. It is true that some psychological and even physiological benefits can accrue through the use of particular methods, but it seems to me that Christian contemplation is something radically different.

In the first place, contemplation is not something that we achieve or acquire; it is something that happens when we are not doing anything else. If we wish to talk about the arithmetic of contemplation, we could say that it follows subtraction rather than addition. We prepare ourselves by stepping back, opting out, letting go, moving away. Solitariness and silence are its best friends. The renunciation of antagonisms, hurtful memories, and angers are among its preconditions. We don't produce contemplation; all we can do is to reduce its alternatives.

The basis of Christian contemplation is the new state of being into which we were initiated by our baptism. We were made children of God, with the right to address God as Abba. By baptism we were immersed into a state of prayer. We don't have to look for it; it preexists our searching. When we are perfectly still, this preconscious state of union with God seeps through to our consciousness and, for a time, circulates through our whole being, like the blood in our veins. Just for a while we are in a different space: perhaps we have stepped over the threshold into heaven, perhaps we have simply taken possession of our own deepest selfhood. Who can tell? It is a different experience that we cannot manufacture, but it gives a clue to who we really are and what our future may be.

We don't find contemplation; contemplation finds us. For this to happen we have to give it room to assert itself. We have to become adept at contemplative leisure, creating a hollow space within us into which God may enter. It sounds easy, but it demands a fairly radical reevaluation of our priorities in life. (February 29, 2018.)

Come, Holy Spirit, stir up within us the boldness to approach God and to cry from the depths of our being, "Abba, Father." Give us the courage to make space in our life for prayer and the energy to bring what we receive in prayer into our encounters with others. For you are the inspiration of all goodness now and forever. Amen.

March 1 ✠ **Correspondence**

As we read the gospels we may be astonished at the number of miracles that Jesus worked, whereas if we were ever to witness a single miracle, probably our life would be changed. But Peter and the rest were exposed to many miracles of different kinds and yet failed to grasp their significance and so, eventually, failed the test when their moment of challenge came.

The problem is, as the Gospel of Mark keeps reminding us, they failed to take to heart what they had seen with their own eyes. The miracles were ineffective in strengthening their faith because there was no correspondence between what was happening on the outside and what was happening inside. As Jesus said to the crowds that came looking for him, "You seek me not because you have understood the signs, but because you have eaten bread and your bellies are full." Even the most spectacular miracles do not work unless they trigger an interior response. This is why, so often, they were followed by misunderstandings and mass desertions.

There needs to be a certain consistency between inside and outside, between what is deepest in us and the practical choices that constitute our everyday life. We need to learn the lessons that life teaches us in order to build within ourselves a structure of belief and value that will serve to guide us in the decisions that we make later on and, thus, serve as a standard against which we can measure our conduct. We cannot allow ourselves to simply float along with the current; we need to burden ourselves with certain principles that define our identity and set our objectives.

This work of having a personal philosophy that is drawn from our past experience and feeds into our present and future living is of considerable importance in arriving at a sense of who we are and what we stand for. In the course of a lifetime, we may not witness miracles, but we do encounter a vast variety of situations from which we may draw forth wisdom and understanding. But we need to step back and reflect, as Churchill once wrote, "to watch the tides and not the eddies."

Jesus' contemporaries saw great signs and wonders and learned nothing from them. Our experience has, perhaps, been a little more ordinary, but we can still draw from it enough to nourish our inner life and to take us some distance along the road that leads to wisdom. But we need to take the time to learn life's lessons. (August 4, 1991.)

Lord Jesus, Word and Wisdom of God, teach us to take seriously the events of our own life and to consider them carefully. Help us to find in our experience pointers to guide us

*to the more abundant life that you have promised. For you
are our Lord for ever and ever. Amen.*

March 2 ⊹ *Corruption*

Pious Mass-goers, if they are attentive, may be shocked by what
they hear in one of the prefaces for Lent. It prays that we may
"rid ourselves of the hidden corruption of evil." We consider
ourselves respectable people and are affronted by the suggestion
that the external persona we have created with so much effort
is in danger of being undermined by interior inclinations that we
dare not acknowledge. We do not want to admit that there are
elements within us that erode the integrity of our faith and practice—like termites that threaten to bring down the whole edifice.

Jesus described those of his contemporaries whose religion
was mainly for show as being like tombstones. Externally everything was bright and shiny, but within they were full of corruption, rottenness, and the stench of decay. Not the most flattering
of images; no wonder his hearers took offense. In the seventh
chapter of Saint Mark's gospel, Jesus gives a long list of defiling
actions and inclinations that flow from the heart. He seems to
have been in no doubt that there is "hidden corruption" in the
hearts of everyone—including ourselves.

It is not the corruption that is the main problem, but the fact
that it is hidden and, therefore, unacknowledged. And, therefore,
unresisted. Corruption works best when it is unobserved. The
first step in neutralizing its baneful influence is to see it clearly
for what it is: an obstacle to our ongoing growth and a barrier
between us and God.

We have the courage to recognize our contrary tendencies only
when two things happen. The first is when we know for certain
that the presence of these instinctual forces makes no difference
to our lovability in the parental eyes of God. The second is when
we are assured of receiving guidance and strength to counter this
natural corruption. All we have to do is to respond positively to

the graces given us and to allow ourselves to be transformed into the beautiful beings God intended in creating us. Hidden corruption is a reality. The good news is, firstly, that it does not have to remain hidden and, secondly, that by God's grace corruption can be countered. (March 26, 2000.)

Lord Jesus Christ, you understand the human heart and know the temptations to which we are subject. Give us the wisdom and strength to resist all forms of evil and to commit ourselves to doing good and bringing your love to all whom we meet. For you are our Lord for ever and ever. Amen.

March 3   ✢   *Critical Mass*

Critical mass is the amount of fissile material needed to sustain nuclear fission. As I understand it, the critical mass of plutonium is about 11 kg. If you have less than that it is relatively safe. Bring two halves of that quantity together, and things begin to happen.

The idea of a critical mass operates in many different areas of life. In social dynamics, *critical mass* is a sufficient number of people in favor of an innovation so that the rate of acceptance becomes self-sustaining and creates further growth. A dissident political group ceases to be a fringe element when it attains critical mass; it then becomes a significant minority. There is a tipping point at which what was previously considered unimportant has to be taken seriously. It is a bit like a plane taking off: it gradually increases speed until it reaches take-off speed, and only then is the nose lifted. There is enough momentum and thrust to safely carry the plane aloft.

There is a kind of critical mass in maintaining good relationships. Without regular contact, a close and warm relationship can cool and become distant. There need be no overt conflict; people just drift apart because the relationship has not been frequent or intense enough to be self-sustaining.

There is certainly a critical mass necessary for us to maintain a good relationship with God. If our prayer has not attained a critical mass, it will not be able to assert itself in our lives. It will either fade away altogether or, if our superego is vocal, it will remain, but under protest: a duty, a struggle, a bore. There will be no fire left; it will likely be subject to further erosion until it reaches the point of being left aside.

Of course, if trouble comes, then there is a surge of prayer, marked by clamorous demands and all sorts of promises. But when normality returns, these are all forgotten and prayer is, once again, exiled to the margins of our lives.

Prayer needs to be more than a start-stop exercise. It needs to be regular, habitual, constant, persevering—even when it yields no instant gratification. If there is a problem in our lives it will eventually manifest itself in our prayer, where we can begin to deal with it in the context of God's unconditional positive regard for us. Our prayer doesn't have to be flash, but it is more than helpful if it is regular. (July 29, 2007.)

Lord Jesus Christ, teach us to pray. Help us to make space in our daily life so that we may enter the inner chamber and come before the Father in simplicity and faith. Make us responsive to the promptings of the Holy Spirit so that the grace of prayer and the fire of love may be kindled within us. For you are our Lord for ever and ever. Amen.

March 4   ✠   **Cross**

In his book on vestment-making, Dom E. A. Roulin lamented the fact that, because it is easy to make, the cross is meaninglessly multiplied wherever there is a space that calls out for decoration. It has become trivialized. Yet in parts of China churches are bulldozed if they display a cross. In territories that were controlled by Islamic State extremists, displaying a cross resulted in a death sentence. For the enemies of Christianity the cross is a potent symbol. Why not for us? Especially since we hear from accounts of exorcism that those who show signs of demonic possession tremble when the cross is brandished before them.

Even in its material form the cross is a sign of contradiction. A check means yes, a cross means no. As a symbol of Christian discipleship, it is a reminder that following the Gospel will often lead us to say no, to oppose the forces of darkness so often manifest in the government of nations and at every level where power is exercised. Injustice, unfairness, and corruption are so endemic that they pass without comment. As Christians, we are given the unpopular mission of contributing to a more just and more fair society. Often we do this by saying no. This is the distinctiveness that marks those who live by the Gospel—a folly and a scandal to many, but the only way by which a more human and more divine society will be brought to birth.

When we speak of the cross, we are referring not to an everyday mishap but to the rejection and persecution that will follow any attempt to live according to the standards Jesus taught. It may take the less dramatic form of prejudice and discrimination or media campaigns that highlight every failing of the church and its leadership, but we would be seriously mistaken if we were to assume that today in our own country there is no hostility to Christian values. We would be wrong to think that the culture of death (as Pope John Paul II termed it) will not resist every effort to throw light on its dark doings. To be a Christian means to be proactive in the defense of goodness and truth and life—and not to be wearied by the opposition this encounters. "Take heart," said Jesus, "for I have overcome the world." (September 14, 2014.)

Lord Jesus Christ, you call us to follow you and to carry our cross. Give us courage to bear the burdens our discipleship imposes and confidence that you remain the master of every situation. For you are our Lord for ever and ever. Amen.

March 5   ✠   Crosscut Saw

Father Finbarr, one of our veterans, loved the crosscut saw and, with equal passion, hated chain saws. What particularly delighted him was to be on one end of a saw on a warm spring day, with burly young men in relays on the other end falling away exhausted. If pressed he would explain the theory that the cutting was due to the weight of the saw itself and to the sharpness of the teeth. It was just a matter of moving the saw back and forth horizontally. Where novices went wrong was in trying to take control of the process, pressing down on the saw and, worse still, by pushing and pulling instead of just pulling. They thought they were speeding things up so that they could finish more quickly. They started the job, but they never finished because they could not develop an even rhythm.

The spiritual life is similar to cutting a log with a crosscut saw. It looks easy enough, and it is easy to begin. It can be a challenge to continue until the work is finished. We should be in no doubt that Gospel discipleship is a strenuous task that demands sustained effort.

The first error we make is to underestimate the importance of rhythm. Our age treasures spontaneity and, perhaps, underestimates the importance of regularity in achieving our goals. We need to arrive at a moderate rule of life by which we ensure that all the things we consider important have a secure place in our day-to-day existence. This means developing a few good habits.

The second error is to be too self-conscious about our practices so that we try to take control of what happens in our spiritual life in order to force a more rapid conclusion. It is much better to work away quietly, trusting that, unbeknownst to us, what we do is slowly bringing us to a better place.

The third error is to forget that we are not alone; there is someone on the other end of the saw. In all our struggles we can be confident of the permanent presence of Christ in our life as a dear friend, a wise counselor, and a strong helper. We don't have to carry the entire burden by ourselves.

We can learn a lot from Father Finbarr and his crosscut saw or, if you prefer, from his devotion to the scythe—which he much preferred to lawnmowers. A balanced rhythm, a steady pace, and endurance: these will bring solid results. (September 9, 2001.)

*Lord Jesus Christ, you have called us to follow in your foot-
steps. Give us the patience to walk slowly and without
drama, willing to invest our whole life in moving gradually
toward the goal you have set before us. For you are our Lord
for ever and ever. Amen.*

March 6   ✠   *Crossing the Bridge*

The proposition of Euclid about isosceles triangles has been
known traditionally as the *pons asinorum*: "the asses' bridge." It
was thought to be the problem that separated the bright students
from the dullards. The image was of a donkey that would happily
trot along the road but would balk at the prospect of crossing a
bridge. This problem belonged in the "too hard" basket.

Our faith teaches us about the existence of God and the resurrection of Christ and thus gives us the hope that there is an
afterlife in which we will enter into communion with the infinite
God. This complex of beliefs is too much for many people. They
are happy to see religion as a custodian of morals and the pro-
claimer of pious platitudes. They are even prepared to hear abstract philosophical monologues from the pulpit. But don't
mention heaven. The afterlife, with its prospect of halos and
white gowns and harps, seems to them almost to belong to the
world of Santa Claus and the Easter Bunny. Most don't take the
trouble to argue against an afterlife; they just carry on as if the
prospect had no relevance to present existence.

Belief in an afterlife is an essential component of Christian
faith. "If for this life only we have hope in Christ Jesus, then, of
all people, we are the most to be pitied." The whole purpose of
human life here on earth is to bring us to the point of crossing
the bridge into eternal life. Only then do we experience the more
abundant life that Jesus came to bring us. If we balk at the bridge,
our thoughts will remain stranded on this side of the river.

It is faith in a future life that empowers us to take risks in the
present. Jesus the Good Shepherd was prepared to lay down his

life for his sheep because he knew that a higher mode of life awaited him. To view our present existence within the horizon of eternity helps us also to endure whatever "slight momentary affliction" we suffer and to be resolute in continuing our journey despite the troubles that we encounter.

Perhaps we need to think more about heaven so that we begin to experience desire for eternal life. This is to cross the bridge in thought and yearning before we have to cross it in reality. (March 5, 2009.)

> *Loving Father, you have called us to a more abundant life to be enjoyed in your presence for all eternity. Strengthen our faith and expand our hope so that we may not lose heart when difficulties afflict us and so that we may have a word of comfort to offer to those with us on the road. We ask this in the name of Jesus the Lord. Amen.*

March 7 ✠ **Crows**

"Consider the crows," Jesus says. Usually translations soften this to "ravens." But of all the birds in the sky, I think the crow must be reckoned as one of the least attractive. Its harsh cry, imitated by the Greek word used, *korax*, is unpleasant to hear. It has no colorful plumage to attract the eye, and its feeding and nesting habits leave much to be desired. If I had been Noah, I think I would have barred crows from entry into the ark.

Jesus tells us that God takes care even of the crows. This seems to indicate that God's love does not conform to human expectations or standards. It extends to and includes those who are ungracious and ungrateful. The undeserving poor. This is hard for many of us who have been infected by the morality virus. We pass through life with a compulsion to label everything we meet as either "good" or "bad." As soon as we have graded something, this colors our whole attitude. If something is bad, then I cannot perceive any redeeming features. This is mainly because I don't want to see anything good in what I have labeled "bad." So, I have to suppress any data that might lead me to change my previous judgment. It is only as I get wiser and, perhaps, older that I begin to doubt the validity of binary judgments. I begin to see that all of us are a mixture of both "good" and "bad" and that the proportion between them varies, if not from day to day then certainly from year to year.

If God thinks that crows are OK, then, clearly, I will have to change my stance. Part of this will involve the acknowledgment that I can never, in this life, know the full story about anyone. Knowing more changes everything. I once knew someone who was commonly criticized for passing through a period of being down in the dumps and grumpy and uncooperative. His condition was obvious. The reason for it was not. He told me his parents were in the process of a very acrimonious divorce; the family was split into virulently opposed parties, and he was in the middle. Who wouldn't be feeling the pressure? But knowing this, as I did, changed the judgment I made. Yes, he was still in bad form, but knowing why this was so meant that it was possible to accept it more in pity than in blame.

With us God knows the whole story. We may be crows in the sight of others, but God still takes care of us. (February 26, 2012.)

Creator God, you have invested our world with a wondrous variety of species, all of them precious in your sight. Help us to be respectful of the reality of other people's lives and not inclined to hasty judgment. Give us the compassion to embrace those who are suffering and the wisdom to welcome those who are different. We ask this in the name of Jesus our Lord. Amen.

March 8   ✠   Curds and Honey

When Isaiah wrote of the birth of the promised Immanuel, he added the note that he would feed on curds and honey so that his growth would be assured. Birth is only the beginning; it is necessary that the newborn child keep growing, physically, mentally, emotionally, spiritually. The same is true of us. Christ is born to us in baptism, but it is necessary that we allow him to grow strong within us during the years that follow. For this to happen we must feed the Christ Child curds and honey.

The curds and honey by which the infant Christ comes to maturity within us are the Scriptures, and especially the gospels. They are the source of strength and sweetness that sustain our spiritual life and allow it to reach a creative adulthood. We need to keep feeding our spiritual life with this food.

The Scriptures are not just records of factual events that occurred in the past. They are documents of faith. They were written to uncover the layers of meaning hidden beneath the interventions of God in salvation history and in the words and deeds of Jesus. They are given to us not merely to inform us but to form us in the likeness of Christ, to strengthen our bond with the spiritual world, to consolidate our faith. "Many other signs did Jesus in the presence of his disciples that are not written in this book. These are written so that you may have faith that Jesus is the Christ, the Son of God, and that having faith you may have life in his name." Reading and pondering the Scriptures strengthens the Christ-life within us.

The thirteenth-century Cistercian author John of Forde wrote that in the hearts of those who love him every day is the day of Christ's birth. And so, every day we must keep feeding the newborn with curds and honey to ensure that he grows strong within us. We need to make the Scriptures our daily bread. (December 27, 2001.)

Loving Father, you have sent your Son to reveal to us the way to eternal life. Give us the strength to choose to follow him, persevering in hope until we reach our eternal home. We ask this in the name of Jesus our Lord. Amen.

March 9   ✠   *Dailiness*

In reflecting on the lives of holy people there is a temptation to focus on dramatic and extraordinary events that support the suggestion that these are people who are spectacularly different. In reality, their response to the extreme situations in which they found themselves was not a matter of sudden heroism, but the result of a slow buildup of everyday goodness and decency.

Most of us are energized by being confronted by unusual challenges; we rise to the occasion. We use some of the accumulated reserves of energy to deal with the situation. This presupposes that there is some proportion between the demands of the moment and the resources we have to meet them. If we have not done our homework, we will certainly fail the exam.

It is daily fidelity to our prime values that prepares us to deal creatively with unusual situations. Years of unexciting exercise and training are required for an Olympic gold medal, a scientific discovery that wins a Nobel Prize, or an invitation to sing before the queen. It is the same with holiness. We become saints not by waiting for an opportunity to display heroic virtue but by responding creatively to the niggling demands that come our way every day. We might ask ourselves a simple question. Do we continue to respond with humility, humanity, and humor to unfair criticism, petty insults, and minor setbacks?

It requires a great soul to take small things seriously instead of being slipshod about what we dismiss as being of no importance. This is not scrupulosity but magnanimity. It means impressing on each moment and on each minor task the character of our fundamental commitment. Instead of being alienated from the tasks assigned us, we engage with them, stamp on them our own signature, and, in the process, ennoble both the task done and ourselves. Do this for a few decades and you too will be ready for the heroic. (July 11, 2006.)

Lord Jesus Christ, help us to see in the ordinary events of every day the summons to respond according to the pattern

*you have shown us. Help us to discover you in our neighbor
and to perceive your Father's loving plan in all that befalls
us. For you are our Lord for ever and ever. Amen.*

March 10 ✠ *Daimonic*

In *Love and Will*, the psychiatrist Rollo May lamented the widespread failure to appreciate the role of the daimonic in human
life. By "daimonic" he understood that upsurge of energy from
deep within us that preexists and is uncontrolled by our reason
or our will. It is the source of all our originality and creativity, but
it has a shadow side that can be a source of destructiveness. It is
only to the extent that the daimonic is integrated within conscious
processes that we become fully operative human beings.

It is very important for our growth that we understand the
destructive potential that is latent within us. People who do awful
things are not much different from us; it is just that this malign
force has been triggered in them by some external event. "There
go I but for the grace of God" is not just pious sentiment; it is
grimly realistic. Within each of us there is a mysterious resistance
to what is beautiful that makes us want to destroy it. A kind of
vandalism that leads us to damage the integrity of something
because its wholeness is tacitly understood as a condemnation
of our brokenness. This is why, even when we know what is good,
we do not do it, or we defer it long enough for the moment to
pass. This is why we can be deliberately hurtful to others, even
at the price of being self-destructive.

Understanding this dynamic takes us closer to appreciating
the tragedy contained in that verse of the gospel: "He came unto
his own and his own received him not." If Jesus is "the joy of
man's desiring," why did he meet with so much hostility and
rejection when he made his appearance? One way of looking at
it is that he became a focus or target for the destructive daimon
latent in his contemporaries. His very goodness and the signs that
he worked before them became fuel for their hatred.

There is a lesson for us in this. When the New Testament affirms that our struggle is not against flesh and blood but against principalities and powers, perhaps it is pointing to a force beyond morality and beyond will that attacks our good intentions. Perhaps we need to be more aware of the power of the daimonic and take steps to diminish its stealth. And then we must seek to neutralize it.

Jesus was not only a doer of good and a teacher of virtue; he was also the focus of divine opposition to evil. He drove out demons, healed those who were under their power, and restored to integrity those who had fallen prey to their suggestions. He remains for us our best hope of winning the battle. (January 30, 1994.)

Lord Jesus Christ, like us in all things, you were tempted by demons and you did not succumb. Drive out from our hearts the impulsions and tendencies that seek to undermine our good intentions and give us that purity of heart which will enable us to gaze on the face of your Father in heaven. For you are our Lord for ever and ever. Amen.

March 11 ✝ *Darnel*

The parable of the wheat and the darnel gives us an interesting lesson in agronomy. Darnel, *lolium temulentum*, is a form of rye grass that is highly competitive; it reduces the yield of any crop it invades. Furthermore, it is dangerous when it is mixed with edible grain because it is prone to ergot, a toxic fungus that causes hallucinations. In its early stages it is indistinguishable from wheat; it is only later that it becomes possible to recognize its presence. The advice given in the parable is good. Do nothing yet; wait for the patches of darnel to manifest themselves and then remove them and throw them on the fire.

The moral of the parable is that we are not yet competent to judge what is of God's planting and what is toxic. If we panic when we discover something that seems undesirable in our midst, then we will be inclined to immediate action—disregarding the collateral damage this may cause. We need the prudence to wait until our intervention has a hope of yielding a positive result.

We live in a world in which good and evil are inextricably entwined. If all our efforts are concentrated on eliminating perceived evil, we may very well be left bereft of real goodness. It is much better to use our energies to promote unambiguous goodness. Unless we know the full story about some situation, we may seriously misread its implications. It is much better to stop and reflect, to take a break before we allow ourselves to condemn. Time may reveal another side to the story. Eliminating everything that appears less than perfect may well mean that very little is left; no harvest follows.

Meanwhile, it is worth remembering that the things that most bother us in others are usually mirror images of our own unexamined conduct. It is not a bad idea to look in the mirror before we criticize or correct. (July 17, 2005.)

> *Lord God, Creator of our world in all its mixity, give us the prudence to avoid rash judgments about others. Give us the patience to tolerate those evils that we cannot eliminate. Give us the hope to believe that all that happens falls within the scope of your providence. We make this prayer through Christ our Lord. Amen.*

March 12 ✠ *Deafness*

The Bible sometimes uses the image of deafness to typify those who are inattentive or resistant to the word of God. God speaks to us at different times and through various channels; if we fail to hear anything, it is because we are deaf at the level of spirit.

The Greek word used in the gospels, *kophos*, can mean either "deaf" or "dumb"—its basic sense is that the person is incapable of interaction with the outside world. When Jesus opened the ears of those who suffered from this condition, he made it possible for them to rejoin society, to reconnect with those with whom they had been unable to communicate.

The rite of baptism traditionally contains a segment that mimics the action of Jesus in curing a deaf man: the priest touches the ears and declaims "Ephphatha!" (Be opened!). And then he prays, "May [the Lord] soon touch your ears to receive his word." The newly baptized person's contact with the spiritual world involves a capacity to hear what God is saying; by baptism our ears are unstoppered so that we become hearers of the Word.

People who suffer from deafness do not know what they are not hearing. They are unaware that turning a page makes a sound, that even a light breeze rustles the leaves, or that birds salute the dawn with a spontaneous symphony of song. They don't know what they are missing. In the same way, we can divorce ourselves from the spiritual world and allow our whole attention to be consumed by the practical tasks in which we are engaged. It feels all right, but only because we don't know what we're missing.

This God-given capacity needs to be exercised. We need proactively to listen for the voice of God, obviously not as an audible sound, but as an interior reality. We need to listen with the ears of the heart. This can be difficult. Our age is full of voices that are not God's, and the din of modern living makes it difficult for us to compose ourselves to hear something different. Even if we do settle, often what we hear is not from God but only the chaotic voice of our own inward dividedness. The only trick that helps is to keep listening. To persevere in silence before God and to say with the prophet Samuel, "Speak, Lord, for your servant is listening." (August 18, 1968.)

Lord Jesus Christ, you cured those who were afflicted with deafness and allowed them to reconnect with those around them. Open our hearts when you speak so that, as we receive with meekness your imparted word, we may be inspired both to sing your praise and to proclaim to others the Good News we have received. For you are our Lord for ever and ever. Amen.

March 13 ✠ *Death*

Understandably, most of us don't want to think about death, and in much of Western society it is a taboo topic. Just as we are constantly finding new names to give to the smallest room in the house, so we employ a range of euphemisms to avoid referring directly to death. When the reality strikes it is disguised as much as possible, and conversation swiftly switches to more uplifting subjects. Yet death is a universal part of human life. I sometimes imagine myself leaning over a crib and saying to a newborn—much to the horror of the bystanders—"I don't know what sort of person you will become; the only thing I know is that one day you will die."

For a large part of our life death is what happens to other people, but as we age the number of dead people in our life increases; grandparents, parents, siblings, and, worst of all, contemporaries. With each death something in us also dies. The part of us which that person alone brought to life by their presence now falls silent.

Spiritual masters sometimes recommend that we keep the reality of death ever before our eyes. Not to become maudlin or gloomy, but to remind ourselves that our time on earth is limited, and that the day will come when we will have to put up the shutters and close shop. If we accept that our time on earth is limited, then we are more likely to try to ensure that we use it well.

I think that one of the reasons for death becoming a taboo topic is that we no longer have a realistic hope for an afterlife. Even at Christian funerals there is often a tendency to concentrate on celebrating a life passed and a corresponding reluctance to refer to a more abundant life that is about to begin. It takes a gulp of faith to affirm that "in death we are born to eternal life." But if we do not accept this, then what is religion about? "If for this life only we have hope in Christ Jesus, then, of all people, are we the most to be pitied." So says Saint Paul.

When we pray for the deceased we are affirming our solidarity with them. Whether this affirmation is a source of comfort or of dread, the fact remains that one day we will most certainly follow them. (November 2, 2011.)

> *God of the living and the dead, keep alive in us our faith in*
> *a future resurrection and our hope that all things will be*
> *brought to a glorious conclusion in Christ. Help us to live in*
> *such a way that we may be ready for the joys of eternal life.*
> *We ask this in the name of our risen Savior, Jesus Christ.*
> *Amen.*

March 14 ✠ *Death Cleaning*

There is a Swedish word bouncing around the internet at the moment: *döstädning*. It means "death cleaning." It involves getting rid of everything that we have in storage that somebody else will have to throw out when we are dead. It is not a morbid exercise, but something that we can begin in late middle age, when death seems an inconceivably distant prospect. It is not a one-time event, but rather a permanent attitude to life that prioritizes decluttering. Its benefits are said to include—and I must confess that I am not a practitioner—a reduction in stress, an increase of efficiency, and a higher level of happiness. As well, it is reported as helping people cope with the prospect of their own mortality.

Whatever the advantages of getting rid of the cherished junk with which we have surrounded ourselves, it is certainly a good idea to consider doing some death cleaning in the house of conscience. This is not an invitation to become scrupulous, but a recognition that as we grow spiritually our standards become higher. Not only do we instinctively expect more of ourselves, but we begin to reevaluate our past life. Especially in the last quadrant of our life, we begin to have some reservations about past choices; they seemed all right at the time, but, under more detached scrutiny, they now seem unworthy of what we expect of ourselves.

What we hope to achieve in the process is a measure of undividedness in our hearts and minds—what the ancients understood as "purity of heart." In the first place this means identifying the compromises that we have made and the rationalizations by which we have legitimated them. Then we have to begin the process of weakening the hold they have on us by generating contrary habits and listening to sound advice. Probably we will not find this easy, and so we will be compelled to supplement our own puny efforts with desperate prayer that God will intervene to bring us to the level of innocence that best accords with the divine plan.

If we clean up our act, we will probably find ourselves under less stress and more able to do what needs to be done. And a further benefit will be that we will face the inevitable prospect of death with some degree of equanimity. (February 23, 2018.)

Lord Jesus Christ, you declared those people blessed whose hearts are pure. Help us to reduce our inner division so that we may love you with all our heart, all our mind, and all our strength. And our neighbor as ourselves. For you are our Lord for ever and ever. Amen.

March 15 ✠ *Debts*

When Jesus spoke about paying back our debts both to Caesar and to God, he hinted at one of the principal challenges we face as human beings. We are born with a double indebtedness: to eternity and to the world of time. It is not so easy to regard both with equal seriousness. Either we participate enthusiastically in this world and pay scant attention to God, or we drift off into some vague spiritual miasma that has little input to the everyday world in which we live.

We would like to be debt-free. To be totally autonomous. To live without obligations to human institutions or to God. To be answerable to none. Yet that would be to deny the reality of human nature. We were created not as isolated units but as parts of a whole, members of a body, depending on one another and all together depending on God. The dream of total independence is not only delusional; it is a denial of who we are. It is much closer to hell than to heaven.

Perhaps we would be much more content to accept our dependence if we thought of it in terms of interdependence. We are perpetually engaged in multiple relationships of complementarity: giving and receiving, speaking and listening, loving and being loved. Every functional community is a delightfully tangled web of such interchanges. The traffic goes in both directions. Even the one who seems only to receive and to listen and to accept love is not a superfluous component to community living; that person is providing the occasion without which others could never feel so good about themselves because they are givers and speakers and dispensers of love. Perhaps, in time, we will grow in wisdom to the point of recognizing that sometimes it is nobler to receive than to give. Afterward, when I express my gratitude and my indebtedness to others, I am consolidating the relationship and laying the foundation for future repayment on my part. This is the debt of love without which no human community is possible. (October 17, 1993.)

> *Creator God, you are the source and energy of our life. Help us to repay our debt of love to you by opening ourselves to share this love with others. We ask this in the name of Jesus the Lord. Amen.*

March 16   ✠   *Deconstruction*

Deconstruction is a term that has a certain currency, although for many it carries with it a sense of foreboding. It seems to indicate the dismantling of what is familiar and the exposure of hidden flaws in what had hitherto seemed relatively blameless. We may even suspect that there is a kind of malign delight in breaking up social constructs and scattering the pieces.

From one point of view this is the fundamental paradox that we find expressed in the New Testament. The teaching of Jesus is more than a collection of moral maxims: it is an invitation to die—and not only to die, but to die rejected and abandoned. Eternal life comes about by death. By the death of Christ, in the first place, but also by our daily dying as it leads up to the ultimate renunciation of all that seems to constitute our life. Of course, we don't want to hear this. It is not a welcome message. It is a scandal to some and stupidity to others, but their umbrage does not lessen the reality of the demand.

We are not permitted to turn Christianity into a feel-good or a do-good religion. It is participation in the life of God as this has been manifested in Jesus Christ. This means that it is something that far exceeds human calculation or evaluation. We are invited to participate in something that is out of our league and will never make much sense if we confine our thinking to the realm of space and time. As God asks Job as he struggles for meaning, "Who are you to dictate terms to the Eternal?" Jesus' words to his disciples are stark: "Whoever loves life in this world will lose it." Although he himself is pictured as shuddering with dread at the prospect of making the transition into the next world, he never waters down the basic principle.

The fabric of this world must be deconstructed if its elements are to find their ultimate fulfillment in the age to come. Our own small lives are to face the same process of disassembly before we will be considered candidates for the glory that is to be revealed. Undoubtedly, a daunting and unnerving prospect. But Jesus says, "Fear not. I have gone before you. Follow me." (March 29, 2009.)

Lord Jesus Christ, you have commanded us to take up our cross and follow after you. Give us the courage to take up this challenge, the perseverance to continue with the journey when times are hard, and the hope that will lift up our hearts at the prospect of what has been prepared for us from the beginning of time. For you are our Lord for ever and ever. Amen.

March 17 ✠ *Defiance*

I offer these thoughts on the Trinity in defiance of a statute of the Cistercian General Chapter of 1230 that prohibited monks from preaching on the Trinity "because of the difficulty of the material." It is always more fun to break the rules than to keep them.

The difficulty inherent in reflecting on the Trinity is not that it is a meaningless topic, but because it belongs to an order of being that is beyond our experience. You might as well ask a blind person to discourse on color or expect someone who is profoundly deaf to appreciate a symphony.

The impossibility of speaking sensibly about this ultimate mystery is diminished by the fact of revelation. That is to say, God's self-revelation. The foundational truth that has been disclosed to us is that the human family has been created as God's image and likeness. If we want to know God, we must try to find a human person. There you will find glimmers, at least, of what God is like. Even in the most degraded and the most malign there remains a scintilla of divinity.

If we were to explore our own experience and ask ourselves what is most precious and most human, we would probably come up with one or other of the rich words that are subsumed under the heading of *love*. What is most human in our lives is the giving and receiving of a complex reality that contains affection, trust, honor, support, attachment, constancy, forgiveness, and utter openness. That is what love is. And that, according to the theologians, is what God is. The key to understanding God is to understand love in all its richness and in all its purity.

Love supposes plurality because it is the bond that unites lover and beloved. In God there is a particular kind of plurality that does not break the inherent unity. A Beloved whose being coincides with that of the Lover and whose Mutual Love is no less than either. Three moments in an eternal lightning flash of being: indivisible and paper-thin, yet wider than the universe.

For us who are created in God's image, the challenge is to realize on earth this community of love. To accept plurality and difference and bring unity to the human family. To become more human and, thereby, to become more divine. Our most authentic mode of existence is to live in the awareness that we come from the Father, that we are brothers and sisters of the Son, and that we are being brought to unity by the love of the Holy Spirit. (June 11, 2000.)

To the Father, the Son, and the Holy Spirit, the source of all blessing, be glory and honor, both now and forever. Amen.

March 18 ✠ *Defragmentation*

In the early days of computers, we were obliged, from time to time, to engage in defragmentation. This involved sorting through all the scattered bits and pieces on our hard drive and rearranging them in a tidy and efficient sequence, so that the computer ran more efficiently.

This is a housekeeping job that we could well do on our own lives. I am speaking of sorting through not merely the physical detritus that mysteriously accumulates around us, but of what clogs up our inner life. Here the saying "If it ain't broke, don't fix it" is bad advice. As with computers, seriously reduced efficiency is always worth addressing. What happens with most of us is that we are inspired by noble ideals, but then we find that we lack the energy to pursue them. The reason we lack the energy is that it is already being used up by warring factions within us. Whenever we make up our minds to do something good, we are immediately assailed by howls of protest from the contrary impulses and imaginations that have made their home within us. For every good intention there are, it seems, a thousand reasons for letting the proposed action lapse. The divided heart is like a fragmented hard drive. It can still perform, but its level of performance is considerably lower than optimal.

Defragmenting the divided heart brings to our inner life a sense of order and harmony. If we are to achieve any degree of personal integration, we have to be able to recognize whatever threatens this inner consistency and work hard to neutralize its baneful effects. The result is peace, and we are unlikely to be able to achieve it by our own efforts. We need help.

The Holy Spirit is the source of our peace, forever prompting our consciences toward greater coherence within our inner life and between our inner life and how we behave externally. The methods used by the Spirit to this end include leading us beyond measured self-assessment into a more exciting adventure, so that we become prepared to commit to realities larger than ourselves and become involved in advancing the kingdom of God in our world. Real peace is not somnolence. It is more like a well-oiled machine operating in deep silence. When we are activated by the Spirit, everything comes together smoothly. The peace we experience is a matter of being fully alive and fully involved in something that transcends mere self-interest. (May 13, 2007.)

Lord God, Creator and Sustainer of all, help us to play our part in your unfolding plan of salvation. Teach us to overcome our divisive tendencies and to open our hearts to be animated and activated by your Spirit, so that in all that we do we may advance your kingdom. We ask this through Christ our Lord. Amen.

March 19   ✝   *Delicacy*

The warrior God of some parts of the Old Testament seems not to spend much time pussyfooting around those who oppose him. He intervenes decisively to wreak destruction. The plagues of Egypt, the annihilation of the Canaanite tribes, and the obliteration of Israel's opponents all attest to a certain spirit of vengeance. In Israel's confrontations with its neighbors there was no doubt about which side God supported. God is presented as an all-powerful defender of some and the ruthless punisher of others. Of course, this is not the only image of God in the Hebrew Scriptures. We are reminded of the mission given to Jonah to save the Ninevites from the punishment due to their ungodly ways, and later there is evidence of a slow outreach toward Gentiles. But often, even alongside the tenderest passages in the prophets, there is a lurking threat of imminent punishment.

A truer picture of God is of One who does not often come on strong, who addresses us less by earthquakes and storms than by the subtle whisper of a gentle breeze. A God who acts in our regard with a certain delicacy, respecting our freedom. Preferring to woo us rather than to compel us. As a result of this delicacy, it is not difficult for us to miss what God is saying; there are other voices—external and internal—that speak more loudly.

Firstly, if we doubt that God continues to address humanity in our times, it may be that we have lost the capacity to hear what God is saying. Our senses may be overwhelmed by the discordant noise that surrounds us, entertaining us and stirring up desires that pull us in one direction or another. The call of God has an absolute claim on us, no matter how undignified the messenger or how quietly the words are spoken. Not to hear that call is our ultimate calamity.

Secondly, let us remember the admonition of Theodore Roosevelt: "speak softly, and carry a big stick." It is the same with God. The fact that God speaks quietly does not indicate that the message can be safely ignored. There are adverse consequences if we choose to decline an invitation to a more abundant life.

Finally, we need to be aware that one thing leads to another. Refusal in small things slowly leads to a larger infidelity. Just as in a marriage, estrangement from God is a slow process; we move away, one step at a time, scarcely aware of what is happening.

God's action is subtle: we may need to pay closer attention if we are to perceive it. (October 6, 1996.)

Lord God, you speak to us at different times and through different means. Help us to listen to your voice, confident

that it brings us the good news of your unfailing love. We
make this prayer through Christ our Lord. Amen.

March 20 ✠ *Delight*

Christianity is not primarily a system of thought or a code of
morality. Rather, it is an invitation to the fullness of life. This is
symbolized by the notion that our ultimate destination is an
eternal wedding feast in heaven. When we sing the psalm that
proclaims that heaven is filled with God's glory, we need to remember what Saint Irenaeus said in the second century: God's
glory is the fully alive human being. Christ came that we might
possess a more abundant life. Heaven is the gathering of fully
alive human beings, rejoicing in the immediacy of God.

Sometimes we may get the impression that Christianity is
more about duty than delight. There are so many rules—our
Catholic Code of Canon Law contains many more regulations
than the Pharisees ever knew. It is easy to become fixated on
legal requirements and to forget the whole purpose of the Gospel, which was, precisely, to communicate "Good News." As
Saint Paul was to say, the kingdom of God is not about fussy rules
concerning eating and drinking but concerns righteousness and
peace and joy in the Holy Spirit. In the last analysis, we are called
to share the joy of God.

When Jesus went up the mountain to proclaim his new law,
the keynote concept was blessedness. In his paradoxical overturn-
ing of everyday thinking he proclaimed that it was the seemingly
underprivileged who were ripe for eternal life. Those considered
to be unlucky, insignificant, or unsuccessful were the ones who
would, by God's action, become happy, honored, and ultimately
satisfied.

Christianity is not a set of rules but a series of promises. This
means that in daily life we need to get into the habit of choosing
what brings the deepest joy and the most enduring peace. As Saint
Augustine used to insist, it is our innate search for delight that

will lead us to transcend selfishness, expand our horizons, and open our spirits to find our joy in the Lord. (October 13, 1996.)

> *Lord Jesus Christ, joy of our desiring, open our hearts to the reality of the spiritual world and fill our spirits with wonderment and deep contentment. May every choice that we make be a choice that leads us to the more abundant life you came to earth to bring. For you are our Lord for ever and ever. Amen.*

March 21 ✠ *Deliverance*

Once a year we have a detailed inspection by the local fire brigade. Part of their job is to point out obvious hazards that would be dangerous in the event of a fire. We know about these firetraps, of course, since we see them every day, but we are so used to them that inertia takes over and we put off doing anything about them. Once they are pointed out, however, we are motivated to remedy the situation.

Wouldn't it be great if we could have someone do a moral inventory of our lives, pointing out the hot spots that might become explosive in the right circumstances? In a sense there would be no real surprises. We are dimly aware of our destructive tendencies and habits, but we have become so accustomed to them that we rationalize them and, so, succumb to inertia. We have a vague hope that some change in our external situation might weaken the hold these have on us. Meanwhile, we leave matters as they are. Our demon is one that encourages us to do nothing.

There are several stories in the gospels in which the arrival of Jesus triggers an outraged response from demons. In the ancient world, a person whose choices were bad, mad, or sad was thought to be possessed by an inner demon. The way to recovery was through the expulsion of the evil spirit. Exorcism. This was an act of power by which Jesus delivered people from the thralldom of evil and restored them to humanity and inner harmony. Such demonic forces not only lead us into wicked deeds, they also prevent us from engaging in the practice of the virtues.

Saint Paul reminds us that "our struggle is not with flesh and blood" but with malign spiritual forces that wage war on those inclined to goodness. It is an unequal struggle that we can never win by willpower alone. We need to be delivered from our demons, whatever language we use to describe them. But first we have to identify them. The point is that we cannot save ourselves. We look to Christ for deliverance from whatever bedevils our efforts to follow him. And that means recognizing that we cannot of ourselves always do what we fervently desire. We need help. And first of all, we need to see what needs doing. (February 1, 2009.)

> *Lord of life, help us to overcome the powers of darkness and death that are at work in our world and within our very being. Show us the way to walk in the light of life and to find our joy in the salvation you offer. For you are our Lord for ever and ever. Amen.*

March 22　✠　*Denarius*

Let us consider the parable about the workers in the vineyard. The daily wage paid by the owner to his hired workers was one denarius, a silver coin that was sufficient for a family to provide for its needs. A day's work earned a day's subsistence at a time when there was no safety net. If you did not work you did not eat. The possibilities for food storage were limited, and building up a reserve fund of money was not easy. Those who were without work were not "idle," as the term is often translated, but unemployed. And being unemployed was not a choice or a vice but a disaster.

In the parable, the owner of the vineyard comes to their rescue, ensuring that they have enough to live on, even though they are not able to put in a full day's work. Clearly he is a kind and compassionate man, remedying their misfortune from his own pocket.

The story is told in such a way that we find it hard not to have at least a little sympathy for those who did a full day's work and received only the agreed amount. Perhaps we need to think again.

Instead of being grateful to have employment and a living wage, everything turned sour for them. They became bitter. Instead of being happy that their neighbors were saved from indigence, or touched by the owner's generosity, they are overwhelmed by a sea of negative feelings.

The ancients called envy "the evil eye" because everything it views arouses fury. This feeling casts its baleful shroud over everything. It does not rejoice with those who rejoice, but is angry at the good fortune of others. We are happy when the millionaire's mansion burns down or the luxury car crashes. We may think that envy is necessarily impotent; it is no more harmful to the powerful than the sulky tantrums of a child. Yet envy does great harm—to the ones who allow this demon to take possession of their lives and cast a blight over every potential source of happiness.

Instead of contributing to the sum total of goodness in the world, envy concentrates on devaluing whatever is praiseworthy, if it is done by others. By bitterness, sarcasm, detraction. It engages in passive aggression to obstruct the good work that others do. It grinds its teeth when others succeed.

We should be glad that others have enough to live on. The fact that it comes from grace and not from works should not upset us, but make us confident that, should we fall on hard times, there will be for us also someone to step in and help us out. (September 20, 2008.)

Lord Jesus Christ, help us to recognize that all that we have is the gift of your grace. Teach us to appreciate what we have received and to be free of the covetousness that ruins our life. For you are our Lord for ever and ever. Amen.

March 23 ✝ *Denial*

Martin Seligman is an American psychologist with a strong interest in plotting paths to greater personal happiness. Part of his work involves examining the causes for the epidemic of depression, which increased twentyfold in the course of the twentieth century. The whole matter is complex. Part of the difficulty is that people suffering from depression attribute their pain to unique features of their particular history; the result is that every instance seems to be different.

Seligman believes that a contributing factor in many cases is the effect of what he terms the "self-esteem movement," which exerts pressure on people to have a positive attitude toward themselves and every aspect of their lives. He believes that this movement cares more for feeling good than for doing well. The result is the denial of anything that could threaten unlimited self-esteem. Negative features of life go unacknowledged and, because they are not owned, nothing is done about them.

Those influenced by this line of thinking feel that it is unhealthy to confront certain aspects of their life: humiliations, difficulties, liabilities, compromises, failures. They are simply pushed away. Effort is expended on changing the feeling while nothing is done to deal with the root cause of that feeling. Sometimes this concerns the way the person has been treated by others, as in cases of verbal, physical, emotional, or sexual abuse. On the other hand, it is not unknown that people contribute to their own unhappiness through what they have chosen to do or through what they have failed to do. We may be victims, but we may also be perpetrators, and it is especially our own complicity in negative situations that we are inclined to sweep under the carpet. We do not want to recognize behavior that is inconsistent with our publicly stated and deeply held values.

A great deal of energy is expended in repressing my awareness of my failures. I create a delusional self-assessment that does not correspond with reality and is not confirmed by a trustworthy confidant. Denial uses up so much energy that less is left for living or for upgrading the quality of life.

Genuine self-regard must be built on reality and on truth. It demands of us the ability to recognize our own limitations and failures, and thereby to be motivated to a sincere commitment to reduce their power over us and to make amends for the harm done to others. It is very hard to ask people to accept that sometimes they are their own worst enemy. (October 28, 2007.)

Lord God, we return to you by the road of truth. Give us the courage to confront what is negative in our life, the strength to do something to improve matters, and the strong faith that by your grace everything is possible. We ask this through Christ our Lord. Amen.

March 24 ✠ *Dependence*

In 1799 Friedrich Schleiermacher published a book titled *Speeches on Religion to Its Cultured Despisers*. The definition of religion at which he arrived was that it was the felt experience of ultimate or absolute dependence. He argued against the notion that religion was primarily a system of morality or a philosophical standpoint. For him religion derived from personal experience, and the shape of that experience was a sense of utter dependence on God for all that we are or can become.

Most of us don't like the word *dependence* because it seems to indicate the status of a child. We become adults by becoming independent; we are taught to be self-reliant. Autonomy is a prized condition. The reason I want to become Emperor of the Universe is that when I reach that position I will be able to do whatever I want. I won't depend on anyone. Perhaps.

A moment's thought is enough to dispel this delusion. Dependence or interdependence is a necessary component of human life. We depend on God, certainly, but we also depend on other human beings. There is both vertical and horizontal dependence. We trust in the providence of God. But we know that Providence expresses itself through the care, concern, support, and service of our brothers and sisters.

When Jesus sent the first disciples on mission, he did not want them to take a truckload of equipment with them. They were not to set up a fully equipped mission center from which they would sally forth to convert the world. They were to go almost naked—without extra clothing or food—so that they would be forced to rely on the generosity of those to whom they were sent. The disciples were instructed to be receivers as well as givers, accepting hospitality in exchange for the gift of their peace and the proclamation of the Good News. Interdependence sets the stage for dialogue. The kingdom is best proclaimed in a climate of conversation and not by monologues. The heralds of the kingdom need also to be good listeners. We know from the gospels that Jesus followed his own instructions, so, perhaps, we also should pay attention to them. (October 23, 2009.)

> *Eternal Father, you so loved the world that you trusted us with your only Son, who came to live among us and to be like us in all things but sin. Help us to rejoice in accepting from others what we cannot provide for ourselves, and make us generous in making our talents and our resources available to those around us. We make this prayer in the name of Jesus our Lord. Amen.*

March 25 ✠ *Detoxification*

When the apostles gleefully reported to Jesus the success of their first mission, he responded by telling them they needed to disengage from their activities, withdraw to a quiet place, and rest. This is a lesson to which many of us today could profitably listen. It is true that we learn by doing; it is also true that sometimes we learn more by doing less. It is not only a case of recognizing our limits and taking due care of ourselves; we need to acknowledge that there is a value in stopping, in being receptive, in reflecting, in listening.

If this message was appropriate for the disciples in first-century Palestine, how much more necessary is it for us today. Many of us overwork. Many of us spend the time when we are not working either in seeking news or entertainment or in extending our networks. We fill our heads with not-very-useful information, opinion, and spin, keeping our poor little brains in overdrive until their critical functions are disabled by an excess of data and give up the ghost.

What we need is a spell of detoxification to clear our head of the accumulated detritus. It is time to take out the garbage. We do not always experience a sense of peace when we are solitary and alone. It can be a time when we become acutely aware of how conflicted we are at a deep level. We may become conscious of imaginations and desires that run counter to our chosen way of life. This is upsetting, but it is a good thing. It helps us to make choices so that we can unravel mixed motivations and take a stand against thoughts, desires, and actions that are inconsistent with the person we want to become. Silence is not always easy, but it is sometimes necessary so that we can fill our minds with noble thoughts and allow our hearts to be filled with the divine peace that surpasses all understanding. (July 20, 2003.)

Lord Jesus Christ, you invite us to enter into the stillness of our hearts to discover there an attraction for all that is good and beautiful, as well as an unwelcome power of resistance. Help us to engage bravely in the spiritual combat so that by your grace we may turn away from evil and do good. We ask this of you who are our Savior and our Lord. Amen.

March 26 ✠ *Diagnosis*

I know an African religious sister who came out from a doctor's office and did a dance in the street. Bystanders joined her and then, after a few minutes, asked, "What are we celebrating?" She replied, "The doctor just told me I am suffering from such and such a disease." Why celebrate a sickness? In this case, as in others I have known, the sister had been ill for years, but no physician had been able to diagnose the cause. She was dismissed as malingering, or as imagining or exaggerating the symptoms. She danced in the streets because a cause had been found at last, and now it was possible to begin thinking about treatment. This was surely an example of where the truth has set someone free. To stand on the solid ground of truth is always preferable to trying to find stability on the shifting sands of evasion.

Many of us go through a stage of feeling a certain malaise either about life in general or about particular aspects of it. We experience a low-level dissatisfaction but are unable to pinpoint its source. We can attempt to distract ourselves from this uneasiness or compensate for it, but it remains as dull accompaniment to everything we do, diminishing our *joie de vivre* and interfering with our relations with others. We need to dig deeper or to ask someone else to do so.

The word of truth is always to my advantage, and attending to it will always lead me to greater freedom and a more complete happiness. Sometimes truth is a bitter pill, hard to swallow, but it is always health-giving. Words of admonition, whether they come from people or whether we read them, can be unwelcome simply because they attempt to divert us from unprofitable and self-destructive endeavors to which we are unreasonably attached. It is hard for me to rejoice when someone wags a finger at me and says, "You need to pull up your socks." Later on, if I had listened to that warning and changed my life, I would be very happy indeed to have escaped a potential pitfall.

These days, amid such a welter of distraction and deception, truth struggles to stay afloat. We need to cut back on our defensiveness and be proactive in searching for answers to the deep questions that every human life generates. When we accept the reality of our situation, we can take a few steps toward improving it. Even if we don't end up dancing in the street, knowing what to do is a cause for celebration. (December 12, 2004.)

Lord Jesus Christ, you came to lead us to a more abundant life. Help us to recognize the obstacles that block our progress and give us the courage and perseverance to confront them and, by your grace, to attain freedom. For you are our Lord for ever and ever. Amen.

March 27 ✠ *Différence*

Vive la différence! In theory we may celebrate those who are different from us, but, in practice, we often feel threatened or, at least, annoyed by them. The grace of God is rich and manifold and produces a variety of gifts. This means that others have qualities that we do not, and they may lack what we so triumphantly possess. Our problem is that instead of delighting in the multiplicity of endowments, we tend to engage in a process of comparison. The more insecure we are about our own gifts, the less likely we are to recognize and exult in the giftedness of others.

In our individualistic world it is very easy to concentrate on our own dreams and projects, so that we fail to recognize that we are only a part of a more excellent whole. Others also have something to contribute. The sun does not shine only on our garden. The sense that we are all members of a single body, each with a different function, seems to have faded. Instead of cooperating to produce something beautiful for God, we enter into competition with those who approach life from a different angle.

We may not want to admit it, but when we see the flourishing of others as somehow diminishing our own prospects we begin to undermine it or try to extinguish it altogether: by violence, by stretching our authority, by bullying, by mockery, by withdrawal. The sight of others enjoying their difference goads us into actions that otherwise we would consider reprehensible.

Do you remember the story of the apostles complaining to Jesus about an exorcist who was not a member of their club? Or when James and John wanted to call down havoc on an inhospitable Samaritan village? Being different isn't necessarily being bad; it is just . . . being different. We don't need to wipe it off the face of the earth. We need to learn to leave it be, to accept difference, to appreciate it, and maybe to welcome it with open arms. In any case, how could we celebrate our own wonderful uniqueness if everybody else were the same as us? (October 22, 2009.)

*Creator God, when you made us in your image and likeness,
you made each of us unique and precious. Help us to respect
and honor all your children, seeing beneath the differences
the humanity in which we all participate and which you sent
your Son to share. We make this prayer through Christ our
Lord. Amen.*

March 28   ✠   *Disasters*

The heavy rain this month and the consequent flooding of our
property are good reminders that we are not in control of everything that happens in the world around us. Most of us spend a fair
amount of energy attempting to exercise control over whatever
has an impact on our lives. If we are successful we end up with a
stout wall that insulates us from anything that might threaten our
equanimity. The problem with this is that we lose the skills needed
to cope with disasters. We go into panic mode too quickly.

The value of disasters is that they demonstrate that we are
not really in control. They help us to perceive more clearly that
much of what happens in our lives occurs at the behest of other
people or is the result of uncontrollable natural forces. If faith is
working its magic in our hearts, we come to realize the importance of dependence on the God who is the source of our being
and the sustainer of our existence. The truth is that we cannot
exist apart from God, yet often our minds are unwilling to grasp
this fundamental need to rely on God. Instead we try to claim a
false independence by building Towers of Babel for ourselves.
When their foundations are undermined and they come crashing
down, we are distraught. As a last resort we turn to prayer and
find there not only a source of comfort but, surprisingly often,
the means to lessen the impact of the disaster. Disaster becomes
for us a school of prayer.

Disaster can also be a school of compassion. If things always
went well for us we would begin to drown in self-approval. To
bolster this unconditional exaltation of ourselves we become

highly critical of the failures of others, blaming them for what is beyond their control and comparing their troubles unfavorably with our own towering competence and virtue. On the other hand, when we experience hardship and failure we tend to become less unsympathetic to others. And when we show genuine compassion to those who experience difficulties we are storing up valuable lessons that will help us cope when more hard times come. Not to want to stand apart from our fellow human beings has the collateral benefit of providing us with support when otherwise we would fall.

In God's providence disasters play an important role in our spiritual development; we should learn to welcome them—at least retrospectively. (September 22, 1993.)

Creator and Sustainer of all that exists, our lives are in your hands, and we believe that whatever happens can serve our ultimate good. Give us a strong confidence in your unwavering love and stand by our side when difficulties arise. We make this prayer in the name of Jesus our Lord. Amen.

March 29 ✛ **Discipleship**

The gospels' preferred term for anyone who followed Jesus was *disciple*. The word ordinarily means "a learner, a student." Our mode of relationship to Jesus is through our willingness to be instructed. The body of the disciples is bound together by their common obedience to the word of the Master; this is the source of their mutual adherence. Without this, the group will soon break apart.

The church is essentially a communion of disciples gathered around God's word: those who hear the word and welcome it, who ponder it in their hearts and practice it in their lives. Those who allow their characters to be shaped by what they have learned from God's self-revelation so that they become a little like God, on the way to being perfect as their heavenly Father is perfect.

This word of God is living and active. It is not simply for our instruction; it generates change within us. By the power of the Holy Spirit, the word of Jesus remains within us, causing us to remember what Jesus taught, prompting us to act according to the beliefs and values of the Gospel and not according to the false philosophy of secular society. It is by changing us that the world is brought to salvation.

This presupposes a willingness to be changed, an attitude typical of genuine learners. As with apprentices in any trade, we have to listen to the instructions of the Master and try to put them into practice. But more than that, we have to stay with the task until it becomes natural, learning to recognize our mistakes and to accept correction. The Word of God facilitates all this for us, if we allow it to do so, if we remain assiduous students.

We may well pay attention to the suggestion of Saint John Cassian: Each day and at every moment we must keep opening up the soil of the heart with the gospel plow. We need to become so thoroughly familiar with the text of the gospels that it takes root in our hearts and from there is able to produce fruit in our lives. If we do this we are true disciples, not merely hearers of the word but also doers of the word. (March 23, 2007.)

Lord Jesus Christ, you have revealed to us the mystery of God's kingdom. Help us to cherish your teaching, to receive it with reverence, and to practice it with diligence. For you are our Lord and Master, now and forever. Amen.

March 30 ✠ **Disproportion**

When Jesus promises that faith the size of a mustard seed can be instrumental in uprooting mulberry bushes and casting them into the sea, he is making a point about the smallness of our efforts compared with the magnitude of divine grace. We are always conscious of how much our occasional good deeds cost us, and we cannot see beyond our own puny contributions. Just as a small measure of yeast is enough for a large batch of dough, so all that is asked of us is not only within our limits but, habitually, does not demand even a mild degree of heroism.

The key component is faith—our connection with God—which makes the impossible thinkable and doable. What we do is often merely a signal to God to intervene, a symbol of the smallness of what we have to offer. A splash of water at baptism, a fragment of bread at communion, a thumbprint of oil in the anointing of the sick. The material components achieve nothing of themselves but become a medium through which the power of God flows. In a similar way, the various gestures by which Jesus heals those who are afflicted with illness or troubled by demons are not necessary therapeutic techniques, but simply signs that the hour has come and salvation is being accomplished on earth.

We are called not to save the world through our mighty exertions, but to be a channel by which the saving grace of God enters in human life and makes things better. Our contribution is relatively insignificant, but it is indispensable. Like the servants at the Cana wedding we have to fetch the water, but the wine we dispense is not the fruit of our labors, but the result of the divine compassion.

So little is asked of us. We are not called to cross the seas and proclaim the imminent destruction of Nineveh. We do not have to endure journeys and shipwrecks and floggings and eventual execution as did Saint Paul. Our task is smaller: we have to do good and avoid doing evil in our own little world. And if even this is too much for us, we have at hand the means of empowerment: our faith. And if our faith is smaller than a mustard seed, then we have the means of growing it further. By regularly opening ourselves to God in prayer our faith expands, and if we keep doing this, the sky is the limit. (November 13, 2017.)

Lord Jesus Christ, increase our faith. Bring to perfection the good work you have begun in us so that your glory may shine on earth. Help us to do our part in bringing your light to all nations. For you are our Lord for ever and ever. Amen.

March 31 ✠ *Diversity*

When the Holy Spirit descended at Pentecost the effect was to blend people from all over the earth into a single whole, bound together by their acceptance of the Good News. The author of the Acts of the Apostles is at pains to stress how diverse this crowd was before Peter got up to speak to them: Parthians, Medes, Elamites, and the rest. And throughout the New Testament, the church is presented as the calling together of those who are different: different in race, in religious background, in function, in religious service, in fervor. Yet all are fused into a single body with one heart and one soul.

Most of us have been formed to accept and love those who are like us and to be somewhat reserved about those who are different. Those who share our culture act and react in ways similar to us, so that we feel comfortable around them. Those who follow different customs are a source of puzzlement to us, and, perhaps, we find their behavior offensive or even hostile. As a result, our first response in encountering them is to hold back. This reserve may quickly transform itself into disgust and rejection. "They are not like us." Without ever getting to know them we push them away. There are, obviously, degrees of rejection ranging from ignoring, snubbing, vilifying, or hating them to open warfare. The fact that they are different from us excuses our mistreatment of them.

Our unease with difference stems from our insecurity about ourselves and our fear that what is different may in some way devalue what we are. When we are comfortable in our own skin we can more readily accept and admire others with different qualities; we begin to understand that uniformity is not God's way. Every snowflake is unique. We can take for granted that the Spirit is at work in us whenever we move to accept, embrace, and rejoice in the diversity typical of God's creation.

Accepting that others are different will usually mean that sometimes we are under an obligation to reshape our behavior if we are to live in harmony with them. This is done not out of fear or shame, but because we value concord and are prepared to do whatever is necessary to preserve the unity of spirit in the bond of peace. The Holy Spirit brings about communion not by some form of magic, but by inspiring individuals like us sometimes to step back from self and make room for others. (June 4, 1995.)

Come, Holy Spirit, draw us into the unity which is of God and for which Christ prayed. Banish falsehood from our midst and strengthen our weakened wills so that we may truly be of one heart and one mind, in Jesus Christ our Lord. Amen.

April 1 ✠ *Divine Forbearance*

It is of the nature of God to be outside time and space. God's overview of creation is not restricted to the present moment and a particular place. It is a global vision that encompasses in complete detail every moment and every location within the entire universe. In a manner unknowable to the human intellect, God is present at all points in the spatio-temporal universe and in the totality. What we experience as a puzzling sequence of staccato events subsists in the mind of God as a smoothly flowing whole concentrated in a single intense point.

We who are caught up in the maelstrom of history are prone to mistaking the real significance of what is happening around us. God, unlike us, knows how to distinguish the tides from the eddies. God interacts with the broader horizons of human history and is not confined within the narrow crevasses of temporality. God's interventions are not stampeded by the dire urgencies of our present situation, but proceed from a calm determination to bring all things to a good and peaceable end by bringing them to completion in Christ.

We are often upset by the fact that we live in a world characterized by a mixity of good and evil. There is a tendency in us to want to strike out to destroy what seems evil to us. This impulse is rash; we may be so zealous to scrape off the rust that we put a hole in the vessel. God, who sees all, acts differently. God is not deceived by an unprepossessing present, but is prepared to wait while what has been planned from all eternity slowly reaches its denouement.

We need to allow God the freedom not to act, to forbear. The pain of present ambiguity may be a scandal for us and can erode our faith and trust and optimism. The pain is caused, however, not by the weight of evil in the world but by the lightness of our faith and the resultant clouding of our vision. We need to grow in likeness to the mind of Christ, recognizing that to all things there is a season. For the moment, we need to wait with God for a little while until the Final Judgment, and then, we shall see, all things will be well. (July 18, 1993.)

> *Creator God, Lord of history, help us to judge all things with the eye of faith. Teach us to have confidence in your providence. Strengthen in us the hope that, in the end, all things will be well. We ask this through Christ our Lord. Amen.*

April 2 ✠ *Divorce*

The ethical system of the New Testament, insofar as it exists, is not based on a philosophical view of human reality and directed to all. It is, rather, proposed for the attention of the few, the committed. It presupposes in persons a high level of discipleship, dedication, and fervor. Much of it comes with the implicit proviso, "If you wish to be perfect." If these ideals are socially imposed when such subjective dispositions are lacking, practice will inevitably falter. It will become a hollow outward form, or it will be abandoned completely.

This is especially true when it comes to moral principles formed around the area of sexual morality. The church is nearly always stricter than the surrounding ethos. The reason for this is that the church cherishes values that are not always accepted in ambient society. Prescribed practice needs to be assessed in terms of the values it expresses.

When Jesus speaks about divorce and remarriage the values at issue are fidelity and commitment. These are two beautiful

human qualities that bespeak a whole galaxy of supportive virtues: understanding, self-giving, communication, tolerance, patience, honesty, compassion, forgiveness, constancy, perseverance.
Taken together, these virtues are part of what we mean when we
use the word *love*. The permanence of marriage is meant to
provide for the nurturance of such qualities by which the two
partners grow into fully mature human beings.

What is to be said when a relationship, far from helping people
grow, becomes abusive, violent, or destructive? What if it
quenches any flame of liveliness? What if it is merely a façade
erected to sustain an illusion of respectability? Must marriage be
maintained at any cost? And if a relationship is irretrievably broken, can the lesson be learned and a new relationship be attempted? These are questions that many have to face. I am not
competent to answer, except to express my appreciation of the
seriousness of the challenge faced by many people and to suggest
that the solutions to these less-than-ideal situations will inevitably be less than ideal. And probably painful as well.

Since Christian marriage is such a high ideal, it would make
sense at the very beginning to embrace two strategies. Firstly, to
recognize that it is worth working on the relationship to avoid
the subtle intrusion of issues that could destroy it. Secondly, a
good marriage will need a high degree of spiritual support; whatever can be done to maintain a vigorous spiritual life will certainly
contribute to a long-lasting and happy marriage. Bringing God
into the marriage may well be the most effective means of safe-
guarding it. (October 5, 2003.)

*Lord Jesus Christ, ever sympathetic to those who struggle,
help us all to live up to the high ideals that you propose. Give
us the courage to face the challenges we encounter in a spirit
of humility and truth and guide us always in the serious
decisions that we face on our journey. For you are our Lord
for ever and ever. Amen.*

April 3   ✠   *Do Not Be Afraid*

The commandment "Do not be afraid" occurs twenty-seven times in the New Testament. That makes it a pretty important obligation. It is arguable that fear is the great enemy of faith for us today.

In the nineteenth-century era of scientific optimism, faith was undermined by doubts and by the suspicion that science would soon explode everything that faith communicated to us. In the latter part of the twentieth century, after a major economic depression and two world wars, it was a hard indifference that faith had to overcome to stand its ground. Now, as we move into the twenty-first century, it seems that what threatens our faith most is fear. There is a widespread apprehension about such things as technology, globalization, terrorism, the increasing power of social media, the non-transparency of governments and their remoteness from the lives of ordinary people, rampant individualism and greed, climate change, and so many other factors that make us hesitant to be confident about the future. Words such as *anxiety* and *pessimism* come to mind.

One characteristic of fear is that it has a foot in two worlds. One foot stands in the world of reality, the other in the world of imagination. Each feeds off the other. I may be afraid of being mugged as I walk along a darkened street, but this fear turns every shadow into a potential assailant. By the time I emerge into the light I am as much a wreck as if I had really negotiated a dangerous path. Reality provided maybe 5 percent of the fear; the rest came from my imagination. Fear is self-perpetuating, and after a while, I am afraid because I am afraid—even though there is no visible reason for fear. Especially when fear is excessive and unreasonable, a residue remains even after the triggering causes cease to operate.

We are not always fully aware of our fears, but they can influence our choices, making life more miserable than it has to be, crippled and overcontrolled. Fears often reduce our capacity to do good, for ourselves or for others. We hold back, thinking that it is safer to do nothing.

The New Testament is against ungrounded fears because they inhibit our confidence and trust in God who cares for us, and in Christ who is ever at our side, and in the Paraclete who infuses in us a spirit of boldness. Do not be afraid; there are fewer things that are out to harm us than we are led to believe. (June 23, 2002.)

> *Lord Jesus Christ, inspire in us a great confidence that all things work together unto good. Help us to survive the inevitable difficulties and failures that life brings, and fill us with the joyful recognition of the wonderful things that are happening all around us. For you are our Lord for ever and ever. Amen.*

April 4 ✠ **Doggedness**

I love Saint Mark's account of the Syro-Phoenician woman's feisty interaction with Jesus. It is a good example of how the gospels aim to do more than tell a story. They are meant to teach, form, motivate, and encourage the reader—in this case, by telling a story about how an impossible request was granted. It gives us instruction on how we should approach prayer in our own life. Jesus tests the woman by ignoring her, giving her a bureaucratic response, and insulting her. Undeterred, and emboldened by love, she doggedly presses her claim until her faith triumphs over Jesus' reluctance.

What messages can we derive from this narrative, which the evangelist presents with so much artistry?

- Faith bids us to take our troubles to Jesus in prayer. It recognizes when we are at the end of our resources.
- Faith makes us bold in expressing forthrightly what we desire to receive; there is no holding back and no attempt to dress up our request to make it more acceptable.

- Faith asks for what is humanly impossible, accepting the truth that "nothing is impossible with God."
- Faith makes us dogged in not giving up, continuing to knock, remembering the victory of the widow over the unjust judge.
- Faith helps us to accept God's timescale; not everything is done immediately, and there is a purpose in the delay.
- Faith sometimes changes us rather than external events; we are empowered to handle what was hitherto beyond our capability.

Just as Jesus attributes the cure of the daughter to her mother's faith, so when we allow the gift of faith to work its magic in us, surprising outcomes may be anticipated. It could be as simple as our becoming more resistant to the power of events to upset us. It could be that we discover problem-solving skills in ourselves or in others. And it may well be that what we ask is simply granted to us. Maybe our faith needs to be purified by becoming more focused.

Faith bids us to live in the context of a loving Father who knows our needs, who covers our liabilities with unconditional love, and who is at work within us to bring us to the fullness of life. In that context, we would be fools not to ask for what we think we need, knowing that we are more likely to receive the hundredfold than not. (August 24, 2014.)

> *Lord Jesus, you have taught us to ask that we may receive, to seek that we may find, to knock to have the door opened. Give us faith that you will hear us when we call and answer when we cry to you. Help us to persevere in prayer and never lose hope in the mercy of God. For you are our Lord for ever and ever. Amen.*

April 5 ✠ *Doing*

When it comes to understanding the great mysteries of our faith—the Trinity, the Eucharist, the forgiveness of sins—we are often unsuccessful. As T. S. Eliot wrote, there is "a strain on the brain of the small folk" (*Murder in the Cathedral*). Even clever people find themselves ultimately stumped. This is especially frustrating in a culture that has no mysteries. We assume that everything is eventually knowable. I use electricity every day. I do not know how it works, but there are people who do know, and it is possible for me to acquire that knowledge if I am so inclined. Knowledge about God is different. I can study theology until I am blue in the face, but I will never master the topic.

The Eucharist is given to us not to know but to do. Jesus said this quite clearly: "*Do* this in memory of me." When he said, "Take and eat," he did not mean, "Study and understand." It is those who eat his flesh and drink his blood who will come to eternal life. It is a matter of doing. The doing itself, the observance of Jesus' command, brings with it a deep sense of rightness, a meaning that transcends rational categories. To the believer it feels right, just as a gratuitous act of kindness or the free letting go of grievances feels right. Greeting a loved one has meaning; there is very little overt intellectual content. It is the act that counts. The formation of the Greek word for *liturgy* clearly indicates that it concerns a work and not a science.

The Eucharist is something that is *done*. This is the vocabulary that is attested from the time of Saint Paul and in so many ancient texts: 1 Corinthians, the four gospels, the second-century *Didache*, and the writings of Hippolytus and Justin. A church that does not *do* Eucharist is a mere shadow of what was known in those times.

In the Eucharist, often repeated, the grace received once in baptism is renewed and activated. We are given access to God in Christ, our sins are forgiven, our vices are weakened. In the well-celebrated Eucharist divisions are eased; we are bound more closely together as members of Christ's single Body, all nourished from a single source.

We know that familiarity often breeds contempt. Perhaps we need to keep refreshing both our theory and practice of doing Eucharist so that it may become for us a vital source of energy in our journey to eternal life. (May 25, 2008.)

Lord Jesus Christ, having loved those who were yours, you loved us to the end. In giving us the sacrament of your Body and Blood, you have provided us with a dynamic means of being united with you and with our brothers and sisters who share this sacred meal. Help us to grow in love of this sacrament and to find joy in its celebration. For you are our Lord for ever and ever. Amen.

April 6 ✠ *Doing Nothing*

In 1977 I was in Papua New Guinea. I was told of a customary practice in the villages before the advent of electricity and electronic media. In the evenings, which fell suddenly in these tropical latitudes, the people would gather around a campfire. The term they gave to this in Pidgin was the equivalent of "Sit down and do nothing." Perhaps they would smoke. If anyone had something to say, it would be said. Perhaps there would be a response. Perhaps not. There was no expectation that anything would happen and no surprise at anything that did happen. It was simply the communal creation of an empty space.

I do not know if this practice has continued. I suspect not. But a moment's thought will probably lead us to think that it was a very civilized exercise and one from which we, in our helter-skelter world, could learn. We so often confuse the urgent and the important that we have ceased to understand the difference between them. The urgent always gets done; the important is often left aside until it becomes urgent. There are so many things to do, we say, and so little time in which to do them. As a result, we don't often take the time to do nothing: to smile at the clouds, to say hello to the trees, to notice that the grass is green. We have much more demanding tasks to worry about and to accomplish.

Mary of Bethany got into trouble with her activist sister for sitting and doing nothing—or, at least, for sitting down at the feet of Jesus and giving all her attention to what he was saying. We will probably be reproached—especially by our own superego—if we try to do the same. We don't want to be seen to be doing nothing.

Many good things grow in the soil of leisure, when both rationality and anxiety are disengaged. It is probably no surprise that Archimedes had his eureka moment when he was relaxing in the bath—not when he was doing his sums in his study. And, more latterly, when asked where he got the ideas for his novels, Don DeLillo replied that they come out of all the time he has wasted. High achievers take note: wasting time can be productive. Doing nothing accomplishes much. (October 6, 2009.)

Lord God, you are the fullness of all that exists. Teach us to empty ourselves of our concerns and activities and to open ourselves to be filled from your abundance. Help us to make space for you in the midst of our overfull lives. We ask this in the name of Jesus the Lord. Amen.

April 7 ✠ *Doublemindedness*

Dipsychos is a term that appears in the Epistle of James and other early Christian literature. It means having a double soul. It refers to the experience we all have had of being pulled in opposite directions simultaneously. This was famously dramatized by Saint Paul in the seventh chapter of the Epistle to the Romans: "I do not do the good I want to do, but I do the evil that I don't want to do." Despite all our best intentions, there is a fifth column within us, undermining our resolutions and seeking to set our feet on a path that is ultimately self-destructive.

Jesus teaches us clearly that we cannot serve two masters; we need to make up our minds whom we will follow. It is probably true that most of us prefer to sit on the fence, unwilling to make a definitive determination, hedging our bets. We think this protects us from heroism and allows us to avoid anything that could be regarded as intense or extreme.

But what are we doing? By delaying a commitment of ourselves, we are perpetuating a state of interior conflict that results not only in mediocrity but also in an unnecessary loss of inner peace. The way of radical discipleship is, undoubtedly, hard, and the door through which we enter into eternal life is narrow. But it is the only way. If we think we can satisfy the spiritual yearnings that are implanted in the human heart by being wishy-washy, then we will soon find out that we are wrong. It is true that not all are called immediately to the same level of fervor, but we are all obliged to take a stand. At baptism we made a commitment to renounce Satan and all his or her pomps and works. That commitment stands. "If the LORD is God, follow him!" We will soon find that despite its demands, an undivided heart bears many fruits that enrich our experience of life. A double soul ultimately yields only trouble. (November 5, 2011.)

> *Lord Jesus Christ, you have called us to walk the narrow way, following your footsteps. Help us to live as true disciples, learning from your example and striving to put into practice what we have learned. For you are our Lord and Master for ever and ever. Amen.*

April 8   ✠   *Dreams*

There are many instances in the Bible where God speaks to patriarchs and prophets through dreams. We may wonder whether God continues to use this medium to inspire people to do what needs to be done to further the divine plan.

We may ask what is special about dreams. Followers of Freud will tell us that, at least sometimes, they are the messengers of our unconscious self, bringing to our attention, whether directly or in code, what we need to hear. We may accept this explanation or not, but the fact that we all acknowledge about dreams is that they are not directly under the control of either our intellect or our will. Dreams only occur when our rational powers have been put to sleep; the gatekeepers are off duty, and so we are likely to have some unexpected visitors.

I myself have had several strong dreams that have been both inspirational and energizing, and I know others who have had similar experiences. One that stands out in my memory occurred about half a century ago. I was passing through a very oppressive time not of my own making, weighed down with high levels of anxiety. One night an acquaintance appeared in a dream and began by saying, "The trouble with you is," and then proceeded to offer a rereading of the situation and a concise diagnosis of the root of my malaise. When I woke up the fog had dissipated. I was standing in the sunlight. The crisis was over. Don't ask me what it means: it happened.

I think messages from God or from our deep self can get through only when "the wild, wanton wits" (as *The Cloud of Unknowing* terms them) are neutralized. Martin Luther used to say that reason was the devil's whore; whenever a good inspiration strikes us, reason is standing at the crossroads to ensure that we do not follow it up. How often this is confirmed in our own experience: as soon as we make a virtuous resolution, a thousand contrary reasons are raised to show that it is not a good idea. We have to learn sometimes to follow a higher rationality.

Maybe we should pay more attention to our dreams or, at least, create within us a zone of silence and emptiness where God can speak if there is a message to give us. (March 19, 2018.)

God of all goodness, at various times and through different media you speak to us to instruct us, to comfort us, and to challenge us. Give us a listening heart, so that we may hear what you are saying, along with a willingness to put into practice what we hear. We ask this through Christ our Lord. Amen.

April 9 ✠ **Duty**

Many of us were brought up with the idea the practice of religion was a duty: something we did whether we liked it or not. It was part of the form of goodness that was superimposed on us when we were at an age when resistance was useless. We had religious duties. Sometimes the institutional church has been complicit in this, insisting that we believe certain things, that we do certain things, and that we do not even think of doing certain other things. The hope has been that by insisting on obligations and inculcating sanctions on those who fail to meet them, the church itself will run smoothly and the lives of its faithful members will mirror that serenity.

If only it were that simple. Dutiful religion quickly becomes a mere social ritual. It lacks the fire of passion, it reduces creativity to ashes, and its hold over its adherents relies on factors external to itself. Eventually, when external circumstances change or when people shrug off the social conditioning of their youth, religion is abandoned. Mostly this is done without regret, although sometimes there is a nostalgia for some of the more colorful rituals associated with religious practice. And sometimes pseudo-religions step in to fill the space. It is not unusual for people to find that they can live very comfortably without God.

This is why it is important that we deemphasize the notion of religion as duty and bring into greater prominence religion as relationship. It is simultaneously a searching after the mystery of the unseen God, a practical response to the call of Jesus, and living in a network with all those other people who have heard the call and who, like us, seek the face of the living but unseen God.

Every relationship, including religion, goes through ups and downs; this is part of human life.

- Sometimes we will be more fervent, and at others we will slacken the pace a little.
- Because relationship is more than a solitary existence, it takes two to tango. Inevitably, there will be surprises and challenges as well as moments of unexpected delight.
- The contours of the relationship will be constantly changing; it will grow deeper over the years.
- Relationship is 24/7; it cannot be reduced to periods of being on duty, leaving other times free.

The church is more a communion than an institution. Belonging to it is less about knowing the right things to do and doing them than about learning the art of love, following Christ and constantly seeking the face of God. (January 23, 1994.)

> *Lord Jesus Christ, you are the way that leads to eternal life. Help us to run gladly along this road with hearts expanded, sharing the joy that you have given us to all whom we encounter on our journey. For you are our Lord for ever and ever. Amen.*

April 10   ✛   *Earthen Vessels*

I often think that Saint James, the son of Zebedee, gets a raw deal. In his feast-day liturgy, the gospel read is not one that celebrates his prompt response to the call of the Lord, or his faithful following in the years afterward, but his momentary lapse when he and his brother come forward to advance their case for priority seating at the eternal banquet.

There can be something instructive for us in this, if we so choose. Saint Paul reminds us that we hold the treasure of grace in earthen vessels. There is no doubt that God's grace works wonders in our lives, but we still have feet of clay.

We are sometimes severe on ourselves—and more often on others—when hidden vices make their appearance in an otherwise fairly blameless life. It is not always clear that we understand the difference between being good and being seen to be good. For the Pharisees and, to some extent, for all of us, being seen to be good is very important. It is as though our efforts at virtue are being reinforced or subsidized by the approval we receive from others; we receive a kind of virtue dividend. A payback for all the effort we have expended in avoiding sin, or at least public sin.

I imagine most celebrities are very cautious about whatever they say or wherever they go, because they know that a single unguarded moment might throw their reputation into jeopardy.

When this happens, there is unbridled delight among the tabloid-reading masses. Yet we need to recognize that we, too, are vulnerable. We may not have much of a reputation to spoil, but we can cause ourselves and our loved ones great grief when some of our hitherto undetected aberrations are published abroad.

We should give less emphasis to being seen to be good and more to being good and truthful and honest. This involves recognizing the inherent tendencies that go against our fundamental orientation. All of us are marred by weakness, blindness, and malice. We will survive, first of all, by owning these liabilities so that we can begin fighting against them. And, as people living in glass houses, being slow to condemn them in others.

Maybe Saint James was ambitious; maybe we are. We will be far from perfect until God wills otherwise. Meanwhile, we can be sure that the Lord does not repent of the choices made. Even though our level of virtue is not as high as we would wish or our reputation as spotless as we would hope that others judge it to be, yet we are still loved by God with a love that is unconditioned by our failures. (July 25, 2016.)

> *Loving Father, you know the clay of which we are made, and you are compassionate with our slowness in virtue and our promptness in delaying the goodness we can accomplish. Teach us to trust in your ever-affirming love, so that we stand in truth before you, unabashed by our own need for your comprehensive mercy. We make this prayer through Christ our Lord. Amen.*

April 11   ✠   *Echo*

As a boy, I was much impressed by the film *The Cruel Sea*, a story about a corvette hunting submarines in World War II. It was memorable because it did not glamorize war, but showed the gritty reality. Also, it contained some mild swearing—unusual in those distant days. Most memorable of all, the action was counterpointed by the *ping-ha* of the ASDIC as they searched for submarines, waiting for an echo that would indicate a lurking danger.

We also, in our relations with others, are always sending out messages about ourselves, often without knowing whether the messages have been received. When an echo comes back—a smile, a word, a gesture—that indicates that we have been heard and understood, we know that contact has been made and we feel a warm glow of solidarity. If there is no echo, all we experience is a sense of dejection, frustration, isolation.

So it is with God. God is constantly pinging us, seeking to attract our attention. Is anybody home? Many texts in the Bible speak of this. "The heavens proclaim the Glory of God." "In various ways at different times God has spoken to us through the prophets." And "In the fullness of time God sent his Son." Christ is the Word, the message of love sent by the Father, audible to the ears of our heart. He is the visible form of the invisible God. God awaits our response.

"He came unto his own and his own received him not." This is probably the most poignant and tragic verse in the Bible. In love the Word went forth from God, but from the many there was no echo sent back to God. The Word was lost in the void of unbelief. But not entirely. Those with faith, those who welcomed the Word and responded, became God's children, sharers in the divine nature. Created to God's image and restored in the likeness of the risen Christ, believers are called not only to receive the fullness of God's love but also by their lives to respond to it and to transmit it. That is our mission: to receive God's word and to respond by communicating to others what we ourselves have received with so much joy and gratitude. (January 5, 1997.)

Loving Father, throughout our lives you call out to us, reminding us of your love and acceptance. Help us to hear your call, to take it to heart, to respond to it, and to share it with others. We ask this through Christ our Lord. Amen.

April 12   ✠   *Ékphobos*

An unusual word occurs in Saint Mark's account of the Transfiguration, one that we meet only once in the Greek Old Testament and in one other place in the New Testament which quotes that text. The word is *ékphobos*, usually rendered as "terrified." This may easily convey the notion that Peter feared for his safety and wanted to escape, as we would if we were terrified. But Peter had just said, "Rabbi, it is good that we are here," so he is hardly hoping to go somewhere else. It seems to me that we have to find another avenue of understanding if we are to appreciate what the word means in this context.

Rudolf Otto, in his landmark book, *The Idea of the Holy*, made the point that the encounter with the spiritual world engenders in us two contrary emotions: fear and fascination. We are simultaneously drawn toward the vision and yet feel constrained to hold back. There is an element of delight mingled with the fear. The fear is not foreboding or dread, but it is a sense of being out of one's league, drawn into an ambience where familiar certainties dissolve, adrift in a strange region without solid points of reference.

If we accept the idea that genuine religion is a matter not so much of feeling good or being good as it is of contact with the spiritual world, with God, then we can expect to feel simultaneously energized by and uncomfortable with such an encounter. We have been launched beyond the sphere of rules, goals, and expectations into the Unknown. Think of all the surprises in the life of Abraham: leaving Ur of the Chaldees, years of wandering, divine epiphanies and promises, the birth of Isaac, the command to sacrifice his only son. Abraham attached himself to God without any security; he had no guarantees except the promise. Who would not feel a little on edge, wondering what demand would be made next?

It seems to me that this is what Peter was experiencing when he was *ékphobos*. A sense of wonderment coupled with an even stronger sense of his own unworthiness. This is what made him make the panicky suggestion that he build shelters for the illustrious trio who had appeared before him. Saint Luke takes a different approach; he says the apostles were overcome by sleep, their faculties disabled. In both cases the apostles sensed that they had stepped over a threshold into the sphere of the utterly different. They were simultaneously fascinated and afraid. This is what *ékphobos* implies. (February 24, 1991.)

> *Lord Jesus, we have not seen you transfigured in glory, but we believe that you are the Christ, the Son of the living God, who died for our sins and rose to save us. Grant that we may remain lifelong disciples, believing with all our heart and expressing our faith through acts of love. For you are our Lord for ever and ever. Amen.*

April 13 ✝ *Elijah*

I remember a song from the 1950s: "Have you ever been lonely? Have you ever been blue?" These are, I presume, rhetorical questions. Implied is the fact that all of us, at one time or another, have been down in the dumps. Part of the problem when we are in that space is that we think that it is all down to us; that nobody else has ever been through what we are experiencing.

That is why I find uplifting the incident when Elijah is in the desert, sitting under a tree and wanting to be dead. He had reason to be a bit down, since Queen Jezebel was out to get him and he had fled for his life. So, he lay down and slept, hoping not to wake up.

Then the story changes. An angel wakes him up twice with a drink and a meal of bread and then bids him to make his way to Mount Horeb, where he will encounter the living God.

When we are oppressed and lacking in energy, pray that God will send us an angel to redirect us and provide us with food to restore our strength and give us heart to go on. The angel will say also to us, "Get up and eat."

We need the bread of community. It is not good to be alone, for when we are low there is no one to lift us up. The following of Christ is not an individual path; it is a journey made in the company of the many who are of one heart and one mind with us. By bearing one another's burdens we are helped through times of personal difficulty, but we are also invited to help others when their path is beset with troubles. A friend once told me that whenever he starts to sink into a mild depression he finds a way out by doing something nice for somebody else. So, get up and eat the bread of community.

We need the bread of the word. Our faith can falter if it is unfed. When faith wanes, troubles multiply. We need the consolation of the Scriptures to broaden our vision and steady our commitment. The word of God is a two-edged sword that vanquishes the tyranny of tired thinking and enables us to reframe and to see beyond the dismal present to a better future. So, get up and eat the bread of the word.

We need the bread of the Eucharist, to enter the sacramental zone, to move into the world of mystery, where nothing is impossible. More often than not we will find the solution to our woes through the action of God, drawing us into self-transcendence. So, get up and eat the bread of the Eucharist. (August 13, 2000.)

> *Lord God, you call us to make the journey to come into your presence. Sustain us as we travel with the word of encouragement and the food that strengthens. Keep us on the right path, confident that each step will bring us closer to you. We make this prayer through Christ our Lord. Amen.*

April 14   ✛   *Elsewhere*

I recently received a copy of a Russian icon depicting the resurrection. Elements from the gospel narratives are arranged around: the earth swirling like the waves of the sea, the stone rolled away, the angel, the women. In the center, nothing. That was the message given to the women. "He is not here. He is elsewhere." This is suggesting the reality of a different universe. The risen Lord is not to be sought within the confines of space and time. He is elsewhere.

The story is complicated then by the fact that although elsewhere, Jesus makes sudden appearances to the women and, then, to the disciples—as many as five hundred, according to Saint Paul. He passes through locked doors, and yet his body is real; he eats and can be touched. So it seems that elsewhere is also here, but invisibly. The two zones coexist and overlap. That is why Jesus can promise to be present wherever two or three gather in his name and to be with his people until the end of the age. He is with us and, yet, cannot be seen.

In his response to Thomas's profession of faith, Jesus makes the surprising assertion that unseeing faith is superior to faith that sees. That our contact with Jesus is deeper and stronger because we cannot see him. This seems to mean that there is a seeing that is unseeing, and an unseeing that is seeing. Two different modes of sight. The intense relationship with Jesus, and through him with the spiritual world, becomes more potent by not being subject to the distraction generated by physical sight. We are the privileged ones.

The power of faith to see what is unseen and unseeable is subject to development. If we want to grow in faith, we have to exercise it. The fundamental way of doing this is to spend time enveloped in nothing. We need to carve out space in which we can be apart from the things of space and time and available for communion with the risen Lord. Even while we remain on earth, it is possible for us also to be elsewhere. (April 27, 2003.)

Risen Lord, remain with us, for it is nearly evening. Be for us a light to our souls, to guide us and sustain us, as we journey to that region where you live with the Father and the Holy Spirit for ever and ever. Amen.

April 15 ✠ *End Times*

It seems entirely probable that the historical Jesus was influenced by contemporary strands of apocalyptic thought—imaginative speculations about the form that the end times would take. And so, in the three synoptic gospels, we have a fiery discourse about the end of the world and the cataclysms that will lead up to it. These, along with the book of Revelation, have provided grist for all sorts of lunatic predictions about the end of the world, but the words of Jesus were never intended to provide a road map to the end. Jesus himself insisted that the day and the hour were not known, but were kept secret by the Father.

The thing to understand about this kind of writing is that it was not meant as a source of factual information; it was more in the manner of exhortation—attempting to motivate us to live lives that would pass muster when the final day dawned. The message given after the evocation of the terrible events of the final age was an exhortation to remain vigilant, to take control of one's life, not to allow oneself to slip into immorality, lest we be taken unawares. We have to be vigilant because the day of reckoning will come suddenly, like a thief in the night.

There is another message, perhaps a subtler one. All the terrible events that, from time to time, make human life unbearable are not outside the plan of God. These are the means by which God's providence brings about the conditions in which the coming of the kingdom will be welcomed. The cataclysmic events that threaten to unseat the cosmic order are not the work of the Antichrist and somehow constitute an attack on the merciful omnipotence of God. By a mystery beyond our understanding, these seemingly destructive forces have a role to play in the bringing about of God's eternal kingdom.

The consequence of this is a message: fear not. Even the worst things that can possibly happen are not outside the providence of God. In ways too profound for us to comprehend, these terrible events will contribute to the ultimate victory of divine grace and mercy. When they happen, we are advised to take precautions to protect ourselves, but to look upon them not in desperation but in a spirit of hope. Fear not. Lift up your hearts, for your redemption is close at hand. (November 17, 2017.)

Loving Father, may your kingdom come. Sow in our hearts the seeds of trust so that whatever tragedies befall us, we may never lose hope in your merciful love. Fill us with confidence in the realization of your loving providence so that we may be at peace even when all around us is in turmoil. We ask this in the name of Jesus our Lord. Amen.

April 16 ✠ **Endurance**

When I was a boy, not long after Noah came out of the ark, there was a radio program called *The Catholic Hour.* It began with the rousing solemnity of Jeremiah Clarke's "Trumpet Voluntary," fading into a deep-voiced enunciation of Matthew 16:18: "Thou art Peter the Rock and upon this rock I will build my church and the gates of Hell shall not prevail against it." It was the best part of the whole program.

It is pretty clear from the gospels that Simon Peter was far from being an immovable rock. In fact, the Greek word *petros,* unlike its Aramaic equivalent, often means a pebble or a small stone. Not much of a foundation to build on. Even after Pentecost, Peter seems to have been as wobbly as a dish of jelly. The text must refer to something other than the immovableness of Peter's faith.

Perhaps we might suggest that Christ's promise more likely refers to the endurance of the Catholic Church throughout the ages. But really, this endurance has often been fairly wobbly. Those who have led the church since Peter's time were probably not much stronger than he was, though their public relations may have been better. Yes, we have had plenty of great popes, but not one of them was immune from human weakness and blindness and malice. The fact that the church has lasted as long as it has is a pointer in another direction.

The persistence of the church is due entirely to the rock-solid fidelity of God. We believe in the church not because it is immune from sin, nor because it conforms to some media-generated standard, but because it is the sacrament by which God brings about the salvation of the human race. The church is imperfect in this present age, and we are frequently made aware of this. But its claim on our allegiance is based not on the performance of its members but on the promises of Christ and the fidelity of God.

The sins and scandals seen in the church are probably the greatest threat to our faith. They present us with a challenge that each of us must overcome in our own way. Meanwhile, we must try to consolidate our faith that just as God does not reject us because of our many sins, so God remains committed to his church and is working to bring it to the holiness that will be its crown at the end of time. (August 21, 2005.)

Faithful God, watch over your church and surround it with your providential care. May it grow ever more effective in leading people from the shadows of time to your everlasting life, so that all may be saved and come to the knowledge of the truth. We ask this through Christ our Lord. Amen.

April 17 ✠ *Energy*

The historian Correlli Barnett's latest and probably last book, *The Lords of War*, defines leadership as "the communication of moral energy." By giving a sense of belonging or inclusion to individuals, and cohesion and identity to the group, the leader generates an enthusiasm for pursuing the goals for which the group was formed. By personal magnetism or attractiveness, true leaders inspire, animate, enthuse, and energize their followers even to the point of self-sacrifice. This concept suits not only military leaders but also football coaches, musicians, politicians, environmentalists, and any who try to achieve social or cultural betterment by directing and enthusing others.

Sometimes we seem to be encouraged to think of the saints as narcissistic practitioners of virtue, people who live lives of solitary blamelessness. But no! Saints are those who communicate a zeal for the kingdom in their own particular sphere of influence. Saints come in all sorts of shapes, sizes, and colors, such as Simeon Stylites on top of his pillar, Basil the Fool wandering naked through a Moscow winter, popes in their pontifical splendor, mothers of families dealing with a thousand domestic dilemmas, tireless workers bringing succor to the neglected. Saints are those who have a positive impact on others. Holiness is a matter of beneficent influence, although it may not always be immediately visible.

Even when unknown, saints have a vibrant role in the church. Like oxygenating bacteria, their unsung contributions lead to a chain of events that culminates in an outcome beyond their imagining. It is true that some of the saints have had visible and hierarchical roles in the church, but many, many more were simple members of God's faithful people, carrying out their daily duties in a spirit of love, illumined by a quiet confidence in an all-caring God.

Maintaining the memory of the saints is a noble Catholic tradition. If we take the trouble to observe their lives, we will find ourselves inspired and encouraged to play our small part in making the world a better place and in building a bridge between God and humanity. They have passed the torch on to us; it is now our task to transmit faith and life to others so that the church is upbuilt and the recognition of the kindness of God begins to dawn in unbelieving hearts. (November 1, 2013.)

Lord Jesus Christ, strength and joy of all the saints, look upon us as we make our way to eternal life and fill us with the energy of your Spirit, so that we may light the lamp of hope in all whom we meet. For you are our Lord for ever and ever. Amen.

April 18   ✝   *Envoys*

When the Twelve are sent forth, they go in the name of Jesus. They are his envoys. They are not licensed franchisees. After time spent with Jesus and their commissioning, they finally depart to be his voice in all the places to which they travel. They are sent two by two to indicate that this is not a personal mission, but a continuation of the ministry of Jesus to which both are witnesses.

In sending them out, Jesus is at pains to instruct the disciples not to rely on human resources. They are to entrust themselves to Providence and to the goodwill of those to whom they are sent. Jesus instructs them to travel light—we might assume that this means being free not only of goods and chattels but also of cultural, tribal, and personal baggage. This is the work of God, and it is not to be hijacked by human beings with their own all-too-human agendas. What is required of envoys is that they speak with the voice of the one who sent them; what the envoys themselves think is of little relevance.

Those who are sent go forth with the authority of the sender. They have power over demons. When they are hauled before kings and governors, they are not to prepare their defense, but to allow the eloquence of the Holy Spirit to speak for them. The task of the envoy is transparency. To allow Jesus to speak and act through them without inhibition.

Just as those whom Jesus sends forth share in his power, so also are they called to share in his cross. They can expect a similar kind of rejection and persecution. In fact, their suffering and death may be the most eloquent part of their witnessing. Only thus can they speak convincingly of the undeviating hope in the resurrection.

The capacity of envoys effectively to bring the Good News to others is dependent on their close union with the One who sent them and own their own invisibility. They must make their own the words attributed to John the Baptist: "He must increase. I must decrease." They may never see the result of their own toil. Sowing and reaping are different responsibilities. But when the harvest comes, sower and reaper will rejoice together. The work in which they played a part was God's work, so ultimate success is guaranteed. (July 12, 2009.)

Lord of the harvest, you send forth workers to carry out your
will that all be saved and come to the knowledge of the truth.
Help us to be willing to accept the mission you give us. Give
us courage to endure difficulties and setbacks. Fill us with
joy and hope at the prospect of the harvest. For you are our
Lord for ever and ever. Amen.

April 19 ✜ **Envy**

A surefire recipe for a miserable life is to allow ourselves to be invaded by envy. Called "the evil eye" in antiquity, envy induces in us a jaundiced view of reality that gradually destroys our sense of well-being and poisons at least some of our relationships. We can recognize envy when we notice that we are feeling sad at another's good fortune: their wealth, their reputation, their talent, their good luck, their apparent spontaneity. If, according to the gospel, a "simple eye" fills our whole being with light, then envy has the opposite effect: shrouding us in a dark pall of sadness.

Envy is sometimes the effect of a childhood in which affirmation was in short supply and love was conditional on achieving some sort of success. It may have seemed to us in growing up that affection would remain the preserve of others unless we entered into competition with them. Whatever they received we perceived as being lost to ourselves. In adulthood the pattern remains. We compete as though there were not enough esteem for everyone.

Because envy is an admission of defeat, it is usually disguised. It presents itself as objective analysis or constructive criticism, aiming to bring the other down without getting our own hands dirty. Invisible though it may be to the one whom it invades, envy is often quite apparent to others, who then respond by withdrawing. In this way, the envious person becomes more isolated and alienated and, thus, prey to an even wider envy.

If we are infected with envy, what can we do? First of all, to recognize it and name it—not to allow ourselves to be drawn into denial. Then we should try to avoid making matters worse. We can learn to silence the impulse to bad-mouth the one we envy. We can refuse to let envy influence our actions. We can attempt to build bridges with those whom we resent. Meanwhile we should build up our own self-esteem, using our talents and striving for a life that is creative and original. And, if all else fails, we can do as Jesus recommends and pray for our enemies. (September 19, 1993.)

> *Heavenly Father, teach us to rejoice always in the gifts you have given us: in creation, in redemption, and in the promise of eternal life. Help us to be magnanimous in our attitude to others, accepting their differences and admiring their gifts. We ask this through Christ our Lord. Amen.*

April 20 ✠ **Epiphany**

The story of the downcast disciples on the way to Emmaus is really the story of an epiphany. There are many paintings by Rembrandt of the moment when Jesus revealed himself to the disciples. It seems to have been a subject that strongly engaged the artist's interests. An outburst of light pushes back the darkness to reveal a serene Jesus who draws into himself the whole attention of his fellow travelers. And it was, of course, the beginning of their mission to proclaim the Good News far and wide.

It is worthwhile to ask ourselves what happened in our own lives to cause us to walk the spiritual path. There are plenty of alternative roads to follow, each with its own attraction. Why did we choose to bear the name of Christian and to place before our eyes the ideal of a life inspired by the values of the Gospel? Saint Aelred of Rievaulx, following an age-old monastic tradition, sees four types of experience that can trigger such a choice: Four different but similar epiphanies. Four different channels of enlightenment.

- In some people, there is a deep and mysterious experience at the very heart of their being. A touch of God. An encounter with spiritual reality that actualizes a deep desire to penetrate further into what has been so momentarily glimpsed. Sometimes this happens very early in life and generates a lifelong seeking after God that is not displaced by periods of indifference or even by substantial failings. Having tasted the goodness of God—be it ever so briefly— nothing else fully satisfies.

- In other people, an epiphany occurs when a word—spoken by another person or proclaimed in the church or encountered in reading—generates a resonance deep inside that enables them to recognize their spiritual identity and to take steps to live in accordance with what they have heard.
- Sometimes the spark is struck by the example of another person's life, whether it be the result of a personal encounter or through reading. Seeing how someone else lives inspires a desire to follow their example as a way to attaining their own deepest personal fulfillment.
- Finally, for some people it is only when disaster strikes and their life is in ruins that they discover the possibility of living differently. When all the cherished projects that have long preoccupied them fall away, they discover something about themselves which has long been latent and now leads them into a new future.

As we make our spiritual journey, Christ will almost certainly appear in a guise that we do not immediately penetrate and at a moment that we do not expect. That epiphany will fill us with delight and energy and change the course of our life. (April 15, 2018.)

Lord Jesus Christ, you see us toiling on our way, dispirited and downcast. Walk with us as we go, open the Scriptures to our searching minds, remain with us and manifest your glory so that we may become your envoys to a not-yet-believing world. For you are our Lord for ever and ever. Amen.

April 21 ✟ *Eucharist*

When we consider the gospel narratives of the multiplication of the loaves, we find four activities of Christ conjoined. He welcomes. He teaches. He heals. He feeds. In the sacramental order in which we encounter the real presence of Christ, we are the beneficiaries of these same four actions. Christ welcomes us, teaches us, heals us, and feeds us. In a mysterious way, if we are attentive, we experience something of the same realities that the crowds that followed Jesus experienced. We do not receive the fullness of these gifts—that is reserved for eternity—but we receive as much of them as we are capable of assimilating.

In our technocratic age we are not very good with symbols. We forget that a symbol contains more reality than its obvious content. A card sent can be a carrier of love and esteem; a flag burned can be considered an act of treason. So, the bread and wine with which we celebrate the Eucharist are more than bread and wine. Eating and drinking unites us with Christ. Because we eat and drink as a group there is a corporate aspect to the action. We are also united to the local community and to the universal church. Because each celebration of the Eucharist is embedded in a proclamation of the Word, we are reminded of the historical Christ even as we celebrate together in his memory. More mysteriously yet, we are given a first access to the eternal banquet of heaven, even as we continue to live within the confines of space and time.

We gather to celebrate the Eucharist as an act of obedience to Christ's command, "Do this in memory of me." This is a memory which is more than mere memory; it is a presence. Invisible though real. It is by the power of faith that we slowly learn to go beyond appearances and become more aware of what is not obvious. And we are called to extend this mindfulness beyond the liturgy into everyday life. As Saint Leo recommended, "Imitate what you celebrate." (June 13, 2004.)

Heavenly Father, you feed us with the bread that came down from heaven to give life to us all. Teach us reverence for this

mystery so that we may receive it in faith and live it in love.
We ask this through Christ our Lord. Amen.

April 22 ✠ *Eunuchs*

The meaning of Jesus' saying about eunuchs and the kingdom
hangs on the translation given to a Greek preposition. The usual
rendering is that there are some who make themselves eunuchs
for the sake of the kingdom. There is a strong argument, however,
that what is meant is that they are eunuchs *because of* the kingdom. This choice is made not on the basis of what might come
about in the future, but because of what has already happened
in the past.

We are, perhaps, familiar with the condition that is called
post-traumatic stress disorder, whereby a seriously negative event
has such a strong impact that it redefines the future of the person
involved. It remains with them, perhaps for a lifetime. In a
similar, although less dramatic, way, a strong positive experience
can have an abiding influence on a person's ongoing choices.

For those to whom it has been given to experience the mystery
of God's kingdom, everything has changed. The finding of the
hidden treasure has begun a process whereby the person becomes
detached from many of the benefits that previously seemed to
make life worth living: family, wealth, career, reputation, even
life itself. The kingdom of God is experienced as an absolute
good in the light of which other realities have only relative value.

During World War I, Joe Young and Sam M. Lewis wrote a
popular song with the title "How You Gonna Keep 'Em Down
on the Farm (After They've Seen Paree?)." The implication was
that the experience of something strange and beautiful would
have the effect of generating discontent with what is plain and
familiar. In a sense, this is what happens when a person experiences what is sometimes called "a touch of God." God reaching
out to them and activating a hitherto dormant desire for the
things of the spirit. Afterward, nothing can be the same. No price

seems too high to pay for the treasure. The choices made in the energy that comes from this experience bear little likeness to the way the person lived before. A new chapter has begun. (August 23, 2014.)

> *Lord Jesus Christ, you enter our lives and, in different ways, you call us to follow you. Give us the strength to accept this challenge and the endurance to carry it through until the end. For you are our Lord for ever and ever. Amen.*

April 23   ✠   *Evangelization*

The gospels make it clear that all are called to be missionaries, to go forth and win disciples for Christ. We may well conclude that the only way to hold fast to the faith is to hand it on. In giving to others we discover the beauty and extent of the gift that we ourselves have received.

I am a little uneasy about campaigns to get God's faithful people to become co-missionaries—by using their credit cards. I know that spreading the Gospel needs human resources and infrastructure, and that all this costs money. I fear that giving money can almost become a pretext for not doing anything else. I don't have to be a missionary, a bearer of the Good News, because I sent a check.

We return to the challenging notion that all Christians are, by virtue of the gift they have received, evangelists, bearers of the Good News, living icons of Gospel truth. Our first mode of evangelization is who we are and how we live. If we are true disciples we will act differently, and other people will notice. We interrupt our journey to attend to the victim by the wayside, we refuse to join the crowd itching to stone the woman caught in adultery, we remain steadfast in our loyalty even when others run away. Alternative actions make people ask, "Why do they do this?" It doesn't matter that no answer presents itself. It is the question that is important; it is a living seed that will germinate when the right season arrives.

us bank

Member FDIC

Official Receipt

DEPOSITS MAY NOT BE AVAILABLE FOR IMMEDIATE WITHDRAWAL.

Cash, checks and other negotiable items received for deposit are subject to the terms and conditions of your Deposit Account Agreement and any other agreements governing use of your account, as amended from time to time. All items accepted for deposit are subject to later count and verification.

Want this receipt via email/text?
Enroll in eReceipts through Online
Banking or with a Banker!

usbank.com

HC 20133 (4/16)   90232175

6,768.40 Ck

5,956.83 Sv

When I say yes to God, I become a doorway through which the spiritual world can find entry into our universe. Without saying anything I embody a hope that gives strength for good and resistance to evil. My mere presence becomes a witness to truths too large to be expressed in words, yet which can kindle a fire in those who, even indirectly, come into contact with them. Every time I choose light over darkness, something of that light passes through me to cast its beam beyond me.

I should not try to measure my missionary impact; "quantitative judgements don't apply," as Evelyn Waugh said. That my role seems small is not necessarily an indication that it is unimportant. In the orchestra, the player of the triangle is usually not the star of the show and probably has less skill than the first violinist. Yet the few moments when the triangle sounds are integral to the whole symphony; without them it is incomplete. We do not have to convert the whole world all by ourselves. We are members of a single body, all working cooperatively according to our particular gifts; we are just as irreplaceable as the prestige performers in the front row. But we are bound to exert ourselves. (August 24, 1999.)

Lord Jesus Christ, you send us forth to proclaim the good news of your Father's love for all that has been made. Help us to embody these glad tidings in the way that we live and interact with people, so that all may be saved and come to the knowledge of the truth. For you are our Lord for ever and ever. Amen.

April 24 ✠ *Evening*

Ralph Wright has published a selection of his poems under the title *Life is Simpler towards Evening.* I have noticed this phenomenon when driving in the countryside. In the full brilliance of sunlight, the disparate objects that are scattered about the landscape often present a jarring picture that is in contrast to the harmony of nature. But as evening deepens, the objects lose their clashing colors and their singularity is softened as they merge with their background.

Our spiritual lives also become simpler toward evening. In the beginning many matters seemed straightforward, and perhaps we were attracted to a radical and reactive form of discipleship in which no expense was spared and no sacrifice was unthinkable. As the years passed, however, this initial simplicity was overwhelmed by complexity. Every day confronts us with new issues. Even within ourselves, we were forced to acknowledge tendencies that we never knew existed. We were baffled by the complexity of doing good in a world full of wounded people, and we were paralyzed, frustrated, and disappointed in our incapacity for a genuine benevolence that is free from darker or more obscure motivations. To live as Jesus lived seems to demand superhuman insight, a high level of diplomacy, and a capacity to tolerate indifference and rejection.

But life is simpler toward evening. After many years of struggle, we begin to notice that our energies are less dispersed. We are less anxious about many things as we become more and more impressed by the notion that only one thing is necessary. Projects, politics, and plaudits figure less in our thoughts, and even spiritual progress is less a concern. Because we are becoming less judgmental, less assertive, and less reactive, we are less upset by what happens around us and more at peace with our neighbor. It becomes easier to consign everything to God's hands, even ourselves. In this gloaming of life, I am reminded of a couple of haunting lines from the Greek poet Sappho's "Evening Star":

> O Evening, you bring home all that bright dawn has scattered;
> You bring home the sheep, you bring home the goat;
> You bring home the child to its mother.

If all goes well with us, the evening of life is a time of homecoming, a time when all the elements of our life come together in harmony, a time of healing, unity, and peace. (May 30, 2008.)

"May [God] support us all the day long, till the shades lengthen, and the evening comes, and the busy world is hushed, and the fever of life is over, and our work is done! Then in His mercy may He give us safe lodging, and a holy rest, and peace at the last!" Amen. (Blessed John Henry Newman, Sermon 20)

April 25 ✠ *Every Day*

An important Greek phrase is added by Saint Luke to Jesus' saying about taking up our cross. We are to do it *every day*. We can see this addition as an invitation to begin each day afresh, to live in the present. Saint Antony of Egypt's remarkable discourse to his followers keeps using the same phrase. The spiritual life is not a stop-and-go undertaking; it has to be consistent. We need to invest effort in it *every day*.

A lot of us go through life somewhat inattentive to the present. Our thoughts tend to swing toward the past or toward the future. The importance of living in the present moment eludes us. So many of our choices are dominated either by the tyranny of memory or by the imagined hope of a better future. As a result, we are always prone to becoming upset because we are faced with situations we cannot change. We cannot do anything about the past because it has passed. The future does not yet exist. What we can do is to interact creatively with the present—not because it is good or bad, but because it is. The present is all we have.

To live in the present mirrors the eternal "now" of God; it is to be fully alive and active as, moment by moment, our life advances. The self is a work in progress, ever evolving, constantly receiving energy from reality as it passes by. We grow by interacting with the real world; fantasy leads only to stagnation.

The psalm reminds us, "If today you hear God's voice, harden not your heart." It is in moment-by-moment reality that God speaks to us—supposing that we listen with the ear of the heart. As Saint John Cassian admonishes, each day and at every moment we must keep opening up the soil of the heart with the gospel plow. *Every day* we strive to hear God's word, and *every day* we make an effort to put it into practice. (June 19, 2016.)

> Lord Jesus Christ, you have called us to take up our cross every day, and every day to keep following in your footsteps. Help us to escape the memories that make us sad and alienated. Help us to have no thought for tomorrow, as you taught. Teach us how to live our life to the fullest every day. For you are our Lord for ever and ever. Amen.

April 26 ✜ *Execution*

On February 3, 1967, under questionable circumstances, Ronald Ryan was hanged at Pentridge Prison in Melbourne, the last instance of capital punishment in Australia. Newspapers at the time carried photographs of his mother's last visit. A little old lady, frail and worn out after a hard life, clutching her rosary beads, coping with a situation that no mother should ever have to face. The photographs, so full of pathos, inspired a great outburst of sympathy and outrage—more for the mother than for the son.

I have often thought back on that coverage as a kind of pictorial commentary on the episode in Saint John's gospel where the mother of Jesus is mentioned among those who witnessed his crucifixion. It was a scene that appealed greatly to medieval piety and was, no doubt, a source of comfort to many. We are not alone in our suffering. The cross has become for us a familiar religious symbol; perhaps it has lost its association as an instrument of torture and death. A hunk of rough-hewn wood used to suspend a man in agony until he died. Enough, one would think, to make any decent person shrink back in horror. How much greater would have been the distress experienced by those who loved the victim. In the case of Jesus, the pain of Mary would have been overwhelming.

Yet there is a kind of serenity in the picture painted by the Fourth Gospel, some sixty years after the event. Mary is presented as standing beneath the cross. She is endowed with dignity, and the mysterious words of Jesus concerning her are probably more than mere domestic arrangements for her future. The whole forms an inclusion with the episode at Cana and seems to suggest a role for Mary within the future church—an indication supported by her presence among the disciples at Pentecost.

Certainly, a continuing role for the mother of Jesus has been part of ongoing Christian experience since at least the third century. As at Cana, she is experienced as an intercessor or advocate with her Son in times of need. As at Calvary, her presence is felt whenever suffering and desolation strike her Son's disciples. Her ongoing role in the life of the church is probably better assayed by experience rather than by abstract thought. And if any of us ever have to deal with the extremes of human suffering, we will probably be grateful to be sustained by the thought of the mother of Jesus at our side. (September 15, 2005.)

> *Lord Jesus Christ, you were condemned to die, an innocent victim on our behalf. Give us the strength to stand by your cross, as Mary did, and to share the pain whenever we encounter the members of your body unjustly condemned and suffering. For you are our Lord forever and ever. Amen.*

April 27   ✝   *Exhilaration*

The picture of the tax collector Zacchaeus climbing a tree in order to see Jesus is heartwarming. It is a good reminder that Christian discipleship is not all doom and duty; it has elements of excitement and exhilaration. In the case of Zacchaeus, desire overpowered respectability. He did not mind appearing silly—perhaps he understood that our word silly derives from the German *selig*, meaning "happy" or "blessed." Is the negative connotation given in our culture suggesting that you have to be mad to be happy?

Saint Luke tells us that King Herod had wanted to see Jesus for a long time. He did nothing about it, and so he missed the opportunity to turn his life around. Zacchaeus acted. He ran out of sheer enthusiasm, was inventive in overcoming obstacles and limitations, and was able not only to see Jesus but to meet him and to receive him into his home.

What a difference exhilaration makes. It spurs to action and leads to conversion and transformation. The treasure found hidden in a field is a source of joy; following that moment of discovery, joy becomes the start of a new life, one that is no longer constrained by self-imposed limitations.

Saint Augustine was convinced that delight was the engine that drives all our spiritual endeavors. Not fear. Not a sense of guilt. Not an overpowering superego. Delight. In a way beyond our understanding we are given to taste and see for ourselves that the Lord is good. Afterward we may well seek to deepen our experience of what we have tasted. Perhaps it makes us a bit mad—or at least willing to do things that are a bit out of the ordinary. I remember a line in a poem by Mary Oliver about climbing a tree in order to feel closer. No doubt Zacchaeus would understand what she meant. (September 9, 2010.)

Loving Father, we want to see Jesus. Stir up in us that desire that will make us seek him more ardently, transcending our limitation and not caring what others think. Help us to seek that we may find. We ask this through Christ our Lord. Amen.

April 28   ✝   *Failure*

Failure can be one of the most profitable experiences we ever have. Because we live in a success-oriented society, failure seems like a disaster. It may well be, but it is a disaster we had to have, and one that grounds the possibility of future advancement.

If we are honest with ourselves, we will begin to realize that we often learn more when things go wrong than when everything seems to be proceeding smoothly. Sometimes it is a matter of unlearning bad habits or learning new skills, sometimes it is breaking our resistance to asking others for help, sometimes it is a matter of learning something about ourselves. Learning about our limitations is always hard, but it can lead us to ground our future efforts more on reality. No one can avoid making mistakes, but we can often avoid making the same mistake twice.

The gospels present Saint Peter in an apparent state of continually making mistakes. He never seems to get it right. He tries to walk on water, he asks the wrong questions and gives the wrong answers, he corrects the Lord when he predicts his own death, and ultimately denies him three times, fearful of the rebuke of a serving maid.

Supposing that Peter had been a successful fisherman, the call of Jesus meant an invitation to become a failure. Not because Peter himself was particularly stupid or incompetent, but because the call involved a state of life that transcended ordinary human capabilities. The failures were not unexpected. They merely underlined the fact that the task could not be completed without help from God. They provided the incentive to rely not on self but on divine help.

Our vocation to follow Jesus involves us in a way of life that surpasses our natural abilities. It is a call to recognize our essential dependence on God and to celebrate that dependence by calling out to God for help. Prayer is the secret consequence of our liability to failure. Because our virtue is precarious, prayer is our only means of avoiding shipwreck. (August 8, 1999.)

Lord Jesus Christ, you have called us to follow in your footsteps. Give us the wisdom to perceive the way that leads to life and the strength to follow it until the end. For you are our Lord, for ever and ever. Amen.

April 29 ✠ *Faith*

One of the most encouraging texts in the Gospel is the promise made by Jesus to Thomas: "Blessed are they who have not seen and yet have believed." That means us. It is not the unseeing that is blessed but the believing, the trusting. Faith is not principally a matter of knowing or seeing; it is the work of the will. We give assent to something that we do not fully comprehend. So, the opposite of faith is not ignorance or doubt, but the withholding of assent, the refusal to take the risk of trusting in God, in Christ, in the Gospel.

Perhaps we do not always appreciate the close linkage of faith with love. Faith makes its presence known through love because love represents the full flowering of faith—expressed in movement toward the other, in self-forgetfulness, in self-giving. The opposite of faith is not a tangled intellectual denial of truth, but coldness, aloofness, withdrawal, self-concern, narcissism.

Normally we cannot really love someone whom we have never met. To have faith in others, we need to get to know them. The mystery of the God-given faith that Jesus declares blessed is that a connection is established between us and One whom we have never seen. The door to the spiritual world opens, and we are invited to enter—but without any tangible supports to help us make the transition. We have to take a leap into what, at one level, is dark and unknown. But some inner drive keeps pushing us. The long meditation on faith in the eleventh chapter of the Epistle to the Hebrews makes the point about Abraham and Moses: faith connects us to the unseen God.

Faith expresses itself in different ways: inspiration, attraction, desire, enthusiasm, energy, endurance, confidence, boldness, joy. We might say that, in practice, it takes its definition from the situation in which we find ourselves. It leaps from where we are and finds its way to where God is; it does not matter how lost we are because the instinct of faith knows the way back to its source. It is from the gift of faith that all spiritual life flows. (March 30, 2008.)

God of all faithfulness, you have called us to know you and to love you and, despite our failures, you continue to reach out to us. Help us to be steadfast in responding to your call

and always trusting in your mercy. We ask this through
Christ our Lord. Amen.

April 30   ✠   **Falling Short**

Last week I had a dream—or was it a nightmare?—that I was
giving a sermon with the unlikely title "The Litany of the Sacred
Heart as an Anthropological Statement." The gist of it, as I remembered afterward, was that since Christ is fully human, all
the titles attributed to him in that litany constitute a revelation
of what human nature is capable of, what is the ideal for each
one of us, since "of his fullness we have all received."

For interest's sake, the next morning I went looking for a copy
of the litany and, after a long search, found a copy. There was
little in the litany to contradict the suggestion made in the dream.
We can be, by God's grace, a holy temple of God, a vessel of
justice and love, a deep sea of all the virtues, the object of the
Father's good pleasure, and so forth. That is what God has made
us to be.

It does not take much self-knowledge to come to the conclusion that we fall considerably short of this ideal. In this we are
not alone. Saint Paul reminds us that "all have sinned and fallen
short of God's glory." We have certainly failed to be beacons of
divine glory in the world, but we are not particularly conscious
of having committed a multitude of great sins. Of course, we
have had our moments of weakness, blindness, and malice. There
have been long periods of selfishness and alienation, but most of
us do not see ourselves as having enough greatness to be great
sinners. Most of our failures are sins of omission. We failed to do
the good of which we were capable.

Why do we leave so much good undone? Maybe the answer
is poignantly indicated in Philip Larkin's poem "Faith Healing":
"In everyone there sleeps / A sense of life lived according to love.
/ To some it means the difference they could make / By loving
others, but across most it sweeps / As all they might have done

had they been loved. / That nothing cures." All that we might have done, had we been loved. We often fall short of God's glory because we have not put ourselves in the way of experiencing God's love. The way back from sin is by opening our hearts in prayer to receive the love of God in Christ Jesus, the Lord. When we feel that we are loved, then we come alive. Then we find ways to express our aliveness by doing good to others. (December 22, 1986.)

God of Love, draw us into your presence so that we may experience for ourselves the length and breadth, the height and depth of your love. May the flame of your love set fire to our spirits so that we may become all that you intend us to be. We ask this through Christ our Lord. Amen.

May 1   ✠   *Family*

There is an embarrassing incident related in the Gospel tradition where the mother of Jesus and other family members decide to drop in when he is teaching the crowds. Informed of their presence outside the house, Jesus proclaims that the hearers of the Word are more important to him than his family and continues with what he was doing. The same priority is illustrated in the call of James and John, who walk off the job, leaving their father to make do with hired help. The mention of Simon Peter's mother-in-law seems to indicate that he left his wife in order that he might follow Jesus.

The negative stories about Jesus' family may, perhaps, reflect the politics of the early church, where there was a power struggle between apostolic leadership (represented by Peter) and dynastic leadership (represented by James, brother of the Lord.)

For us, however, such narratives can serve as a reminder that Christianity is a religion of choice. Essentially, it is not permanently inherited from our parents, even though we may receive it from them at an early age. We have to make a choice—if not at the beginning, then certainly later on and, perhaps, more than once. Inevitably choice requires renunciation. To choose one option is to leave other options unchosen.

Choice requires the setting of priorities. When Jesus said, "Seek first the kingdom of God," he meant it. He promised that we would receive a hundredfold in return, but the renunciation was still nonnegotiable. We cannot serve God and mammon. This is a hard teaching, and we would prefer a challenge that would leave us with more wiggle room. But it seems that the only way to set out on the road that leads to eternal life is through the narrow gate that leads to an even narrower path.

What is paramount is that we give priority to hearing God's word and allowing it to shape our life. We can be reasonably sure that God will not ask of us more than we have the capacity to give. With the challenge comes the grace, and with the grace comes the consolation that nothing that is given to God is ever lost. We can take comfort in this, but sometimes the going will still be hard. (September 23, 2014.)

Lord Jesus Christ, when you call us to leave all to follow in your footsteps, you are calling us to a more abundant life. Give us the courage to respond to your invitation and the perseverance to remain with you in good times and in bad. For you are our Lord for ever and ever. Amen.

May 2 ⊹ *Fasting*

One of the scandalous things about the lifestyle of Jesus' first disciples is that they were rather casual about the rules of fasting practiced by the more fervent of their contemporaries. The controversies continued in the early years of the Christian church. Of course, it was not only fasting. The dispute covered the whole gamut of rituals and customs that surrounded fasting. The question really concerned the continuing relevance of the ancillary customs that had attached themselves to the practice of the Torah. The telling metaphor that Jesus used was that of new wine and old wineskins. The new cannot fit into the old; both will be lost. The new age, triggered by the coming of the Christ, demands new institutions and new structures. The purpose of fasting is to express a spirit of waiting for the coming of the Messiah; when the Messiah comes, fasting ceases to have a function.

This is an instance of discontinuity in God's dealings with us. Often it happens that God asks of us to let go of the good things that we have, so that we may reach out to grasp what is even better. Abram had to leave Ur of the Chaldees in order to become Abraham, the father of many nations. If he had stayed where he was, his shop in Ur might have done very well, and he might have died a rich and happy man, surrounded by swarms of grandchildren. But he would have missed his moment. He had to leave and begin afresh in order to achieve the ultimate greatness to which he had been called.

I do not underestimate the value of practices that bring us closer to God and increase our willingness to be generous in responding to the call of the Gospel. But sometimes, after months or after years, these practices can become so routine that they lose their energy to motivate us. This is really the moment for a bit of discernment. We need to ask ourselves whether we leave things as they are, or whether we seek alternative ways of serving the purposes embedded in what we had been doing. It is not always easy to arrive at the answer immediately; sometimes we need to experiment in order to find out what seems to be working best. Sometimes we need to seek counsel. But, first, we need to be aware that God frequently calls us to change our blameless ways because there is something even better awaiting us. (September 2, 2016.)

> *Lord God, you call us to yourself through a lifelong journey that has many twists and turns. Help us to keep our eyes fixed on our goal, so that we may be ready to reorient ourselves whenever the pressures of life cause us to wander off the track. We ask this through Christ our Lord. Amen.*

May 3 ✠ *Father*

When Jesus instructs us to address God as Father, he does not intend this to be taken as the apotheosis of the beliefs and values of a patriarchal society. The everyday term *Abba* belongs more to the breakfast table than to the throne room. In encouraging us to use it in speaking to God, Jesus is emphasizing that we may dare to inject into our prayer a high level of intimacy. This represented a rereading of the theology of the Hebrew Scriptures—the universalization of the singular closeness permitted to Abraham and Moses and a few others.

It seems to me that part of the reason why Christianity was largely victorious over paganism in the age of Constantine was its emphasis on a God who was loving and who calls forth love from us, so unlike the multitude of capricious and demanding deities who had to be served and placated. Our relationship with God is not so much specified by external laws and regulations; it is a matter of heart speaking to heart—to recall the motto chosen by Cardinal Newman: *cor ad cor loquitur.*

This devotional aspect of Christianity is not something to be spurned in favor of a more "rational" approach. In fact, devotion has been described by Edward Schillebeeckx as the living skin of religious experience (*Essays: Ongoing Theological Quests*). It is not to be identified with sentimentalism or pietism. Feeling is integral to human experience. Unfeeling religion easily becomes harsh, rigid, and judgmental. When people cease religious practice because it is boring, arid, or sterile, it is really because feeling has fled from their exercises of piety.

Feeling is not everything, but it is not nothing. We do not have to be able to explain it rationally. We are more likely to continue in prayer if it is marked by a sober sense of being content and comfortable in the presence of God; there may be storms on the surface of our life, but deep down we are possessed by an assurance of God's unconditional love, confident in being accepted as we are, and unashamed of our ongoing need for forgiveness and mercy.

When the son of Philippine president Ferdinand Marcos was stopped by a policeman for speeding, the outcome was certain. The policeman was sacked. This example may serve as an extravagant image of God's attitude toward us: "If God is for us, who could be against us?" "Even though our hearts condemn us, God is greater than our hearts." Our many sins and failings may not be enough to get us into trouble. That is because God is our Father. (July 28, 2013.)

Loving Father, open our hearts and minds to be mindful of the many events in our life that bear witness to your unchanging love for us. Help us to go through life confident that we can never move outside your loving acceptance and your powerful help. We ask this in the name of Jesus, your Son. Amen.

May 4 ✠ *Fear*

Martin Seligman has given us a recipe for a healthy and happy life: to recognize one's highest gifts and to use them at the service of something greater than oneself. Three ingredients: recognition of gifts, their employment, and a higher vision. If I sing like a nightingale, I need to acknowledge that gift, to develop it, to discipline myself to protect it, and then to use it not merely for self-congratulation, but to bring joy and uplift and, perhaps, healing, to others. If I don't I will be unhappy, and maybe I will become ill. Those who do not use their gifts in this way become frustrated and resentful, projecting their problems onto others, blaming them, and ultimately withdrawing their services and themselves from involvement with others.

We find the same principle in the parable of the Talents. The servants are given money as a stake to begin an enterprise in their master's name. The qualities required of them are honesty, industry, energy, and initiative. Presumably the master recognized these gifts in them; otherwise he would have been throwing his money away. The servant who failed to yield a profit tells us why: he was afraid.

Not all fears are harmful, but many have a paralyzing effect that inhibits us from realizing our potential. Many unreasonable fears come from a hyperactive imagination. Let loose, they can create an alternative world that overpowers our relationship with reality. Tsunamis happen, but that is no reason to avoid taking a walk along the beach. A vivid imagination can be our friend in allowing us to see around corners, but, like a horse, it needs bridle and bit to ensure it does not carry us off to where we don't want to go.

We must value our gifts and own our responsibility to deploy them. We build up the boldness to do this if we allow ourselves to be seduced by the vision of something greater than ourselves. Our gifts are not merely for self-gratification. They are meant to serve others, to serve all others, to serve the cosmos. And if something is worth doing, as Chesterton noted, it is worth doing badly. Even if our goal is lofty beyond what we see as our capacity, we need not fear that God who has given the gift and inspired the vision will not bring to completion any good work that we have begun. If fear forces us to bury our talent, then our life will be pretty miserable. (November 16, 2008.)

Lord Jesus Christ, give us a spirit of boldness so that we may gratefully use the talents you have entrusted to us to advance your kingdom. May we play our role in reducing suffering in the world, and in being bearers of Good News for all. For you are our Lord for ever and ever. Amen.

May 5 ✠ *Fear Not*

When Jesus comforted his followers with the words "Fear not, little flock, for it has pleased your Father to give you the kingdom," he was saying something to which we also might well pay attention. We do not always admit to our fears; we act as though we are not under their influence, even though it costs a lot to keep up the façade. Fears cause us to hold back, to keep something in reserve, to have a Plan B ready, just in case.

It has been said that fear is a greater threat to faith than doubt. Doubts can be assuaged by the comforting presence of someone who gives us a guarantee. Fear, on the other hand, cripples our sense of solidarity and our *joie de vivre*. Faith is allied to courage and confidence and perseverance. Fear undermines all these qualities and makes us timid and tentative. We lack the boldness that is necessary to do the unexpected and original.

Often our courage drains out of us because we feel that we are in a minority; we are only a little flock faced with a great task. Here it is good to remember the story of Gideon in the book of Judges. The Lord sent away the men of Gideon's army until no more than three hundred soldiers remained. With these Gideon was commanded to face the hosts of Midian and Amalek, which were as thick as a swarm of locusts. The victory that followed was not Gideon's but God's. "Nothing is impossible for God."

It is probably true to say that the grace of fervent Christian living is welcomed only by relatively few. The Gospel places demands on us that may sometimes seem excessive. But the work is God's. We play our part. Often that will mean acting in a way that is the opposite of heroic, working with the few resources that are at hand. But nothing is impossible for God, and we can be sure that "it has pleased the Father to give you the Kingdom." (August 12, 2001.)

Loving Father, send us the Spirit of boldness, that we may stand before kings and governors, not quaking with fear but firm in our faith. Give us the confidence that you are accomplishing your plan to bring all things to completion in Jesus, your Son. We make this prayer in his name. Amen.

May 6   ✠   *Fence-Sitting*

There is a great scene in the Bible where Joshua assembles the entire population at Shechem and tells them, "Choose today whom you will serve." Unsurprisingly then, and throughout their history, a large proportion of the people preferred to sit on the fence and keep their options open. We don't have to go back thousands of years to discover this tendency. We can find it in ourselves. In many matters we prefer not to give our full commitment until we accumulate more data and, especially, until we can know for certain how things will turn out.

What a difference it would make if there were fewer fence-sitters, if more people were committed, intense, passionate, and energetic. It doesn't take many wholly committed people to galvanize the rest. It is not unusual for administrators of all kinds of institutions to be champion fence-sitters. They will change something only if a bomb is put under them. When from below there is a dense enough push for change on a particular issue, then they will act, if only to guarantee a quiet life for themselves. If we want to produce a more just society or a more transparent administration, we have to organize. Organization needs organizers, people passionate enough to bestir themselves.

The model on which some theoreticians base their reflections is that of the church as a perfect society. It doesn't take long to discover how hollow is this claim. In every age, and not only ours, the church has had it limitations, and the ranks of the clergy have not been restricted to bright angels of virtue. The spottiness of the church reflects the inherent condition of all its members; in this age we cannot expect to find only saints. The point is that this is no reason to withdraw our support or our fidelity. If God can cope with the church's imperfection, there is no reason for us to bail out. Or to remain inert.

In Western countries more people are becoming obese; the danger is that our thinking becomes flabby as well, and we leave that task to others. We go with the flow. Drifting with the current will not take us anywhere good, nor will we find much excitement if we keep sitting on the fence. Maybe we should take the risk and try a little initiative to make the world and the church better places. (August 24, 2003.)

Lord God, you call us to fight the good fight and to be active in redeeming the times in which we live. Rouse us from our slumber and give us the courage to engage with the issues of

*our day, and guide us by your Spirit of wisdom and pru-
dence. We ask this in the name of Jesus our Lord. Amen.*

May 7 ✠ *Few or Many?*

Jesus seemed reluctant to respond to the disciples' query about
how many would be saved. Perhaps this reticence can be seen as
having a moral purpose, as if to say, "Don't you worry about the
number of the elect, just make sure that you are included among
them." In this case, even though the twelve disciples were his
closest followers, they were being admonished that there were
no guarantees, no privileges, no reserved seats. They, like everyone
else, had to maintain their efforts to enter through the narrow
gate and to keep walking on the demanding road of discipleship.
Yes, they were invited to the wedding feast, but they needed to
wear the appropriate wedding garment. They needed to keep
their lamps filled with oil. They needed to stay awake. And the
same applies to us.

Maybe we can approach matters from another angle. Perhaps
"few or many" is a false formulation. Perhaps the phrase should
read "few *for* many." Some are called to play a more heroic role
for the sake of the others. They are the salt that seasons the
whole, the leaven that causes the entire dough to rise. Maybe we
should think of salvation less in terms of individuals passing the
examination at heaven's gate and more in terms of the whole of
God's faithful people entering into the life that Jesus has won
for them. The whole Body of Christ will be saved, and, by God's
grace, the different members of that Body will all have different
and distinctive parts to play in the process. Just as Christ gave
his life for the sake of the many, those members whom we call
saints make up in their own lives whatever was left undone in
the work of the Head. In the same way that Saint Paul affirms
that an unbelieving husband is saved by a believing wife, so the
faith of the "little flock" has a positive outflow to those to whom
the Good News has not arrived.

Every small deed done for God is an ecclesial act. It is not merely a meritorious act that belongs to the individual who performs it; it is an ecclesial act, continuing the work of Christ. Its effect is to bring closer the day when all will believe and rejoice in the knowledge of the truth. (August 25, 2013.)

> *Loving Father, you so loved the world that you sent us your only Son so that all who attach themselves to him might come to a more abundant life. Keep us firm in our faith and joyful in hope so that our lives may become an expression of Christ's love. We ask this in the name of Jesus the Lord. Amen.*

May 8 ✠ *Finishing*

Discipleship is not something into which we enter on the spur of the moment. It is meant to be a cold-blooded decision. Jesus talks about building a tower. He advises us to look before we leap, to know what we are getting into, not to start what we cannot finish, and once we start to keep going until we finish. All these suggestions make sense. We would do well to follow them. Finishing is more important than beginning. And more challenging.

Since any relationship, including that of disciple and master, is a two-way process, we are entitled to ask whether the Lord follows his own instructions. Does he practice what he preached? Saint Paul tells us that we are God's building. Did God consider the potential liabilities when we were chosen and called? The psalmist tells us that God knows the dust of which we are made so, I suppose, we have to expect that God knew something of our weakness, blindness, and malice before beginning to deal with us. So even those ugly things in us, about which we scarcely dare to think, were taken into consideration by God. God was not buying a pig in a poke.

God is always working to complete the good work that has been begun—to avoid the possibility, raised by the psalmist, that enemies will say to us, "Where is your God?" Our growth in holiness is God's work; we are not permitted to think that God is uninterested in its outcome.

Jesus also talks about calculating the odds before we go to war, whether our ten thousand have a chance against an enemy's twenty thousand. Here again, God is not uninformed or unprepared. Those predestined are called, and those called will certainly be saved. If God is for us, who can be against us?

From God's side, all is settled. We who walk by faith and not by sight cannot always perceive this; we are sometimes afflicted by hesitations and doubts. We have to remember that what seem to us to be serious obstacles to completing the work of sanctification are, in God's sight, no more than pesky flies on a summer's day. They can distract and annoy, but ultimately they are not life-threatening. God will bring to completion the work that has been begun and, in reality, in Christ the bulk of the work is already finished. (September 5, 2010.)

> *Loving God, you have called us to follow Christ and to walk the road to a more abundant life. Help us to keep making progress on this path, confident that you go ahead of us and accompany us, and that you provide a remedy for all our mistakes. We make our prayer in the name of Jesus, your Son. Amen.*

May 9   ✠   *Foreign Cows*

There is an Irish proverb that says, "Cows from beyond the sea have long horns." What it means is that we more readily attribute greater authority to whatever is strange and unfamiliar. A shaven-headed Tibetan monk in exotic robes is obviously wiser and more spiritual than the parish priest or my next-door neighbor. Or so it seems. There is another similar proverb: "Familiarity breeds contempt." And Jesus himself lamented that prophets were not received in their own country.

Perhaps we need to be critical of such an attitude because it leads to the conclusion that if God were to speak, if God were to call us to conversion, it would be by means of something strange and dramatic. We want to be spiritually entertained. We find the still, small voice by which God habitually addresses us too unemphatic, ambiguous, and, perhaps, too respectful of our freedom. According to legend, the disciples of Saint John the Evangelist were dissatisfied with his continual preaching on the theme "Love one another." They hoped for something a bit more scintillating.

God speaks in various ways, and we need to listen for them all: through conscience, through those closest to us, through the liturgy, through what we read, even through homilies. And, as Saint Augustine points out, God can speak to us through the rebukes given us by our rivals or enemies. God continues to address us, but somehow the message doesn't get through to us because we are hoping for something different. God does not communicate to us an overwhelming insight into the meaning of life. The message is simply for today, and it is often a very minor revelation of a step that can be taken. Perhaps slightly to upgrade our own life. Perhaps to offer something to somebody else. Perhaps to step back from an unseen danger. The word comes to us simply. It is so easy to ignore. But to take our cue from it may well be the beginning of a major grace in our life.

When it comes to problem-solving we will usually find that a complex situation is resolved not by a single complicated intervention, but by a dozen insignificant little interventions, each untying one of the knots that binds us fast. The steps toward a more abundant life are not exotic but familiar, everyday gestures that collectively have more punch than the big intervention for which we were hoping. (July 18, 2016.)

Loving Father, you enter our lives in many different ways, and your words of comfort and challenge are often very subtle. Help us always to listen to the promptings of your Holy Spirit so that we turn away from evil and become the persons you intended us to be. We ask this in the name of Jesus our Lord. Amen.

May 10   ✠   *Frivolity*

There is an attractive rusticity about the Cana miracle as told in the Fourth Gospel. It could easily be the subject for a Brueghel painting. Jesus' friends are not only poor and unlearned, they are also thirsty. Those of us with a more refined sense of propriety may be offended by the event; the miracle seems frivolous to the point of scandal. In a world full of human suffering, why squander a miracle on such a trivial benefit? If Judas had been present he might have said, as he querulously remarked at the anointing at Bethany, "Why this waste?"

The evangelist is smarter than we are. He sees the miracles that Jesus works not just as a temporary fix to a problem or an entertaining demonstration of power, but as "signs." The miracles point to something beyond themselves. As is often said, it is the thought behind the gift that matters. One rose can serve as a sign of love just as effectively as a hundred roses.

The signs that Jesus worked were perceived as signs only by those with faith. Many years ago an older brother pointed out to me the difference between dogs and cats. If you point, the dog looks in the direction you are indicating; the cat looks at your hand. The cat does not recognize the pointing finger as a sign; the dog does. To those with faith the miraculous wine gives a message of the all-powerful love of God revealed in Jesus. The believer follows the sign to the object it is indicating. To the unbelieving it is simply a matter of extra wine—and the prospect of a bigger hangover.

All that Jesus did to signal his Father's love is marked by both gratuity and abundance and brings in its wake happiness and rejoicing. The miracle at Cana may be insignificant in its contribution to world history, but it made some people happy. And that is an achievement that does not deserve to be labeled "frivolous." And, as a sign, the incident points beyond the present to a more profound celebration when with Christ we will drink the new wine in the kingdom that is to come. (January 15, 1995.)

Lord Jesus Christ, you came among us to share our joys and our sadness. Help us to become ever more conscious of our solidarity with all, and inspire us to be a source of joy and happiness to those who are a part of our life. For you are our Lord for ever and ever. Amen.

May 11   ✠   **Fruit-Bearing**

Jesus makes the point that the only way that a seed can produce its fruit is by dying. Death is the doorway by which we enter into life. It is not easy for us to appreciate how this stark message can be termed "Good News."

When we are in the midst of life, full of gratitude for God's beautiful gifts—enjoying the resources we have, the love in which we share, good health and life itself—it seems like a cruel sentence that we must relinquish all of these in order to obtain what Christ has promised. Like some of the first disciples, we are inclined to complain, "This is a hard saying; who can bear it?" Such a precept is indeed a narrow gate, the eye of a needle at which we affluent camels balk.

No wonder that there is a near-universal tendency to water down the costly demands of the Gospel discipleship. We try to transform Christianity into a feel-good or do-good religion, a means of enhancing our present life.

Real Christianity is unthinkable unless we understand it in terms of a future life. "If for this life only we have hope in Christ Jesus, then, of all people, we are the most to be pitied." Faith is necessarily connected with the unseen realities of eternal life. This future existence, "which eye has not seen, nor ear heard, nor has it entered our heart to imagine," is what gives meaning to our present experience of suffering and will make even our death seem tolerable. When Jesus bids us take up our cross, it is not intended as a call to a life of misery or a summons to annihilation; it is, rather, an invitation to give priority to the highest gifts of God, to set our hearts on things that are above and not on those which are on the earth.

The seed that dies does no more than relinquish the mediocre level of existence with which it is familiar in the process of moving to the more bountiful stage of its natural life cycle, bearing fruit. Death in all its myriad forms is a natural element in life as we know it. The Good News to which our faith leads us is that our final death is not the end, but rather an entrance into a higher, more fruitful, and, ultimately, more satisfying form of life. The tender compassion of our God has prepared for us something far better than anything we have yet experienced, and it is worth losing anything and everything in order to obtain it. (Undated.)

Lord Jesus Christ, help us to understand that your call to the cross is not folly or scandal but a call to entrust ourselves to the power and wisdom of God. Strengthen our faith so that in times of trouble we may remain full of hope and optimism. For you are our Lord, for ever and ever. Amen.

May 12 ✠ **Gate**

In the late 1970s, while I was in the Philippines, a late-night exchange of anecdotes led my companions to conclude that I had been visited by a *kapre*, the cigar-smoking giant that lives among trees and can sometimes be heard whistling in the darkness as it comes to observe humans. Wide-eyed with wonder, my informant told me that, above all, I was not to accept the invitation to follow the *kapre* because I would be led to a tiny hole in the ground and, if I entered, would suddenly find myself in a cavernous space from which there was no exit.

In the intervening years I have occasionally pondered the significance of the image: a small hole leading to an immense space. It is probably an indication of the belief that our familiar earth is not far distant from another, more mysterious zone, and that there are places on earth that are much closer to heaven than others. The Celtic tradition calls these "thin places." These are sacred places where God seems nearer to the believing heart and where prayer comes more readily.

In the liturgy for the dedication of a church building, the edifice is described as "the house of God, the gate of heaven." The material building, whether grand or rustic, is seen as the doorway to heaven. A gate is for passing through. Nobody stops at the gate or even takes much notice of it. The mind is fixed on what is ahead. The church building, likewise, is intended to take us beyond itself into the invisible world of spirit. It does this in two different ways. Either it leads us through images—the artwork suggesting an alternative vision of reality and a reminder of the content of our faith—or the church building can help us to pray by its bareness, its lack of distraction, its call to a concentration on deeper and loftier realities.

In his Rule, Saint Benedict decrees that the place of prayer should be what its name indicates and, therefore, nothing else should be done there or left there. When we enter a church, we should allow ourselves to be drawn beyond its material details, seeing it especially as the gate of heaven—an invitation to lift up our hearts and to seek the realities that are beyond and above. Even the humblest building can have a sacred character, giving us access to the vastness of the sphere of God. We go to a church because we want to meet God, not to comment on its architecture. (September 9, 1999.)

> *Loving Father, you have imprinted on our souls the affirmation that we are citizens of heaven; this is our homeland. As we make our way on this earthly pilgrimage, keep us mindful of where our journey ends and teach us to act in a way that expresses our heavenly identity. We ask this in the name of Jesus the Lord. Amen.*

May 13   ✠   *Gentleness*

I happened to see the final episode of a reality-TV series entitled *The Edwardian Country House*. Although those involved were only play-acting, and the series was heavily scripted, there were strong emotions at the end. Those who played the bosses were weepy that after three months their role was ending; those who played servants couldn't get away fast enough. Not a bad reminder that, for all the rhetoric, being a servant is not much fun. I heard of a bishop who was honest enough and blunt enough to omit the prescribed words "me your unworthy servant" because he felt them to be untrue.

Those who are paid to serve on a nine-to-five basis can assume the appropriate attitudes during work hours and hang them up with their uniform when they are off duty. Real servants are on call 24/7; they live over the shop, as it were. Their needs and preferences are considered unimportant. That is probably why we no longer have many such people—effectively, they are slaves.

It is very rare to find a person who has sincerely internalized the qualities of a servant: hardworking, nonassertive, self-effacing, obliging. This is the quality that is designated in the New Testament by the words *meekness* or *gentleness*. The best way to define this quality is by thinking of its opposites: harshness, violence, bossiness, imperiousness, assertiveness, heavy-handedness, and so on. To eschew such ways of interacting with others demands great strength of character. It means living by the fruit of the Holy Spirit, in the way set forth in the Beatitudes. It is not so easy to offer the other cheek when struck, not so easy to go the second mile, not so easy not to take offense when insulted. To be gentle means being very strong.

I can compel you by power, but I can draw you by gentleness. I can drive you by force, but I can lead you by gentleness. I can crush you by arrogance, but I can nurture you by gentleness. I can destroy you by vengeance, but I can forgive and heal you by gentleness. This is the way of Christ. This is the litmus test we can apply to ourselves, whether we be leaders or followers. (October 19, 2003.)

> *Jesus, meek and humble of heart, teach us the way of gentleness. Help us to use whatever authority we have with the*

utmost respect for others, as a sincere service of the com-
munity and not as a convenience for ourselves. Help us also
to respond to hostility with meekness and humility, and let
us make peace before the sun goes down. For you are our
Lord both now and forever. Amen.

May 14   ✠   GIGO

Eating habits have changed in the last thirty years. In a country like Australia, where the quantity of food is more than sufficient, we have begun to pay attention to what we put into our mouths. We like our milk to come from contented cows and our vegetables to be grown organically. We wear our spectacles when we shop for groceries so that we can scrutinize the labels to ensure that the products we purchase adhere to the high standards we have set ourselves. This is a long way from a period when suppliers were able to put sawdust in strawberry ice cream to make it grittier, or colorants in tea to give it a deeper hue. We are more conscious that we are what we eat, and so we take steps to ensure that our diet is appropriate.

Perhaps we are not so careful about what enters the mind. The things that we allow to be introduced into our thinking also have a role to play in shaping who we are and what we will become. Because many of us suffer from a chronic tendency to boredom, what we seek, above all, is to be entertained. Light amusement, we think, is simply a means of relaxation. It does no harm. We need to question that. Entertainment always comes embedded in a system of beliefs and values that, often enough, it seeks to communicate to the recipient. Every dictatorship knows the value of using popular media to transmit a message. And of suppressing any freedom of expression which might undermine the total credibility of the party line. Cartoons can easily be subversive; a politician drawn with a boozy red nose is not taken seriously because we mindlessly imbibe what the media want us to believe.

In the early days of computers we were warned of the GIGO principle: garbage in, garbage out. Computers are not infallible. They depend on how they are programmed. If the data is wrong, the conclusion will also be wrong. It is the same with humans. If only bad data goes in, then the conclusions we draw and the decisions we make will inevitably be blighted.

You may say, "I don't have much exposure to mass media, so I am safe." Perhaps. Media usage is generally underreported. We don't want to admit how much of our day is passed under its influence, directly or indirectly. Garbage in, garbage out. If we want to upgrade our lives we need to look at the quality of what enters our mind. Maybe we need to dig deeper. Perhaps to ask questions before we swallow: what are they selling? Perhaps we need to turn to cooler media for balance: reading, reflection, adult discussion. (January 25, 2004.)

> *Creator God, you have endowed us with reason so that we may find our way to you and learn to live a wholesome life with others. Give us a discerning mind, so that we can perceive what is good and noble and uplifting, and the courage to turn aside from all that debases your creation. We ask this through Christ our Lord. Amen.*

May 15   ✠   **Give**

One of the tricks that professional writers and speakers use is occasionally to throw in an unusual word that jolts us back into attention. They know that there is a danger that our concentration will lapse if it is unstimulated for too long. This can be a misfortune because, sometimes, the most important words are simple and familiar.

I would suggest that one such word that we encounter often if we read the Bible is *give*. It is frequently applied to God. God gives gifts to his people: life, the promises, identity, guidance, protection. In the Fourth Gospel especially the word is used so often that translators try to spice up their text by using different renderings. There is an advantage, however, in sticking with the simple expression, which leads us to the conclusion that the nature of God is to give. It is our nature to receive from God.

Christ is God's self-gift to humanity. "God so loved the world that he gave his only Son." He came to reveal God's giving nature. In his time on earth he gave to others teaching, healing, peace, comfort, courage, abundant life. Above all he gave himself; he is our Immanuel: God-with-us. Not only was Jesus God's gift to the people of Palestine two millennia ago, he is also given permanently to us by the power of the Holy Spirit. He continues to bestow his gifts on us through grace. Interiorly when we are at prayer. In the Scriptures. In the church. In the sacraments.

When Jesus was speaking to the Samaritan woman he exclaimed, "If only you knew the gift of God." I suppose he would say the same thing to us. If we can get some inkling of God as giver, then perhaps we would pay more attention to our present possibilities of receiving whatever we need to flourish. Nothing is impossible for God; it is only our lack of faith that closes our hearts so that we cannot receive what God is preparing for all who love him. (August 4, 2002.)

Eternal Father, you gave us your Son, you give us your Spirit. Help us to open our hearts to receive your gifts so that our lives may be forever marked by praise and thanksgiving. We ask this in the name of Jesus the Lord. Amen.

May 16   ✠   *Glory*

I have seen a device advertised as a means of personal defense. It is an exceedingly bright light that startles, blinds, and disorients a potential attacker so that the user can take the opportunity to escape. I don't have one, but the advertisement is a good reminder that light is not always a friendly force. Sometimes we are happier in the shadows of twilight.

There are three kinds of brilliance: one that oppresses, one that dazzles, and one that attracts. Light that oppresses makes us conscious of our own poverty and dirtiness. The brilliant know-it-all is not a comfortable companion because we are constantly being excoriated for our inexcusable ignorance. Light that dazzles us is light that takes up all available space so that it is as though we cease to exist. We are lost in admiration, yet we feel unwilling to approach. Light that attracts is that which appears at a distance and which draws first our eyes and then our feet to itself. We see it and want to come closer. Like Moses and the burning bush, first the extraordinary sight seizes our attention, then we feel compelled to move toward it, and then, as we approach, we are filled with a delightful sense that we are in the presence of the sacred and hasten to remove our shoes.

The glory of God is the attraction by which we are drawn toward the ultimate mystery. An encounter with it kindles in us a desire that can never be satisfied. The more we experience the infinite variety of the divine, the more we desire it. Our desire is never satiated. When our desire reaches out to God, so Saint Bernard tells us, it is like throwing oil on a fire; it burns ever more fiercely. Desire for material things disappears once we possess them. Being drawn into the glory of God has the effect of making us desire to be drawn ever more intensely into the mystery. Pseudo-Denys describes this ongoing penetration as like the action of a corkscrew: going ever deeper into a single and simple reality, but always finding something new. Even though we remain somewhat fearful in the presence of the all-holy God, we are fascinated and spellbound by it, and desire ever more.

This encounter with God's glory is the means by which we are also sanctified. "With unveiled face we all gaze on the Lord's glory; we are transformed from glory to glory into his very image as by the Lord who is Spirit." (October 24, 2009.)

Loving God, you have planted in our hearts the desire for eternal life with you. Help us to set lesser desires aside and to follow more earnestly on the road mapped out for us by your Son, who is our Lord for ever and ever. Amen.

May 17   ✠   *Gnats and Camels*

Jesus' remonstrance to the Pharisees that they were straining out gnats and gulping down camels is a colorful reminder that sometimes the relative importance we assign to things is unreal. If there is any lesson we need to communicate to those in our care, it is surely that some things are more important than others. If the house were burning down, would we rescue our computer or our cat? The choice we make would indicate our priorities.

There are relatively few things that are really of prime importance in our life. One undoubted claimant to this title is certainly our life, both present and future. "What would it profit persons if they gained the whole world and lost their lives"—or "their souls," if you prefer. Surely this would be a case of ultimate stupidity. We let go of a permanent good in order to grasp something transitory.

Father Adolfo Nicolás, the former general of the Jesuits, was asked what was the most serious problem facing the world today. He replied, "the globalization of superficiality"—a phrase that Pope Francis has also used. Our capacity and willingness to look beneath the surface of things is slowly being eroded by our preoccupation with trivialities: with non-news, entertainment, and a move away from rationality. In so many cases the frenzies whipped up by the media are examples of "much ado about nothing."

Many of these pursuits that seize our attention are relatively harmless in themselves, but they consume time and distract us from looking at matters that really call out for our intervention. Polishing the bronze on the *Titanic*! Some in the Vatican seem more concerned about red shoes, lace albs, and baroque miters than with financial scandals and sexual abuse. Straining gnats and swallowing camels!

We ourselves are not immune from similar temptations. The things that upset us most are usually relatively minor and will probably be forgotten in a short time: small instances of sloppiness, perceived insults, different points of view. If some of the energy we use in brooding over such shortcomings were employed in creating a cleaner environment or a more contented community, the world would soon be in a much better state. As it is, we fritter away our resources in making a fuss about things that don't much matter. Learning to let some things pass without reacting will probably be a step in the right direction, contributing to both inner peace and social harmony. (July 18, 2014.)

> *Lord Jesus, you taught us that it is useless to wash our hands when our hearts are unclean. Free us from concern with things that do not matter and help us to devote our energies to cooperating with your plan to bring all people into your kingdom. For you are our Lord for ever and ever. Amen.*

May 18 ✠ *God the Enemy*

In his book *Religion in the Making*, Alfred North Whitehead distinguished three successive phases in our perception of God. At first God is a *void*: merely a three-letter word with no linkage to our experience of reality. If we grow spiritually, then God becomes for us an *enemy*—One outside ourselves who makes demands on us. We have to stay with this image of God until we become sufficiently respectful of the otherness of God that God can become for us a *companion*.

It is the middle phase that is challenging, the disjuncture between life as we have designed it and a higher life to which we are being called. Mostly, we don't want to take the step upward. We enjoy staying within our comfort zone. Sometimes the surest indication that the grace of God is at work in us is that we begin to resist and rebel. We could call it the Jonah syndrome. As long as God remains silent we are at peace; if God begins to speak to us, to call us, to send us on a mission, our instinctive response is to take a jumbo jet to the ends of the earth.

Many of the prophets show a similar reluctance to accept their mission, and, if we are honest, we will probably find symptoms of it in ourselves. God's plan for our growth often begins with disengaging us from what currently occupies our attention. Like the fishermen and the tax collector in the gospels, we can be called to start a new chapter in our life, often enough one for which we have not been prepared. To arrive at any real state of friendship with God, we have to learn to coexist with God the enemy.

The story of Jesus' encounter with the Syro-Phoenician woman in the Gospel of Mark follows this pattern. At first Jesus ignores the woman's pleas; he does not want to initiate contact. When he does respond, it is to insult her. This apparent hostility does not dislodge her faith but strengthens it. She is undeterred. And so finally he gives in and grants the cure for which she had been asking. From God the void to God the enemy; from God the enemy to God the companion.

I am reminded of a story about Saint Teresa of Avila who, after a narrow escape, remonstrated with God, "If this is the way you treat your friends, it's no wonder you have so few!" Even the saints experienced stormy weather, and we certainly will. But if we doggedly refuse to be deflected by the way God seems to be dealing with us, then it is not unrealistic to expect that eventually the sun will break through the clouds and things will begin to appear in a different light. (August 3, 2011.)

Loving Father, keep alive in us a firm trust in your providence. Help us to see that even our trials and misfortunes serve your loving purpose and that when you seem to be absent, it is only an invitation to seek you more intensely. Hear us now and sustain us always in Jesus Christ our Lord. Amen.

May 19 ✠ Good Friday

The death of Christ, which forms the focus of our reflections today, is not simply a matter of commemorating an historical event. It is a reality in which we all participate because Christ's death reveals something about human nature itself. The death of Christ was a necessary consequence of the incarnation. The one thing of which we could be certain concerning the newborn

Jesus lying in the manger is that one day he would die. How he would die and at what age were hidden, as are the details of our own end. But death itself was certain.

So, Christ's death was not an unfortunate accident caused by the weakness or perfidy of a few individuals—or even as a result of the collective guilt of the whole human family. It was, as Saint Peter is quoted in the Acts of the Apostles as saying, "according to the deliberate intention and foreknowledge of God." It was part of God's plan because—as Saint Irenaeus later wrote—"what was not assumed was not healed." The only way in which that most powerful enemy of humankind could be rendered impotent was for Christ to demonstrate by his resurrection that death was unable to overcome God's love.

Death is not external to human nature—a foreign intruder. It is a necessary element of our destiny. What we see from our perspective is the end of the first phase of our existence. We do not have eyes to perceive that it is not only the termination of earthly life, but also a transition into another mode of being. In death we are called to let go of the many good things that have previously constituted our life, not in despair, but in the sure and certain hope that the greater good of resurrection awaits us.

There are many minor deaths throughout life when we are called to release our hold on one moment in order to move to the next. Perhaps the most basic of all sins is the refusal to keep letting go, not wanting to move on. We cling to the past and ignore the present. Yet eventually everything will have to be left behind. Perhaps we might ponder the words of one of Albert Camus's characters: "Who could have believed that crime consists less in making others die than in not dying oneself?" Maybe we need to learn the art of dying. (April 17, 1981.)

Lord Jesus Christ, dying you destroyed our death; rising you restored our life. Keep alive the flame of hope in our hearts so that we may always be confident that what awaits us in the future is God's banquet of eternal life. For you are the Lord of the living and the dead, both now and forever. Amen.

May 20 ✠ *Graciousness*

In China I have never had to stand in the subway. Perhaps misled by my white hair into thinking I am much feebler than I am, someone has always stood up and offered me a seat. At first I was reluctant to accept the offer. Maybe I was vaguely affronted at the implied suggestion that I was as old as I am. In any case, the thought came upon me that I had to learn to be gracious in responding to the thoughtfulness of these strangers. The strategy I developed was that I turned on my most regal smile and contentedly sat down, even though it was only a matter of minutes before I alighted.

We hear a lot about generosity in giving, especially just before the collection is taken. We hear much less about graciousness in receiving. Yet the two virtues belong together, and jointly they constitute an important strand in the weaving of the social fabric. Activists that we are, it is important to be generous; perhaps we need to reflect a little on the nobility of being a gracious receiver.

Graciousness has a family connection with gratitude; the two words have the same foundation. What makes the act of receiving gracious is the gratitude that is expressed in some way by the recipient. Gratitude is more than the utterance of conventional politenesses. It is not enough merely to say "thank you." We have to feel something and to instill that feeling into the words we say and the gestures we perform. Feeling grateful binds the receiver to the giver. It does not necessarily involve the incurring of a debt, but it is a possible foundation for the strengthening of future relations.

We all know the importance of the dual commandment to love God and neighbor. Perhaps we can express part of this obligation differently. We are called to be grateful to God as well as grateful to our neighbor. Whereas gratitude does not add anything to God, it does add something to us; it helps us to realign our relationship with God, putting it on a sounder basis. Salvation is not something that we achieve; it is a gift given to us. Our response to it is not a cry of triumph but a heartfelt feeling of gratitude graciously expressed. (March 11, 2018.)

Lord God, give us gracious hearts to acknowledge the gifts
we have received from you and from others. Give us a true
sense of humility to recognize our neediness and boundless
gratitude in response to your ongoing giving. We make this
prayer in the name of Jesus the Lord. Amen.

May 21 ✠ **Gradually**

One of the most dramatic incidents in the Gospel tradition is
the episode where Jesus drives out from the temple the hawkers
and moneychangers and all the animals. It was a scene that offered great scope for a painter such as El Greco to portray the
contrast between the fiery anger of Jesus and the fearful flight
of the traders. The incident has also been welcomed by preachers and moralists and self-styled reformers, who see in it an
obvious call to reform and purify.

I would like to ask a different question. The Jerusalem temple
was the center and focal point of Jewish religion. The Third
Temple, which Jesus visited, was a magnificent edifice already
forty-six years in the building and with work continuing. How
did it get to be in such a mess? The outer court had become a
marketplace with cattle and sheep and birds, buying and selling,
moneychangers and all the melee they implied—people milling
around, networking, haggling, shouting. Not quite the place of
prayer that its history suggested.

The temple was seen as an outpost of heaven, it did not belong
to the earth. It was extraterritorial, like a diplomatic mission. It
was understood as a holy place, the house of God. The word *temple*,
like the words *template* and *temperature*, has its origin in the San-
skrit term *temp*, which signifies the mark on a rod that serves as a
measure and ensures conformity. A temple is a place on earth that
mirrors the heavenly sphere. That is why some temple complexes
(including perhaps Stonehenge) try to reproduce on earth the pattern of the stars. A temple is meant to be is reserved place: nothing
unholy is to be stored there or done there.

To return to our question: how did the temple become so defiled? The answer: gradually. Step by step. Item by item. Convenience displaces reverence, and by a series of small compromises a slow erosion begins. The holy site was assessed by secular categories; its sacred character disappeared from view. What harm could there be in taking a shortcut through its precincts?

We may well be familiar with the process in our own lives or in the life of communities. There is a self-legitimating spiral of decline, each step dictated by common sense. When we close our eyes to the mystery, the voice of conscience is quietly silenced and soon we don't even remember what we have lost. The time has come for a prophet and a whip. (November 9, 2014.)

Lord Jesus, lead us into the presence of the mystery of God. Teach us to have reverence for the realm of the Spirit so that we do not allow our familiarity with the sacred to lead us into inattention. Make us true worshippers in spirit and in truth. For you are our Lord for ever and ever. Amen.

May 22   ✟   **Gratitude**

The story of ten lepers being healed and only one coming back to give thanks can serve as a useful reminder of the importance of gratitude as a lubricant of social life. Human beings are social animals, and the only way that we can flourish is in a state of inescapable interdependence. We are constantly giving and receiving services that are rendered at some cost to the one who serves. It is only appropriate that the recipient acknowledge this in some way, at least by saying, "Thank you."

We are aware that the giver invests both thought and effort in preparing a gift, and so givers are greatly esteemed. Perhaps we are less conscious that there is also an art in receiving what another gives. When we receive a gift we become indebted to the donor. In some cultures we are obliged to reciprocate with a gift of comparable value. Even when the gift is gratuitous, honor demands that we repay the giver by the manner in which we accept the gift. The word *gracious* comes to mind. To receive a gift graciously involves acknowledging the joy that it brings us, at the very least with a smile. We honor the giver by manifesting our appreciation of the value of the gift—whether it be its objective value or simply what it means to the recipient. And we recognize the thoughtfulness and generosity of the giver. We should invest as much in receiving a gift as the giver invested in preparing it.

In a culture where all are encouraged to be doers, perhaps we need to place more emphasis on being good receivers. People who are conscious that everything that they are, as with all that they have, must come from other people—and ultimately from God—are less likely to be self-centered and antisocial. They are blessings to any community of which they are a part. On the other hand, nobody wants to be around ungrateful people: those who are so possessed by a sense of entitlement that they cannot recognize generosity in others or feel any inclination to reciprocate.

We have been the recipients of many blessings. May we also be among those who take the trouble to come back and give thanks to God and to others for what we have received. (November 15, 2017.)

> *Lord God, giver of all good gifts, we thank you for the blessings with which you have enriched our life. Grant us the humility to recognize the services others do for us and the nobility of spirit to repay them with our gratitude, our prayer, and our willingness to reciprocate. We ask this through Christ our Lord. Amen.*

May 23 ✠ *Gravity*

In the liturgy there are many references to the glory of God. Most of us would be hard-pressed to give an exact definition of what we mean by this term, despite the fact that the Swiss theologian Hans Urs von Balthasar has written seven volumes under the title *The Glory of the Lord*. Most of us would probably think of glory in terms of brilliance, radiance, splendor. A bright light that dazzles and subdues those touched by it. Like rays coming from the sun.

There is another way of looking at God's glory, not as outgoing but as in-drawing. The glory of God is the divine power of attraction, the gravitational pull to which all created beings are subject. As Newton noted, the effect of gravity is to pull the moving object into rest. Our restless hearts yearn to find their resting place in God. Like Ignatius of Antioch, we long to exclaim, "I hear the murmur of waters calling out, 'Come to the Father.'" Do we hear the inward voice of Jesus speaking to us? "Come to me. Come to the Father. Allow yourself to be drawn. If I am lifted up, I will draw all people to myself." To submit to this ultimately irresistible attraction is to become fully alive, fully human. As Saint Irenaeus wrote, the glory of God is the human being fully alive; and the life of us all is to see God. In that happy state we will say, like the apostles at the Transfiguration, "It is good for us to be here."

God is an ocean of vast unknowable infinity, and yet the waves of this sea are permitted to crash upon the shores of time, as God is revealed in various epochs and in different ways. And in the last times God sent the Son, a veritable tsunami of uncreated love. As with all waves, the effect of divine revelation is to create an undertow, a rip, that if unresisted will carry us off into the infinitude of God, and we will see God face-to-face and so be transformed from glory to glory into the very likeness of Christ.

"For in the mystery of the Word made flesh / a new light of your glory has shone upon the eyes of our mind, / so that, as we recognize in him God made visible, / we may be caught up through him in love of things invisible" (Preface I of the Nativity of the Lord. (Undated.)

Lord, Creator, and Sustainer, let your glory shine on earth. Let us see your face and we will be saved, so that in all things you may be glorified. We ask this in the name of Jesus the Lord. Amen.

May 24 ✝ *Greed*

Saint Augustine was reluctant to accept the common notion that infants are innocent. It is not innocence, he believed, but impotence or an incapacity to impose their will. This helplessness is the source of the tantrums we sometimes see in very young children. They cannot get what they want, so they make themselves as unpleasant to others as they can.

Greed begins at a very young age. It begins with seeing something as desirable, as wanting to have it, to reaching out, grabbing it, possessing it, and attempting (at least) to consume it. The tendency transmutes itself from a simple biological urge for food to every other source of relief for our native neediness, and thence to the satisfaction of our social aspirations: our acquisitiveness, our ambition, our desire for prestige, our vanity. Like infants, we are not at all amused when we don't get what we want. Frustrated greed easily leads us to let others know how we feel. We do this through displays of anger, aggression, violence, revenge. The untrammeled desire for money and other things is the root of all evil.

What I want for myself involves my denying it to others, since there is not enough for everyone. But there is irony here. As the Irving Berlin song reminded us, "After you get what you want, you don't want it." We move on to the next thing. You might recall that Ethan in John Steinbeck's *The Winter of Our Discontent* concludes that you can never have enough money; you either have no money or not enough. And wasn't it the Beatles who sang, "Money can't buy me love?" Greed remains hungry even when the monster is fed. Meanwhile, having acquired what we wanted, we worry about losing it, and if that should happen, we grieve over its loss. The moment of bliss is brief indeed.

Wise people in every religious tradition urge us to remember the transitoriness of all that momentarily gratifies us or is the object of our multiple desires. Nothing lasts forever. Too much concern about such things weighs down the heart and prevents us from acquiring the kinds of skill that will make us really happy and becoming grateful for what we have, be it ever so humble. No wonder Saint Paul says that avarice is a kind of idolatry.

In several prayers of the liturgy, we ask that we may use the good things that pass in such a way that we may hold fast even now to those that endure forever. That's a good balance, isn't it? (July 21, 2016.)

> *Lord God of heaven and earth, from you all creation has its being and on you all that lives is dependent. Help us to overcome our lust for possession so that we may find gratification in what we already have and a generosity that is willing to share with others who have less. We ask this through Christ our Lord. Amen.*

May 25 ✟ Grievance

Evagrius of Pontus listed among the principal impedances of prayer the remembrance of past wrongs done to oneself. Just as we settle to spend time quietly with the Lord, we are disturbed by the memory of the harm that someone has done to us. As soon as we empty our minds of other distractions, this memory leaps in to fill the void, bringing with it feelings almost as strong as those generated by the original affront. Immediately our prayer ceases and we are left seething.

In such cases it is useless to ask whether there is just cause for the grievance. Inevitably we will convince ourselves that we were totally blameless, the innocent victims of another's thoughtlessness, misjudgment, abuse, or persecution. That is not the right question at such a time. The fact is that every person is subject to some degree of unfairness or worse; it is a normal component of humanity's fallen state. This is not to justify ill treatment nor to ignore our obligation to respond to it, but simply a reminder that we should expect sometimes to be its target. The question we need to ask concerns how we are to deal with it.

And deal with it we must. Otherwise our grievance will fester and infect our whole life so that, eventually, we may reach the point of being defined by it. If we become obsessed with the wrongs done to us, there is danger that our whole outlook on life will be blighted. We may become permanent victims. It may happen that our memory of events becomes distorted. We may exaggerate the malice of others and diminish our own complicity in what happened. Above all, we may overlook the fact that by continually revisiting the source of our grievance we may be perpetuating its malign impact on us. The ongoing memory may be more harmful than the triggering event itself.

The New Testament concept of forgiveness invites us to let go of the bad event. Here I am thinking mainly of everyday hurts; more extreme instances may well need professional help. For the usual abrasions caused by social living we need to make a stand and refuse to admit the remembrance of such troubles to haunt our awareness. We need to make a choice. First we have to deal with the situation, if it needs dealing with; sometimes this involves doing a reality check on our memories; they tend to become inflated over the years. Otherwise we refuse to think about it, set the memory aside, and allow time to heal the pain.

Above all, I need to be mindful of the fact that nurturing everyday grievances harms only me; the perpetrators escape scot-free. (August 24, 2014.)

Lord Jesus Christ, you suffered the shame of the cross as an innocent victim of human malice. Help us to be prepared to share in your passion without being defeated by it. And give us confidence that in all these trials we will overcome because of God who loves us. Hear us Lord, now and forever. Amen.

May 26 ✝ *Grime*

One day I was sitting in an airport, vacantly waiting to board the plane. A young woman came and knelt down beside me and started working on a potted plant, washing and wiping its leaves and cooing quietly into it. When she had finished, I asked her what she was doing. She said it was her job to go around the various terminals, tending the indoor plants. The atmosphere inside an airport terminal is toxic for plants, and it was her responsibility to try to offset the stress that crippled the plants' well-being. And she showed me the grime that she had wiped off the leaves.

I muttered to myself that nobody cared about the grime that I was absorbing from the atmosphere, but, then, I was not a permanent resident of the terminal.

Later I began to think of how toxic our cultural ambience can be and how crippling the effect of its toxic influence. For better or for worse, most of us are exposed to mass media and social media for several hours every day. Some of the messages we receive are overt—maybe even strident—and these can, if we care to take the trouble, be submitted to a fact check and a value check. But other messages are subtle. They work gradually beneath the level of consciousness, undermining our beliefs without openly confronting them. Raising suspicions where there is no evidence to support the claims. Presenting issues in a way that shepherds us to the desired conclusion, as in push-polling, where the question is submitted in a form that predetermines how it will be answered.

Without our noticing it, we are slowly being overlaid with a layer of intellectual and moral grime. We are less able to see our way clearly through the welter of different opinions, and our moral compass swings too wildly from side to side to give us a firm direction to pursue.

We need to make opportunities to wipe away the grime. To step back and activate our conscience. To reacquaint ourselves with the words of Jesus and the teaching of his church. To celebrate a Sabbath in which we shut down the voices that are trying to inhibit our freedom. We need to be still to allow ourselves to see that God is God. To taste and see that the Lord is good. (March 13, 2018.)

Lord God, free us from all that will distort our vision or cloud our judgment. Open our minds more fully to your truth and give us a heart that is ready to love and be loved. We make this prayer in the name of Jesus our Lord. Amen.

May 27   ✠   *Growth*

Most of us have a positive reaction to the word *growth*. It echoes the nineteenth-century myth of progress, which seemed to suggest that everything was in a state of evolution toward something bigger and better. Yet growth is not an unqualified good. To grow to be two meters tall means that you will be always bumping your head on the door frame. Do you really want to keep expanding your girth until you resemble a blimp? What about warts? What about cancers? These are all instances of growth. This leads us to say that only that growth is good which fosters the general well-being of the person. Otherwise growth is best avoided.

Perhaps we have heard about champion athletes who have sacrificed everything to achieve excellence at their sport, only to face emotional or physical decrepitude when retirement imposes itself even before the midpoint of their lives. Perhaps we know businesspeople or academics who work so hard at furthering their careers that they neglect their health and their family, and maybe fail to see hidden gifts and talents that call out to be developed.

Not every avenue of growth leads to a happy outcome. When we think of working toward a different future, we have to ask ourselves whether this will make us happier, more balanced persons or whether it will merely isolate us, alienating us from those around and boosting our futile sense of self-importance. At an early stage an unwise choice may feel like a liberation from both past and present, but we may be progressively moving into a delusional space that impairs our true sense of who we are.

It is all a matter of discernment. To try to become what God intended us to be at the moment of our creation. Not to redirect our vital energies into channels of our own choosing, but to seek to invest our small efforts in the same direction that God is empowering. The growth willed by God always leads to innocence and integrity. Anything else is unworthy of us. (June 12, 1988.)

> *Creator God, help us to become what you have made us to be. Show us the way that leads to a more abundant life and give us the strength to travel it. We ask this through Christ our Lord. Amen.*

May 28 ✠ *Hammers of God*

In the 1930s it was decided to build a new temple in the heart of Bangkok. The authorities found a large statue of the Buddha in an outlying area and transferred it to the new site. To the horror of the watching monks, the statue proved heavier than expected and the chain snapped as the statue was lifted into the courtyard. The statue fell with a great crash. The monks who rushed in to assess the damage were astounded to find that the stone was only a coating; inside was another statue, made of 50 tons of gold, worth about two billion dollars, give or take a few cents. The precious statue had been covered with stone to protect it from marauders.

Perhaps some of us are like that statue; the way we present ourselves often hides who we are. And so our golden heart is concealed. What others see is a façade, a mask, a persona, a role—they never see us as we are. After a time we begin to accept their assessment. No doubt our lives are relatively blameless, but they lack the sparks of originality and spontaneity that would kindle a flame. Our public virtue is a burden that we sometimes dream of casting away.

The first thing that God has to do is to save us from ourselves, to deliver us from this inner tyranny that is ruining our happiness. This means cracking open the stone shell so that the heart of gold is revealed. Sometimes this is brought about by a big fall that utterly destroys the outer layer. More often the work is done by a more gradual process. God sends workers with hammers to chip away at the surface of our life until the reality is revealed.

It may be a guileless child or Balaam's donkey. It may be like the cock that crowed to hold up a mirror to Simon Peter.

The false self that is about to be shattered is the source of two opposite problems. The first is complacency; we begin to accept the press releases we issue and, so, begin to accept that we are as good as we want others to believe. The opposite danger is that we are weighed down by an interior sense that we are hypocrites, not a quarter as good as the sparkling image we project. The reality is that we are neither as good nor as bad as our image suggests. We need to get rid of that image. Meanwhile, God's hammers are working to bring us to a fuller truth—to reveal our heart of gold. As we read in Jeremiah, "Are not my words like fire, says the LORD, and like a hammer that shatters rock?" (December 10, 1995.)

> *Loving Father, open us to accept the many ways in which your providence leads us to reality. Remove falsehood from our vision of ourselves so that we may recognize that your loving mercy accompanies us through all the changes of our life, forming us to be truer images of Christ. We make this prayer in the name of Jesus the Lord. Amen.*

May 29   ✠   *Happiness*

Psalm 4 asks, "What can bring us happiness?" Our inner identity is clearly indicated by the way we answer that question. Is it money, or power, or friendship, or security, or love? These are all good things, useful and even essential for a sound level of contentment. All of them, however, are precarious. Today we enjoy them; tomorrow we may well lose them. Possession that is only partial is unsatisfactory; it always seeks more. Possession that is liable to loss can never be absolute. Wars, natural disasters, and civil disturbances can, in a single day, rob us of the assets that took a lifetime to accumulate.

Another psalm says, "In God alone is my soul at rest." This verse may remind us of the famous sentence in *Confessions* that

Saint Augustine addressed to God: "You have made us for yourself and our hearts are restless until they rest in you." We will
remain forever dissatisfied until we learn to look beyond the
things of time to seek what is above. "Here we have no abiding
city." All things are transient; only God remains.

Our faith reminds us of all this, but, because eternity surpasses
our capacity for understanding, we allow ourselves to live as if
heaven did not exist. We do not reject the notion of eternal life,
but we set it aside in order to concentrate on things that are
nearer and more comprehensible. We say, "A bird in the hand is
worth two in the bush."

Léon Bloy once said, "Joy is the most infallible sign of the
presence of God." If we really open our hearts and our lives to
God, we will begin to experience a little bit of heaven on earth
as the joy that floods the spirits of the elect begins to take root
in our souls. Perhaps then we begin to understand why Jesus
summarized the effects of discipleship in terms of happiness.
"Happy are the poor, the meek, the persecuted . . ." It is God
alone who brings true contentment. (October 14, 1990.)

*Eternal Father, you have called us to share your joy and to
take our place at the banquet of eternal life. Teach us to keep
our eyes fixed on the end of our journey, and help us to follow
the example of your Son, who is the way to truth and life.
We ask this in the name of Jesus our Lord. Amen.*

May 30 ✠ *Hard Times*

One of the particularities of Jesus' invitation to discipleship was
that he never disguised the fact that following him would involve
blood, sweat, and tears. His disciples must carry the cross, their
future will be "not without persecution," and they may have to
endure the birth pangs of the New Age. We may ask ourselves,
"Why does it have to be so hard to follow the way that leads to
more abundant life?"

Jesus' warning of hard times ahead is particularly relevant in our times. We live under the influence of the nineteenth-century myth of progress in which all things are seen to come under the evolutionary umbrella. Everything is always getting better. That would be wonderful if it were true. Our experience of life, however, leaves us in no doubt that all of us undergo struggles and compromises and failures. We waste our time and energy going up blind alleys and wandering around, lost. We can be crippled by regret and guilt. We can be misunderstood and treated unfairly. Jesus is telling us that such undesirable setbacks are normal. We had better get used to them.

We may not allow ourselves to be deterred by the obstacles we encounter. Perseverance is always a challenge, but, in any endeavor, it is absolutely necessary if progress is to be made. We will be often tempted to change direction and seek an easier path, but that is usually delusional. The only change that will make a difference is that we change ourselves: change our outlook, change our habits, realign our expectations to reality.

It helps if we do not lose sight of our ultimate destination. The kingdom of God is beyond all knowledge and experience, yet it is promised as the fulfillment of all that makes us human. Even in the bleakest of seasons we do not travel alone. We walk with an immense throng of fellow pilgrims. And Christ is in our midst as our guiding light, providing us with all we need to arrive home safely. God is faithful and will not desert us. (November 18, 2001.)

Heavenly Father, help us to keep our hearts fixed on the things that are above and to seek first your kingdom of righteousness and peace and joy in the Holy Spirit. Help us to surmount whatever obstacles we encounter so that we may come with joyful steps to the feast of eternal life. We ask this in the name of Jesus, the Lord. Amen.

May 31   ✠   *Hardness of Heart*

There is a wonderful Greek word in the New Testament: *sklero-kardia*. It sounds like a fatal disease, and so it is. It is hardness of heart. Commonly, when we say people are hard-hearted, we usually mean that they are not softhearted; they are austere, unapproachable, harsh, severe, uncompassionate. But the term used by the New Testament goes deeper than that. It refers to a person who has no understanding and, hence, has lost the capacity to be moved, to be changed, to expand. Such a condition experiences no regret and can see no reason for changing direction. Particularly in the Gospel of Saint Mark it is used of the disciples; Jesus accused them of losing the plot. "You do not yet know, you do not understand, your heart is hardened." They just don't get it.

Imperviousness of heart takes many forms. All of them are perfectly obvious to others, but, unfortunately, we don't seem to be able to identify them in ourselves. Let us say a little about some of the different embodiments, remembering it is not a binary condition. There are different degrees, and different manifestations can coexist and overlap.

- *Forgetfulness of God.* There are so many important and urgent things that cry out for our attention that often they consume all our energies. As a result, we become impervious to any sort of spiritual stimulation, and, for all intents and purposes, we live as practical atheists.
- *Entertainment*: The world is full of amusing things to do, and it is easy enough to spend vast amounts of time being entertained. Progressively, as a result, we lose not only the taste for spiritual reality but even the capacity to be aware of it.
- *Lack of Self-Knowledge*: Without the investment of time and energy in plunging beneath the surface, we become spiritually illiterate, uninterested in and unable to be concerned about anything beyond our immediate concerns and projects, strangers to our own inner world.

- *Lack of Self-Acceptance*: If we don't truly know ourselves, then our self-esteem is based on how others view us. As a result, we are constantly trying to win their approval; we never really graduate into autonomous adulthood.
- *Loveless Life*: When we lose contact with reality, life becomes meaningless and dull; we tend to project our self-rejection onto others. Genuine self-giving and other-receiving love is absent from our lives—and that is why we are so harsh and unsympathetic.

I suppose it is worthwhile praying for a receptive heart, a heart open to receive from God and from others. As a result, we are blessed with the gifts of wonder, gratitude, and empathy. And we become a little more human. (January 6, 2010.)

> *Lord God, take away our hearts of stone and give us hearts of flesh. Help us to be more open to the inspirations and influence of your Holy Spirit and give us a willingness to make ourselves accessible to all whom we encounter. We ask this through Christ our Lord. Amen.*

June 1 ✝ *Harvesting*

In a well-remembered saying, Jesus exhorts us to pray to that Lord of the harvest that he would send workers to bring in the harvest. In many parts of the church today this injunction is taken seriously. There seem to be fewer vocations now than there were forty years ago. There are many reasons for this: smaller families, demographic changes, changes within the church, scandals such as sexual abuse, alternative openings for service, and, in the case of the diocesan priesthood, the unpopular requirement of celibacy.

What we need to remember about the work of harvesting is that it is the final stage of a long process. The soil has to be prepared, the seed sown, and growth monitored before we can begin to think about bringing in the sheaves. And, meanwhile, the weather plays an important and uncontrollable role in bringing about a successful outcome. The failure of the harvest is due most often to defects in the earlier stages. Likewise, a successful harvest is scarcely to be credited to the harvesters alone. It is a corporate victory. Many have contributed to it.

Jesus noted this when he said, "One sows, another reaps." Reaping or harvesting is a joyful time, as we can see from boisterous harvest festivals celebrated in many cultures. But sowing is a work done in blind faith, not knowing whether the seeds will germinate or to what extent they will come to fruition. The sower sows. The outcome is necessarily unpredictable. But "those who sow in tears will reap with joy."

When we apply this extended metaphor to the church today, we have to say that there is certainly a need for harvesters. But we must go further and affirm that the need for sowers is even more intense. God's faithful people are urgently called to labor in the darkness of faith to bring about the coming of God's kingdom. This means persevering in sowing seeds of goodness in soil that is not equally receptive. We will not necessarily see the harvest of what we have sown; this falls to the purview of the Lord of the harvest. We simply do our bit and let natural processes take over. (October 18, 2011.)

Lord of the harvest, send forth sowers to sow the seed of your word in the hearts of all. Let the favorable rain of your grace sustain the seed as it grows to fruition. And when the season is right, send forth reapers to bring in the harvest to the glory of God and the joy of us all. For you are our Lord for ever and ever. Amen.

June 2   ✣   *Hatefulness*

As a small boy I was told to be careful with postage stamps that bore the king's head. To place them on the envelope upside down was considered an act of treason. I don't know if this advice was factual, but I have spent the rest of my life avoiding this jeopardy. The point is that human beings have a tendency to create crimes and sins out of virtually nothing. We define sin as lawbreaking and then accord to any law that happens to pop into the heads of legislators the power of sanction over any who disregard it.

I wonder: would it work to define sin in terms of its human impact rather than in terms of law? If the lawyers lost out and physicians took over, sin would be redefined as anything that was hazardous to health. If the psychologists intervened, sin would be anything that impaired our sense of well-being. Everybody would be able to define sin however they like; probably everyone would have a different catalog of sins.

My own view, at the moment, is that sin is anything in us that is truly hateful. Sin is what turns the comedy of life into a tragedy. If you think about it for a moment, do such behaviors as murder, avarice, infidelity, disloyalty, dishonesty, mendacity, and any kind of moral inconsistency bring anything but sorrow to humanity in general? Perhaps they impart a momentary thrill to their perpetrators, but their ongoing impact is to tangle the lives of all whom they touch. If we accept Saint Augustine's dictum, "Hate the sin, but love the sinner," then these behaviors are eminently hateful. They do not make us happy. They drive a wedge into our hearts that will eventually split us apart. A double life is double trouble.

World War I was prompted by a single murder. Think of the hardship inflicted by the greed of the wealthy. How many families have been ruined by thoughtless infidelities? Sin is hateful because it is inhumanity. It is not just breaking the rules—like putting a postage stamp upside down. Sin causes suffering, whether immediately or ultimately, however it attempts to disguise its true nature, however it is spun by clever words into seeming something good. Sin is whatever is truly hateful.

Christ came to heal the weakness, ignorance, and malice that are endemic to the human condition and are the ultimate causes of sin. He does this in four ways; by the sacramental action of the church, by the admonitory action of the Scriptures, by the inspirational action of good example, and by the invisible action of the Holy Spirit in our souls. When hatefulness departs, we become entirely lovable and find also that the commandment of love is not so difficult. (December 19, 2010.)

Loving Father, you created us in your image and likeness, but we have fallen from grace and exiled ourselves far from you. Call us and give us the strength to make the journey back to your loving embrace. We ask this through Christ our Lord. Amen.

June 3 ✠ *Hats*

I grew up in the golden age of Westerns, when footage of men on horses shooting each other was considered appropriate entertainment for small boys. To help me understand the mayhem on the screen I was given a hermeneutical key: those in white hats were "goodies"; those in black hats were "baddies." And so we cheered when the black hats were shot and sighed with relief when the white hats rolled out of danger at the last minute.

In the real world it is not so easy to distinguish between good and bad—partly because men have stopped wearing hats! There are other criteria that have evolved in different social groups that are just as inaccurate: race, politics, gender, money, religion. It makes it easy if we live in a world of prejudgments; we don't have to think. Then a trope developed in novels whereby the stereotype flipped and displayed the opposite qualities: the prostitute with a heart of gold, the severe clergyman with secret vices. And this is very much what sells tabloids even today.

In his parables, Jesus overturns such facile expectations about good and bad people. He makes the point that things are much more complicated. In the story of the two sons in Luke 15, both the rebel son and his elder brother are at fault, but in different ways. In another parable, both the son who said no but repented and the one who said yes and did nothing leave something to be desired. Some may say that Jesus is calling us to judge people on what they do rather than on what they say. More likely he is returning to the theme raised in the Sermon on the Mount: not to judge at all.

It is true that the strictly observant Pharisees are condemned as "hypocrites" or play-actors because their practice did not come from their hearts. God can see this. I cannot. If I start judging others, I am putting myself in jeopardy. Saint John Cassian says that we tend to condemn in others what we refuse to see in ourselves. Psychologists would say that what is repressed in us is projected onto others. It is better that we don't judge at all.

In any case, we all have two hats, black and white, which we wear interchangeably. We hope we will die wearing the white hat, but it doesn't really matter. All alike need God's indulgent mercy. (October 1, 2017.)

God of infinite compassion, have mercy on your people who struggle to choose what is good. Help us to discern what truly leads to life and give us the energy to maintain our course even when the going is rough. We ask this through Christ our Lord. Amen.

June 4 ✠ *Hearers of the Word*

In 1941, the great theologian Karl Rahner published a book in which he tried to isolate the quality that sets human beings apart from the rest of creation. His conclusion was that only a human being can be described as a "hearer of the word." This title refers not merely to our ability to make use of language but, more especially, our capacity to hear the Word who is beyond all words— the self-revelation of God. As human beings, we are open to receive the gift of God's self-outpouring and, so, to enter into dialogue and communion with God.

If an openness to the divine is the essential characteristic of the human race, then it is obvious that whatever promotes this openness is also working to make us ever more human. The converse is also true. Whatever causes us to draw back from our attraction to transcendent reality and the spiritual world reduces our humanity. As Saint Augustine wrote at the beginning of his *Confessions*: You have made us for yourself and our hearts are restless until they rest in you. Resting in God allows us to be more fully alive as human beings.

The Bible is the story of God's self-revelation. Since the creation God has spoken to us in many and varied ways, not to communicate information but to initiate and sustain a relationship. Part of the history of salvation, as it is revealed in the Bible, is that some people accepted the invitation, whereas others resisted. It is possible to traverse the Bible and notice which of its personages hear the word and live in communion with God and which choose to go their own way. The greatest hearer of the word was Mary, the Lord's mother. She so fully received the gift of God's self-revelation that the Word became flesh in her body. For us and for our salvation, the invisible and apparently silent Word assumes a human voice to become our teacher and guide to eternal life.

Because we are capable of hearing the word, a response is expected of us. Sticks and stones and cats and dogs are, certainly, the outcome of God's creative word, but only humans can speak a word back. When God speaks to us an answer is expected. It is to be hoped that, like Mary, we also will say, "Yes, be it done to me according to your word." Thus, not only are we hearers of the word but we become doers of the word. (December 18, 2005.)

Loving God, you have spoken to us throughout our history and invited us to share your life. Give us the wisdom to respond positively to your invitations and the strength to remain faithful to the path you trace out for us. We ask this in the name of Jesus, your Son, our Lord. Amen.

June 5   ✠   *Heaven*

Cardinal Newman wrote about heaven that it was like an eternal liturgy in which we join the angels in ceaselessly celebrating the wonderful works of God. C. S. Lewis responded that an endless liturgy sounded more like hell than heaven. If we take the book of Revelation as our guide, then Lewis is closer to the truth; it says that in the heavenly Jerusalem there is no temple.

One of my warmest images of heaven derives from my experience as a small child going to the Royal Melbourne Show, which was, in those days, much more spontaneous than it is now. It was a holiday from school and thus imparted a sense of freedom and exhilaration. Everyone seemed to be in a good mood, not only my immediate family but also the thousands who poured into the Showgrounds from all over the state. It was a time of color; people matched the blossoms of spring by donning their glad rags. There was, in the eyes of a child, endless variety, with a surprise around every corner. The fact that it lacked a hospital, a school, and a church meant that there seemed to be no sickness, no ignorance, no need for redemption. Bliss! No doubt, as an adult, I would find it less than a total delight, but to a child, it was entrancing.

Jesus said that the kingdom of heaven is designed for little children. So perhaps my experience so long ago mirrors what will be our future. Heaven will certainly be crowded. The book of Revelation mentions 144,000 plus a numberless throng. The "abode of the blessed" sounds like something pious, but it simply means that only happy people live there. There are no hospitals in heaven because the well-watered tree of life provides leaves for the healing of nations. There will be no schools, no need for one to teach another because all will know the Lord directly. Best of all, there will be no temple. God will no longer seem to be an object outside ourselves, but we will be invited to participate in the very life of God.

But there is a difference. Show Day came to an end, and it was back to school the next day. In contrast, heaven is not ruled by sun and moon; there it is endless day because God is light. With a reality far exceeding all images, heaven will be our happy home forever; this is what is prepared for those who love God. (November 1, 1995.)

Loving Father, strengthen our faith so that we really believe that you have prepared a place for us in heaven. Grant us a vibrant hope that is ready to endure much to obtain what you have promised. Fill us with a love that conquers all fears and inspires us to spread contentment and joy wherever we are. We ask this in the name of Jesus our Lord. Amen.

June 6 ✠ **Hell**

Imagine that you have been given a ticket to be present at Wagner's operatic epic that goes under the title of the *Ring* cycle. What would be your response after fifteen to sixteen continuous hours of Wagnerian music? For some people it is sheer bliss, the climax of a lifetime. For others it is total agony, beginning not more than a few minutes after the curtain rises.

In one sense this operatic experience illustrates the difference between heaven and hell. Contrary to the popular imagination that heaven and hell are not two distinct places separated by a vast abyss, it seems to me that heaven and hell occupy the same space. What is different is to be sought in the responses of different people to what they are experiencing. As with the opera, for some people it is sheer bliss, the climax of a lifetime. For others it is total agony, beginning not more than a few minutes after they arrive. The separation is caused by differences in the minds and hearts of those present.

If we, ordinary people, were somehow compelled to attend the whole opera, it would probably be sensible to do some preparation, to acquaint ourselves with the narrative and its background, and to try to drum up a bit of understanding and appreciation of the type of music it embodies. This way we could make the most out of what otherwise might be an unpleasantly challenging situation.

It is a little like this in the afterlife. Heaven is way out of our league, and we will be totally uncomfortable there unless we try to adapt ourselves now, so that later we can appreciate and enjoy its specific character. This process is what the New Testament terms *metánoia*, a radical reeducation of mind and heart so that we conform to what is anticipated in citizens of that place. Its details are concisely mapped out for us in the Beatitudes. Adopt these attitudes, and the afterlife will be total bliss. Continue the way we are, and our afterlife will be marked by awkwardness and alienation. We will not belong. It will be like arriving at a Holocaust commemoration in an SS uniform, or going naked to a papal audience. But worse. Those who choose not to prepare a wedding garment will not only find themselves excluded from the feast but will have no one to blame but themselves. (August 23, 1996.)

Lord Jesus Christ, you have called us to the feast of eternal life, and you yourself are the way by which we can arrive. Help us to follow more closely in your footsteps so that even now we may begin to experience something of the joy that follows opening ourselves to the presence of God. For you are our Lord forever and ever. Amen.

June 7 ✠ **Heteronomy**

Heteronomy is a word associated with the eighteenth-century philosopher Immanuel Kant. It refers to an action or state that is not fully autonomous, but is under the control of another. As the idea, if not the term itself, slowly percolated down to popular culture, it has generated the belief that there is something fundamentally wrong about being dependent on others. Thus we believe ourselves entitled to autonomy in every significant aspect of our life.

This expectation has led to our culture giving a priority to choice in every department of life. We want to be able to choose between different brands of toothpaste, notwithstanding the fact that they are all manufactured by the same company and only the packaging is different. Sometimes people adopt a particular fashion in order to trumpet their uniqueness, apparently not noticing that thousands are wearing the same mass-produced brands. It feels good to think that we are being distinctive, even though the difference is delusional.

This trend blinds us to the necessity and advantage of cultivating interdependence. "No man is an island." We are born, nurtured, and sustained in our journey through life by the generosity of others, and our life will become most meaningful to the extent that we accept our responsibility to give unstintingly of ourselves to those around us. Independence and individualism are all very well in short bursts, but when they isolate us from others they lead to much unhappiness.

In the book of Genesis humanity is given its special status when God breathes on us. The breath by which we live is not ours but God's. For as long as it remains we are alive. If it departs, we give up the ghost; we die. We may like to believe that we are the owners of our life, but it is not so; we are mere renters. That is why we speak of a "lease of life." The ultimate lord of our life is God; our lives are most fully human when we acknowledge this truth and live in accordance with it. To worship God and to follow God's law are not optional extras; they are constituent imperatives of human nature.

We depend on God. We depend on others. We were made for interdependence. Our happiness depends on living in harmony with these fundamental realities. (October 5, 2008.)

Loving Father, in you we live and move and have our being. Teach us to find delight in living your law of love, so that we may experience the full freedom that belongs to the children of God. We ask this in the name of Jesus our Lord. Amen.

June 8 ✠ Highway

When Jesus referred to himself as "the way," we must take the expression to mean that he was talking about a highway and not simply a boulevard. A boulevard may be very pleasant for sauntering, but it is necessarily aimless. A highway has the objective of leading as directly as possible from one place to another. It is meant for purposeful traveling. It is an invitation to begin a journey.

Jesus leads us deep into the mystery of the Godhead, on condition that we follow him. This is not as easy as it may sound. Following Jesus means negotiating all the counterintuitive twists and turns that beset the would-be traveler from the world of space and time moving into the swirls of eternity. We have the sense that we are constantly out of our league, forced to engage in matters that are beyond our competence. But we would be in even more trouble if the road on which we are traveling did not exist.

The journey we are making is accomplished not by the steps of our feet, but by a changing of the dispositions of our heart. We have gradually to become new persons: more softhearted, obliging, nonjudgmental, nonassertive, nonreactive. Ready to live as Jesus lived when he was among us. This is a task that is accomplished not by introspection or naked willpower, but by doing the kind of things that Jesus did and commanded. If not clothing the naked and visiting the imprisoned, at least being thoughtful to those around us, responding to their needs and listening to their stories. It is not beyond possibility, though it takes an effort.

This highway leads to eternal life. If we follow it to the end, we will be drawn into the infinite attractiveness of God. Already in this life we will catch glimpses of what awaits us, glimpses that motivate us to keep walking, despite the doubts and difficulties that assail our progress.

There is something else. Christ the highway leads to the discovery of God. This same road also leads us to a richer knowledge of ourselves. In Christ we see the potential of our nature, what we ourselves will become by grace. Created in Christ's image and likeness, we will discover our true and unique identity only by following him, adhering to his teaching, and allowing ourselves to be drawn into ever-deeper union with him and through him with God the Father. (April 3, 2013.)

Lord Jesus Christ, you are the way that leads to the fullness of truth and a more abundant life. Give us the courage to follow this way despite its challenges and help us to guide and encourage those who make the journey with us. For you are our Lord for ever and ever. Amen.

June 9 ✝ *Hildegard*

As a nine-year-old boy, my father was pulled out of his warm bed and dragged outside and told to look up and remember what he was seeing. It was Halley's comet. He always hoped to reacquaint himself with this phenomenon but, sadly, died before it reappeared.

Halley's comet is the image that comes to mind when I hear of Hildegard of Bingen, a Benedictine nun born at the end of the eleventh century and following a spectacular trajectory through the eighty or so years of her life. She was a woman with an extraordinary combination of gifts. She excelled not only in philosophical and theological speculation and in mysticism, but also in music, art, writing, and practical administration. Notwithstanding these outstanding attributes, she seems also to have been a humble and prudent person, prepared to recognize and respect the gifts of others and able to use her own talents for the benefit of all.

I think that we can look upon Hildegard as a good example of the flowering of human qualities that follows a full acceptance of Christ's invitation to a life of discipleship. We may think of this as the hundredfold that we are given, even in this life. Notwithstanding the persecutions that seem to beset the path of the fervent, there is a net advantage.

Too often, perhaps, we concentrate on detachment and deprivation as the marks of a dedicated disciple. Especially in the West, our idea of full commitment is stamped with the sign of the cross. This is undoubtedly part of the package, but only part. The parables of Jesus leave us in no doubt that we are intended to make use of the talents we have received and not leave them hidden underground, unrecognized and fruitless.

God's will is that we become all that was intended for us at the moment of our creation. To fail to reach the full flowering of our gifts is the ultimate tragedy, not only for ourselves but also for the world. Each of us is sent with a mission to fulfill; it may not be as spectacular as Hildegard's, but it is important. We are meant to provide a unique piece in the jigsaw puzzle of universal history; if that piece is missing, the whole is incomplete.

When Hildegard was professed as a Benedictine nun, it was prayed that God would bring to perfection the good work begun in her. That prayer seems largely to have been fulfilled. The same prayer could be offered for each of us. May the gifts we have been given come to full flowering and fruiting, so that in all things God may be glorified. (September 17, 2010.)

> *Creator God, you have called us all to proclaim your glory through the brilliance of our lives and through our commitment to goodness and truth. Help us to follow—at least from afar—the example of Saint Hildegard and so play our small part in the realization of your plan. We make this prayer through Christ our Lord. Amen.*

June 10   ✠   *Holiness*

Particularly in the priestly tradition of the Old Testament, holiness is understood as being separated from ordinary usage. It is untouchability. The message to the Israelites while God was in conversation with Moses was "Keep your distance." Anything that set foot on the mountain was to be stoned to death. And you will remember the incident when the ark of the covenant was being carried back to Jerusalem and the oxen stumbled. Uzzah stretched out his hand to steady the ark and was immediately struck down by God. He had touched what was holy.

When the Son of God pitched his tent among us, holiness became accessible. Indeed, Jesus himself took the initiative in reaching out to those who were suffering and touching them. The presence of God was no longer predominantly fearsome. It became attractive. "If I be lifted up I will draw all people to myself." The message that Jesus brought was "Come to me." It was not a distancing. It was a call to universal neighborliness. Whoever is a true disciple of Christ is a neighbor to everyone.

Christ said of himself, "Whoever sees me, sees the Father." It should be possible for the Christian to say, "Whoever sees me, sees Christ." We are meant to be images of Christ, icons of Christ. We have been sent forth by him as he was sent forth by the Father. The impossible task that we have been given is to be windows into the spiritual world through which the radiance of God's acceptance and love shines forth.

Such a mission is, thankfully, less a task or a call than a gift from God. We are invited to unwrap the gift that has been given us when we received the faith and to unfetter its intrinsic radiance. Our role is to shine, to be radiant. To be witnesses to something that is greater than ourselves.

When Jesus prays for his disciples in the words, "Make them holy in the truth," it is a prayer that the Father hears. The work of holiness is being accomplished among us today, not through any merit of ours, but by the powerful work of grace. How does God bring to completion the plan of salvation? By gifting us with a holiness that we do not deserve. We have only to allow it to do its work, and we will be transformed and others will receive the benefit. (September 17, 2005.)

Lord Jesus Christ, you prayed that your disciples would be consecrated in the truth. Look upon your church today and bring to fulfillment this promise of holiness, so that through the actions of its members the world may come to believe that you are the source of all goodness and life. For you are our Lord for ever and ever. Amen.

June 11 ✝ *Honesty*

Forty years ago, on this day, I gave a sermon on the Feast of Saint Peter and Saint Paul. I asked the question then, "How would it be if Peter and Paul were members of our community and we had to deal with them on a daily basis?" I think that the question is worth asking again.

I suppose that our immediate response would be that it would be wonderful to have two such great saints in our midst to compensate for the low standards we perceive around us. They would lift the tone of the whole community and be a focus of love and appreciation for all. Perhaps.

One of the singularities of the New Testament presentation of these saints is that it does not pull its punches. Considering that these are the very foundations of the church, the accounts we have of their performance are breathtakingly honest. With regard to Peter this is especially so in the Gospel of Mark, notwithstanding the fact that Papias tells us that Mark was Peter's mouthpiece. It is as though the prince of the apostles had no qualms about letting us know his shortcomings. Paul is equally frank. "Let nobody think of me beyond what they can see or hear from me."

Peter seems to have had serious defects both of temperament and of character. He was more like a rolling stone than a solid bedrock on which the church could be built. I am not sure that I would have trusted him with the keys to the house, much less with the keys to the kingdom. My choice would have been James, the Lord's brother: solid, reliable, predictable. Jesus knew both of them, and he chose Peter.

As for Paul, conflict dogged his steps. Wherever he went there was trouble, as if he were one of those strong-minded persons who cannot abide people of less keen intellect and, as a result, cannot live without contention. Yet Paul was "a vessel of choice," not elected by anyone, but chosen by God.

If they lived here, I think that we would have given both of them a hard time. This is because we equate holiness and perfection. Perfection belongs to God alone, and all of us, including the saints, are woefully imperfect. Asking perfection of anyone is unfair.

What we need to recognize in Peter and Paul is their holiness. God chose them, and they responded. It was by God's grace that they were set apart, and it seems God was in no hurry to bring them to any perfection that could lead to self-congratulation. If we are honest, we may recognize our lives in theirs. (June 29, 2009.)

Infinite God, you alone are without limitation or blemish. Help us to bear with patience our own imperfections and those of the people around us. Give us the confidence to accept that your power exults in our weakness. We ask this through Christ our Lord. Amen.

June 12 ✠ **Honor**

I often wonder how the bystanders reacted to Jesus' interaction with lepers. It was a disease that inspired repugnance rather than pity. It was thought to be contagious, and so those suffering from it were excluded from the community, including their own families. It was thought to have been a punishment from God for something they had done, and so the social stigma was deepened.

What would it have been like to have lived as a leper in those days? I suppose, if we want to find out, we could ask those who suffered from AIDS in its early manifestations. They were forced to live isolated from daily contact, without respect, without honor.

Most Western cultures have lost an appreciation of the notion of honor. We often attribute the title "honorable" to persons by virtue of their office, whether they be honorable in fact or not. Yet Saint Benedict in his Rule makes the point that we should give honor to every person. The stranger who turns up at the front gate is to be received with honor, with the greatest honor being shown to the poor. The monks are told to live in a state of mutual respect, giving a higher priority to wishes of others than to their own preferences.

When I honor other persons, I am giving them permission to be what they are, and I am assuring them that there is no need to playact or to present a respectable façade. In some sub-Saharan cultures the morning greeting is "I see you." It acknowledges the unique otherness of the person and celebrates it. It is the diametric opposite of what is expected of job applicants, trying to make themselves into exactly the person they imagine the potential employer wants to see.

Honor is more than respect. Respect recognizes a person's office, what they have, or what they have done. Honor is about what a person is. I honor others by being open to them and offering them hospitality in my life. Pure honor is nearly always gratuitous; we do not offer it in the hope of receiving anything in return. It is drawn forth from us spontaneously by the recognition of the high value of the person. Honor motivates us to give space to the other person, moving back to allow them to expand. It gives them the precious gift of our time, making ourselves as accessible to them as we would the pope if he dropped in to see us. Above all, it is listening to them, paying attention, and responding. Honor is the Golden Rule on steroids. (January 8, 2010.)

Creator God, you have made every human being in your image and likeness, and you love each of us with a particular affection. Help us to see, respect, and honor the uniqueness of each person we meet, treating them as we ourselves would wish to be treated. We ask this in the name of Jesus our Lord. Amen.

June 13   ✠   *Hot and Cold*

It seems that there are two extremes of sinfulness, one hot and the other cold. Hot sinners are the ones about whom we learn through the mass media; cold sinners sin in secret. One day in a train I noticed an elderly and goggle-eyed gentleman reading a tabloid newspaper blaringly headlined "Youth Orgy on Beach." I wondered to myself who were the greater sinners, the kids enjoying themselves or the gratifyingly scandalized readers of the newspaper. Or the observer passing judgment on both. There is less moral distance between the riotous and the self-righteous than is commonly believed.

In the parable of the Prodigal Son, Jesus places before us the examples of a hot sinner, in the person of the younger son, and a cold sinner, in the stay-at-home elder brother. One point that the parable makes is that the father's love embraces both. We probably feel more sympathy for the wild and adventurous brother rather than the one who resentfully bound himself to duty, but each in his own way was defective in responding to his father's affection. Yet there is no diminution of that love for either of them. Both are loved unconditionally.

Look how tender the father is toward the elder brother. He comes away from the party and goes out to him, listens to his complaints, and then reasserts his love—"You are always by my side and all I have is yours"—without in any way reversing his welcome to the sinner.

The Good News is this. God loves hot sinners. The Good News is also this. God loves cold sinners—even Pharisees. We need to understand that whatever the mode in which we express our resistance to God's love, God does not cease to hold us close. Whether our sins are hot or cold or tepid, God's love for us endures, constantly drawing us back and calling us in, to sit at the high table at the banquet of eternal life. (March 14, 2010.)

> *Loving Father, may we never doubt the inclusiveness of your love or the wideness of your mercy. May we learn from receiving such love how we are to welcome, accept, and include all our brothers and sisters, excluding none from our compassion and forgiveness. We ask this through Christ our Lord. Amen.*

June 14 ✠ *Humility*

In Patrick White's novel *Voss*, the ornithologist Palfreyman opines, "I am glad that my knowledge of astronomy is very poor. . . . To understand the stars would spoil their appearance." Underlying this statement is an appreciation of the fact that sometimes we can know too much. An excess of knowledge can cause feeling to lose some of its intensity. This sometimes happens when people experience a conversion: with all the best intentions, they try to build on the experience by studying theology. Alas! More often than not their studies dry up their devotion, and their enthusiasm wanes.

One of the lessons of wisdom is to know when to stop searching and to appreciate the value of what we already have. Wisdom teaches us to recognize when we are confronted with a reality that is larger than ourselves, that we can never master. All we can do is begin a slow apprenticeship through which we learn how cramped is our knowledge and how vast is the truth that we have yet to discover.

Those who have truly encountered God are filled with a sense of wonder at the mystery and, simultaneously, confounded by a sense of their own insignificance. Think of Moses before the burning bush, Isaiah swept into the presence of the all-glorious God, Jeremiah entrusted with a mission beyond his choosing. Think of Simon Peter crying out, "Depart from me for I am a sinful man." Or the centurion: "Lord I am not worthy." Truly to have encountered the divine holiness makes us aware of our limitations and the liabilities we carry.

This sense of littleness is what opens us up to be filled with the gifts of God, who looks with favor on the lowliness of his servants. God has turned his back on those who are wise and learned in their own sight and revealed the mystery to the little people: those who are not much in the sight of the world but who approach what is holy with awe and reverence.

Humility is not primarily a social virtue, the opposite of arrogance. It is the necessary consequence that follows an encounter with the loving holiness of God. After that it doesn't matter much what status others assign to us. (June 4, 1989.)

Lord Jesus Christ, meek and humble of heart, teach us to recognize that we have nothing that we have not received. Teach us true gratitude, which encourages us to use your gifts in the service of others to the praise of your glory. For you are our Lord for ever and ever. Amen.

June 15 ✝ *Hundredfold*

Jesus' promise that his followers will receive a hundredfold for all they have given up probably needs to be submitted to a reality check. Does it really work out that way? Especially as Mark's version has the addendum "not without persecutions"—perhaps meant to be interpreted as "despite persecutions." Do those who have left everything to follow in the footsteps of Christ really receive much more than they have given up?

Medieval monastic writers often referred to the monastery as a "cloistral paradise." At first glance, this perspective seems to be the result of wearing rose-tinted glasses. Sometimes, at least, the day-to-day life of the monastery is more akin to the purifying effects of purgatory than to the serene bliss of heaven. A monastery is a place of labor and self-denial rather than of eternal rest.

Perhaps the idea that the monastery is heaven on earth is meant to be taken in a developmental context. The purpose of the monastery is to *become* heaven on earth. In a sense, this is true of every authentic Christian life. By laboring to become more Christlike, we begin a gradual process by which our attitudes are transformed. We begin to see things in a different light. It is not a question of changing our immediate environment to eliminate all potential sources of friction, but of changing ourselves, so that progressively there is less that can disturb our equanimity. We are at peace because we have chosen not to be upset. This usually involves the commitment to a triple renunciation: to be nonjudgmental, nonassertive, and nonreactive.

Even when we have found a way of living with others that is reasonably harmonious, we have another battle to fight; we have to find peace within ourselves. As we progress through the spiritual life, growing toward perfection is largely a matter of growing in genuine self-knowledge. Such growth generally involves a reevaluation of our behavior in the past. We begin to experience a great dissatisfaction with the choices that we once made, the things that we once did, the motivations that once inspired us, and the willful omissions that limited the good we achieved. As we enter the final quadrant of our life, such thoughts inject a certain bitterness into our hearts. We feel no better than hypocrites and may begin to doubt whether we deserve to receive mercy from God. This is perhaps the last obstacle we have to hurdle. But, by grace, we can surmount it. If we are willing to let go of any claim to personal merit and to place all our hope in the mercy of God, then, one day, we may very well open our eyes and discover that, indeed, we are living in heaven on earth. (July 11, 2009.)

> *Lord Jesus Christ, you promised that those who followed you will receive a hundredfold even in this life. Give us freedom of heart so that we may discover the treasure you have hidden in even the most ordinary moments of the day. May we rejoice in your presence, even when everything seems dark. For you are our Lord for ever and ever. Amen.*

June 16 ✠ *Immaculate*

Saint Augustine summarized his theology of grace in a concise axiom to which he often referred: Everything that Christ was by nature we can become by grace. This remarkable affirmation reveals his appreciation that the spiritual life is not so much a task of being "good." It is, rather, a gift of becoming divine, divinization. We are called to become "sharers in the divine nature" according to a phrase in the Second Epistle of Peter that is repeated at the offertory of every Mass. Of Christ's fullness we have all received: grace for grace. We are constantly being transformed from glory to glory by the radiance of the risen Christ.

One way of understanding the Catholic doctrine about the mother of Jesus is to see in her the full realization of God's plan for us all. By grace she became everything that her Son was by nature—exactly as we are called to become. If we may extend Augustine's saying, everything Mary was by grace we also may become by grace. As Saint Paul reminds us, "It is not a matter of the one who runs or the one who works but of God showing mercy."

Mary is considered the preeminent recipient of grace, the model of the church in the order of faith, hope, and charity: "all glorious, without stain or wrinkle or anything like that, but holy and immaculate." This seems far above our league, yet we can say, "All that Mary was by grace we also may become by grace." As members of the body of the church, we are called to participate in the holiness of our Head. As Mary was. She, therefore, is for us a "model of holiness," as the preface for her feast proclaims. She was immaculate by grace; we also may become immaculate by the power of that same grace.

But we, poor banished children of Eve, are far from blameless. Our consciences stand in testimony that often we have sinned and fallen short of the glory of God. Is divine grace sufficient to neutralize human malice? Yes. God exists outside space and time and sees all temporal reality as present in a single eternal moment. Nothing is beyond the loving and reparative power of God. Even logical impossibilities. That is why the church addresses God as "restorer and lover of innocence." All we have lost is restored to us so that we too may become immaculate. In heaven, we will all be garbed in brilliant white robes, such as no earthly fuller could produce. God will, once again, look upon his creation and find it very good. Because nothing is impossible for God. (December 8, 2017.)

Creator God, you have made us in your image to share in the fullness of your Son. Open our hearts to receive the grace you wish to communicate to us, so that we may be daily transformed into your likeness, and all our sins forgotten. We make this prayer in the name of Jesus our Lord. Amen.

June 17   ✠   *Imperfection*

Many of Jesus' contemporaries would have liked him to present himself in a more heroic mode. His ordinariness was an affront to their expectations of a triumphant messiah. They were looking for a glorious epiphany, and what they got was something more humdrum and down-to-earth.

People of my generation grew up with a triumphal image of the church: a noble (though misunderstood) history, marked by an unfailing defense of eternal truth, peopled by heroic witnesses of impeccable holiness, and governed by an unbroken line of wise and saintly pontiffs. It has been a bit of a struggle for us to accept the reality that such assumptions are false, that the church has always been imperfect (to say the least). Vatican II stated that the church is on the way to holiness, not that it has already arrived. The fact that we are all still traveling means that there is plenty of scope for disedification and scandal.

The Gospel of Mark leaves us in no doubt about the failings of Jesus' first disciples so that we are not surprised that they ran away when they were needed most. Add to this the fact that the Acts of the Apostles lifts the veil on some of the bickering that went on in the early church. What we know of the next two thousand years is that there is ample evidence of weakness and blindness and malice at all levels. Our times are no different.

The church is composed of sinners—people who struggle with the same uncreative tendencies as ourselves. Those whom we regard as holy have not exchanged this flawed humanity for an effortless perfection, but have drawn from their personal contact with Jesus the willingness sometimes to put themselves out in order to do a little good. The fact that we are less than we would desire is not a reason for feeling discouraged or for turning aside. It simply means that we need to rely more fiercely on the grace of God and put ourselves more regularly in the space to receive it. And, then, to act upon it. (June 29, 2008.)

Lord Jesus Christ, you alone are holy. Help us to return often to you so that we may be encouraged by your friendship, guided by your wisdom, and strengthened by your ready help. For you are our Lord, for ever and ever. Amen.

June 18 ✠ **Improvisation**

I wonder if we are losing the art of improvisation, with the result that random acts of goodness seem to need to be corralled, so that jointly they add up to something significant. I remember hearing an expert speaking about parish missions. He went through the necessary components: media saturation, division of labor, networking, strategy, tactics, follow through. . . . My head was beginning to spin. Are we putting too much trust in organization, and is there something sneaky about it? Who pays for it? Are people being tricked into doing more than they would otherwise have wanted? After the Bali bombing a torrent of donations poured into the Red Cross. Only a trickle reached the victims—the agency reckoned maybe 10 percent—and the rest was spent on administration, bank charges, wages, postage, and so forth. The disaster was financing the Red Cross rather than vice versa.

We tend to think that big is beautiful and the most effective way to get things done is to capitalize on economies of scale to create a large organization. The spin-off from this is that we tend to underestimate the disproportionate impact that simple acts of kindness often have.

When Jesus gave instructions about evangelization to his immediate followers, he insisted that you don't need a caravan of flunkies to proclaim the Good News. Just go as you are, do what you can, speak from the heart. And don't expect 100 percent success, at least not immediately. They were to be the sowers of the seed. Others would come later to reap the harvest.

The principal instrument of evangelization is a believing heart made visible on a face marked with joy and love. You don't have to be a card-carrying member of the Union of Apostles. Remember the incident in the gospel about the exorcist who did not belong. All that is needed is that you have heard the Good News, have accepted it, and feel the urge to communicate glad tidings to those willing to listen—and to some who aren't.

Inevitably this is not part of a master plan for the salvation of the world. It is spreading the Word in a manner that seems somewhat random and improvised. It seems to be taking the initiative away from the professionals and entrusting it to God's faithful people, transmitting the faith by their everyday interactions. And that may be a good thing. "See how they love one another," they say. "Religion is caught, not taught." (July 13, 2003.)

> *Lord Jesus Christ, you send us forth to a world filled with lights contrary to the Gospel to allow the radiance of faith to reach to the ends of the earth. Give us a spirit of boldness to speak of what we know and a love that will make us willing to share what we have received. For you are our Lord for ever and ever. Amen.*

June 19 ✝ *Incarnation*

Human life begins as a single cell, dependent on its immediate environment. The miracle of life is that it remains itself, even as it develops. The single cell multiplies and diversifies, forming a more complex organism, until it becomes independent. And so it comes to birth. But growth continues. The care and nurturance hitherto provided internally in the mother's womb needs to be continued externally in the bosom of the family—ideally by those biologically similar to the newborn. A helpless infant becomes the center of a complex of nurturing activities lasting maybe half a lifetime. This involves more than food and shelter. Just as our body grows by absorbing matter from its environment, so we continue to develop by the emotional, mental, and spiritual formation we receive from those around us.

It is not so difficult to grasp that the Word of God expressed himself in human form by a physical body. We sometimes forget that this taking flesh meant that the Word of God was also expressed in a social body—inextricably located not only in space and time but also in a family, a race, a nation. By the incarnation the Word became human and, in so doing, put himself at risk, entrusting himself to a particular family not only for the necessities of life but for the formation appropriate for a man of his time.

We may like to think that the family of Nazareth was exceptional, and it probably was. Yet, if we consider the genealogies given us in the gospels, we can see more than one scoundrel in the background, and none whose virtue was not tarnished by some failing. Perhaps we demean Jesus' family by insisting too much on their perfection—as it happens, in stark contrast to what is conveyed to us in the gospels. Part of being human is living with perceived imperfection, our own and that of others. Part of growing up is learning to deal with imperfection or somehow bypassing it and not being laid low by it.

Jesus was like us in all things except sin. The holy family of Nazareth was probably closer to us than we are inclined to think. The source of holiness was not a merely human achievement, but God within, acting to bring to perfection the good work begun in conception and meant to continue throughout life. (December 27, 2009.)

> *Lord God, you created us with a view to our sharing in your divine life. Help us to embrace the example which your Son has given us so that we may come to share ever more intensely in the divine nature of him who came to share our human nature. And we make this prayer in the name of Jesus our Lord. Amen.*

June 20 ✝ *Inclusiveness*

One of the lessons that Jesus was constantly teaching his disciples was that no one was unimportant. This is the message behind his welcoming of small children and his harsh condemnation of any who would scandalize these "little ones." In the kingdom of God no one is unimportant. It is the same message given in the parables. The loss of one coin out of ten is a call to turn the house upside down looking for it. The loss of one sheep out of a hundred demands that the many are abandoned in the search for the one that strayed.

The feast of the kingdom demands that all be present. This is sometimes a difficult truth to accept. We acknowledge that God wills all to be saved and to come to the knowledge of the truth, but, inwardly, we believe and we hope that some will be excluded. Yet, for God, it is not good enough that 99 percent are saved; a 1 percent loss is unacceptable. The parable of the Good Shepherd demonstrates this.

It is important that we do not identify being saved with being "one of us." There is a nominally Christian sect that has adopted the name "Exclusive Brethren" as an indication that their identity is derived not from the membership but from those who are outside. We may be faintly amused at such presumption, but we are probably a little bit guilty of the same fault. If we say, "You have to be one of us if you are to enjoy God's favor," our way of thinking deserves the rebuke addressed to Peter: it is human, not divine.

It is good for us to pray for the coming of the kingdom, as we do in the Lord's Prayer. It is good for us to be proactive in drawing others to that kingdom. This does not mean converting others to be more like us. First of all, it means accepting the mystery of God's radical inclusiveness by which all are brought into a unity in Christ. This is a vast cosmic drama, but we participate in it by acting locally, by breaking down local barriers that exclude. Ninety-nine percent inclusion is not enough. Our aim is nothing less than full inclusion, even if that means embracing some whom we would have thought belonged outside. (August 12, 2014.)

> *Loving Father, your will is that all are to be saved and come to the knowledge of the truth. Help us to be less discriminating in the welcome we give and the love we extend. Help us to work for the unity for which Christ prayed. We ask this in the name of Jesus the Lord. Amen.*

June 21   ✣   *Incredible*

In Lewis Carroll's *Through the Looking-Glass*, the White Queen famously declared, "Why, sometimes I've believed as many as six impossible things before breakfast." Maybe the idea of impossibility has slipped from our sight. In our world of rapid scientific and technological advances, it is easy to assume that everything is eventually knowable and nothing impossible. It seems as if it is only a matter of time before we can deal with the many things that puzzle us today. We have lost the sense that there are realities which are beyond our imagination.

The miracles of the Gospel are examples of what many people reject on the basis that they are impossible: walking on water, multiplying loaves and fishes, curing incurable diseases, raising the dead. Even otherwise stalwart believers may try to find "natural" explanations for the events described so that we are not precipitated into the sphere of the supernatural. The greatest miracle of all was the resurrection. That Christ rose from the dead and was seen by many witnesses is something that defies scientific analysis. It is unthinkable. This is why, some years ago, an Anglican bishop was heard to declare that the bones of Jesus were still somewhere in Palestine.[1] Belief in the resurrection is the greatest challenge and measure of our faith. We remember what Saint Paul wrote: "If Christ be not risen our faith is in vain."

More troubling to many than Christ's resurrection is the prospect of our own future rising from the dead, so that we may take our place in the company of the saints for all eternity. We are often embarrassed by talk of heaven; even at funerals many prefer to focus on the life now finished than on the fact that death signals our entry into eternal life. We have removed heaven from our notion of religion and reduced it to a matter of mere morality.

Christian faith is more than being good. It is confidence in a loving Creator who has destined us to share the more abundant life of heaven. Not a matter of harps and nighties, but a veritable banquet, where all our yearnings are satisfied and our tears dried. A region where harmony and intimacy reign. Where all the moments of our life are one and death is no more. Eye has not seen nor ear

---

1. Soon afterward, his cathedral was struck by lightning.

heard nor can the human heart conceive what God has prepared for those who love him. We cannot fully comprehend what it means, but, by faith, we accept its reality. (August 11, 2002.)

Loving Father, you have created us to share your life for all eternity. Keep alive in us the hope of this more abundant life, especially in difficult times when faith seems to falter. We ask this through Christ our Lord. Amen.

June 22   ✠   *Indefectibility*

Following yesterday's papal election, it is natural that our thoughts should turn to the universal church and the role of its chief pastor. Since the nineteenth century the role of the Bishop of Rome immediately conjures up the notion of infallibility, not necessarily taking into account the restrictions that hedge it about nor avoiding the misunderstandings perpetuated by both its advocates and its antagonists.

I would like to change the focus somewhat and concentrate on a neglected quality that belongs to the universal church: indefectibility. This teaches us that at least a remnant of God's faithful people will persevere in authentic faith until Christ returns, and that whatever is truly essential to the church will remain intact. Obviously, there will be heated discussion about what is truly essential. For the moment, I would like to let that question pass.

Let me offer an unconventional image of ecclesial indefectibility. I see it as being like an old drunk returning home from the pub after a night's boozing. Sometimes he sings. Sometimes he weeps. Occasionally he becomes aggressive toward bystanders. As he walks he wobbles and wavers. Then he sits down in the gutter and rests. Afterward he stands up and remembers where he is going; he makes his uncertain way onward and finally arrives home. There you have a metaphorical rendering of the church's history. You can stop the film at any moment and focus on what is happening then and make a judgment, or you can watch the whole saga and say, "Whatever the ridiculous reverses of the journey, eventually he made it home."

If we attempt to sanitize the church's long history, in the manner of authoritarian governments everywhere, we risk generating unrealistic expectations about the present. The indefectibility of the church is testimony to the fidelity not of its members but of God. God never deserts his people. As individuals our record of fidelity is not great, but as a group we give witness to a certain homing instinct which pulls us back toward our correct course whenever we go too far astray. Like Saint Peter, our first leader, we are often unfaithful, but God remains steadfast and true. Foibles and failures abound in the church. What sets us apart is not our blameless behavior but our active memory of Jesus Christ and our hopeful vision of our way home, the road that leads to eternal life. (August 27, 1978.)

Lord Jesus Christ, shepherd and guardian of your faithful people, inspire in us a bold hope for the life of heaven and a deep longing to enter into eternal life. Protect us from the dangers we encounter, and keep alive in us the memory of where we are going. For you are our Lord for ever and ever. Amen.

June 23 ✠ *Infiltration*

During the 1940s the archbishop of Sydney proposed the creation of a Catholic university. He was blocked by Archbishop Mannix of Melbourne, who did not want to establish a parallel system but preferred to "infiltrate" the existing one. Using the notion of infiltration was typically daring. The term was usually applied to Communists finding a nest within the trade unions.

In a similar way, God's plan to bring humanity to its fullest potential was not to be accomplished by external marshaling but from within, by infiltration. As a race we are often like poor sheep, willing to be driven one way or another, not only by force but also by subtler but no less brutal means of persuasion. This was not the way God chose. When the Word became flesh, he did not allow himself to be numbered among the powerful of the land, but was content to take his place in the heart of the ordinary people in a town from which nothing good was expected. When, eventually, his special gifts were recognized, his "authority," the observers were surprised that such a quality could adhere to a man whose background seemed to indicate that he was nothing special.

The lack of temporal power—"my kingdom is not of this world"—meant that whatever influence Jesus exerted over others was not due to external force or overwhelming logic. It was because he caused an echo in their hearts. "Were our hearts not burning?" In some way, he empowered them to recognize the deepest strand of their own humanity and to respond to it. He taught them to acknowledge the interior attraction by which they were drawn to God.

Jesus saved us by his solidarity with us. He infiltrated our world and served as a leaven by which it could rise to God. He speaks to our freedom. We cannot be dragooned into eternal life; we must go willingly. And what motivates us to make that choice is the meeting with one who is like us in all things except sin.

What he was we are called also to become. Not to harangue people into heaven, but by our simple companionship to make available to them the gifts we have received. To infiltrate their hearts and then begin to make them aware of the Good News by which we live—sometimes even using words. (December 6, 2009.)

Lord Jesus Christ, you became one of us to be our means of entering into eternal life. Open our hearts to receive the gift you came to offer us and make us ever more willing to share that gift with others. For you are our Lord for ever and ever. Amen.

June 24 ✝ *Influence*

Last month I was privileged to be at a meeting of 237 Benedictine abbots and assorted hangers-on. My accommodation was in a nearby religious house. This meant a short walk to attend the sessions. As it happened, a Greek orthodox monk representing the patriarch of Constantinople had similar accommodation and we often walked up together. We had several interesting conversations, but it was a single gnomic sentence in one of them that remained in my memory: "The only way to have a good influence on others is through humility."

I immediately thought of so many promising politicians whose credibility has been eroded by perceived arrogance. Too much certainty, too little self-doubt. Too much self-interest, too little altruism. Too much adversarial conduct, too little working toward consensus. When a politician is thus perceived, nobody is going to believe anything they say.

At the funeral of a very bossy person, it is sometimes said— ironically, I believe—that they were very humble in the presence of God. Perhaps. Here we need a reminder that the vertical and horizontal aspects of our spirituality need to match. A person who is truly humble before God will be like Moses, "the meekest man on earth." An arrogant person who comes before God will not shed their self-glorification; they will be like the Pharisee in the temple whose prayer was simply a litany of self-congratulation.

Jesus emptied himself and became humble like a servant. This was not a self-glorifying title like the papal "servant of the servants of God," but a reality. He came not to be served but to be a servant, to the extent of giving his life for the redemption of others. The humility that Jesus modeled for us was not inaction— a summons to be shrinking violets. It was a call to action. Nobody wants servants who are merely decorative; their job is to work.

There are two complementary aspects of humility. The first involves the recognition of our own gifts in the context of the opportunities that confront us; this owning of our gifts leads to their employment for the benefit of others. The other aspect is being able to cope with the labor, the suffering, and the diminishment that often accompany our efforts to make the world a better place. Not to lose our nerve in the face of indifference, misunderstanding, envy, or persecution.

To persevere in the employment of the gifts God has given us, because they are gifts God has given us, does not inflate the ego, but keeps us grounded in a spirit of service that has as its focus something greater than ourselves. Such humility will certainly result in a wholesome influence on those around us. (October 21, 2012.)

Lord Jesus Christ, meek and humble of heart, teach us to learn from you the way of humility and truth. Keep us from arrogance and pride and give us the wisdom to delight in associating with the little ones who are most welcoming of your kingdom. For you are our Lord for ever and ever. Amen.

June 25   ✠   *Infrastructure*

We are probably all acquainted with a proverb sometimes attributed to Benjamin Franklin: "For want of a nail the shoe . . . the horse . . . the rider . . . the battle . . . the kingdom was lost." Military campaigns are won or lost less on individual feats of derring-do than on the boring and grinding work of logistics—getting the stuff you need to the right place at the right time. Most real wars end up being wars of attrition: one side trying to wear down the other. Whoever lasts the longest is victorious. This image may serve as an unwelcome reminder that we have to lay down foundations before we start to build anything. And that includes building a spiritual life. There are some basic things to which we have to attend before we can hope for much progress.

The text of Job 7:1 was often cited in early Christian tradition, recognizing that our life on earth is like a military campaign in which constant challenges to our security are to be expected. Indeed, some Latin versions translated the Hebrew word meaning "military campaign" as "temptation." Our whole life is lived in a permanent state of temptation—one in which we are constantly faced with the choice between the way that leads to a more abundant life and the way of death. Unless we intend dying young—and it is too late for most of us to hope for that—we can take for granted that our spiritual warfare will be more a matter of resisting an enduring sense of weariness and futility than of dramatic engagements with the enemy.

It is important that we try to put in place good habits that will keep us supplied with all that we need to continue the warfare. This means making time on a regular basis for prayer and *lectio divina*. Without such dedication any sense of discipleship, any commitment to mission, any participation in worthy group activities will be more prone to failure. We probably need more time in solitude to allow for spiritual recuperation and, perhaps, the realignment of priorities. If we have access to wise counsel, we will be protected against the stupid ideas that sometimes take root in our heads. Developing such good habits is not very exciting, but it is an important bulwark against our being assailed by temptations that, at the time, seem overwhelming—because we have not prepared ourselves to face them. (February 9, 2003.)

> *Lord God of Hosts, keep us on the path that leads to life. Strengthen us to recognize and reject all that would cause us to drift away, and keep alive in our heart the fire of hope. We ask this through Christ our Lord. Amen.*

June 26 ✠ **Innocence**

A beautiful liturgical prayer dating from the fourth century addresses God as the "restorer and lover of innocence." The order of words indicates that there is no other way of being innocent than by having innocence restored. Surely a wonderfully paradoxical statement. Innocence does not exist except by God's gift to the guilty. You may ask, Are not babies innocent? The answer that Saint Augustine gives is this: No. They are not innocent, but merely ignorant or impotent. If they are blameless it is only because they lack the capacity knowingly to make mischief. Innocence is not merely the absence of guilt but the presence of a quality that is exceeding beautiful, without stain or wrinkle.

This is surely the content of what Saint Paul calls "justification." The infinite goodness and holiness of God cannot be contained within the Godhead, but spreads itself abroad. It is contagious. To the extent that, through faith, we are in contact with God, we cannot help but catch some of the qualities that are typical of God. They rub off on us. As we walk with God we become imperceptibly more like God.

The restoration of which the prayer speaks is so radical that it constitutes a new creation. It is not a repair job that leaves structural defects that are out of sight but still weaken the whole. It a new creation; there are no scars or reminders of past failures. Everything sparkles. And there is joy in heaven because this is God's professional specialty: to make all things new.

God is outside space and time. What we perceive as occurring at different times and in different places is perceived by God as a single dense instant, in which all space and time is compressed. Creation and re-creation are simultaneous from the vantage point of eternity. As the liturgy often announces: Today is the day of creation; today is the day of redemption; today is the day when all things come to completion. Today God has restored us all, not to a lost innocence—since we never had it to lose—but to an innocence that is so bright that it obscures every impediment to its own radiance. (November 3, 2011.)

> *God, restorer and lover of innocence, may we come before you confident in your power to make right all that is wrong in our lives. Give us the faith to open ourselves to your healing mercy and the generosity to pass it on to others. We ask this in the name of Jesus our Lord. Amen.*

June 27 ✝ **Integrity**

Integrity is a much-prized quality. I find it interesting that there is no adjective corresponding to the noun. Integral means "belonging to the whole" and "integrated" seems more psychological than moral. When we talk about persons of integrity we are speaking of those who practice what they preach, whose shadow side is well and truly subdued, and whose promises can be trusted. The fact that there is no related adjective that we can quickly fasten on people seems to indicate that we do not have much occasion to use it. If the whole truth be known, there is difficulty finding ten just persons not only in the city of Sodom, but elsewhere. So, integrity remains an abstract phenomenon rather than an observable characteristic.

There are four special characteristics typical of the ideal of integrity.

- There is harmony and collaboration between the interior and exterior zones of a person's life. Thoughts, speech, and actions all adhere to the same high standards.
- The heart itself is undivided; through many years of self-discipline, internal fragmentation and conflict is ended.
- There is consistency in the practice of goodness from day to day and from year to year.
- There is an absence of actions and reactions that are split off from conscious priorities and are being controlled by sub-personal tendencies.

It is obvious that complete integrity (if the pleonasm may be excused) is rare, and even unlikely, this side of eternity.

What we need to do is accept that our humanity is a work in progress. This means that we have to recognize our lack of integrity, be dissatisfied with it, and desire to improve matters. If our faith is firm, this will lead us to prayer. Inner division will inevitably trigger temptation, and, statistically, temptation has a good chance of making us stumble. When we fall, we have the opportunity to learn the lesson of asking for forgiveness and then, in welcoming it, to learn something of the gratuity of love. Finally, after years, our persevering faith will encounter the healing power of Christ and we will begin, suddenly but slowly, to become whole. To become what God always intended us to be. Eventually. (October 23, 2000.)

Creating God, you have formed us in love to journey toward greater closeness with you. Cleanse the eyes of our soul so that we may see more clearly the way ahead. Give us the strength to continue when the traveling is rough. Fill us with hope so we desire ever more urgently to arrive at our destination. We make this prayer in the name of Jesus the Lord. Amen.

June 28 ✠ *Interiority*

I must confess that I am a bit of a snob when it comes to religion. Sometimes, when traveling in the United States, I have had the opportunity of watching some of the many religious channels that are available. My reaction to most of them is "Thank God, I am not religious." At least I am in good company. Jesus himself affronted the religious people of his day by his failure to fast, to observe the rules of ritual cleanliness, to keep himself aloof from sinners, and, above all, to observe the Sabbath scrupulously. He manifested a cavalier attitude to all the niceties by which his contemporary coreligionists trumpeted their piety.

Genuine religion, as Jesus pointed out to the Samaritan woman, is a reality that operates at the level of spirit and truth. It certainly involves external realities, but these are only approximations of what is deeper and more interior. In the sacraments, the visible sign is meaningful only because it points to an invisible gift of grace. Even the practice of virtue carries a certain ambiguity with it: does it spring from the heart, or is it a calculated scheme of the head?

Religion, at its best, is an inner imperative that proceeds from the deepest center of our humanity, being created as it is to God's image. God has placed this instinct or desire at the level of spirit, before ever we come to the point of making religious choices. As we read in the sixth chapter of Saint John's gospel, the Father is continually drawing us away from the familiar world into the invisible mystery of the divinity. This is not a movement we ourselves generate but a gift of God, common to every human being. Whether we can cope with the externals of religion or not, what is most important is that we respond positively to this drawing. We do this by descending to the depths of our own interiority. By listening to our conscience. The Desert Father Abba Pambo responded to a question about the way to salvation with these words: "Find your heart and you will be saved." The hullabaloo of religious practice may or may not immediately appeal to us, but first we have to descend to the level of the heart and follow what arises from there. (August 11, 1985.)

Loving Father, in many and varied ways you draw us to yourself. Help us to give our assent to this drawing so that by coming closer to you we may become a source of life and love to all around us. We ask this through Christ our Lord. Amen.

June 29 ✝ **Internet**

The kingdom of God is like the internet—a vast spider's web of interconnecting threads, crisscrossing everything that exists and binding all things together. Some of us would prefer the kingdom to be like a Nuremburg Rally, with everyone lined up and marching in step along a prescribed route. In that perspective the kingdom seems chaotic, but that is because God transcends the rigors of sequential logic; in it the impossible becomes doable, and cause and effect are no longer married.

The Fourth Gospel, in particular, celebrates linkage. Jesus speaks of his unity with the Father and, for good measure, throws in his relationship with the Holy Spirit, the Paraclete, the Spirit of Truth, the Advocate. Jesus also identifies with the disciples as the vine to its branches, as a shepherd to his sheep, as bread for the hungry, and the road to the traveler. He is light and life to the world, the truth or meaning of all that happens. Christ is the one who simultaneously descends and ascends, the one who comes into the world and the one who goes out from the world, the one who dies, yet is alive.

Inevitably we are confused if we try to line up all these images and metaphors and arrive at a synthesis. The problem is not only that the pieces don't seem to fit together; they are in constant motion. As soon as we think we have established some stable connection between two, both of them move.

The resolution of our puzzlement comes when we cease to impose logical categories on the presence of Christ in the cosmos and open ourselves to the poetry of God's creation. All that exists is in a state of movement, uncoordinated to the unskilled eye, but wonderfully symphonic in accordance with the plan of God. All created reality must come to a head in Christ—to use the term employed in the Epistle to the Ephesians and much loved by Saint Irenaeus. To switch to the terminology of Teilhard de Chardin: Christ is the Omega Point, the ultimate destiny of all creation. In him we will come together because we belong together. Our separateness is illusory. Our task here on earth is to discover and recover this native unity, and the only way this can happen is through union with its source. In Christ we are connected; apart from him we fall apart. (May 7, 2009.)

O God, Creator and Sustainer of the universe, you are the source and the energy of all that is. Help us to recognize your loving plan in the world around us, and strengthen us to conform our lives to the rhythm of its realization. We ask this in the name of Jesus, your Son, our Lord. Amen.

June 30　✠　*Invisible*

No one can observe the coming of God's kingdom. Although we are often warned that the Day of the Lord will come upon us like a thief in the night, this is not the reason why we do not see it coming. The hiddenness of the kingdom is not due to its creeping up on us stealthily, but because it has already arrived. The kingdom is present yet invisible: present and active, though remaining unseen. And it is unseen because we lack eyes capable of perceiving it.

Bats can hear more than we hear; eagles can see more than we see; dogs can scent more than we smell—yet we are ever so confident that there is nothing beyond what we can hear, see, or smell.

Even so, it is not so easy to convince people of the reality of the spiritual world that, in some way, permeates our tangible universe and yet remains unseen. When we proclaim, "The kingdom of God is among us," the response is, "Don't tell us, show us."

Even ardent religious practitioners struggle against this invisibility. The transcendence of the utterly other God is a difficult message to communicate. Perhaps we try to replace the unseen God with idols, or to channel the deep spiritual impulses of the heart into external rituals. Or we dumb down the mystery, reducing the teaching of Christ to systems of morality or metaphysics. Maybe we strive to create "useful" religion in which good works predominate over the more fundamental obligation to be entranced by the mystery of the all-holy God.

The apparent absence of God gives power to the persecutor's hand. "If he be the Son of God, let him come down from the cross." How many horrific acts are perpetrated on believers and unbelievers alike while God remains silent! Where is God when all this is happening?

Believers are called to be the interface between the unseen God and an unbelieving world. Even though their faith is far from perfect, from their contact with God they are empowered to reach out to those in need. To make visible the proactive compassion of a loving God, who is the source of an energy that allows them to do what otherwise would seem impossible. God becomes more visible by our love. (November 16, 2017.)

> *Unseen God, show yourself to us who seek your face so that we may point the way to those who are searching for an unknown God. Let your glory shine on earth. May your kingdom come. Let your face shine on us, and we shall be saved. We make this prayer in the name of Jesus our Lord. Amen.*

July 1   ✠   *Ite missa est*

Many Mass-goers (and some celebrants) would probably say that their favorite part of the Mass is the dismissal. They see this as a chance to get back to business as usual. As though coming out of a coma, they reach for their cell phones to see what has happened in their absence.

Not so. The dismissal should be like the alarm going off at a fire station. Suddenly all are flung into action. Those present at Mass are being told to go forth and change the world. The presupposition is that they themselves have experienced something and have been changed by the liturgy. They are being exhorted to communicate to others what they have received. Pope Leo the Great used more formal language: "Imitate what you celebrate."

The gospels remind us that being sent forth is an integral part of discipleship; mission is not reserved to specialists. This does not mean that we all have to obtain passports and head off to the ends of the earth; it is simply a matter of being a carrier of the Good News to all whom we meet within our own sphere of activity. Sometimes we need to be reminded that our faith is not passivity, but an incitement to action. There is a danger that we may see the practice of religion as a kind of pious consumerism; we aim to receive as much as we can and give as little.

We are sent forth as witnesses. This does not mean that we become soapbox orators, constantly haranguing others, usually about their morality. That is a fairly blunt instrument. A much subtler mode of witnessing is being willing to engage others in serious conversation. This does not mean monopolizing the microphone, as it were, but being willing to interact. This involves listening considerably more than talking, and not just sponge-listening, but actively receiving what others say. First we have to establish a mood of solidarity, and then evangelization will eventually find an opening. Often our actions will speak more loudly than our words, as was expressed in a catechetical axiom of the 1960s: "Religion is caught, not taught."

In our own simple, sympathetic way, we can be an influence for good in the people around us. As Jesus taught, we are to be the salt of the earth. Salt is something that is used only in small quantities, not to impose its own taste but to liberate the natural taste in the food to which it is added. A little is enough. Small acts by small people sometimes have larger-than-life results. (July 16, 2006.)

> *Lord Jesus Christ, you have sent us forth to proclaim the Good News to all people. Deepen our understanding of the message you have brought us, and give us the confidence and courage to communicate what we have received to those who sit in darkness and desolation. For you are our Lord for ever and ever. Amen.*

July 2   ✠   *Jonah*

What could the phrase *sign of Jonah* mean? In ordinary usage, *Jonah* is used of someone who brings bad luck. Those who are more familiar with the Bible might guess that since Jonah was a prophet who refused to participate in a mission of mercy and needed some dramatic persuasion, perhaps the sign of Jonah is an indication that however fierce our rebellion, God can find a way around it. That makes Jonah a sign of hope for all of us. From another angle, what was demonstrated in the case of Jonah was the irresistibility of divine mercy. If God decides to saves the Ninevites, intractability on the part of his messengers will not halt the process.

Yet there is another way of reading the metaphor. The prophet resists his mission because he knows that it is unlikely to generate success. He is overruled. Death intervenes, and he spends three days and three nights in a mobile underworld. Then he rises from his entombment and begins to preach. Miraculously the preaching is effective beyond all expectation, even beyond all possibility. The Ninevites undergo conversion from the greatest to the least, and the plan of God is fulfilled.

Jesus spent about three years traversing the length and breadth of Palestine, calling for repentance and conversion. Although he made a great impact by his signs and wonders, there was not a great wave of conversion. Things continued very much as they had before. There were a few who changed their ways and followed him, but even the privileged Twelve were still very deficient in faith and without understanding.

Jesus came unto his own, and his own received him not. So great was the hostility directed toward him that he was eventually condemned. Death intervenes, and he spends three days and three nights in the tomb. But then he rises and a new era begins. The Holy Spirit descends, and those who previously cowered timidly behind locked doors surged forth and began to preach with an effectiveness beyond all expectation.

The sign of Jonah is the sign of God's mercy working its wonders despite human weakness. (July 21, 2014.)

God of all nations, you call all peoples into your kingdom, and you invite us all to proclaim the Good News to the ends of the earth. Give us the boldness to trumpet Gospel values by our manner of living and by the love and kindness we show to all. We ask this in the name of Jesus the Lord. Amen.

July 3   ✠   *Joseph*

According to his contemporaries, Jesus was a nobody because his father was a nobody. A builder in a small village. In fact, the gospels seem to agree with this assessment because they have little historical data to impart on Joseph's life and death. Just the theological fables of the infancy narratives. Perhaps we should take comfort in this. Joseph's life was ordinary, obscure, and laborious—just like ours.

There is something more that is worth pondering. Psychologists tell us that those who grow up with a tyrannical or abusive father often find it almost impossible to apply this term to God. Or if they do accept the conventional usage, they paint their picture of God in colors that are far from flattering. Their image of the divinity as Father takes its form from their own childhood experience and not from the teaching of Jesus.

Without attempting to strain out the gnats of scholarly debate, it seems pretty certain that the application of the term *Father* to

God is an innovation of the New Testament, and that the usage devolves from Jesus himself. If you think about it, it is surely remarkable that the word *Father* is applied to God 184 times in the 4 gospels. I counted them! This makes the usage something very characteristic of the primitive church's proclamation of the Good News. We have become so accustomed to speaking of God as Father that some of the sparkle of its use has been dulled.

For Jesus to have come up with the term *Father* to describe his experience of the divinity means—if the psychologists are to be believed—that he must have had a very good relationship with his own presumed father. When Jesus tried to find words to describe what he had experienced of God, he drew from his everyday experience within the family. God was like . . . Joseph!

God does not present as a celebrity, existing far above our heads. There is, as Julian of Norwich noted, a certain "homeliness" about God. He is like Joseph, manifesting his deep, personal love for each one of us in the midst of lives that are ordinary, obscure, and laborious. It may be that we are nobodies, but that is the way that the Son of God also chose to live. (May 1, 2013.)

Lord Jesus Christ, you taught us to call upon God as Father of us all. Help us to live in this awareness, knowing that we are greatly loved by God and that we are called to extend this love to all our brothers and sisters. For you are our Lord for ever and ever. Amen.

July 4 ✠ *Joy*

Of all the attributes of God, the one that is often neglected by theologians and preachers is God's joy. So weighed down with so many inhibitors of joy are we, that we cannot begin to conceive the utter joyfulness of God. As a result, we are not much moved by the prospect of sharing in that state; eye has not seen nor ear heard nor has the human heart conceived what God has prepared for those who love him.

God is a boundless sea of happiness, a Trinity of blessedness, a communion of joy. This joy is not subject to diminishment by the action of others nor by any intrinsic limitation or weakness. God is the only one who can truthfully sing with Edith Piaf, *"Je ne regrette rien"*—there is nothing for me to regret.

God created us to share that joy, placing man and woman in a garden of delights. But we fell from joy, preferring an independent life of pain and tragedy, hiding from the source of our own ultimate happiness.

God would not accept our fallen state and constantly sang to us the songs of Zion, trying to wean our hearts from sadness and remind us of the blessed homeland to which we are called. Through prophets and sages, he strove to open our hearts to receive his messengers of love. The angel appeared to Mary and said, "Rejoice!" And then, in the last times, God sang the Song of his own joy, the Word who is the living expression among us of all God is.

And so the Word was made flesh and God's joy lived among us. Jesus, a man overflowing with attractiveness of divine joy. Not only the "man of sorrows" of whom some speak, but one who said, "May my joy be within you." He lived a life that we are called to imitate so that we might become sharers in the divine nature. So filled with joy was Jesus that the sadness of death could not overcome it. He rose, conqueror of death, breathing out on the world the Spirit of joy.

Joy is the most infallible sign of the presence of God. God is joy, and those who abide in joy abide in God and God in them. (January 4, 1981.)

Father most holy, show us your face and we shall be saved. Unveil to us the mystery of your love, and fill us with the gift of your Holy Spirit so that all that we do may be radiant with your joy. We ask this in the name of Jesus our Lord. Amen.

July 5   ✟   **Judgment**

I have often thought that the Final Judgment needs better public relations. When the topic of the Final Judgment is addressed, most of us think of it as bad news and start quaking in our boots. The one thing we would prefer to avoid beyond all others is to be brought before the judgment seat of God.

Wait a minute! Perhaps we have been listening too much to hellfire preachers trying to make us fearful with their bloodcurdling denunciations. Haven't they heard? "It is the will of God that all are to be saved and come to the knowledge of the truth." God's plan for the universe is not about to be thwarted by the weakness, blindness, and occasional malice of people like us. Is God's work of creation-redemption-glorification to be brought to nothing?

The Final Judgment is the conclusion and culmination of God's work of salvation. In it all things are brought to a head in Christ and God becomes all in all. This is not some petty tribunal that has an itemized list of every wrong move we have made, every misjudgment, every giving way to malice and unkindness. This is the supreme moment of God's exalting mercy over judgment. The triumph of God's steadfast love, finding us guilty and yet acquitting us—not only declaring us to be just, but rendering us worthy of such a declaration. And our bumbling efforts to be good will be celebrated.

Since we have all sinned and fallen short of God's glory, none of us goes before God blameless. In a sense, it doesn't matter. Playing around with a famous sentence in the New Testament, Saint Bernard declares: God's love covers the multitude of our sins. God is not like a nagging parent. Jesus has not sold out to the scribes and Pharisees. The Final Judgment is the triumph of God's unconditional and parental love over pathetic human sinfulness. What will happen to sinners who remain fixedly unrepentant? I don't know. God knows. (August 23, 2014.)

God of mercy and compassion, Creator, Redeemer, and Judge, teach us to look forward to that day of glory when

*you will bring all things to completion in Christ and call all
your sons and daughters to share the wedding feast of heaven.
We ask this in the name of Jesus our Lord. Amen.*

July 6   ✠   *Kairos*

Time is a great mystery. It surrounds everything we know. Our
present experience is buttressed by the memory of times past,
on the one side, and by an anticipation of the future, on the other.
Yet time is irrelevant to God, who perceives the whole of evolving reality in a single point.

Yet the term *kairos* as it is used in the New Testament indicates a privileged point in time in which God acts, a time of
special grace and opportunity. God's time, *kairos*, is not just a
tick of the clock. It is a moment of energy. This moment does
not observe events inertly; it is an active player in human history.
The moment in which God's self-projection intervenes in earthly
affairs changes the course of events. Nothing is ever the same
afterward. This is a time which we may not anticipate or attempt
to forestall, but for which we must wait in patience.

Waiting in patience means that we have to bear with imperfection—in ourselves and in others. We are all too ready to scrape
off the rust, forgetful that if we are too vigorous we will destroy
what we attempted to save. Perhaps the time for conversion is
not yet. We may not preempt the action of grace. Especially
regarding others. As Saint Augustine wrote: Don't despair of
those who are now what you used to be.

Such a stance demands a large measure of trust in the workings
of Providence. Proactively to wait for the call of grace and to
respond to it with energy and perseverance. There is a time to
wait and a time to act. A time to do nothing and a time to be
engaged. What matters is that we try to act in God's time and
not by human reckoning.

God's time is an open doorway to eternity. What is done in
God's time is inevitably easier, more powerful, more lasting, and

more life-giving. Living in God's time is an introduction to the Time beyond time, when our lives will be fully overlaid with the glory of the risen Christ and all will be well. (September 23, 1990.)

> *God, beyond all ages, Creator of our world and of our race, teach us to know your ways and to be alert to your calling. Free us from the burden of our sinful past and fill us with hope for that day when all will be revealed. We make this prayer through Christ our Lord. Amen.*

July 7 ✠ *Kindliness*

In the prayer for the Mass of the Seventh Sunday in Ordinary Time, now inexplicably suppressed, a very simple request is made of God: "Keep before us the wisdom and love you have revealed in your Son. Help us to be like him in word and deed." We pray for the gift of attention in our everyday activities so that we do them, as it were, under the eye of Christ, conscious of the way he lived and trying, in our own small way, to live according to the principles his life embodied.

Jesus showed us how to be perfect as our heavenly Father is perfect. This consists not in attempting to mimic God's inalienable works of power, but simply in being a force that leads to a more abundant life. We are called to imitate our Father who is kind to the ungrateful and the wicked, to be full of compassion, slow to anger, and rich in mercy.

Treating others well often involves ensuring that our conduct flows from what we are, from the choices we have made about the kind of life we lead and the kind of person we are. Often it means refusing to be triggered into an automatic reaction to what we perceive other persons are or to what they do. Just as God's actions are an overflow from the divine nature—good is self-diffusive—so we should try to shape our behavior so that it expresses who and what we are.

The English word *kind* means beneficent; it also indicates the source of that positive attitude to others: our shared nature. *Kind* is an old word for "nature." When we are kind, we are acting according to our nature; when we are unkind, we are acting contrary to what we were created to be. Relating positively to others is a concrete expression of the truth that we share the same human nature; we belong together. In a sense, we can never go wrong by treating others extravagantly well; it shows that we have learned something from the magnanimity of God. To the extent that we have experienced God's unconditional love for us, we will more readily become kind and loving to those around us. We will become more like what we were created to be. (February 23, 1992.)

Creator God, you have made us to live in harmony with those who share our nature. Help us to be attentive to the example of Jesus and to imitate his wisdom and love in our way of dealing with others. We ask this in the name of Jesus the Lord. Amen.

July 8   ✠   *Kingdom*

Persons who are seriously defective in one of the senses—those who are tone deaf, color blind, or anosmic—do not know what they are missing. They are aware of their disability only by hearsay. When they pay attention to the world around them, they believe that they are perceiving the whole reality. All of us do. Yet dogs have a keener sense of smell, which is why they are employed as sniffers. Bats have a much sharper sense of hearing, and eagles have an astonishingly powerful sense of sight. We perceive only a portion of reality, and we are not aware of what we don't perceive.

This means that we can never be certain that what we cannot sense lacks reality. "There are more things in heaven and on earth than this world dreams of." It follows that the burden of proof lies on those who proclaim the nonexistence of God. A vague agnosticism is, at least, more honest.

In response to Pilate's question, Jesus said, "My kingdom is not of this world." Not *of* this world, yet *in* this world, for "the kingdom of God is among you." Jesus spoke allusively. The kingdom is both here and not here. The two thieves crucified with Jesus saw things differently. One saw what was taking place before his eyes; the other perceived a deeper reality that was beyond visual perception.

What we know of the kingdom of God we know only in part, in parables and riddles. Sometimes the spiritual world breaks in on us. We have "intimations of immortality," but the conclusions we draw from these are neither evidence-based nor comprehensive. Perhaps our sense of God is more bound up with the intuitive right side of the brain than with the analytic left side.

Because we are insecure with the hidden nature of the kingdom, we sometimes seek to construct a visible substitute, what Malcolm Muggeridge called "The Kingdom of Heaven on Earth Incorporated." This is what Pope Francis terms "spiritual worldliness." Perhaps he forgot that the call sign of Vatican Radio is a triumphalist ditty called "*Christus vincit*": "Christ is the Conqueror, Christ is the King, Christ is the Emperor."

We need to keep in mind that the "kingdom" of which Christ is king is that described in the Beatitudes, or, as Saint Paul affirms, it is a realm of "righteousness, peace, and joy in the Holy Spirit." When we pray for the coming of the kingdom we are not craving earthly domination but, as the preface of the Feast says, we are praying for the rise of truth, life, holiness, grace, justice, love, and peace. I'll drink to that! (November 24, 2013.)

Lord Jesus Christ, you came to serve and not to be served, and you lived on earth a life that was ordinary, obscure, and laborious. Help us to learn that in your kingdom the first will be last and the least shall be first. For you are our Lord for ever and ever. Amen.

July 9 ✠ *Knowledge*

The Greek philosopher Plato made a distinction between *opinion* and *knowledge*. In these terms we could perhaps say that we live in an epoch in which opinion is far more influential than knowledge. Evidence is ignored; what matters more is how deeply you feel about a topic. As a result knowledge and the search for knowledge are being sidelined. And we are fast losing the capacity for sustained and systematic thought.

This is probably true in matters of faith and spirituality. We may recite the Nicene Creed every Sunday at Mass, but we probably don't have much of a clue about what it means or how it might be relevant to our everyday lives. It may well be that, in the past, too much emphasis was given to knowing the details of Catholic faith and tradition, but today the danger is that we know too little.

Jesus was moved with deep compassion when he observed that so many of the people who followed him were like silly sheep. He did not upbraid them but, as Saint Mark tells us, began to teach them. We do well to note the number of times that Jesus is said to have taught the crowd, using a variety of methods. Jesus was concerned not simply to impart an incomprehensible moral code; he wanted his followers to understand what it was all about. How often, in Mark's gospel, does Jesus rebuke his closest disciples precisely for their lack of understanding. In addition, the church has always taken seriously its teaching mission. Those faithful to their pastoral responsibility have been assiduous in explaining and expounding the full content of what we believe.

The organs of social communication often expose the Christian faith and the Catholic Church to ridicule. We may well find ourselves unable to defend what we believe simply because we lack the knowledge to do so. At this point we need to recognize the obligation to depart from the ranks of the silly sheep and start to try to arrive at an adult understanding of what we hold to be true.

We don't have to become experts in theology, but we should try to find out what the church really teaches. This is relatively easy to do. In the *Catechism of the Catholic Church* we have an authoritative exposition of Catholic belief and practice to which we can easily refer whenever we have a question. It is not a book for children, nor is it likely that we will read it through from beginning to end. But it is a reliable reference that should have a place in every home. (July 17, 1994.)

> *Lord Jesus Christ, you had pity on the crowds and set your-*
> *self the task of teaching them. Inspire us to keep deepening*
> *our knowledge of our faith so that we may stand firm against*
> *contrary suggestions and be in a position to help others find*
> *their way. For you are our Lord for ever and ever. Amen.*

July 10 ✠ *Lamb of God*

I had been merrily singing the *Agnus Dei* for decades before I really asked myself what the term meant. Then I was in Indonesia and they started singing the *Anak domba Allah*, and it suddenly struck me what a curious term it is. Why is Christ called the "Child Sheep of God?"

There are lots of lambs in the New Testament: the paschal lamb, the sacrificial lamb, Isaiah's lamb led to the slaughter, the triumphant lamb of the book of Revelation. None of these seems to fit in this context. Perhaps the Greek is a less likely translation of the Aramaic *talya*, which also can mean "a servant." That would make a bit more sense in the light of the Servant Songs of Isaiah.

What does this lamb do? Traditionally his function is translated as taking away the sins of the world. That is perfectly acceptable, both linguistically and theologically, but there is an alternative. Both in Greek and in Latin, and maybe in Aramaic, the verb used can also mean "to carry" or "to bear." This give us a different picture of Christ. Not as one who triumphantly eliminates sin and its effects, as it were, from outside, but as one who takes upon himself and within himself the whole burden of human sinfulness. "On him has been laid the iniquity of us all." He is one like us in all things except sin, and so he must endure all the consequences of human malice. He bears the weight of the world's sins.

Jesus was conscious of belonging to a sinful race, and he chose to walk a different path. And he calls us to follow. We may not close our eyes to the reality of sin, lest it sneak up on us and overcome us without our offering more than token resistance. To follow Christ is to struggle against sin's baleful effects in us, around us, and all over the world. It means that we prefer integrity of life over the ways of crookedness and deceit. We must hold ourselves aloof from systems of tyranny and dehumanization. We must make the effort to reduce suffering in whatever form it presents itself to us.

Like Jesus, we must be willing to bear the sin of the world; we must bear one another's burdens, in small matters as well as in global issues. We receive within ourselves some of sin's toxins, and, by the power Christ gives us, we neutralize the poison and simultaneously improve the lot of others and unknowingly cooperate in the work of our own salvation. (January 20, 2008.)

> *Lamb of God, who bears the sins of the world, help us to bear one another's burdens in the confidence that your grace will give us strength. Give us a joyful confidence in the active power of goodness that you have unleashed on the world, to bring everyone to salvation and to the knowledge of the truth. For you are our Lord for ever and ever. Amen.*

July 11   ✛   *Lassitude*

"Better to reign in hell than serve in heaven" is the leitmotif of Milton's Satan. It seems to me that this attitude embodies a grave untruth. It seems to suggest the possibility that infernal existence can be interesting, exciting, even heroic, evoking from hell's denizens the ultimate response of courage and endurance. Not so. Hell is not an alternative form of life, but it is the diametric opposite of all that life implies. It is a lethal lulling into unending lassitude.

Hell will be the sum total of all the numbing, debilitating, enervating, narrowing forces that even now limit our liveliness by cutting us off from benefits outside ourselves. Hell will condemn us forever to a lonely life of selfish and solitary dissatisfaction. The idea that hell will be a lively place is utterly wrong. The poets notwithstanding.

The purpose of reflecting on hell is not to gain information about what shape that damned future might take, but to generate an insight into how we might be able to create such a state for ourselves while still on earth. As Milton noted, "The mind is its own place, and in itself / Can make a Heav'n of Hell, a Hell of Heav'n." We have an obligation to ourselves to make our lives as little hellish as possible. This means that we habitually choose life over death, growth over stagnation, love over coolness, movement over sloth, rest over restlessness. Hell is the absence of free choice.

It is precisely from a drifter's life of lassitude that the Gospel summons us. We are to leave aside the feelinglessness and the fear that hold us back from interaction. We have to shake off the fog of forgetfulness that befuddles our minds and the practiced indifference that hardens our hearts. We are called, above all, to be alive: to feel, to think, to love, to act, to endure.

Whatever form the afterlife may take, we are faced every day with a choice between heaven and hell. The more we make an exit from a state of lassitude, the more we make our actions the result of conscious and rational choice, then the more we are becoming free citizens of heaven and not monsters of that other place. (August 21, 1977.)

Lord Jesus Christ, you are the way that leads to eternal life. Inspire in us a vivid hope to share in that blessed state and the openness to receive even now some foretaste of what awaits us in heaven. For you are our Lord for ever and ever. Amen.

July 12 ✠ Law of Life

I have often wondered to what extent the accounts of Jesus' opposition to the law that we find in the gospels were influenced by the teaching of Saint Paul. Paul lived and died and wrote his epistles before the gospels were composed, and I think that it is not unlikely that his approach to the law would have had some influence on the evangelists as they composed their narratives. Maybe Jesus' resistance to the sterner details of observance would have been less apparent to his contemporaries than appears in the texts as we have them.

In any case, the tradition associated with the book of Deuteronomy insists that the "keeping" of the law will issue in a long life, good health, well-being, peace, happiness. In other words, the purpose of the law is to safeguard and enhance life. Jesus' conflict seems to have been with those who divorced legal observances from human reality. For example, he refused to take seriously those who inflated nibbling on a few grains to the bringing in of the harvest. As Saint Paul noted, these were men who were "zealous but without intelligence." Their scrupulous literalism is stupid.

I remember an incident in 1951, when an ambulance driver lost his job for breaking the speed limit. The fact that he had saved the life of the little boy in the back by a timely arrival at the hospital was considered irrelevant. He had broken the rules. End of story. And don't we all know instances where the law gets in the way of life.

Life is not just a state that exists before death. Life is a state of growth; nongrowth is not much better than death. For the most part both civil law and canon law aim at preserving the status quo, and, as a result, they can often restrict or inhibit growth. The law of God is different. This law existed for the sake of life. Since Jesus came to offer us a more abundant life, there would have been no conflict unless distorted minds created it. (October 30, 2009.)

Lord Jesus Christ, you came to fulfill the law of Moses by making it a servant of a fuller righteousness. Grant to your church, and to those who lead it, the wisdom to use their authority to promote life in all its variety, so that your Body may not be lacking in any spiritual gift. For you are our Lord for ever and ever. Amen.

July 13   ⊹   *Lazarus*

In the parable of the Beggar and the Banqueteer, Jesus points to a polarity that exists among people: we can have too much or too little. The rich man dines sumptuously every day, while poor Lazarus goes hungry.

In the first place, it is against the dulling of conscience that this parable is warning us. We all know that a comfortable life often leads to a form of complacency that induces a miasma of forgetfulness. Not only forgetfulness of God but also of the big moral questions that confront us. At the same time, we have to admit that severe deprivation also can absorb our attention so that God is excluded. This is, no doubt, why the book of Proverbs prays, "Give me neither poverty nor riches, but just the food I need."

But it is the rich man who stands accused. He had lost the awareness that the choices we make today stand for all eternity. What happens today is not somehow a rehearsal; rather, it is the reality and, in a sense, it is irreversible. No doubt what happens today will be repeated tomorrow and then the day afterward. Incrementally it will become part of who we are. It is easy for the big little-sin to be transmuted into a little big-sin and thence into a big big-sin. We don't notice the slide or the change that it effects in us. Slowly our behavior shapes what we will become.

Only in hell, when it is too late, does the rich man see the error of his ways. Like the goats at the Last Judgment, he protests that he didn't realize that this was not a drill; it was the real thing. His request that his brothers be alerted to this danger is greeted coldly: "They have Moses and the prophets; let them pay attention to them."

The message of the parable is rather grim. We have sufficient resources to discern the ultimate significance of our actions. If we consistently choose to act in a way contrary both to our humanity and to the law of God, we cannot expect that all will be remedied at the snap of our fingers. We need not only a change of heart but also a change of behavior. And the sooner the better. (October 25, 2009.)

Lord God, you fill the starving with good things, but the rich you send empty away. Open our eyes to see the needs of those around us and open our hearts to share our resources with those who have less. For you are our Lord for ever and ever. Amen.

July 14 ✠ *Leadership*

I recently read in a newspaper that [British] Prime Minister David Cameron is said to be a lineal descendant of Moses. A lot of good that seems to be doing him! I am probably a lineal descendant of monkeys, but that doesn't mean that I like peanuts.

In any case, the figure of Moses, as presented in the Old Testament, is scarcely that of a typical model of leadership. Taking forty years to lead the people from Egypt to Palestine does not seem to indicate a well-thought-out plan. In addition, Moses was shy and reluctant to become involved; he preferred that his brother Aaron take the lead. He had a tendency to micromanage his responsibility until his father-in-law suggested a devolution of his authority. He frequently became discouraged and angry at the recalcitrance of his followers. At the waters of Meribah he failed to show his own faith in the Lord's continuing guidance.

What made Moses a leader was quite simply the fact that he was the Lord's choice, despite all his inadequacies. Choosing an unsuitable leader, as Jesus did with Simon Peter, allows for the possibility that the main credit for the success of the undertaking is given not to the leader but to the Lord. The story of the exodus from Egypt and the eventual arrival in the Promised Land has only one hero: the Lord. It was God who smote the Egyptians, divided the waters of the Red Sea, provided manna, and gave the law. All this was God's work. Moses was merely a (mostly) faithful instrument of God's proactive fidelity. Moses' strength was his union with God and his willingness to keep moving forward despite all the difficulties he encountered.

Is it unnecessary to say that the work of God is principally God's work? We are privileged to be involved, but we should not be too anxious to take over the reins and direct it according to our own perceptions. We expect humility in religious leadership. This involves more than eschewing the ridiculous pomp and ceremony of previous generations. It means being prepared to listen and to follow what others suggest. It means being very cautious in accepting the absolute rightness of their own ideas, thinking that every thought that comes into their heads is an inspiration of the Holy Spirit and that every plan they hatch automatically becomes the will of God. This is close to blasphemy and is a much greater obstacle to the onward march of God's people than the timidity of Moses ever was. (July 14, 2009.)

Lord God, in baptism you called us out of the region of darkness into your own wonderful light, and you have given us your Son to be our leader and guide in all the vicissitudes of life. Open our hearts to heed the teaching of Jesus, and give us the strength to put it into practice. We make this prayer in the name of Jesus our Lord. Amen.

July 15 ✠ *Leap*

After the crucifixion, the disciples went fishing. A shadowy figure appeared on the shore, giving instructions, and someone said, "It is the Lord." And Peter leaped out of the boat into the sea. If we take a snapshot of this action, we get a good image of what is involved in the life of faith.

It begins with an appearance, something unexpected that breaks into our life. There is a great deal of obscurity and darkness about such appearances. At one level they do not seem to make a lot of sense; at another they fascinate, drawing us into themselves. We ask ourselves, What does this mean? At this point we are called to make a judgment. To turn away and go back to doing what we had been doing, or to investigate further. Think of Moses at the burning bush; a puzzle attracted his attention, and then he went closer to examine this phenomenon.

The more we ponder the mystery, the deeper the ambiguity. The only way to settle the issue is for us to make a choice. We do not have 100 percent certainty. We have to accept that we operate on the basis of probability. And so we take a leap. Those around us look on our action with dismay; they see the sight but prefer to remain safely on the sidelines of any action. So the leap of faith is a significant step; it is what separates true believers from mere observers. Yet for those who take the leap there is never absolute certainty that they are doing the right thing; at the back of their mind is the doubt that perhaps what they are doing is very foolhardy.

The leap of faith makes contact possible. It is by risking everything that we are able to encounter the risen Lord. And from this encounter our life begins to be changed.

Faith has a tendency to metastasize. It wants to take over our whole being. It wants to colonize our whole life and to evangelize the world in which we operate. It ceases to be a private thing between me and God, and even though there is not total clarity, my faith becomes a force by which God touches and blesses the world. And it all began with one risky leap. Since this is a leap year, perhaps that means now is the time to act. (April 25, 2004.)

God of light and darkness, you call us out of the gloom of unbelief into the luminous twilight of faith. Train our eyes and our hearts to see clearly, so that we may walk more boldly on the paths that lead to your kingdom. We ask this in the name of Jesus our Lord. Amen.

July 16   ✠   *Liberation*

On one occasion Saint Bernard subsumes the whole complicated process of spiritual growth under a single word: *liberation*. If we look at the activity of Jesus while he walked this earth, we can see that this was the benefit he brought to the people. Liberation from the power of evil spirits, liberation of those who were crippled by illness or disability, liberation of those restrained by the hardness of their own hearts. He did not merely enunciate a cold code of morality which placed the bulk of the responsibility on a person's own action, but formulated a philosophy of love—to deliver those whose hearts were leaden from their loveless lives.

For us, it is important that we have full faith in Jesus' continued work of liberation. Christ continues to act on us with a view to bringing us to the freedom and joy characteristic of God's sons and daughters. The difficulty comes from the fact that he does not consult us about what will best serve this purpose. His liberating initiatives often occur beyond our understanding of our own situation. This is because one of the liabilities from which we need to be delivered is our lack of complete understanding of who we are, where we are going, or what the constraints are that bedevil our progress. We may think we know, but we don't. Sometimes the very issues we crave to be solved are, without our knowing it, doing life-giving work on us. Just as in times of trouble we discover who our real friends are, so hardship often brings out the best in us. Part of our deliverance involves God's wresting control from our hands so that our blind willfulness does not lead to destruction.

God's providence surpasses our petty plans and private projects. It sets its gaze on our ultimate good and seeks to lead us to that more abundant life which eye has not seen, nor ear heard, nor human imagination conceived. The Lord says to us, "My ways are not your ways" because there are ways that seem right to us but lead only to despair. The paths that lead to life are often hard and austere. We need to trust Providence. As Saint John Cassian wrote, we need to believe that "every circumstance, favorable or unfavorable, is designed by God's providence for our good." (October 24, 1982.)

Creator and Ruler of all, help us to trust in the kindliness of your providence, so that whatever befalls, we may believe that nothing can separate us from your love. We make this prayer in the name of Jesus the Lord. Amen.

July 17   ✠ *Light*

What is the first commandment? Well, if you start reading the Bible at the beginning you will find that it is "Let there be light." God spoke these words into the dark turmoil of primeval chaos, and everything that is good and beautiful followed from them.

This would seem to indicate that the fundamental moral precept is "Let your light shine," and the worst crime we can commit is either inhibiting the radiance of our own inner light or extinguishing the light of others.

When Jesus declared himself to be the light of the world, he was not only asserting that in him everything is radiant and there is no darkness, but also promising to help us find our light and let it shine. Jesus did not intend himself to be the only light, but a light that enlightens others—in the sense of empowering them also to become radiant. As an example, we might think of Gustavo Dudamel, the Venezuelan musician and conductor who expressed his own musicality not simply by being a star performer, but by helping hundreds of his young compatriots to discover the music within themselves. That is a very superior grade of musicianship. In like manner, we can say, the Light of Christ is such that it enables our light to shine more brilliantly.

Jesus cautions us against putting our light under a tub. Whatever humility is, it is certainly not a denial of God's gifts. In fact, as the parable of the Talents insists, leaving those gifts unused is a serious sin. From one point of view it is the only sin: not letting our light shine. For evil to thrive, it is sufficient that good people do nothing. If we don't shine, others are deprived of light.

The largest deterrent is our timidity. Perhaps we have been criticized so often that we are fearful of owning our particular giftedness. Perhaps we are too unsure of ourselves to step out onto the stage. We hold back. This is not a wise choice. We will find that gifts unused become a festering sore of resentment that can poison all our joy in living. What was meant to add a sparkle to life becomes rotten, like food long left uneaten.

"Let your light shine before all so that they may see your good deeds and glorify your Father in heaven." (Undated.)

Lord God, in you is the light of life, and in your light we see light. Help us to recognize the gifts you have given us so that we may use them for the advancement of your kingdom and for the benefit of all our brothers and sisters. We ask this in the name of Jesus our Light. Amen.

July 18 ✠ *Linearity*

One of the most hurtful mistakes we can make is to assume that human life advances in a straight line. Always making progress. A bank-issued money-box I had as a child came emblazoned with the slogan "Great oaks from little acorns grow." That may be true, but even the sapling oak does not always grow at the same rate, nor is the absence of obstacles guaranteed. Likewise, the image of climbing Mount Carmel, used by Saint John of the Cross, is taken by some to mean that all they have to do is keep climbing and they will reach the summit.

The hazard that the belief in linear progress engenders is that we are unprepared for the failures and reverses that are an integral part of a fully human existence. The trouble is that we have only one life; there is no chance for rehearsal, and, inevitably, we miscalculate and make mistakes. Sometimes serious ones. Usually, but not always, these errors are reversible, but they often leave behind a residue of regret, a reduced sense of confidence, and sometimes much confusion and pain. We want to keep going forward at a steady pace, and we are horribly disappointed when this doesn't happen.

Normal human life is made up of a series of small deaths. We grow out of what is familiar, and we are forced to become accustomed to what is strange. Puberty and adolescence constitute an intermediary phase through which we must pass to reach adulthood. Youth gives way to maturity and then to senescence.

We don't always handle the transitions well. Some aptitudes decline, and weakness sets in. Such is life.

More shattering are the moral reverses brought about by the choices we make. We willfully take the wrong direction, we embrace a course of action that harms us, we turn aside from a life-enhancing challenge. Our life ends up in a blind alley; we seem to be going nowhere. We have either to go back to where we deviated from our course or to sit down in the middle of the road and weep.

The tragedy that we contemplate and, perhaps, overdramatize is the common lot of humanity. We all make mistakes, we all take wrong decisions, and sometimes we all act in shameful ways. Such is life. We need to be prepared to do what needs to be done, to make the most of opportunities inherent in the present situation and set our minds and hearts on the goal of eternal life. When Humpty Dumpty has a great fall and the pieces can't be reassembled as they were, this is a golden opportunity to put them together in a new way. We will often be surprised and delighted at the result. (June 8, 1986.)

> *Loving Father, all that happens in our life is contained within the embrace of your providence. Help us to endure the humiliation of our many failures without becoming discouraged, confident in your capacity to bring forth good from everything. We make this prayer in the name of Jesus our Lord. Amen.*

July 19   ✠   *Linkage*

When I was a very small boy my family went through a Monopoly phase: we played at every opportunity. Although I was usually on the sidelines when the siblings played, after they had left for school, I would play the game with my guardian angel. Needless to say, I won handsomely every time. It is easy to pull the wool over an angel's eyes; it is harder with flesh-and-blood brothers and sisters.

I suppose this is why the linkage of the two commandments of love is important. We may think that we are serving the God whom we cannot see, but this perception is verified only by the quality of our interaction with visible brothers and sisters. Fanatics who are involved in terrorist acts claim to be serving God, but few of us would be likely to give them the benefit of the doubt. We say, "What sort of God would command killing and maiming and destruction?" We are less acute in assessment of our own acts of mini-terrorism. When our religious zeal generates resentment, fortifies prejudices, and is punitive toward those who do not observe our favorite precepts, surely that also cannot be from God. Surely such zeal qualifies for Saint Paul's categorization: "Zeal without knowledge." We may not cause mass mayhem by our acts, but we can be destructive on a domestic scale; we can easily slip into the habit of being terrorists of the tongue, as Saint James reminds us.

Religion cannot be divine if it is antihuman. God is unwilling to become an accomplice to any act that derives from hardness of heart, whether by commission or omission. God is not like my guardian angel in the Monopoly game, reduced into silent compliance with whatever I want. God is uncompromising about the need for justice in all our dealings with others; we must leave our gifts before the altar if a brother or sister has some claim to make on us. We may not avoid giving others their due by playing the game of Corban—declaring the goods we owe to be sacred to God and, therefore, exempt. God is not fooled. God's absolute uprightness and all-seeing eye keep us honest. (October 27, 2002.)

God and Father of us all, teach us to express our love for you by our acts of kindness toward our brothers and sisters. May the loving respect and active concern we receive from you be mirrored in the way we treat one another. We ask this through Christ our Lord. Amen.

July 20 ✠ **Little Ones**

Jesus rejoiced that deep, spiritual mysteries were reserved for the little ones. Mistake-prone Simon Peter seems to have been one of them, since Jesus declared, "Flesh and blood has not revealed this to you but my Father in heaven." Jesus seems to be saying that the deep secrets of God are hidden from the wise and intelligent. Does this mean that we should strive to be unwise and unintelligent? If we think so, then we are faced with the fact that unintelligence is listed in Mark's seventh chapter as one of the vices that comes forth from the human heart and defiles.

Perhaps we can solve the dilemma by saying that the divine mysteries can be touched not by the analytic left hemisphere of the brain, but only—and then imperfectly—by the intuitive right hemisphere. We cannot master the mystery, but we can taste it. We accept and believe first, and then we begin to understand a little. Book learning will take us only so far; we need to taste and see.

You might remember the story of Saint Augustine, who was pacing the seashore trying to see clearly some point about the Trinity. He had a vision of a little boy who had dug a hole in the sand and was running back and forth with a shell to fill it with seawater. The great theologian explained that this was impossible. The boy replied, "Likewise, it is impossible for you to comprehend the Trinity with your puny intelligence."

The little ones have access to God because they do not attempt to present themselves as anything other than small created beings, dependent on God for their very existence. God resists the proud but gives grace and light to the humble. It is obvious that God's faithful people, whose lives are ordinary, obscure, and laborious, are closer to the heart of the church than those who strive to be served rather than to serve. The question that confronts us all is this: how can we, who love being big, succeed in becoming one of the little ones? (July 16, 2014.)

Lord Jesus Christ, you call us to imitate your meekness and humility. Help us to renounce all arrogance and pride. Give

*us a surer self-knowledge. Teach us to rejoice in the company
of the simple and pure of heart. For you are our Lord for ever
and ever. Amen.*

July 21 ✠ **Lizards**

I often think that we are spiritual lizards. Naturally cold-blooded,
lizards need to be allowed to lie in the sun. Slowly their sluggish-
ness recedes, and they begin to experience a rise in energy levels
so that they can start moving around to look for lunch. The same
is probably true for most of us in our spiritual life. We need to
be warmed up before we can hope to develop much enthusiasm
for investing effort in living spiritually.

The gospels leave us in no doubt that Christian discipleship is
not merely a matter of obeying rules and doing all the right things.
The following of Jesus engages us in the task of living a life
marked by unlimited love—love of God, love of our neighbor,
love of our enemy. We all know what love is, and we have some
experience of its positive effect on our lives, but growing into a
love that is without frontiers is something that seems practically
impossible.

Here we can learn something from the lizard. To charge our
relationship with God, we have to put ourselves in a space where
we can experience God's love. This means we have to make the
effort to spend time in the sunshine, allowing God to warm us
up. Almost always it takes an effort to spend time in prayer, but,
as Saint Gregory the Great once remarked, prayer is usually
better at the end than at the beginning. Our spiritual blood has
started to circulate. We go forth with a little more energy to live
as Christ lived. Even though it is hard to get started and things
move slowly, our exposure to God is having an effect. We may
be the last to notice.

Most of us take a while to arrive at a deeper level of prayer.
That is normal. We learn to wait patiently. Meanwhile we can,
perhaps, take comfort in the words of the psalm: "My soul lies

in the dust, by your word revive me." We will find for ourselves one day that prayer is an agent of transformation in our lives. That is why we need it on a daily basis. (October 31, 1988.)

> *Loving Father, you know that often our hearts are far from you. Draw us back to you, fill our hearts with your love, and help us to be good news to all whom we meet. We ask this through Christ our Lord. Amen.*

July 22 ⫝̸ *Loss as Gain*

The philosopher Karl Jaspers once wrote in *Way to Wisdom*, "When everything is lost, but one thing remains: God is." It is a startling conclusion, but one that is often verified in experience. We find in ourselves the energy to seek and find God only when everything else falls apart, when the comfortable world we have carefully constructed crumbles into dust. We may think this demolition is the result of hostile intervention from outside. More often, however, it is the result of its own inherent instability; nothing here on earth is meant to last forever. But when everything fails, God remains, if only we are prepared to open our hearts so that we may see more clearly.

This is why, in the gospels, those who truly encounter Jesus are those who approach him conscious that their world has fallen apart: the sick, the disabled, the bereaved. In their poverty and need they are prepared to make room in their lives for the God who surprises. "God fills the hungry with good things, but the rich are sent away empty." Jesus shatters our delusions about what is truly valuable when he proclaims, "That which is highly esteemed among human beings is an abomination before God."

If we feel that God is absent in our lives, perhaps this is because our lives are too full of other things. Material possessions, knowledge, expertise, reputation, and even the love of those closest to us can so fill our lives and shape our sense of self that we feel no real need for God. It may be that even our religious practice becomes an asset, adding something to our complacency.

When we already have all that we desire, there is nothing left to hope for. But beware. Maybe, like Job, we have to lose everything before we are in the right space to receive a blessing from God. And perhaps then we will discover for ourselves that when everything is lost, God remains. (September 17, 1969.)

> *Lord, teach us to receive all good things from your hand with both gratitude and detachment, knowing that the Giver is more important than the gift. And arouse in us a firm confidence that even when everything else fails you remain at our side as a comforter and a source of strength. We make this prayer through Christ our Lord. Amen.*

July 23 ✠ *Magdalene*

Mary of Magdala must have been a very holy woman because, as the gospels tell us, seven demons had been driven from her. According to the ancient way of looking at things, our bad behavior is caused by resident demons—some seven or eight of them. These interior forces were thought to prompt the various vices to which we succumb: anger, lust, sloth, avarice, and the rest. The only way to inward peace and spiritual progress is to confront these demons and neutralize them. This is the contest that, for many of us, occupies most of our life. Mary of Magdala, in contrast, seems quickly to have arrived at a point of innocence that we can scarcely imagine—since she had been delivered of all seven demons.

No doubt it was this purity that powered her attraction to Jesus and motivated her to become one of his disciples, following him on the way to Jerusalem, being formed by listening to his words, and remaining faithful even to the horrific moment of his death. She was one of the women who came to the tomb and was privileged to have the truth of Jesus' resurrection revealed to her, with the mandate that she was to go and announce the good news to the apostles. Because of her importance as a witness of the resurrection, Pope Francis upgraded the liturgical celebration of Mary of Magdala from a memorial to a feast.

Mary Magdalen herself was something of an expert in resurrection, since she had been raised from servitude to her interior demons to the liberty of God's children. And, in our own small way, we are called to follow in her footsteps. Progressively to silence the inner voices that lead us into sin and away from God, to put ourselves in the way of growing in wisdom by giving due attention to the words of Jesus, and to allow ourselves to be filled with boldness so that we may proclaim the glory of the resurrection to an unbelieving world—sometimes using words. (July 22, 2016.)

> *Loving Father, help us to be true disciples of Jesus, willing to learn from him, following him faithfully even to the end. Open our hearts so that we may receive from him the promise of eternal life so that, filled with confidence, we may proclaim the Good News to all whom we meet. We make this prayer in the name of Jesus our Lord. Amen.*

July 24   ✝   *Magnanimity*

The wonderful story of the anointing at Bethany places before us an example of extravagant devotion. A year's wages poured our purposelessly in a single exuberant gesture. It seems a bit over the top. Like the bystanders we may ask, "What's the point of it?" We are willing to pretend that we see it as an affront to the poor, but, really, we are uncomfortable with the action because it shows up, by contrast, our own minimalistic generosity.

What is clearly exhibited here is an outward expression of a deeply felt devotion and love. It is of the same species as the act of the widow who put her last two coins into the temple treasury, but it makes a bigger splash. Big money speaks to us. In both cases, love prompts the gift of the entire self. It is not the amount of money that matters but the love that pours it forth. We never sing, "I love you with half my heart," even though that may be closer to the truth. In a sense, real love is indivisible; it is either whole or it is fake.

As religious persons, our attitude to life is a reflection of our image of God. If I see God as generous, I will strive to be generous. It is all very well to speak about the love of God, but the word *love* is used in so many contexts that it has ceased to mean very much. Perhaps it is better to seek other words to describe how God treats us. Think of the magnanimity of the Prodigal Son's father, proactive in seeking both sons, more than willing to forgive both their different vices. Over the top in his affectionate reception of erstwhile sinners. If this is what love does—and the example of the two women seems to demonstrate something similar—then, as Jesus said at the conclusion of another parable, "Go and do likewise."

We know that small-mindedness is a vice and large-heartedness is a virtue, but perhaps we should think more about this polarity in shaping our choices. Acting magnanimously makes us like God, with whom there are no divisions, no frontiers, no barriers. And it calls us to pour our whole self into what we do, to act exuberantly. The measure of real love is that it is beyond measurement. If we can measure our response, it is not love. That is why the extravagant action of the woman at Bethany makes sense. (June 17, 2007.)

Creator God, you so loved the world that you gave us your only Son. Help us to open our hearts to receive your gifts, to recognize them, and to be ever grateful to the Giver. And teach us to be large-hearted in our dealings with everybody so that through us your love may transform our world. We ask this in the name of Jesus our Lord. Amen.

July 25   ✠   *Mayan Calendar*

We are being told by the half-crazed media that, according to the Mayan calendar, the world is due to end on December 21, 2012.[2] If we accept that, then that gives us about three years to get our act together. In that case, it seems that the words in the gospel

2. It seems that, in fact, the world did not end on that date.

apply to us: "Before his generation has passed away, all these things [that is, the final apocalypse] will have taken place." Many people are titillated by the prospect of an imminent disaster, mainly because they see themselves as safely beyond its reach. "It could never happen to me," they say. And so they procrastinate, like Noah's contemporaries who kept eating and drinking and having fun right up to the time when the flood struck.

The purpose of the dire warnings we find in the Sunday gospels that are read as the liturgical year draws to its end is not predictive but admonitory. We are being exhorted to live as though the end of the world were on the point of arriving. We are being told to stay awake and remain alert.

I think that this annual warning does not mean that we should live in trembling expectation of a cosmic cataclysm. It is telling us that we should not postpone taking control of our lives until something dramatic occurs. If we suddenly found ourselves in a war zone, or if our lives were thrown into confusion by a terrorist act or natural disaster, how we respond in such circumstances would probably depend on how we were living when everything was calm. The best defensive preparation for war is not bayonet practice, but building up a healthy culture that can adapt and respond to whatever form hostile action takes. A healthy body is more likely to resist the plague than one that is infirm.

Jesus solemnly warns us, "You know neither the day nor the hour." This means that we are expected to live as though the day of reckoning were just around the corner. We may see the necessity of getting our own act together, but it is more than that. It is bestirring ourselves to spread the Gospel before it is too late, increasing the amount of goodness in the world, and seeking to repair some of the ravages of sin. The call to keep the end time in awareness is meant to stimulate, not to paralyze. (November 15, 2009.)

Lord Jesus Christ, you have commanded us to remain vigilant in expectation of your coming. Give us the eyes to see your presence in the most unlikely places and the hearts to respond to you as we would hope to respond when the Last Day arrives. For you are our Lord for ever and ever. Amen.

July 26 ✠ **Meekness**

If asked what qualities were most hated in politicians and unacknowledged rivals, many would reply in terms of arrogance, hypocrisy, deceit, pompousness. People do not use such terms about themselves, only about others. It is as though we resent the fact that others are taking up too much space, leaving not enough for us. By their seeming self-importance they appear to be underlining our relative unimportance. As they increase, we feel ourselves decreasing.

The virtue that is opposed to such self-inflation is meekness. The word itself is not often used and even less praised. It seems to bespeak a mouse-like timidity. We often take for granted that meek persons are afraid to assert themselves, allow themselves to be trampled on by more dominant personalities, and don't stand up for their rights. This is wrong. Meekness requires great strength of character. We can always find means of self-assertiveness, whether by active or passive aggression. Meekness is the virtue by which we voluntarily relinquish control over a particular area in order to achieve a greater benefit, such as harmony, or peace, or the personal growth of somebody else. It takes a strong will to restrain oneself when we feel a strong urge to intervene.

The penalty for the first and every subsequent sin was shame. This is expressed in not wanting to be seen naked, as we really are. So, we dress ourselves up. We cover our bodies. We cover our feelings. We cover our deepest convictions. We cover our aspirations and expertise. This is self-rejection. It is not meekness.

It is good to remember that Jesus said, "Learn of me, for I am meek and humble of heart." The gospels present Jesus as a fearless man, unafraid to be different or to engage in controversies and confrontations. Meekness is not incompatible with boldness. Think of his driving out the buyers and sellers from the temple.

His message was sufficiently challenging for the established authorities that it led to his being put to death. Yet he spoke of himself as "meek."

True meekness grows out of love: we give way to another out of respect and affection. We get joy by giving joy. Meekness is a sign that we are growing out of infantile and adolescent self-centeredness and learning to locate life in a context broader than our own immediate feelings. Another word for it is *maturity*. (July 7, 2002.)

> *Jesus, meek and humble of heart, increase in us the sense of belonging to one body. Teach us to make room for others. Help us to rejoice with those who rejoice and to comfort those who grieve. For you are our Lord and Master, now and forever. Amen.*

July 27 ✠ **Memory**

The English writer Julian Barnes had been married for thirty years when his wife was diagnosed with cancer. She died thirty-seven days afterward. He wrote a memoir, *Levels of Life*, about the years of grief and acute loneliness that followed his bereavement. At one stage he considered suicide but rejected the idea. If he killed himself, his wife would die a second time because the intimate memory of her that possessed him would perish with him. "If I have survived what is now four years of her absence, it is because I have had four years of her presence." In some strange way, she often seemed more present to him after her death than when she was alive.

Memory becomes presence. This is one way of understanding what happens when we celebrate the Eucharist as Jesus commanded us, "Do this in memory of me." When two or three gather in his name, Jesus is present, even until the end of the age. Memory becomes presence.

The symbolic meal of bread and wine is stamped with Jesus' signature. On a psychological level, it is an opportunity for us to come together and revive our corporate memories of what he did and taught. That is why the Eucharist is never celebrated without a reading of the gospels. In coming to Mass we make time and space for Jesus to reenter our lives. Memory becomes presence. We have an opportunity to present our needs to him and receive from him guidance and comfort and healing.

On a sacramental level, the power of the Eucharist to enhance our lives comes from the action of Christ, not from the diligence of the participants. We encounter Christ in the Eucharist because he is already there, awaiting our arrival. The external ritual we share makes actual the gracious activity of God in Christ, reaching out to save and sanctify the world. When we hear the word and eat the bread and drink the cup, it is as though Jesus walks among us. This is the mystery of faith. Memory becomes presence. (May 26, 2013.)

> *Lord Jesus Christ, give us the grace to imitate what we celebrate. Remain in our memories and keep alive in our hearts the hope of eternal life. For you are our Lord for ever and ever. Amen.*

July 28   ✝   Mental Betrayal

Our instinctive reaction to learning of genocide and concentration camps and torture is to think, "I would never have been involved in that." Even on a smaller scale, whenever we hear of people behaving badly, our first response is to ask, "How could they have done this?" It is a rhetorical question; we don't expect an answer. Yet there is an answer, and that is "Very easily." It is not so difficult to be drawn into the most repugnant behavior as long as we arrive there in small increments. In our blindness we claim to be blameless because we did not notice that we were sliding downhill. We claim not to have recognized the consequences of our actions.

Heinous crimes do not begin without preparation. They begin in the mind, when we start giving assent to thoughts that we

272 Balaam's Donkey

would never allow others to read. We do not know where these thoughts begin, but their fruit begins to manifest itself in the negative judgments we make of others. Progressively we begin to transform those who are different into enemies, people unworthy of our respect, care, or consideration. We see ourselves as their victims in some manner, and we feel obliged to pay them back by working for their destruction. We do not allow ourselves to be aware of how far we have traveled because each small step is rationalized, denied, and justified.

The process begins with mental betrayal. We have already said no to these people in our hearts. Then follows a legion of small actions: omitting, forgetting, delaying, procrastinating, dismissing as unimportant; these slowly segue into passive aggression. From there verbal or physical violence and abuse is only a hair's breadth away.

This is why the ancient monks placed so much emphasis on being vigilant about our thoughts. They are harmless wisps of imagination in themselves, but they change the way we feel about others, they shape our attitudes, and before long they begin to dictate our actions.

Think of the parable of the wicked tenants who began by refusing to pay rent and ended by murdering the king's son—and ensuring their own destruction. Small beginnings can have tragic endings. (October 3, 1999.)

> *Loving Father, send your Holy Spirits to purify the thoughts of our hearts so that we may live as Jesus taught, loving you and our neighbor with the love that is your gift to us. We ask this through Christ our Lord. Amen.*

July 29 ✢ *Meta-experience*

Judith Wright's poem "Grace" speaks of those privileged moments in which we catch a glimpse of a world beyond the ordinary spheres of space and time, a mystery that "slants a sudden laser through common day." Like the apostles on the mountain of Jesus' transfiguration, we become subtly conscious of the hidden reality that pervades everything around us. For an instant we see the world in a different light, and we are astonished that we feel so much at home in its radiance. It is as though we sense, dimly, that we were made for this, and that every other experience is thin and transient.

There are many clever people who cast doubts upon the existence of God or the reality of a spiritual world that transcends the limitations of sense and intellect. On this topic, arguments can continue indefinitely without any clear result. What is often ignored in such trivial debate is the fact that many people have "intimations of immortality" that they experience as invitations to penetrate deeper into a zone of reality that lies outside the reach of science and intellect. They have a certainty that comes not from reasoning but from experience. Or, better, from meta-experience, since what they feel goes beyond any ordinary experience. It has an energy that prompts them to make choices that are generous beyond any human measure.

Part of the power of meta-experience is that it cannot be manufactured, prolonged, or repeated. It cannot be harnessed to a particular ideology or made to serve a particular purpose. It is ultimate gratuitousness, with no before or after. It may be compared to an outrageously radiant sun shining through a narrow window into a dark place; so bright that everything else disappears. Yet the light is not oppressive. It inspires awe, certainly, but it also exercises a powerful attraction that bids us draw closer, just as the burning bush called out to Moses. By it we are invited to enter a place of warmth and acceptance that relocates the rest of our life in a different context.

Like the apostles, we are happy to be summoned to ascend the mountain; it may be a hard climb, but at the summit, we may be privileged to see Jesus glorified—to look through a window into heaven. And then we have to come down. (February 28, 2010.)

Lord Jesus Christ, you allowed your faithful disciples to catch a glimpse of your glory so that they would be strengthened for the struggles ahead. Help us to grow in awareness of your presence in all that we do or endure. Show us your face, and we shall be saved. For you are our Lord, for ever and ever. Amen.

July 30 ✠ *Metánoia*

The Sermon on the Mount is often included in anthologies of world literature because of the nobility of its language and the loftiness of its sentiments. It can happen, however, that we are so dazzled by its beauty that we fail to appreciate the very considerable challenges that it embodies. If this discourse called us simply to upgrade our behavior, it would be hard, but not entirely outside the realm of possibility. The impossibility comes from the fact that it is demands of us a complete transformation of our way of looking at the world and embracing a different set of values and attitudes.

The Greek word used in the Gospel tradition is *metanoia*, sometimes translated as "conversion" or "change of heart." What it means essentially is a change at the level of *nous*, or intellect. Walking the way of Christ is impossible without a complete change of attitude. "Let that mind be in you which was in Christ Jesus," says Saint Paul.

The Beatitudes put before us a person who takes a different stance from that embraced by many of our contemporaries: detachment from riches and status, renunciation of violence and vindictiveness, willingness to resolve conflicts. They call us to be gentle, merciful, proactively peaceful, pure in heart, and able to endure sorrow and persecution with equanimity. Live like this, and your whole life will be a proclamation of the essential message of Jesus.

But how can ordinary people aspire to such high ideals? We have to change. We have to become pupils in the school of Christ to learn a whole new way of living. This means spending substantial time with Christ by regular and reflective reading of the

Gospel. Not just reading bits, but starting at the beginning and spending maybe a year, slowly pushing forward, paying attention to every word and trying to allow the voice of Jesus to touch our hearts. We will almost certainly discover that we are slow learners. Even so, we are learning something, and with time we may very well become different. (February 3, 2008.)

> *Loving Father, open our eyes to the way of life embraced by your Son. Allow us to be attracted by his wisdom and generosity and his kindness to all. Help us to embrace the values he embodied and to live our lives as other Christs. We ask this in his name. Amen.*

July 31   ✠   *Military Service*

The text of Job 7:1 has been much quoted through the centuries. "Is not human life on earth a military service?" The noun has been translated in various ways, but the principal idea seems to be that our life is not a honeymoon. It doesn't take much experience to come to the conclusion that mortal life is marked by toil, servitude, emptiness, misery, disease, and death. Not all the time, of course, but even in our happiest moments we have no certainty that the grim reaper is not lurking behind the next corner.

To those of us who have been brainwashed by the happy-face philosophy promoted especially by advertising, this is very disturbing. To some extent we believe that we are entitled to be happy, and if we are not, somebody else is to blame. The book of Job reminds us that suffering is a universal component of human existence. The fact that we would prefer it to be otherwise is not a valid reason for disputing the truth of the assertion. In a consumer society the appetite for acquisition knows no limits; no matter what we have, we want more of it or something else. "After you get what you want, you don't want it." On this basis it would seem that those who are truly content with a little will be content most of the time. Those who are not will be always unsatisfied.

Jesus seems to concur with Job when he says, "In the world you will have distress." But then he adds, "But be of good heart; I have overcome the world." Because the complex consumerist system in which we live can never deliver on its promises of happiness, we are compelled to look elsewhere. This means negating the claims that the world tries to impose on us. It means taking our principal point of reference from somewhere else. By what means is this accomplished? "This is our victory over the world: our faith."

Faith is the word we use to describe our connection to the spiritual world, with God, with the person of the risen Lord. When this relationship grows strong within us, we are in a position to disencumber ourselves from the tentacles of commercial and political influences. Faith is our source of strength to do and to endure. It is a counterweight to all the loud voices seeking to exploit us. Faith is a force for freedom. (February 8, 2015.)

> *Loving Father, amid all the troubles and uncertainties of life, it is you who are our refuge and strength. Confirm us in faith so that we walk with joy on the road your Son has shown us and so find our way to the happiness of eternal life. We ask this in the name of Jesus our Lord. Amen.*

August 1   ✠   *Mirrors*

I wonder how we managed before mirrors became widespread. Without them it is hard for us to know how we are, at least on the outside. We may see in mirrors a kind of metaphor for the function of the prophets. They tell us how things are on the inside. Sometimes what they say confirms what we think about ourselves, but more often it seems that they are the bearers of bad news.

The Epistle to the Hebrews begins by saying that God has spoken to our ancestors and sent messages through the prophets. It did not seem to do much good. "Was there ever a prophet whom your ancestors did not persecute?" Under one pretext or another the prophets were maligned, rejected, and subjected to violence. The people failed to dance to the tune of John the Baptist and, later, accused Jesus of being possessed by a demon. We can sit back in our armchairs and ponder the fact of the prophets' rejection. It seems that only false prophets with welcome news, such as the pampered prophets of the royal temple, were popular. Sometimes the personality of the prophet or his lifestyle provided ammunition for the attack, but these objections were merely pretexts for rejecting the message. We have to admit that real prophets are never comfortable people to be around.

Mostly prophets denounce, as Jeremiah pointed out. They challenge the status quo. They call for change. Their promises of good times were always conditional on such change occurring. Their challenge comes not from some arcane information but because they hold up a mirror. Remember the story told by Nathan to the adulterous King David, ending with the punch line, "You are that man." This is what prophets do. They hold up a mirror and say, "This is what you are, this is what you have become. You may fool others, you may deceive yourself, but this is the truth. 'You are that man.' "

Throwing a brick and breaking the mirror changes nothing. We can reject the messenger. We can reject the message of truth. But the day of reckoning will come eventually, perhaps in a more vehement form.

Who is the prophet in my life? Probably it is the person to whom I am least likely to listen. The person who does not buy into my PR propaganda and is not entirely convinced by my self-congratulatory utterances. What that person is saying to me is, "Change your ways." It is probably in my best interest to listen. (December 7, 2008.)

Loving Father, time and again you have spoken to us through your servants the prophets, but we have not listened. Open our minds to receive from you the word that will lead us to salvation. Remove from our hearts whatever will impede your message of love. We ask this in the name of Jesus the Lord. Amen.

August 2   ✠   *Misery*

Medieval authors often referred to the human condition as one of *miseria*. This was not so much the subjective state usually understood by our English word *misery*, but an objective state resulting from our being far from the glory for which we were destined. We live under a cloud because our self-actualization is far from complete. We are unfulfilled.

Theologians of a certain bent prefer the term *original sin* to describe this condition. We are born in a state of alienation from God that preexists any act of the will. As a consequence, we are also alienated from our deepest self. The result is that any attempt to live a spiritual life is bedeviled by reluctance, heaviness, and boredom. And any suggestion that we curtail the satisfaction of our desires by compliance with the commandments is met with resistance and rebellion. We don't need theologians to tell us this; we know it from our own experience.

The problem with the term *original sin* is its inclusion of the word *sin*, which implies that this condition of *miseria* is somehow our own fault. That in some way we are responsible for it. It is true that this prevoluntary state is the seedbed from which personal sin sprouts, and it is also true that with each act of consent the power of sin grows stronger, but this state in which we are born is not of our own making. The story of Adam and Eve, together with the imaginative attempts theologians have made to make sense of it, are simply efforts to explain this universal human disability.

The mystery of disorderly incompleteness that we daily experience is an aspect of our developmental nature—we exist in a lifelong process of growing toward that which we are to become. We are not there yet. As a result, all the dynamic elements in our nature are not yet operating in harmony. Whether it is public knowledge or not, we are all in a bit of a mess. And how does God look upon us? As Julian of Norwich wrote in *Revelations of Divine Love*, "With pity and not with blame." Human misery prompts in God the response of mercy—or, as the medieval said, our *miseria* was met by God's *misericordia*. Original sin and its consequences serve as a lure that attracts God's mercy. "Why was this man born blind?" the disciples asked. Jesus answered, "So that the power and mercy of God might be manifest in him." (March 3, 2013.)

> *Loving Father, look upon us in our incompleteness. Do not allow the weakness and blindness and malice that seethe beneath the surface to ruin our lives, but deliver us from all that restricts or restrains our heartfelt response to your love. We ask this in the name of Jesus our Lord. Amen.*

August 3   ✠   **Mist**

On these misty mornings I am reminded that one of the great images used of spiritual experience is the cloud or the mist. As it happens, in Middle English, *misty* and *mystical* were seen to be related terms and shared a common adverb, *mistely.* We find the image of the cloud strongly present in the exodus, where the presence of God is signified by a cloud during the day and by a pillar of fire at night. Both Origen and Gregory of Nyssa have reflected on this at length.

The cloud may be understood as an intermediate state between darkness and full illumination. As such it becomes a potent symbol of how our spiritual lives waver between light and its absence. Our vision is limited. We do not see God face-to-face, but we walk as in a mist, relying more on hearing than on sight, relying on God's word for guidance for our uncertain steps.

In another sense the cloud represents the bafflement experienced by our reason when confronted with the reality of the infinite God, when our highest knowledge of God is to experience that God is beyond knowledge. It was about this that a fourteenth-century English writer composed a treatise: *The Cloud of Unknowing.*

And yet there are rare moments in our life when the clouds part for an instant and we catch a fleeting glimpse of what is beyond. As on Mount Tabor, before the astonished eyes of the disciples, the Son of God sometimes appears in something of his native radiance, overwhelming us by his presence and drawing forth from the deepest center of our being a wholehearted and yet confused adoration. This experience of the transfigured Christ begins the process of our own transformation.

But then the moment passes and we are, once again, enveloped in a cloud that seems denser than before. Having caught sight of the divine radiance, we experience more deeply the darkness of our habitual state. As with the apostles, we must come down from the mountain to plod forward in faith, praying that we do not deny in the gloom what we have seen in the light, but recognizing that to be in the light is both the substance of our vocation as Christians and its culmination. (August 6, 1982.)

> *Lord Jesus Christ, we have seen your glory. Since you have called us to live in the light, guide our steps and strengthen our wills so that we do not turn aside to lesser lights, but fix our gaze on finding the light that is life eternal. For you are our Lord, for ever and ever. Amen.*

August 4   ✠   *Mixity*

One feature of childhood, whether childhood ends at adolescence or remains throughout life, is that issues are judged on a black-and-white basis: you are good or bad, right or wrong, guilty or innocent, one of us or one of them. One of the lessons that we are compelled to learn before we pass into a mature adulthood is that binary options rarely reflect the reality of life. Things are more complicated than we may have anticipated.

Whether we begin with ourselves or with others, we eventually come to the conclusion that human life is a necessary mixture of contrary and conflicting tendencies. Making snap judgments is not only unfair but usually results in wrong conclusions.

To begin with an obvious truth: where there is light, there is shadow. The brighter the light, the darker and deeper the shadow it casts. When we encounter a highly gifted person, our tendency is to assume that their whole life is a breeze. They have nothing to worry about. Yet this is not true. Even in the noblest of spirits there is, more often than not, a tragic flaw that keeps their feet on the ground, a thorn in the flesh, such as Saint Paul describes it. To simplify another life, so that it is exclusively an object of either envious admiration or unknowing rejection, is to deny the mixity of all human existence.

In classical thought virtue stands as the midpoint between two opposite vices. Generosity is braced by prodigality on the one side and meanness on the other. Prudence is halfway between recklessness and timidity. Temperance is always a matter of avoiding both too much and too little. Even so, recognition of virtue would be easy enough if the scales were static. This is not the way it is. Situations change. What is too much today may be too little next week.

Accepting mixity means recognizing that different responses are needed in different seasons. What is prudent when everything is going well may be excessive when life is difficult. There is no iron-clad rule for living virtuously; our choices need to be responsive to the changing circumstances in which we find ourselves. In particular, we need to avoid being too hard on ourselves or on others when things go bad. The wheel will turn. It was said that one of the reasons for the superiority of the Australian cricket team a few years back was that they kept faith with players who lost form. Eventually they reaped the dividend when a man bounced back. If we are wise, we accept mixity; we learn to wait for the opposite quality to make itself visible. And it nearly always happens eventually. (July 18, 1999.)

God of simplicity, help us to find peace in accepting the dividedness of our nature. Teach us how to discern what is good, and strengthen our wills always to seek first what leads to your kingdom. We ask this through Christ our Lord. Amen.

August 5   ✠   *Moderation*

One of the most solidly attested propositions about Jesus is that he was in conflict with the Pharisees. This does not surprise us because, throughout the gospels, the Pharisees are treated as hypocrites, enviously plotting the downfall of the crowd-pleasing Jesus. And, so, today the term *Pharisee* is regarded as an insult. But it was not always so.

If the scribes were considered to be the experts in the theory of the Mosaic Law, the Pharisees were its faithful practitioners. The Torah was considered to embody no less than 613 commandments, ranging from universal obligations to details of ritual. The worthy aim of the Pharisees was the strict observance of all these rules. They saw this as a way of reflecting the holiness of God in their everyday life. You would think that they would be the natural allies of Jesus, as against the Sadducees, who were more worldly and political and less overtly religious.

Maybe the lesson we can draw from Jesus' response to these religious perfectionists is that it is possible to be too virtuous. Maybe excessive virtue is not such a good thing. First of all, it disguises our native neediness and makes us attribute our success in being good to our own efforts and not to the grace of God. Then it makes us complacent, over-pleased with ourselves and reluctant to accept any evidence that might weaken our self-approval. This leads us to a defensive tendency to be harsh in our judgments of others. Consider the Pharisees' criticism of the disciple for "harvesting" on a Sabbath: picking a few grains and eating them. Or their nitpicking over the niceties of Sabbath observance when it was a question of restoring a fellow human being to health. They strained out the gnat and swallowed the camel.

The problem with perfectionism is that it obsessively sucks up all available energy and diverts it into one or two areas, and not necessarily those that are the most important. "These things you should have done without neglecting the others." Good works are good in moderation; only truthful humility can be allowed to run untrammeled. (September 3, 2016.)

*Lord Jesus Christ, Master of the Sabbath and of all human
regulations, teach us to discern the path that is most human
and most divine. Help us to live dependent on your grace
and holy inspirations. For you are our Lord for ever and ever.
Amen.*

August 6 ✠ **Morality**

The key to understanding the moral teaching of the gospels is
the recognition that it consists not in advocating the fulfillment
of various rules, rituals, and prohibitions, but in the progressive
liberation of the heart. The conduct of a person who is free from
the vices that debilitate will be marked by honor, integrity, goodness, and truthfulness. Without such qualities good behavior is
no more than conformity to external expectations.

Jesus taught that moral disorders are not something that can
be negated by external actions or rituals. Since evil comes forth
from the heart, it must be at the level of the heart that the first
steps to counter it are taken. This means that, before ever desires
have been expressed in overt actions, an effort must be made to
mute their influence. On the understanding that we are in the
process of becoming whatever currently fills our minds, it makes
sense that we must dare to become conscious of the drift of our
thoughts. Jesus was quite severe about thoughts: he seemed to
consider adulterous imaginings almost as serious as the actions
themselves. While it is not possible for us to control what comes
spontaneously into our mind, we must make the effort to eliminate unworthy thoughts as we become aware of them, before
they begin to have a corrupting influence on us.

Jesus repeatedly demonstrated by word and action that we
need to base our discipleship on more than rules and rituals,
however useful these may seem. It is a morality that begins on
the inside and then shapes what happens exteriorly. When the
crowds acclaimed Jesus' teaching as having "authority," they were
affirming that what he was saying, challenging though it was,

corresponded to their own experience. Actions are nearly always ambiguous because we cannot see the intention that governs them. Real goodness not only embraces the virtuous act, but also involves the interior dimensions of the external deed—in essence, the love from which it springs. (February 14, 1993.)

Lord Jesus Christ, you call us all to holiness in thought and word and deed. May your Spirit guide our thoughts, govern our words, and strengthen our deeds so that our lives may be a source of comfort and challenge to all whom we meet. For you are our Lord for ever and ever. Amen.

August 7 ✠ Most Vicious

The BBC magazine *Focus* has just published the results of its research on the seven deadly sins. After surveying people in thirty-five different countries, it came to the conclusion that Australia was the most vicious of all the nations investigated, in that it scored highly for all the vices. It is nice to know that we excel at something. We managed to win the gold medal in only one vice, and that was envy. I am not sure how valid this unenviable finding is, but it is worth considering.

Envy is often conflated with jealousy, but there is a difference. Jealousy is overprotectiveness of what belongs to me; envy involves a desire to acquire or destroy what belongs to another. Envy is the fruit of self-comparison and self-dissatisfaction. I become envious by comparing myself with somebody else. I forget that comparisons are valid only between compatible things; I cannot compare my musical ability with someone else's engineering skills. They don't match up. I can, however, compare how much money I have with how much money you have—or seem to have. Envy bases itself on isolating an area of competition, inflating its importance, and then making measurements.

The problem is that envy reduces the totality of a life into visible and quantifiable elements. Qualitative differences that are unseen do not enter into the equation. If, instead, I were to concentrate on celebrating my highest giftedness and appreciating what is unique and original in myself, I would feel no urge to make any comparisons with the different giftedness of other persons. There is no competition. I am what I am. They are what they are. There is scope to celebrate everyone.

Envy is the diametric opposite of love. We are so insecure that we hate what is good in others because it seems to pose a threat to our well-being. We feel that their success makes us look like failures, particularly if they come from the same background as ourselves. We begrudge them their good fortune, even when it is the result of sustained effort such as we are too lazy even to consider. Envy drives us to diminish their achievements, and in so doing we diminish our own. Called "the evil eye" in antiquity, envy makes us look on everything with bile. Envy makes us miserable. It alienates us from ourselves, from others, and ultimately from God.

The gospel tells us that Jesus came unto his own and his own received him not. We may ask why it was that his neighbors at Nazareth greeted him with a lynching party instead of a parade. The answer is simple. They were envious of his growing reputation. God help us if we are, in fact, the most envious nation. (January 31, 2010.)

> *Creator God, help us to appreciate the many gifts with which you have endowed us. Give us the boldness to develop our talents as means to bring happiness and healing to those around us. And open our eyes to appreciate the different gifts that we can find all around us. We ask this in the name of Jesus our Lord. Amen.*

August 8 ✝ **Moving On**

Toward the end of my last year of high school, one of my teachers decided to improve our French language skills by having a series of debates. The topic that I was given was "My last day at school will be sad." Fortunately, I was assigned to the negative side. My argument was that school was just a preliminary and preparatory phase of a much more interesting and exciting after-life. It would be great to have done with it and move on to the real thing.

I wonder how you would debate the proposition "My last day on earth will be sad." I would hope that you would use the same argument. Life, as we now experience it, is merely a preliminary and preparatory phase of a much more interesting and exciting afterlife. There may well be sadness, but this will be mainly on the part of those left behind; they will miss us—I hope. But for us, "life is not taken away but changed." Death is an inexorable part of a natural process that started with our birth. Billions of people have already passed through that portal; we will be no exception.

Jesus compares death to a grain of wheat in the process of producing an abundant crop. The only way that this can happen is that the grain of wheat must break free of its restraining cara-pace and allow the full expansion of the vital force hidden within the husk. Unless it die, the grain of wheat will not yield a harvest. So long as we remain in this present stage of life we are not producing our full potential.

Inevitably, the prospect of making this transition generates a sense of dread in us. Just ask the wheat grain how it feels. But we will have the courage to face death creatively if our faith in an afterlife is firm. Jesus himself agonized over the suffering that lay ahead of him, yet he was empowered to embrace it by his conviction that, before long, he would drink new wine in the kingdom of God.

I heard of a simple old Irish monk who noticed a younger monk obviously weighed down with gloom and sadness. Coming up to him, he whispered in his ear words that he had probably uttered often to himself. "Cheer up, brother; you'll be dead soon." (March 18, 2018.)

Lord of the living and the dead, keep alive in us the hope of eternal life. May the words and example of Jesus inspire in

*us a confidence that neither death nor life can separate us
from your love. We make this prayer through Christ our
Lord. Amen.*

August 9 ✠ **Myanmar**

I recently had occasion to speak with people actively engaged in
evangelization in Myanmar—Burma, as it used to be named. It
is a predominantly rural country with a population of some 43
million, divided among seven ethnicities. It is 90 percent Bud-
dhist, and Christians number less than 5 percent; in the whole
nation Catholics are fewer than in many dioceses. Yet, despite
being socially disadvantaged, there are many converts and more
than a hundred seminarians.

I was told about a dynamic body of catechists. Boys and girls,
aged twenty to twenty-two, who are unable to continue their
education but enroll as catechists. After six months' training,
they go forth two by two into remote villages, where they live
for most of a year, teaching, nursing, preevangelizing, witnessing.
Their lives are not so romantic. They are all city people; they
have to live in jungle villages outside their ethnic territory. As
strangers, they are powerless, living under the threat of violence
and rape. There are many health issues; so far, seven of them
have died from malaria. Yet, when they return at the end of the
year, the majority of them reenroll and, after a break with their
families, return to their missions.

As it says in the Acts of the Apostles, "These people have been
turning the world upside down." They are not sorry for themselves. They are not victims. They have shed every sense of entitlement. They are realistic about the dangers, but they are
committed, enthusiastic, and joyous. Their deepest desire is to
penetrate ever more deeply into their faith.

I wonder how we compare when it comes to commitment,
enthusiasm, and joy. Perhaps we may find our attitude to our
faith more characterized by boredom, uninvolvement, self-pity,

and gloom. Shame on us who have robbed the Gospel of its fire in favor of comfortable indolence! In fifty years' time, when people look back on this period as a crossroads of history, they may ask us, "What were you doing then to change the world?" I wonder what our answer would be—if we are still around to give one. "And gentlemen in England, now abed, / Shall think themselves accursed they were not here" (*Henry V*). (September 6, 1998.)

> *Lord God, source of every good gift, give us a fully-fledged faith that brims with confidence and joy. Help us to expand our horizons and to share in Christ's mission to proclaim the Good News to all peoples and nations. We ask this in the name of Jesus the Lord. Amen.*

August 10   ✠   *Nakedness*

Before the Fall, the dress code at the Garden of Eden was remarkably informal. It was only after their act of disobedience that Adam and Eve experienced a sense of shame on account of their bodies and sought to conceal themselves. The harmony of creation was disrupted. The relationship with God, with each other, and even with themselves was shattered. And so began a long history of covering up. The truth had to be dressed up, disguised, diluted. What you see is not necessarily what you get. Concealment became a way of life.

"These people honor me with their lips," God complained through Isaiah, "but their hearts are far from me." We have become so accustomed to hiding behind a manufactured mask that we are often fearful of a fully open relationship—even with God. We hide behind our practices of piety and hope that God does not notice. It was for their play-acting, and not for overt moral failures, that Jesus criticized the Pharisees.

So often in the psalms we encounter the lament addressed to God, "Why do you hide your face?" Yet it is not God who hides from us; we are the ones who hide from God. Saint Augustine often laments in the *Confessions*: You, O God, were present to me, but I was not present to you. Trying to present ourselves to God as other than what we are is like trying to access a computer with the wrong password. God does not relate to the false self. We have to present ourselves naked to God, stripped of all self-deluding subterfuge and allowing God to see us as we are.

To give us confidence to appear before God in all our littleness, God has chosen to be unveiled before us. Jesus Christ is the visibility of the unseen God. In him we see the bared reality of God. He is the humanity of God made evident, our humanity. Like unto us in all things but sin. He calls us to come out of the bushes and be seen as we are, no longer fearful of rejection, but confident that we are held in God's all-embracing love. We can let ourselves be seen just as we are. There is no longer any reason to feel ashamed. (June 9, 1991.)

Lord Jesus Christ, we come before you with our inherent weakness and our long history of infidelity. Reveal to us your Father's all-embracing acceptance, and let us be strengthened by the conviction that in all that befalls us you stand beside us, unashamed to be our brother. For you are also our Lord for ever and ever. Amen.

August 11 ✠ **Negotiation**

Sometimes we think of the prayer of petition as simply a matter of submitting our request and sitting back to await a response. It seems like a bureaucratic formality, like filling in a government form online. Such an approach is contradicted by Jesus' instruction to keep on asking, to keep on submitting our request. This is not mere mindless repetition, such as was rejected in the Sermon on the Mount; it is something more. Neither is prayer a matter of trying to arrive at the right formula, as though hoping to find the right button to push.

Jesus encourages us to bring our raw, unprocessed needs and desires directly to our Father. Not to censor them or dress them up, but to speak them out as honestly as we can. This is the first step in what can be a long process.

When we express a desire, the words we use cannot convey the full personal meaning that drives the petition; the words are true enough, but they are crass. It is as though we sense something is lacking in our communication. And so we enter into a kind of dialogue—a dialogue with ourselves in the presence of God. A dialogue with God. It is like a tennis match; our prayer goes back and forth between us and God, becoming more nuanced with each exchange. Slowly our prayer changes. We change. We become possessed by a deeper peace, more confident that whatever comes of our prayer, it will be for our ultimate good. Think of how Jesus prayed at Gethsemane; at the beginning, he was troubled and falling apart. After a long spell of praying for deliverance "using the same words," he goes forward to meet his betrayer, renewed now in confidence and courage.

Prayer does not always directly change events; it changes persons. And changing persons usually has an impact on how events unfold. (July 25, 2004.)

> Lord Jesus Christ, Master of prayer, teach us to approach our Father with confidence and boldness, willing to be changed so that the loving plan of God, which surpasses our understanding, may be fulfilled in us and through us. For you are our Lord for ever and ever. Amen.

August 12   ✝   **Newton**

Newton's third law of motion states, "For every action there is an equal and opposite reaction." The applicability of this principle goes far beyond physics. It is also true in the spiritual life. The only way that we can advance in one area is to renounce another. If we are at a crossroads in life, it does not matter whether we choose to take one direction or whether we choose not to take the alternative. The result is the same. Choosing and rejecting are two sides of the same coin.

This means that attachment to God inevitably demands detachment from us. We cannot serve both God and mammon. We cannot hope simply to add a spiritual layer to our life without it displacing something else. There is no cheap grace. I wonder whether it is not an unwillingness to pay the price that commitment demands that makes some of our contemporaries prefer the vaguely spiritual to concrete participation in a particular religion.

When Abraham was promised the land, it was at the price of his leaving Ur of the Chaldees and living a nomadic life for many years. When Jeremiah accepted the call to be God's prophet, it meant accepting to live a single life, isolated by the mission he had accepted, the object of scorn, rejection, and hatred. When Andrew and Peter followed Jesus, they left their boats and their livelihood behind.

To the extent that we are enriched by some spiritual grace we will find ourselves called to some measure of poverty. The more time and energy we devote to spirituality, the less time and energy will be available for various useful or delightful temporal concerns. If we are unprepared for the impoverishment, the enrichment will not happen.

There is another way in which Newton's principle applies. Where there is brilliance, there will be shadow. Tabloid newspapers love to reveal the dark side of high achievers: I suppose this is meant to make the rest of us feel better. But we need to have a more compassionate understanding of the complexity of human life. Those who excel in one or several areas are liable to suffer serious defects in other zones of their personality. Nobody has every possible talent; if we applaud the gift then we must be prepared to tolerate its complementary liability. We should not expect champion athletes to be role models as well. It is easier for us on the sidelines to propound high standards than it is for them to meet them. We are being unfair to them, and eventually this unfairness will rebound on ourselves to make us more miserable about our failures than reason demands. (January 3, 1993.)

God of light and darkness, we are confused by the complexity of our own being, in which good and evil tendencies are mingled. Help us to accept ourselves and to be willing to accept others, knowing that all things work together unto good for those whom you love. We ask this through Christ our Lord. Amen.

August 13 ✠ **Niceness**

When I was a small boy I used to like running my thumb down the notes of a piano, delighting in the rippling cascade of sound that resulted. No single note stood out; all were merged in the total sequence. Sometimes it is like this when we listen to the Scriptures and hear a series of virtues or vices. We get the general idea, but we don't pay much attention to the individual items in the list.

Take, for example, the list we hear in the Epistle to the Colossians: compassion, kindness, humility, meekness, patience. "Yes, yes," we say, "we agree with all that." But do we have a clear picture of what sort of person is being described? Probably we have just a fuzzy impression of a good or nice person, without any clear notion of what this involves. Let me do a riff on these five qualities so that we can all ask ourselves to what extent they are found in us.

Firstly, am I *softhearted*? This is probably a more idiomatic rendering of the Greek expression *bowels of pity*. Obviously, it is the opposite of hard-heartedness. It is a strongly feeling word that indicates one is moved by the suffering of others. An easy touch.

Secondly, am I *obliging*? The word used refers especially to a pleasant and practical kindness, a willingness to help. It is well covered by the French word *serviable*, a willingness to be of service.

Thirdly, am I *nonjudgmental*? The Greek word emphasizes the interior or mental aspect of humility, rather than its behavioral expression. Mental arrogance is usually expressed by a tendency to pass harsh judgments on others without bothering to collect evidence or to see both sides of a story.

Fourthly, am I *nonassertive?* Meekness or gentleness refers not only to smoothness in action but also to attitudes that leave room for others to be themselves; a self-restraint that freely steps back a bit to enable others to expand. A willingness to yield control in the trivialities of everyday life.

Fifthly, am I *nonreactive?* The word used refers to the opposite of being short-tempered. It means slow-burning, the willingness to reflect before reacting, an attitude of seeing immediate events in a broader and longer context.

How well do my attitudes match those mentioned in the epistle? If there is a good level of correspondence, then this means that I am probably a very nice person; one who lives peaceably and is easy to be around. To the extent that I am lacking in these qualities, perhaps I need to consider initiating a change in how I express what I am. Others will be grateful. (January 19, 2018.)

> *Heavenly Father, keep before our eyes the model of humanity that you have shown in the life and teaching of Jesus your Son. Help us to become, every day, more like him. We ask this in the name of Jesus our Lord. Amen.*

August 14 ✠ *Nonjudgment*

One of the sins that good people like us commit most frequently is making hasty judgments about the actions of others. It is easy for us to slip into the habit of condemning others without taking the time to hear the full story. Progressively we ease into a permanent attitude of condemnation, our lips pursed in a grimace of disapproval as though we were sucking lemons.

In court the judge sits high above the crowd, garbed in a distinctive robe that sets him or her apart from mere humanity. In criminal cases there is no familiar small talk between the judge and the accused. Distance is maintained. In the same way, this is what happens when we adopt a judgmental stance before other people: we distance ourselves from them. They are not like me. They are different. They don't belong. The rush to condemn others grows on that distance, legitimates it, and increases it.

It is probably true, as Saint James seems to say, that it is especially in our speech that we fail in our duty of love and respect for others, not only by what we say, but also when we fail to give expression to what is appropriate and even necessary. Sometimes it seems impossible to restrain a negative opinion. It forces its way into a conversation, even if there is no direct linkage to the topic. There is a bitterness that craves to be expressed and to win the approval of others—at least by their failure to rebut it.

We will never control our tongue unless we exercise some vigilance over our thoughts. "From the abundance of the heart the mouth speaks." Bad-mouthing others stems from thinking ill of them. Saint John Cassian notes that often we criticize others for the very faults of which we are ourselves guilty—though we are unlikely to admit it. Psychologists tell us that what we deny in ourselves and then repress, we usually project onto others. If we want to reduce hasty judgments of others, the best way is to start judging ourselves. Self-knowledge is the best cure for undue criticism.

We are to be merciful to others as God is merciful to us. Why is God merciful? Because God knows the whole story and looks upon our sins, even our sins, with pity more than blame. (March 2, 2015.)

> *Merciful Judge, have pity on us as we stand before you conscious of our many failings. Give us a compassionate heart that does not judge but seeks to minimize the guilt of others, being willing to absorb its malice rather than pass it on. Hear us, through Jesus Christ our Lord. Amen.*

August 15   ✠   *Now*

The eighteenth-century spiritual writer Jean Pierre de Caussade is often remembered for the phrase "the sacrament of the present moment." He was alert to the fact that many of us fail to deal with the challenges we are now meeting because we are too concerned with reliving the past or with making provision for the future. We have all encountered tourists who cannot take seriously any place they visit because whatever they see is compared unfavorably with what they have seen elsewhere in the past. Perhaps we can learn from such idiocy the importance of living in the now and making the most of it.

Sometimes it is our memory that inhibits us from fully interacting with the present. We carry around our particular collection of grievances and allow the troubles of the past to influence the way we feel and act in the present. Remembering the unpleasant surprises of the past can lead us to attempt to exercise total control over the present so that the unexpected is excluded. The result is, of course, a very dull present, lacking adventure, not calling forth new talents, more dead than alive.

On the other hand, we can be preoccupied with the future, trying to accumulate sufficient resources to see us through any crisis. What we forget is, as one of John Steinbeck's characters remarks, we can never have enough money; we either have no money or not enough. Avarice is an endless anxiety—and it is not only about money. Whatever it is, we want more of it. We are afflicted by chronic discontent, which becomes a kind of existential dread that casts a pall over every experience. This is why Jesus taught us to have no care for the morrow.

After many years of marriage, my father used to soothe my mother's occasional bouts of chagrin with words he learned from the liturgy: "This is the day the Lord has made; let us be glad and rejoice therein." Possibly a good lesson for all of us. As an old song expressed it, "Yesterday's troubles are over and done. Don't think of tomorrow, it hasn't begun. . . . Making the most of each day." De Caussade would certainly have agreed. (August 1, 2010.)

God of all times and seasons, help us to see your loving hand in all that happens today, whether it comes as comfort or challenge. Let nothing dissuade us from believing in your love. We ask this in the name of Jesus the Lord. Amen.

August 16 ✠ *No Wine*

The time of Jesus and the apostles was probably very much like our own in that there was no shortage of problems: war, oppression, violence, betrayal, human misery, and suffering of all kinds. In fact, the times seemed so bad that many of those who lived through them were convinced that the world was coming to an end, just as many of our own contemporaries believe.

In the presence of such weighty concerns, we might wonder why the Fourth Evangelist bothers to preserve an account of events at a village wedding. Here we have to remember that Saint John was not a historian. The events he narrated were intended as signs pointing to a deeper meaning. The key to understanding this incident is to focus on Mary's statement, "They have no wine." The statement points to a more universal resourcelessness. What we are meant to conclude from the outcome of this intervention is that the divine action begins only after the wine has run out.

In our youth, perhaps, we thought that life was a simple lineal progression, a process to be started and then allowed to run its course without many complications. We believed ourselves to be masters of our own destiny. That was fine as long as the wine lasted. We believed that it would continue indefinitely and looked down on those who seemed to be laboring under difficulties. Despite what we thought at the time, God was scarcely present in such a life; it was under the tyranny of ego.

We soon discovered that ego has a way of wilting. The more unrestricted its exercise, the more quickly it reaches the end of its potential. The wilder the party, the sooner the wine runs out. We are left without resources. We think that this is the end, whereas it is really the beginning. Helder Camara in his poem "Put Your Ear to the Ground" wrote that God "is far less likely / to abandon us / in hardship / than in times of ease." The action of Christ in our regard is limited by failure to recognize our need for it.

So we have to be prepared for the wine to run out; we cannot afford to lose our nerve when things look bad. If we are going to do a parachute jump and we become afraid at five hundred feet and jump too early—splat! We have to wait for things to get much worse. Maybe five thousand feet, and behold, the parachute opens and we land safely. (January 19, 1986.)

> *Lord Jesus Christ, you come to our aid when we are left without resources. Help us to retain our confidence in difficult times so that we never lose hope in the mercy of God. For you are our way to eternal life, for ever and ever. Amen.*

August 17   ✠   **Obstacles**

Pope Benedict has recently got into hot water with some commentators because of his apparent assertion of the distinctively Christian character of universal love. This is a love that goes beyond family, tribe, or nation and reaches out to embrace all as neighbors, a love that accepts no limits but is always pushing against its boundaries, a proactive and forgiving love that includes enemies and renounces all violence, aggression, and revenge.

Such an ideal is precisely that: an ideal. This means that we all fall short of it, sometimes seriously, sometimes for long periods, sometimes destructively. That, however, is no excuse for not trying to make such universal love a little more than rhetoric.

Each of us is confronted with serious existential questions. How can I come a little closer to the ideal? How can I increase the power of love to shape my everyday activities and so to form my character? The simple answer to both questions is this: by tackling love's most manifest obstacles. "But what, kind sir," you may say, "are these obstacles?"

Let me offer a first round of targets for our reforming zeal: ambition, competitiveness, envy, jealousy. You may be familiar with some of these. Such vices control my choices so that my first priority is getting ahead of others, keeping them down, denying them access to goods, services, territory, honor, power, and, ultimately, happiness. By depriving them of these benefits I think to make these advantages more available to myself or, at least, not to feel bad about my own deficits. My mantra is "Their gain is my loss," and I act as if that outcome must be avoided at all costs.

If this is not completely successful, I need to call up my reserves to defend against these perceived rivals: gossip, rumor, lies, detraction, calumny, defamation. They may or may not influence the attitudes of others, but they certainly dominate my own. Progressively these perceived competitors are excluded from my sympathy and become the targets of opportunity for my anger, aggression, violence, and cruelty. In a last-ditch attempt at self-preservation, I am prepared to sacrifice others and feel no shame.

It is easy to know the advantages of growing in universal love, but it is a challenging task to attempt. Where do we start? Get rid of the obstacles. Even that is a formidable undertaking. The only way we approach this ideal is by staying close to Christ and being formed by him, to love as he loved. (September 24, 2006.)

Lord Jesus Christ, you have commanded us to love as you love, with our whole heart and with all our strength. Show us the many ways in which we can grow in love, and give us the energy to reach out to others, even when times are difficult for ourselves. For you are our Lord for ever and ever. Amen.

August 18   ✠   **Ocean**

Freud's description of religious experience as an "oceanic feeling" is a good pretext for describing God as an ocean as, centuries ago, Ruysbroeck did. On the maps oceans appear as stable masses of blue. If we have ever had experience of the ocean, we know that this does not reflect the reality. Oceans are in a state of constant flux; the tides come and go, the waves roil over the entire surface of the earth, the colors change from hour to hour. There is not a molecule in the vast mass of earth's oceans that remains still for more than a moment.

And God? Well, we believe that God is beyond change, but our perception of God is always changing. If we try to hang onto a fixed image of God, we will find our faith crumbling in the face of inevitable changes in our life. The image of God that sustained us in our youth needs to grow with us so as to serve as the basis of our faith in later years.

This means remaining in contact with God through the many changes and reversals of fortune that we experience. This is sometimes difficult. Today God seems not to be in the same location as yesterday. We have to look somewhere else. Of course, it is not God who has moved; we are the ones in perpetual motion. Every day we have to take a new sighting to reestablishing our relationship. This is why looking, seeking, and desiring are among the most significant elements in our religious response to life. If we don't seek, we won't find.

Every day we need to start afresh, to hear the invitation, "Come and see." Every day we need to taste and see for ourselves how good God is. This is a noble objective, but it is a challenge; yet those who struggle to keep seeking will certainly find. Saint Gregory the Great reminds us that in spiritual affairs everything is back to front. Normally desire precedes possession and disappears when its object is attained. In prayer desire grows stronger the more contact we make. That is why we often find that prayer flows more easily at the end than at the beginning. We just have to overcome our inertia, get started, and stay with it. (January 17, 1982.)

> *God of infinite variety, teach us to seek you where you are to be found. Help us to find you in whatever circumstances we may be, so that we may grow strong in receiving your acceptance and love. We make our prayer in the name of Jesus the Lord. Amen.*

August 19 ✛ **Offense**

What is sin? Many of us would define sin in terms of its being offensive to God. But if we were to ask ourselves why adultery, theft, and covetousness are offensive to God, perhaps we would be stuck for an answer. Sin offends God because it is an offense against ourselves. Not only does it reduce our capacity and inclination to do good to others, but it also acts as an inhibitor to that ongoing growth which will enable us to become the kind of person that God created us to be. Sin is offensive because it prevents our self-actualization. The demand for present pleasure and profit has blinded us to the ultimate destiny for which we were created.

Perhaps we need to think less of sins (plural)—sinful acts—and concentrate more on sin (singular), the state that results from our history of wrongful choices. In the Bible there are four great symbols for the ongoing effects of sin. Sin is uncleanness. Sin is sickness. Sin is being lost. Sin is a weight on heart and mind. Taken together, these symbols give us a picture of what human life alienated from God looks like. It is self-dissatisfaction growing into self-rejection and even self-hatred, often projected onto others. It is a sense of incapacity, weakness, and discomfort, like the pain of a body that has ceased to function as intended. It is confusion and a sense of ultimate directionlessness. It is a darkening of the intellect and a weakening of will, a blinding of conscience and the heavy burden of immovable guilt; it is inertia and stagnation. Apart from God, we cannot become fully human.

These are symbols of the state of alienation from God: they are not meant as statements of cause and effect. Sin expresses itself in an estrangement from the ultimate Good progressively expressed in reluctance, resistance, and rebellion. Trying to live independently from God results in an estrangement from humanity—a loss of fundamental identity and a reduction in our total vitality.

Christ came to restore our humanity by healing our relationship with God and by helping us again to live as one undivided people. He does this by leading us along the way of self-acceptance so that we no longer feel unclean, by building up our strength so that we are no longer held back by weakness, by being for us the road that leads to eternal life so that we are not lost and confused, by lifting from our hearts and minds the heavy shroud of anxiety and guilt. By helping us to become fully alive we become fully human;

by becoming fully human we become fully participant in the divine. (February 12, 2018.)

> *Lord Jesus Christ, you are our way, our truth, and our life. Guide our lives according to the truth of what we were made to be so that we may come to that more abundant life that has no limits and that lasts forever. For you are our Lord for ever and ever. Amen.*

August 20 ✠ *Omission*

If I were to ask you to draw up a list of the world's greatest sinners—present company excluded—I wonder who would be on it. Maybe Hitler, Stalin, Alexander VI, Henry VIII, Herod, and the kind of people reported in our tabloid newspapers: pedophiles, drunks, venal politicians, drug lords, and so on. Such sinners are important to us because in comparison with them we feel ourselves to be relatively blameless. Thank God I am not like the rest of humanity.

Imagine a man sitting back in an armchair boozily watching a football game. An angel comes down from heaven and announces, "You're off to hell." The poor guy replies, "You've got the wrong man; I didn't do anything." The angel replies, "That's why you're going there; you never did anything."

It is one of the scarier aspects of Saint Matthew's depiction of the Last Judgment that the people who are sent off with the goats are those who didn't do anything. They sauntered up to the judgment with a smile on their faces, only to discover that they had it all wrong.

We were made in the image of the Creator God, and one of our primary responsibilities is to reproduce in our own small way the creativity of our Maker. We were not made to be stones or drones, but active cooperators in furthering the work of creation. We have all been given talents, and with that gift comes an obligation to use what we have for God's greater glory. Talents are given us to be developed; we need to provide ourselves with oil to keep our lamps burning. And, furthermore, we are expected to be proactive in discovering avenues by which our talents may be employed.

It is no excuse to say, as those about to be sent off with the goats tried to say, "We were not aware." The point is that this willful nonawareness is at the heart of our sin. We pass down the road on the other side, averting our gaze from the fallen traveler who calls out for our help. This is more than a moment of inattention; it is a strategy of avoidance. It is a refusal to engage our conscience in the choices we make. We may fool ourselves, but God is not misled. We are as responsible for the things we do not do, as we are for what we do. So perhaps we need to revive our list of great sinners. (Undated.)

> *Creator God, give us the willingness to make full use of the talents we have received so that we may be faithful servants of your loving plan for all that you have made. Help us to use our gifts to meet others' needs. And never let us lose sight that all we have comes not from ourselves but from your loving kindness. We make this prayer through Christ our Lord. Amen.*

August 21 ✠ Once

A character in Nikos Kazantzakis's 1954 novel *Christ Recrucified* asks rhetorically, "Must Christ be crucified in every generation?" It is a response to the sight of so much suffering by good people and the killing of a truly noble soul. The sentiment reflects how we feel sometimes when confronted with pain, persecution, and rejection. Yet the answer to the question must be no. The New Testament affirms that Christ died once for our sins, and this single death is sufficient to atone for all the hateful things humanity has inflicted on itself. The Greek word is *ephapax*; its very abruptness closes the question. Christ's saving death is a one-off event that does not have to be repeated and never can be repeated.

Yet Christ himself warns us that we cannot escape the cross if we are to be his disciples. But he commands us not to take up his cross but to take up our own. We do not have to repeat Calvary, but we cannot escape our personal and corporate measure of suffering. Suffering is the most universal of human experiences; nobody escapes it. But we are to be inspired by the example of Jesus and strengthened by his grace to carry whatever burdens life lays on our shoulders: weakness, sickness, fragility, incompetence, failure, sin. We do not have to seek the cross; it will find us quickly enough.

Does the Christian have to bear more of the cross than the pagan? Not an easy question to answer, since there is no metric for assessing suffering. But we can say that the follower of Jesus may be empowered to give more than the unmotivated, to go the extra mile, to lend without expecting repayment. And it is not unknown that mysterious forces of evil sometimes have fervent Christians in their sights. The ancient martyrs are not the only ones who have to suffer for the name of Christ, even if, sometimes, the real reasons for persecution are concealed.

We do not have to repeat Calvary, but our faith may well bring us some collateral hardship. In such times we will discover that we are not left alone, bereft of consolation. Christ will be with us even more powerfully as a dear friend to comfort us, a wise counselor to guide us, and a strong helper to assist us in our attachment to what is good and our resistance to what is evil. (August 7, 2015.)

Lord Jesus Christ, you have called all your disciples to bear the cross and, so, to experience for themselves the power of resurrection. Give us the courage in this vocation and the strength to remain full of hope in every trial that life brings us. For you are our Lord for ever and ever. Amen.

August 22   ✠   Originals

The book of Revelation portrays the inhabitants of heaven as vast in number and of infinite variety. The 144,000 are mentioned and, behind them, an uncountable number of persons of every race, nation, and language. Painters who attempt to depict the scene usually settle for two or three rows of detailed figures fronting an anonymous and amorphous multitude all dressed in identical white garments, with standard-issue halos.

What will astonish us and fill us with joy when we arrive in heaven is to discover the wondrous multiplicity of stories. Every saint is an original. There are no stereotypes, no duplications; each is a unique triumph of divine grace. I think that many biographies of the saints—especially those that veer toward hagiography—do an injustice to them, forcing them into a conventional mold of sainthood that has little to do with the flesh-and-blood reality of their lives. To present them as models of ideological or institutional conformity is patently false. They are revered precisely because they went beyond common norms; they were discontented with prevailing standards and chose to live by a different law. They were nonconformists who refused to become complicit in the prevailing tepidity. In a certain sense, they were rebels.

The originality of the saints is not self-designed or self-chosen but flows from their openness to the creative hand of God. It involves patiently removing the obstacles to the call of God, and a lifelong fidelity to being formed by the mysterious workings of Providence. No saint has all possible virtues—some are incompatible—but their uniqueness stems from the unique interplay of virtue and vice, of darkness and light, of innocence and repentance. Every saint is an original, with a unique call and a unique history composed of what they did and what they endured, their successes and their failures, their joys and their sorrows. Saints cannot be compared. Nor should they be slavishly imitated; their vocation is not ours.

Like the saints, we walk an eminently simple path. We must strive to become what God intended us to become when we were created. Our innate gifts and talents are unique; our changing circumstances are unique. Our task is to hear God's call in our life and to pursue it faithfully. If we do this we will be among the vast multitude of heaven's citizens, with a unique story to tell of how God's grace has triumphed in us. (November 1, 2017.)

Creator God, you have made us to fill a unique place among your saints. Give us the wisdom to become aware of your call, the faith to embrace the task you have entrusted to us, and the perseverance to remain faithful even when things go against us. We ask this through Christ your Word. Amen.

August 23   ✠   **Orphans**

Without Christ we are orphans in the spiritual world: unsupported, out of our depth, and not knowing where to turn for help. *Orphan* must be one of the most desolate words in the language; it implies that we are deprived of the presence of loved ones, the guidance of elders. We are bereft, alone, lost, powerless, and left behind. The future will inevitably be bleak.

Christ has promised that we would not be left orphans. Thanks be to God. We will not be abandoned. He will remain with us, not visibly but spiritually and really. By the action of the Holy Spirit there will continue to be at our side an advocate, an encourager, a cheer-leader supporting us, guiding us, and helping us. Saint Bernard says that Christ remains with us in three ways: as a dear friend, as a wise counselor, and as a strong helper. Because we have access to love and wisdom and strength, we are no longer orphans. We belong in the spiritual world; we are members of the household of God, fed at God's table, sustained by God's love.

Christ has promised to remain with us, but we must also exert ourselves to remain with him. There are many ways of contacting Christ, but we need to be proactive in making use of them. We meet Christ in the silence of prayer. We meet him when we consult our conscience about ways of behaving. We meet him when we open the Scriptures and allow the Word to bathe us in its light. We meet him in the celebration of the liturgy. We meet him in taking care of the needy: the poor, the sick, the imprisoned. We meet him, if we wish, in the everyday jocularity that binds us together with those we love. Christ is never far away from us, but we have to make the effort to initiate an encounter.

In the normal course of events, our sense of communion with Christ broadens out over time to make room for others, in the giving and receiving of love, wisdom, and practical help. Without our being fully aware of it, we are becoming more Christlike in our interactions and in the manner in which we respond to situations. There is, however, a condition. We must remain with him who has remained with us. With Christ at our side we are far from being orphans. (May 21, 2017.)

> *Lord Jesus Christ, Immanuel, you have promised to be with us until the end of the ages. Help us to be more aware of your presence so that by the enabling of your grace we may stand at the side of all who need our help. For you are our Lord for ever and ever. Amen.*

August 24   ✠   **Orthopraxy**

Education has been whimsically defined as whatever remains after you have forgotten everything you ever learned at school. When the fact that the circumference of a circle is $2\pi r$ has vanished from consciousness, along with all the other items of information so laboriously memorized, is there anything left? If you had a good education, then perhaps there might remain a love of learning, a taste for quality, a sensitivity to beauty. If not, then perhaps none of these.

Every learning seems to have two distinct phases. The first is a controlled environment in which one receives from another information of which one had been ignorant. This is the mug-and-jug stage. The jug pours facts into the mug. This is an important foundation. We can go no further until we have mastered the data and acquired the skills of dealing with it appropriately. It is the same in mathematics, in languages, in art, in cooking, in paddling a canoe. Good learners, however, go beyond beginnings and develop the knack of completing the job, not under direct instructions, but from their own resources. Often they will follow the training they received, but gradually they will develop new ways of doing things.

The same is true of learning to be a Christian. We are disciples in the school of Christ, but eventually we have to graduate. This means that more is expected of us than merely memorizing his teaching. We are required to put it into practice in the unique and unrepeatable circumstances of our own life. We see that Jesus spent time teaching the apostles but then stepped out of the picture, leaving them to carry on the work without him. "It is expedient for you that I go," he told them.

Catechesis is necessary, but we have passed beyond that stage. It is time for us to put into practice all that we have retained of our faith after the catechism is forgotten. We are still learners, but our learning comes through experience. The time for gathering nectar has passed: now we have to change it into honey. Thanks be to Christ, who has sent us his Spirit to guide our thinking and sustain our acting. (April 30, 1989.)

Come, Holy Spirit, fill our hearts with your abiding presence. Teach us to choose paths that lead to life. Strengthen us with courage to put into practice what we have learned. Sustain and encourage us when the way is rough. Amen.

August 25 ✝ **Outcomes**

Since the seventeenth and eighteenth centuries we have lived in a world that has given increasing importance to the role of science. The linkage between cause and effect is regarded as a primary tenet of rational knowledge. Our first question when something happens is "Why?" If we do not know, then we expect that we will be able to find out. We are sure that an answer exists. Science is a systematic gathering of all the fragments of human knowledge of cause and effect so that it becomes possible to predict outcomes and, so, to produce desirable results.

We have been formed by this scientific culture, and so we expect that effects will inevitably follow causes. We transpose these assumptions into the spiritual life and presume that appropriate effects will follow once their causes are in place. We think that if we do the right things, right results will follow automatically. We are baffled when we hear that bad things can happen to good people.

If we read the gospels carefully we will come to the conclusion that there are no predictable outcomes: the first will be last, the humble will be exalted, and the rich will be sent empty away. Most paradoxical of all, Jesus himself is rejected by the people he came to save, and executed as a criminal. It is clear that the normal rules do not apply.

Yet, learning that God is not just another predictable factor in the chain of cause and effect is not all bad news. "With God nothing is impossible." This means that even when things appear bleak to us, there is more than a glimmer of hope. God's determination to bring his creation to a glorious completion is unwavering, though the means of achieving this are not to be confined within the hard categories of human reckoning. This is God's task; our task is to have confidence that—despite appearances—God's purpose has not been derailed and, in the end, all will be well. (June 16, 1985.)

> *Creator of the world, help us to accept your governance of our history and your lordship over all that happens. Give us the courage to live in the mystery of your providence and the joy of knowing that you will never abandon us. We ask this through Christ our Lord. Amen.*

August 26 ✠ **Outposts**

A familiar text in the Epistle to the Philippians proclaims that we are citizens of heaven. The consequence of this is that, in a sense, we are aliens in the earthly city. We are surrounded by a culture that is not our own and from which we have to make an effort to remain distinct. The beliefs and values which are specific to us as Christians are not necessarily embodied in the society in which we live. This is especially so in a post-Christian era, when the language of Christianity may continue, but its substance has been diluted. Easter is observed, but as a festival of chocolate.

One way of understanding our situation is to see ourselves as members of a diplomatic mission sent from heaven to represent our home country. We are outposts of heaven. The responsibility that we have is to present to an under-believing world the pattern of life that Jesus taught that aims to create heaven on earth.

The charter by which we live is the Gospel, and at the heart of the Gospel we will find the Beatitudes. These texts, as they have evolved, are much admired for their inspiring vision, their noble language, and their serenity, but the challenges they embody are often left aside as unrealistic. Nobody is happy to be poor, the meek and the gentle inherit nothing, and many who mourn are inconsolable. Great poetry, but impractical.

It must be said, however, that the deep resonances these texts inspire in the heart indicate that, in some way, the Beatitudes show us the shape of authentic humanity, as created by God. And so we find ourselves perched on a paradox. The heavenly life prescribed for its citizens is vastly attractive, but it is virtually impossible in the living conditions of earth. It would be nice if it were otherwise, but that is the reality.

By way of response we may say that the Beatitudes represent an ideal; they are meant to generate within us a deep sense of dissatisfaction with the very different manner of living that we experience on a daily basis. They are meant to make us desire something better. And it is desire that makes us take the first feeble steps that begin the journey of a thousand miles. We yearn to be the kind of people to which the Beatitudes refer, and this yearning takes us in two directions. First it opens our eyes to the possibility of some small progress. Then, and more importantly, it teaches us to look to God in prayer for the help we need to attain the impossible goal. (November 1, 2000.)

Loving Father, at the invitation of Jesus your Son we have become members of your household. Teach us to cling to the sources of genuine happiness so that in seeking the things

that are above we may serve, in our own small way, as point-
ers for all who desire your heavenly kingdom. We ask this in
the name of Jesus our Lord. Amen.

August 27 ✠ **Package Deal**

Part of the reason why many people have difficulty in accepting church doctrine—whether it concerns the Trinity, the question of heaven and hell, or contraception—is that church teaching is a vast network of interrelated doctrines that has developed in different geographical zones over two thousand years. If that is not enough, most of this massive body of teaching has been developed and consolidated in a largely internal dialogue among people with nothing better to do than study theology or ethics. And it is not immune from political wrangling; some of the early councils were slanging matches between the rival centers of Christian thought: Antioch and Alexandria. If you remove one brick from this towering edifice, there is a fear that the whole lot will come tumbling down. Even if a particular doctrine is wrong or based on bad science or muddled by mistranslation, it has to remain in place.

That is the church we have inherited. It may have passed muster in the 1950s, but, it seems to me, the impetus behind Vatican II is driving us to examine what can be done about it. Today church teaching is becoming ever more remote from the ordinary lives of God's faithful people. They accept it as part of a package deal, but they are unable to profit from the potential richness of the magisterium because that function has become more like policing than teaching.

We live in an age of sound bites. It is inconceivable to many that anything can be true if it cannot be explained to a seven-year-old in thirty seconds. Take many news stories: climate change, economics, toll roads, toxic dumps, stem cells, nuclear power. Honestly, are we capable of making a solid judgment on any of them? Of course, we have opinions, but more often these are secondhand convictions, hand-me-downs from our favorite pundits of binary politics. Remember what Jesus said to Nicodemus: if you don't understand the physical world, how can you hope to understand the spiritual world?

Perhaps we need to concentrate first on our core beliefs: the love of God made present in Jesus and the ethical primacy of love. For the rest, we accept the package. If, however, some issue touches us directly, we need to have the patience to think the matter through sequentially, to take steps to ensure that we are not merely rationalizing our own preferences, and finally to check with our twin guides: conscience on the one hand and common teaching on the other. And then go back to our core beliefs. (August 27, 2006.)

Lord God, we live in a world where light and shadow mingle. Attune the senses of our heart and form our conscience so that we may see more clearly the way that leads to a more abundant life and learn to live surrounded by many things we do not understand. We ask this through Christ our Lord. Amen.

August 28 ✠ **Paint Can**

If you have ever tried to open a half-used paint can, you know that it is not a matter of simply lifting off the lid. More often than not, the lid has been stuck fast by paint allowed to dribble over the rim of the can. As a result, you need to use some sort of implement to prize the lid from its moorings. You go around the lid, raising one part at a time until the whole is ready to be lifted off.

I often think that God's work in bringing us to conversion has something in common with opening a can of paint. God's word often needs several attempts before it can lift us out of the fixity of our faithlessness into the freedom of grace. This means that results are not always sudden and dramatic but are, more often, slow and incremental.

God is always at work, but not according to any timetable we might devise. When the Day of the Lord dawns, it will do so with a decisiveness that brooks no delay, but for the time being, God's action is subtle and patient and not always with visible outcomes. God has respect for the freedom of persons and so accepts that a change of heart cannot be brought on suddenly. It needs time and patience, and sometimes it requires the use of a series of initiatives to bring about the desired result.

Saint John Chrysostom was a golden-mouthed preacher, and when he spoke crowds flocked to his cathedral in Constantinople to hear his eloquence and imbibe his wisdom. But, an observer remarked to the saint, it didn't seem to make much difference to the way they lived. Their morals were not improved. "Yes," John replied, "they continue to sin, but they sin less boldly." They sin less boldly. The lid remains on the can, but he has inserted his implement and it is starting to lift. There is much more to be done, but a start has been made.

Saint Augustine, John's contemporary in the West, stretched his conversion over a period of seventeen years. Later, from his own experience, he thought that we should never write anyone off as beyond redemption. It is just that it may take a little longer. We could well take his words to heart: "Let us not forget what we were once, and then we will not lose hope for those who are now what we used to be." (October 12, 1991.)

God of infinite patience, help us to open ourselves to your unceasing efforts to bring us to conversion. Give us the courage to take the small steps that are possible for us today, that will bring us a little closer to the goal that you have in mind for us. And we ask this through Christ our Lord. Amen.

August 29   ✛   *Paraclete*

The *Oxford English Dictionary* gives one of the meanings of the verb *preach* as "to give moral advice in an obtrusive way." I suppose that is why we don't much like listening to sermons. It is very easy when preaching to exhort others to pull up their socks, but it is not so easy to do it ourselves. It may be that I don't claim to know all that is wrong with me, but I know enough to become discouraged even to think about the labor involved in any substantial level of amendment.

I think that we can all be mightily encouraged by Jesus' promise that he will send us a paraclete: an advocate, an advisor, an encourager, a friend, someone who is always at our side and on our side, someone who sees our troubles and works with us to improve the situation. We are not alone. We have someone with us who can handle anything that comes our way. We might think of the role of the Archangel Gabriel in the book of Tobit. An ideal traveling companion to have as we face potential dangers. And remember, the Paraclete whom Jesus sends is much more sensitive and strong than any archangel.

The Gospel teaching about the Paraclete is a reminder that any improvement that takes place in our life comes about by our corresponding with grace given us. Of itself, willpower is not enough. It can bring about a temporary improvement, but that is about all. It operates a bit like the old-fashioned whalebone corset. It holds the flab in, but then the flab simply appears in another place. Maybe we can grit our teeth and badger a particular vice into submission, but while we are doing this, a different vice makes an entrance through the back door. While I am waging a winning war against anger, lust, envy, or avarice, the far more serious vice of pride may well sneak in unobserved. When God acts, the remedy is total.

By God's generous gift, the Paraclete is our companion on the journey. Our Friend helps us to remember all that Jesus said and did, encourages us to do the same, and supports us throughout all our bumbling efforts to live a life worthy of our divine vocation. The Paraclete is a life coach par excellence, preparing us for eternal life. (April 4, 1986.)

Come, Holy Spirit, fill the hearts of your faithful. Be our companion on the journey, teaching us how to observe all that Jesus taught and keeping alight in our hearts the flame of hope and confidence. Amen.

August 30 ✠ *Parousia*

In the early church, Sunday—the Lord's Day—was considered both the first day of the week and the eighth day. Because it is the first day, we look back and remember the life, death, and resurrection of Jesus and are instructed by his teaching. Because it is the eighth day, we look forward to the end of time when Christ will come again, the Parousia. Most of us are familiar enough with the act of remembrance, but we are less accustomed to looking forward to Christ's final coming and the culmination of God's work of creation.

Whatever has a beginning will have an end. While the world of space and time continues to exist, we do not know how or when it will cease to be. Science and theology can establish a great deal about earth's beginning but can only guess about how and when it will end. Of course, this has provided a fertile field for doomsayers to sow their febrile speculations, but the fact is that we know neither the day nor the hour, nor anything else about it.

The hour may be unknown, but we know something of the how. In the funeral liturgy it is asserted that at death, "life is changed, not ended." The afterlife is not a quantitative continuation but a qualitatively different mode of existence. This is on an individual level. In the same way, when the end comes for all, it will be a matter of qualitative change, a transformation. "Beloved, we are now God's children. It has not yet been shown what we shall be; but we know that when he appears we will be like him, because we shall see him as he is."

That day will not be one of sadness; it will be a glorious day, when God's work in creation and Christ's work in redemption will celebrate their triumphant finale. Life will be better when Christ comes again. Changed but not ended. Christ has died.

Christ is risen. Christ will come again. Let us reaffirm our commitment to the invisible world outside space and time into which all creation will be drawn at the end of time. Happy indeed are those who will be called to the supper of the Lamb. (November 28, 2010.)

> *Creator of all, Master of all ages, teach us to see our life as a journey toward your kingdom. Help us to value the good things with which we are endowed as means to guide us toward those higher realities that await us in our eternal homeland. We ask this in the name of Jesus our Lord. Amen.*

August 31 ✠ *Patience*

Patience is our most accessible means of living the way Christ lived. We rarely include its opposite in our list of negative behaviors, yet chronic impatience destroys both our sense of self-worth and our communion with those around us. Franz Kafka once wrote, in *Aphorisms*, "Impatience got people evicted from Paradise . . . and impatience kept them from making their way back." That makes failures in patience pretty serious.

Patience is the real battleground where the reality of our faith is tested. Failure in faith is not so much a matter of disputing one or other item in the Creed, but whether we are able to acquiesce in the idea that Divine Providence is, in some way, guiding or allowing everything that happens to us. It means believing that God is acting for our salvation through the events that constitute the daily grind.

Part of the difficulty comes from the fact that patience is such a domestic virtue. It is not so hard to live under the delusion that we would rise to the occasion, were heroic challenges to appear on our horizon. It may be easy for me to believe I would rather die than deny my faith while, at the same time, mentally murdering a coworker with a booming voice and an empty mind. Patience concerns how we act in our everyday situations. In its perfect form, it is marked by four characteristics. Firstly, it is tough, able to endure hardships, contradictions, and insults. Secondly, this endurance is not only exterior; it is animated by an inner quietness that does not succumb to the external storm. Thirdly, patience may go further and be content to bear with the situation and even, like the apostles, be happy to endure outrage for the sake of Christ. Finally, if it reaches the heroic level, it may, in the spirit of the Sermon on the Mount, go the extra mile and ask for more.

If we wish to minimize evil in the world, our best means of accomplishing this is to absorb it within our own lives, like Christ, to bear the sins of the world. Not to react to the petty prickles of social living, but with a quiet mind to embrace the way of Christ, making sure that the suffering inflicted on us is not reprocessed and then passed on to others. (April 18, 1984.)

> *Jesus, Lamb of God, you bear the sins of the world, and through your patience you have shown us the way to a more abundant life. Give us strength to bear our trials with fortitude. Give us wisdom to see your providence at work. Remain with us in times of suffering so that we do not lose heart. For you are our Lord forever and ever. Amen.*

September 1   ✠   *Patrick*

Saint Patrick is sometimes trivialized by being associated with shamrocks and leprechauns. Although he is well-known as the apostle of Ireland, his inner life is less recognized, notwithstanding the fact that we have eloquent testimony of this in his writings.

Patrick was, above all, an outsider. From the time of his abduction into slavery, when he was a mere youth, until the end of his life, even when he became bishop, he walked a lonely path. His life was a continuous going forth, moving onward, never putting down roots. He wrote of himself in his *Letter to Coroticus*, "I live among barbarians, a stranger and exile for the love of God."

Even within the church he was an outsider. Although he was the grandson of a priest and the son of a deacon, he was uncatechized. His methods of evangelization were condemned, his episcopal ordination opposed, his youthful sin exposed to his shame. His only support came from his intense spiritual life and his openness to God.

Although the church is, deep down, a communion, those entrusted with a God-given role of speaking out often have to tread a solitary road, driven forward by their unique sense of divine vocation and sustained only by their faith. Just as missionaries are always leaving behind the communities they have founded and moving on to new territory, so prophets never belong. Because they are pushed out to the margins of society, they see what is wrong more clearly than those engrossed in administration. It is because prophets are outsiders that they can better understand what needs to be done.

Saint Augustine wrote that often our enemies are more likely to speak the unwelcome truth to us than our friends. Perhaps it would be helpful for most of us if we were less defensive, if we listened to the remarks of those who are different or indifferent, even of those who are hostile, and try to discern whether God has sent them to us for the purpose of our amendment. We don't have to like prophets, or admire them, but we are obliged to pay attention to what they say. (March 17, 2010.)

Loving Father, give us the courage at your call to go forth from what is familiar and to reach out to what seems strange and beyond our understanding. Help us to be bearers of the Good News to all we meet. We ask this through Christ our Lord. Amen.

September 2 ✠ *Peace*

Peace is a beautiful concept in every language. In Hebrew, *shalom* evokes the ideas of completeness, ease, and prosperity. In Chinese, *ping* highlights social harmony. The Latin *pax* is more a matter of mutual agreement and good order. What are we to think when Jesus declares, "I have come not to bring peace but the sword"?

The benefit of peace that Jesus bestows is of an order different from these conceptions of peace. "Not as the world gives peace do I give it." This peace surpasses our understanding. It can coexist with hardship, poverty, conflict, and social upheaval. It remains constant even in times of war.

We might therefore define this peace as a freedom from determination or dependence of this-worldly factors. It is an inner freedom from disturbance, no matter what is going on around us. It is like reverse-system air-conditioning. You set a temperature, and that is what you get. It doesn't matter what the weather outside is like. If it is hot, the unit cools; if it is cold, it heats. The peace of Christ comes from a certain emotional, mental, and spiritual independence from what is going on around us. It derives from having given preponderance to spiritual factors in our life. To the extent that our deepest self is hidden with Christ in God, nothing temporal can shake its calm—a few brief flutters may be the worst we feel.

Peace is not primarily an absence of disturbing forces, nor is it merely a state of soul. It is primarily a relationship. When Christ is with us we have nothing to fear—so long as we are also with Christ. This necessarily involves us in being peacemakers—proactive, preemptive peacemakers, bringing to others what Christ has brought to us.

Christ's gift of peace is the gift of himself: accepting us as we are, loving us, forgiving us, energizing us, and, in the last analysis, divinizing us, making us like himself. Whatever he is by nature, we become through grace: sons and daughters of God, brothers and sisters to all. (April 30, 2013.)

Lord Jesus Christ, bringer of peace to our troubled world, make us agents of your peace, willing to bear hardship and humiliation in order to maintain the unity of your body in the bond of peace. For you are our Lord, forever and ever. Amen.

September 3   ✠   *Peacemaking*

The Lord's gift to us is peace. Each Eucharist recalls this as we receive the gift and exchange it with one another. I wonder, do we ever think to ask the question: what is peace? For most of us it is a matter of not being disturbed: harmony, quietness, inner serenity—whether it concerns a person, a family, or a nation.

I have in mind a half-remembered text from the book of Proverbs that tells us of three things that disturb our peace: a nagging spouse, a leaking roof, and a smoking fire. This leads me to suppose that, practically speaking, my peace of mind is often subject to disturbance by outside elements over which I can exercise no control. If this is true, then it leads to the conclusion that there can be no peace until all have peace, and thence to the proposition that there can be no genuine peace without justice. Until wrongs are righted and abuse stopped, there can be no peace.

Christ came to bring not peace but the sword. The peace that Christ gives us is not a tranquilizer but a stimulant, an energizer. We are called not merely to possess peace but to create peace. "Blessed are the peacemakers," Jesus said, "for they shall be called children of God."

We make peace by practicing proactive justice: inclusively, systematically, universally, fully. We become peacemakers by recognizing, respecting, and promoting the rights of others. Not necessarily dramatically or loudly, but cold-bloodedly in whatever situation we find ourselves. There can be no peace in the body if one member lacks peace; there can be no peace without justice. To make peace, we have to take upon ourselves the task of attending to what is wrong.

The gift of peace is the call to make peace by a zeal for justice, following the example of Jesus. This often means venturing beyond the frontiers of strict justice into the wider region of love, kindness, compassion, and forgiveness. We won't be very successful as peacemakers if we do not practice patience, bearing one another's burdens and, like a poultice, drawing out the malice from the sins of others and being willing somehow to absorb it within ourselves, without complaint. (May 17, 1998.)

> *Lord Jesus Christ, Prince of Peace, make us your collabora-*
> *tors in bringing peace to the world. Give us the courage to*
> *address injustice wherever we find it, and provide us with*
> *balm to heal those who have been wounded in life. For you*
> *are our Lord for ever and ever. Amen.*

September 4   ✠   *Pearl of Great Price*

From time to time it is not a bad idea to ask ourselves what is most precious in our lives. What is of supreme importance to us? What would we want to have with us if we were all alone on a desert island?

Possessions are important, but they can be lost, stolen, or broken—or they can go out of fashion. Health is very important, but it remains precarious; all it takes is a broken bone, a misfiring neuron, or a genetic quirk to make our future seem very dim. Ambition may energize us for a while, but the higher we rise, the harder we fall, and nobody stays up forever. Power may seem sovereign, but a week is a long time in politics. All of these desirable goals lack permanence, and at some stage we will have to survive without them. We are very foolish if we allow ourselves to be defined by them.

We may think that the right answer is "love." Yes, it is; but it is not necessarily everything that claims that noble name for itself. Love, too, can be impermanent. Parents die. Friends and siblings can become estranged. Partners can break up, and children joyfully flee the nest. Alone again. The question may be posed: is there a love that is not subject to decay?

Saint Paul gives the answer to this in his famous hymn to *agape*. The love that comes from God and transforms the human heart will last forever. We need to distinguish this from lesser loves, which are self-centered, maybe to the point of narcissism. We can know *agape* by the features it displays. It is respectful,

hospitable, nurturing, growth-fostering, liberating, engaging, supporting, forgiving, self-forgetful. Truly a pearl of great value.

How do we arrive at this summit of love? A brief answer might
be, by living a long time. There is no trick we can learn that will
enable us to reach this point quickly and effortlessly. We can
expect it to be the labor of a lifetime. If there is anything that
will help us to focus our energies and progress along the path to
love, it is the pursuit of wisdom.

Wisdom is the kind of understanding that comes from experience and from empathy; it is not merely the fruit of knowledge
or science. It involves the unconditional acceptance of reality in
all its contradictory complexity. It demands the gift of discernment: the keen eye that distinguishes what is whole from whatever is tainted by untruth, unfreedom, or inhumanity. Everlasting
love is an unprejudiced passion that leads to the nonpossessive
embrace of whatever is good, noble, and honorable. Surely, a
pearl of great price. (July 24, 2005.)

*God of all ages, keep before our eyes the impermanence of
all that surrounds us, and kindle in our hearts the desire for
that which lasts forever. Instill in our hearts the love that
gives meaning to our life by opening us to you and to all. We
make this prayer in the name of Jesus your Son, who is our
Lord for ever and ever. Amen.*

September 5   ✠   **Penance**

Over the gateway leading to a particular European monastery are
inscribed the words, "Unless you do penance, you will all likewise
perish." Fortunately the inscription is in Latin, so, I suppose,
most of those passing through this portal are unaware of the stern
message that is being beamed at them.

The idea of "doing penance" is not particularly popular today;
it is associated with a self-punishment that seems to have been
fed by an exaggerated sense of guilt, unmitigated by any appreciation of the developmental aspects of human behavior. We link

the practice of penance with the season of Lent but are rarely given any plausible reason why self-denial is good for us.

Here it is probably useful to return to some of the passages in Saint Paul's epistles where he makes a contrast between the "flesh" and the "spirit." Commentators rush to inform us that by *flesh* Paul was referring not only to the body and its instinctual tendencies but also to human nature itself. This was considered to be reluctant or resistant to be ruled by the spirit and, ultimately, to be in a state of rebellion against God. Fleshly desires are, of course, prime manifestations of our unspiritual state, but Saint Paul never intended to set up a dichotomy between the physical body and the spirit. The struggle he envisaged was a moral dilemma, not an expression of dualism.

Saint Paul is following the rabbis in understanding that our decisions are influenced by two contrary tendencies. One is life-giving; the other leads ultimately to death. Each day, as the book of Deuteronomy reminds us, we are faced with choices with serious consequences. Each choice that we make leads either to life or to death. Although, obviously, some matters are more important than others, nothing is neutral. We are admonished, "Choose life." It is not always easy. The pleasurable response to a sugary drink may seem to enhance our life at the time, but we know that ultimately it is another small step toward illness and, ultimately, death.

Penance is really about getting our priorities right, not allowing ourselves always to be swayed by immediate gratification when there are negative consequences down the track. First, however, we need to be motivated by recognizing that the right choice is not usually the easy choice. This means adopting a different mind-set about what is worthwhile. And, as it happens, that is an alternative (and better) translation of the term usually rendered, "Do penance." (October 17, 2011.)

Lord Jesus, you instructed us that to enter the kingdom of God we must have a change of heart. Open our eyes so that we may begin to see things differently and so, animated by

the values of the Gospel, we may live as you lived and act
as you acted. For you are our Lord for ever and ever. Amen.

September 6 ✠ *Periphery*

At Epiphany we celebrate the periphery. During the Christmas
octave, our attention has been centered on the Word become
flesh, the newborn at Bethlehem. At Epiphany the periphery
takes center stage. Sages arrive from the East. Caravans of camels cross the desert, and dromedaries come from Midian and
Ephah. The pantomime picture portrayed on our Christmas cards
illustrates a central truth of our faith. Christ came to bring peace
and healing not only to those who happened to be close by, but
also to those who are far away. To all he cries out in the words
he addressed to his first disciples, "Come and see."

There is no division between insiders and outsiders in the
kingdom of God. The kingdom is not located in or limited by
time and space. All have equal access. "God's will is that all are
to be saved and to come to the knowledge of the truth." This
was clearly demonstrated in the life of Jesus. If there were any
who had privileged access, it was those on the margins: the poor,
the oppressed, the unclean, tax collectors, Samaritans, and sinners of all stripes. Jesus entered into life-giving dialogue with the
periphery. None was excluded.

The Fourth Gospel announces the incarnation in the well-
known phrase "The Word became flesh." But it is quick to add,
"And we have seen his glory." When we try to create an image of
glory, we probably think in terms of a sunburst with golden rays
emanating from a central point. But there is another aspect of
glory: its power to attract. Glory is also a vortex, drawing to itself
whatever it touches. Crying out in the streets, "Come and see."

The kingdom of God is not an intimate dinner party. It is an
immense banquet to which all are invited. Including us. For our
part, we need to listen to make sure we hear the invitation. Although we live on the periphery of faith and morals, we are still

summoned to the feast. We are meant to be part of it. The eternal banquet will not be as joyous if we fail to arrive.

Heaven will be enriched by our presence just as the church on earth is enriched when outsiders enter into the conversation, even if it is by way of fair criticism, pointing out that the emperor has no clothes. The church is renewed to the extent that it opens its doors to those outside, when it welcomes those on the periphery. All have been called. Those whom God has invited, let no one exclude. Jesus said, "If I am lifted up I will draw all to myself." (January 7, 2018.)

> *God of all nations, you call together all your sons and daughters to feast in your kingdom. Give us a spirit of magnanimity that excludes no one and welcomes all. We ask this in the name of Jesus our Lord. Amen.*

September 7 ✠ *Permeability*

When someone close to us dies and the outward grieving of the funeral has ended, we are left with the overwhelming impact of the absolute finality of death. We look around, and the person is not there. There is a mute absence where, so recently, there was a living, and perhaps lively, presence. A fire door has abruptly slammed and a relationship is severed—relegated to the dim echoes of memories and the fading mementos of happier days. Silently and privately, we who remain grieve—perhaps not so much for the deceased as for that part of ourselves that has died with them.

At times like this it is worthwhile asking ourselves what our faith has to say about the situation. It is only faith that can give us an assurance about things that are beyond our experience. It is only faith that allows us, as Saint Paul admonishes the Thessalonians, to comfort one another in this matter.

Our faith insists that the boundary between the world of space/time and the world of spirit is permeable. Jacob's vision of the ladder connecting heaven and earth showed angels descending and ascending. An indication, it seems to me, that our world is in constant communication with the spiritual world and with God, who stands at its center. In death, "life is not taken away but changed"; the fact that we do not understand in what form life continues does not indicate its unreality, but only the limitations of our intelligence. What happens after death is not only outside our experience, but also inaccessible to our understanding so long as our existence is subject to the conditioning of space and time.

Lazarus, Jairus's daughter, and the widow's son at Naim were all raised from death to life. They returned to what they were before they died. They continued with their life as if nothing had happened. And eventually they died. Jesus' resurrection was quite different; it was not a return to life but the transition to a new and higher mode of human existence. What is revealed to us in Jesus' resurrection is that our ultimate destiny transcends our human span on earth. We will attain, by God's love, a spiritual future, the form of which we cannot know. We can, however, be reasonably certain that our relationship with the dead continues in some subtle form that, perhaps, sometimes manifests itself to us in unguarded moments. Those who have left us are sometimes felt to be still with us. (March 9, 2008.)

Lord of the living and the dead, keep alive in us the hope of eternal joy and the confidence that we will be united with all those who have gone before us into eternal life. Help us to look forward to that heavenly banquet where with them we will sing forever of your love and mercy. We ask this in the name of Jesus our risen Lord. Amen.

September 8   ✝   **Perseverance**

One of the commonest reasons for giving up religious practice is boredom. Where religious practice seems to be booming, it is because a lot is happening. The so-called megachurches, with highly participative services accompanied by professional musicians, seem to generate a lot of noise with the kind of enthusiasm that is lacking in the staid weekly worship at a parish church. We may ask, however, whether this is an appropriate way of dealing with the widespread religious indifference of our epoch.

Enthusiasm does not last. After two or three years, the flow of biochemicals slows and people go back to acting on the basis of the beliefs and values they previously had. While it is true that a bit of drama can help lubricate the process of conversion, once the transition is made there is a need for consolidation. True conversion is a slow, ongoing, and cold-blooded process that involves gradual changes in our way of viewing things and making evaluations. It calls for a renegotiation of many elements in our lifestyle: attitudes, activities, relationships.

Perseverance is not a strong factor in our culture of immediate gratification. We vainly flip through television channels to find something that will hold our attention; we leap from one topic to another on the internet, unsure of what it is for which we are looking. Fashions come and go; the latest cars predictably boast a plethora of "new" features. The idea of a lifelong commitment has come to seem vaguely unrealistic. How can we make sure that we persevere in our faith and practice?

In the first place, we need to welcome the unwelcome thought that final perseverance is not a given in any sphere of human activity. We need to be soberly realistic about the precariousness of our faith and pray often for stability in belief and practice.

Secondly, we will more likely continue our journey if we have traveling companions. The support of our local faith community will help us to pass through the inevitable challenges to our continuing commitment.

Finally, we need to ensure that our religion is not merely a social or institutional obligation but a matter of a personal relationship to Jesus Christ. This we achieve both through an interactive encounter with him through our regular reading of the gospels and in our regular periods of silent prayer.

By such means does final perseverance become possible. (August 5, 2004.)

Lord Jesus Christ, you have taught us that those who perse-
vere to the end will be saved. Help us to produce good fruit
through patience in following your footsteps, and fill us with
a vivid hope of the abundant life that you came to earth to
bring. For you are our Lord for ever and ever. Amen.

September 9 ✠ **Persistence**

When the Lord instructed his disciples about the art of prayer,
he placed great importance on persistence. We should continue
with prayer despite its apparent pointlessness, even though we
cannot find words that express what it means, notwithstanding
the fact that it seems to go unanswered. The kingdom succumbs
to violence; we have to keep hammering on the door.

If we consider the example of the woman trying to shake the
unjust judge out of his inertia, we can imagine all the possible
pretexts she may have considered for giving up. "What's the use?"
she may well have said to herself. Obstinate laziness is usually
only moved from above, by a higher power, not from below. How
many people have worn themselves out trying to extract an ounce
of compassion or common sense from desk-bound bureaucrats?

Jesus is telling us that, though prayer may feel hopeless, perseverance will eventually yield fruit. *Eventually* means in God's time,
not in ours. Prayer takes much proactive persistence and requires
a great deal of energy, while fatalism, passivity, letting events follow
their natural course, and cutting our losses seem easier.

From the context of the parable we can see that the model of
prayer that Jesus proposes is not intended to favor a particular
type of personality, one characterized by bullheaded stubborn-
ness. Rather it is admonishing us to adjust our image of God.
Despite appearances, God will not fail to bring about justice. If
there seems to be a delay, it is not because God is indifferent to
the plight of the oppressed. If there is a delay it is because it is
part of the solution—and not part of the problem. The delay can
be pedagogical or tactical. Just as in many sports there is a single

moment in which an action will produce the desired result, so jumping the gun usually renders an intervention ineffectual. God acts speedily at the right moment to produce the best result. The fact that we do not agree with the timing means nothing.

The message is clear. Keep praying. God is listening. God will act. Don't try and grab the controls because you don't understand the whole picture. Trust in God, for God is faithful. (October 21, 2001.)

> *God, ever faithful to your promises, look upon our neediness and let this cup pass from us. Strengthen our faith in your unchanging goodness and ever-present power so that in all that befalls us we may never lose hope in your mercy. We ask this through Christ our Lord. Amen.*

September 10 ⊹ **Phototropism**

I am often fascinated by the phenomenon of plants turning to face the sun, sometimes following its trajectory across the sky. I think that the flower opening up its petals to receive the full radiance of the sun is a good image of an important aspect of human reality. We come to a fuller liveliness by being exposed to the light that beams from eternal day. Spending time in the presence of God makes us beautiful. "Look toward God and be radiant," the psalm sings.

It is from this exposure to the light that we receive the energies needed to live according to the impossible standards set by the New Testament; relying on our own meager resources will yield only frustration. Unlike plants, our divine phototropism is not the automatic response of nature; it requires the free assent of our wills. It is deliberate. To the extent that we fail to take the opportunity to enter into contact with the spiritual world and be with God, we will lack the energy to do good and our lives will be lusterless.

Our resistance to the instinct to look toward the light is deep-seated. We close our eyes and block our ears to the very reality that will bring us to a more abundant life. We hide from God and then affirm that it is God who hides from us. "This is the judgment. The light has entered the world but people loved darkness rather than light, because their works were wicked. All who do evil hate the light and do not come to the light lest their works be exposed. Those who accomplish the truth come to the light so that it may be revealed that their works are done in God."

The Word made flesh is the outshining of eternal life, the light that shines in the darkness. Those who follow that light will have eternal life. Our task is clear: To act as our nature indicates. To open our eyes to the deifying light. To look toward God and become radiant. "Sleeper awake, rise from the dead, and Christ will give you light." (April 3, 2011.)

Lord Jesus Christ, in you is the light of life, and in your light, we see light. Open our eyes and our hearts to perceive your action in our world and help us to follow your light wherever it leads. For you are our Lord for ever and ever. Amen.

September 11 ✠ *Pinocchio*

One of the childhood images that has stayed with me is from the film *Pinocchio*. It is of Geppetto, the puppet's maker, searching for him in the pouring rain and crying out in a grief-stricken voice, "Pinocchio! Pinocchio!" Looking back, I am surprised that a Disney film could cause such *angst*. I seem to remember that Pinocchio had been naughty and had run away. It was then that he had fallen on hard times. In a sense, Geppetto was well rid of him; he was undeserving of such concern.

Sometimes it is only loss that reveals the extent of love, just as grief at bereavement brings to the surface a love long submerged in the trivialities of daily interaction. I found the image of the rain-soaked Geppetto coming back to me as I pondered the three parables of loss that Saint Luke has included in his fifteenth chapter.

In each case the focus is not on the one lost, but on the one seeking what was lost. The wandering sheep represented only 1 percent of the total, the lost denarius only 10 percent, and the lost son only 50 percent. In two of the three cases the ones lost were responsible for separating themselves from safety and getting themselves into trouble. Particularly in the case of the lost son, the separation is aggravated by bad behavior, wasting his inheritance on prostitutes and living riotously. We would probably say that he was undeserving of any special treatment—and it seems that he himself came to recognize this.

The parable, however, is not about the son, nor about his brother, but about the father. It was meant to make the point that God's love for us is over the top. It is superabundant. To love extravagantly and gratuitously is the only way God knows. There can never be any question of a measured, merit-based love. "God makes the sun to rise over the wicked and the good, and the rain to fall on righteous and unrighteous alike."

These parables teach us that God may be defined as the One who seeks what is lost—just as Jesus defined his mission as calling not the good but sinners. Many of us may remember how this aspect of God is celebrated in the long poem by Francis Thompson, *The Hound of Heaven*: "Who wilt thou find to love ignoble thee, / Save Me, save only Me?" (August 5, 2007.)

> *Heavenly Father, we have wandered far from your house and allowed ourselves to lose sight of your love. Call us back, and give us the strength to change the direction of our life and to start again to journey toward our heavenly home, with steps made light by the remembrance of your care for us. We ask this in the name of Jesus the Lord. Amen.*

September 12 ✠ *Prayer*

Most of us, when we consider working on a deeper religious dimension to our lives, think in terms of improving our knowledge or upgrading our behavior. This will not happen unless first we lay down an experiential foundation. Without personal contact with the spiritual world, our religious efforts will soon falter. We may well believe that faith without works is dead, but we need to recognize that faith without prayer is dying.

The gospels offer us a coherent picture of the qualities of prayer, based on the example and teaching of Jesus. Among other qualities, four stand out. Prayer is to be intimate, honest, confident, and persevering.

Jesus' own prayer to the Father was intimate, and he invites us to follow his example and share his family access. Empowered by the Holy Spirit, we can call God *Abba*, addressing One whom we recognize not only as the source of our very being, but also as One who loves us dearly.

Because God is our Father, we can be perfectly upfront with him about all that concerns us. There is to be no holding back in order to present ourselves as better than we are. The great mystery inherent in God's love is that it stems from what God is and not from what we are. No matter what sort of mess we have made of our lives, God's love for us does not flicker.

This undeviating acceptance is the basis for our confidence that our prayers will be heard. Prayer never has a negative result. If we ask for a stone, God will give us bread. If our petition is for snakes and scorpions, we will receive fish and eggs. An answer will come, though maybe not in the form we expected.

God is outside time. Our prayer will be heard at a time of God's choosing. This means that we have to keep on praying, knocking, and seeking until the season arrives when God will act. Think of how Saint Monica prayed for her son Augustine's conversion, and her prayer was heard. After seventeen years. (July 25, 2010.)

Lord Jesus, you taught us to pray with boldness. Guide us in our journey of prayer, and give us the courage to keep on praying when all seems lost. For you are our Lord for ever and ever. Amen.

September 13 ✠ *Promises*

The way that Saint Luke has chosen to present the backstory of
the incarnation is to give priority to the theme that God is faithful to promises made long before. His genealogy stretches all the
way back to Adam, as if to intimate that the promise realized in
Jesus was already implicit from the creation of the first human
beings. This would seem to suggest that the incarnation was not
consequent on the Fall, but something eternally conceived even
before primal light first shone in chaos. The process begun in
creation will reach its denouement only at the end of time, when
all things are brought to a head in the glorified Christ.

The incarnation is not a bolt out of the blue, but the result of
an agelong period of preparation. It is the turning point of history.
The birth of a son is announced, the direct gift of God in a way
surpassing all those other favored births by which God intervened
in the life cycle of his people and realigned them to his purposes.
We think of the birth of Samson, the promise made to Ahaz of
the birth of a child to be called Immanuel, and, especially, the
commitment made to King David that his throne would never lack
an heir. All of these are subtly recalled in Luke's narrative. The
child to be born is the fulfillment of the promises made of old.

Saint Thomas Aquinas teaches that theological hope is based
on the acceptance of two truths: that God is willing to do something and that God has the power to accomplish that will. In
recalling the promises God has made to his people, Saint Luke
indicates that it has been God's constant will to bring his creation
and his people to the fulfillment initially intended. Given human
weakness, blindness, and malice, is God able to bring this about?
The gospel reminds us that the promise made to Abraham was
based on the premise that "nothing is impossible for God."

Saint Luke tells his story for a reason. That is to fortify our
hope that God is able to deliver on the promises made to us, that
God is faithful. In dark days, it is possible for us to doubt whether
the plan of God is really being unfolded in our case, or in the
church of today, or in the world. There is much contrary evi-

dence. Yet the promises that have been made really are indications that God is present throughout our speckled history, in bad times and not only in good. God is present and active, well able to bring to completion the good work that has been begun. This is our hope, and it is our hope because God has promised and nothing is impossible for God. "Uphold me, Lord, according to your promise, and I shall live; do not disappoint me of my hope." (April 10, 2018.)

Lord God, bring to fulfillment the promises you have made from of old. Pour out your Holy Spirit on all who follow the way of your Son, and bring us all together to everlasting life. We ask this through Christ our Lord. Amen.

September 14 ✠ **Prophets**

The saying about prophets not being welcomed in their own country has been a solace to many of those who are alienated from the community in which they live. They seem to believe that anyone who is not accepted must automatically be regarded as a prophet. Perhaps they forget that there are many reasons why people are rejected or feel rejected. Sometimes it is because of their bad conduct or wrongful attitudes. Sometimes we can be complicit in our own marginalization, knowing that there is a certain freedom that comes from living on the fringe.

Neither acceptance nor nonacceptance is a guarantee of the authenticity of prophecy. There were plenty of false prophets during Old Testament times—in fact, Elijah slew more of them in a single day than there are true prophets—and most of those false prophets were very popular. Real prophets were outsiders, scorned by the people and persecuted by the authorities, but they remained tireless in bringing the word of God to those to whom they were sent. The genuineness of prophecy is not assayed by its reception. The only criterion is the truth of its message. The proof of the pudding is in the eating. Real prophecy is more than information: it speaks to the heart, it communicates energy. It is self-legitimating.

The word of God has the power to produce results beyond the prophet's capabilities: Moses was not a good speaker, Jeremiah was only a boy, and Isaiah was a man of unclean lips. Yet when they uttered the words that had been given them by God, they spoke with authority—the same quality the crowds later recognized in Jesus. True prophecy has power; false prophecy is nothing more than mere words, a puff of wind with no substance or endurance. Real prophecy has substance. Those who do not listen to the ones God sends set themselves not only against the prophet but also against the authority of God. "This is judgment: the light came into the world and people preferred darkness to light."

We are all prophets, and we can know that our message is true if it touches the hearts of our hearers, if it brings with it a surge of energy, if it leads them to a fuller faith. If, on top of that, we suffer persecution for the sake of the Gospel, then surely this adds extra credibility to our message. (July 4, 2017.)

> *Father in Heaven, you continue to speak to your people at different times and in varied ways. Help us to welcome the word in whatever form it comes to us, to ponder it in our hearts, and to put it into practice in our lives. We ask this through Christ our Lord. Amen.*

September 15   ✠   *Providence*

Most of us have heard about sibling rivalry, and perhaps we have seen some obvious examples of it. The biblical story of the patriarch Joseph is an extreme case. As we know, Joseph's birth broke the spell of childlessness suffered by Rachel, the favored wife of Jacob. As a result, he was always special in the eyes of his father. His older brothers were not pleased with this and burned with an envy that soon turned into hatred. They plotted to kill him but, instead, sold him into slavery. Joseph was exiled to Egypt. He continued to suffer misfortunes until, one day, his luck turned and he became the all-wise manager of the country's fortunes and, eventually, the savior of those who had betrayed him. It was through Joseph's intervention that the line of Jacob secured continuance.

Most of us do not want to experience such undesirable events, but the lesson we can learn from them is that, even though the worst happens, good can result. Viewed retrospectively, Joseph's misfortunes were the building blocks of a life lived to great purpose. I wonder: can we look back on our own lives and see such somersaults of fortune, perceived disasters yielding unanticipated benefits?

There is a world of difference between a naïve optimism and the theological certainty that all things work together unto good for those who love God. A belief in God's providence is not a blindness to sometimes-horrendous reality. Nor is it an invitation to fatalism. It is the overriding confidence that God understands the totality of our situation much better than we do ourselves; our purview is limited.

It is true that God saves us by mighty acts of deliverance. It is also true that God saves us by causing us or allowing us to pass through hard times. By breaking open the complacent carapace of our lives, God exposes us to influences that force us to backpedal, to change tactics, to learn new skills, to move into unexplored territory. Mostly, this is an unwelcome change, but, despite our grimaces, it is beneficent. We are being delivered from the self-imposed limitations that have hitherto inhibited our lives. We are being freed from the moribund staleness we have embraced and invited, if not to be reborn, at least to begin a new stage in life.

All that comes from the hand of God is good; if we can accept this our lives will be both happier and more purposeful. (July 8, 2009.)

Creator and sustainer God, in love you have made the world, and in your love you guide it to a joyous culmination. Give us faith and hope that will sustain our confidence when life is difficult, and strengthen us by your grace to respond in love to whatever befalls us. We ask this in the name of Jesus our Lord. Amen.

September 16 ✠ **Purple**

Twice in the year the ministers of the liturgy don purple vestments: Advent and Lent. This may lead us to think that the two liturgical seasons are similar. But this is not correct. It is true that both seasons call us to be more attentive than we are at other times, but the direction of the attention is different. In Lent we look back at our past. In Advent we look forward to our future.

In Lent we are invited to become more conscious of the compromises that have bedeviled our efforts to be good over the years. It may be that when we were young we considered ourselves relatively blameless and all our good deeds admirably free from mixed motives and subtle malice, but, as we grow older and wiser, we begin to comprehend that not everything was as sparkling crystal as it seemed at the time. We become subject to waves of regret and bouts of salutary bitterness over lost opportunities, confused intentions, and rampant selfishness. Since we cannot change the past, we cannot undo what was done. We cannot seize now the opportunities that have long since faded. We must be content to learn from our ancient imperfections and to trust ourselves to the mercy of God. Lent is the time when we look back to discover how total is our need of God's compassionate mercy and forgiveness. This realization purifies the soul, opens us to receive the bounteous love of God, and gradually restores lost innocence.

Advent is different. In Advent we look forward to the resurrection of the dead and the Final Judgment. Can we really look forward to God's judgment? Of course! At that time a great book will be opened, and every single good deed that, by God's grace, we have done will be read out. From the chocolate biscuit we shared with a younger sibling when we were four years old to the smile we offered a stranger a few minutes ago. Every single good deed! And as each item is read out, the angels will sound their trumpets, the 24 elders around the throne will toss their golden crowns in the air, and the 144,000 of the elect with the vast crowd of those who are saved will fill the air with a resonant cheer. Again and again and again. That is what the Last Judgment will be like. Anticipating it fills us not only with hope and endurance and patience, but also with a deep and lasting joy.

In Lent we look back; in Advent we look forward; but wherever we look, we find the infinite mercy of God. (December 4, 2017.)

> *Bounteous God, Creator, Redeemer, Sanctifier, bring to completion the good work you have begun in us, so that in all things you may be glorified and your name may be hallowed in all creation. We make this prayer in the name of Jesus our Lord. Amen.*

September 17   ✝   *Pygmies*

We belong to the church of the pygmies, and we had better get used to it. There is no point in hoping that everyone with a significant role to play in the church will be some kind of spiritual giant. To be such is neither their gift nor their function. This has always been the way, beginning with the Twelve. Many East Asian traditions place considerable emphasis on the role of the guru, an enlightened one who awakens the spiritual instinct in disciples, who reads their inner states and guides them to a higher state. There may be some exceptions, but this is not the normal job description of the standard Christian minister.

In his lifetime Jesus was often to be found with no-hopers, sinners, and underachievers. That is why most of us feel perfectly at home in his presence. It is the presence of Christ in the hearts and lives of his faithful people that constitutes the church. The various officials are merely doorkeepers whose job is to provide access, to let people in, to pass them along to the One they are seeking. They may be decked out in gold braid and a smart hat, but they are uniformed nobodies. Their job is to open the door and step aside. The action happens inside.

It is of no special consequence if priests lose their shirts in a casino, or bishops are photographed entering premises with dubious reputations, or nuns are found drunk in the park. We make no judgment. This could happen to any of us and, as persons, they are no different. Jesus tackled such situations head-on and simply advised, "What they say, do; what they do, do not." It should not surprise us that Christ has chosen earthen vessels to convey to us something infinitely precious.

It is the presence of Christ that constitutes the church. "Christ is now at work in the hearts of all through the energy of his Spirit." It is the immediacy of Christ in the lives of the little people that carries weight; everything else may well be self-important frippery: it does no great harm in most cases, and if it is damaged or lost, the outcome makes little significant difference to anything. "It is the spirit that gives life; the things of the flesh are useless." (November 3, 1996.)

> *Lord Jesus Christ, help us to take seriously the idea of church as the gathering of your little ones, the poor, the disadvantaged, the wounded. Teach us to avoid worldly standards and to love everyone, no matter how they present themselves, knowing that in each of them you are present. For you are our Lord for ever and ever. Amen.*

September 18   ✠   **Quality**

If you ever read *Zen and the Art of Motorcycle Maintenance*, as I did many years ago, you may have come away from the book with a new appreciation of the word *quality*. As I remember it, Robert Pirsig was making the point that there are layers of meaning undergirding the everyday realities with which we interact and which, in some way, determine the value of those realities. In its most obvious form it is the contrast between what something really is, its quality, and how much of it there is, its quantity. In this approach we hear echoes of ancient philosophical debates about the relative values of what is seen and what is unseen. In human affairs, also, "quantitative judgements don't apply." One rose can be invested with more love than five hundred.

All this is by way of reflecting on Jesus' statement that giving a cup of water in his name is sufficient to obtain salvation. Although many of us have a tendency to dream about heroic actions, the prospect of actually having to perform them terrifies us. We admire the martyrs for their courage in enduring torture but prefer to go to heaven in economy class. The possibility of a cut-price fare to heaven, however, is not so obvious. The gospels are full of calls to heroic discipleship, leaving behind family and resources so that "naked we can follow the naked Christ," as the ancient saying exhorts us. And that following can lead only to Calvary. That is not where we want to go.

We suppose that the applause will be very faint when we enter heaven on the basis of our having given a cup of water. It is nothing compared to the sufferings of Maximilian Kolbe, or the wisdom of Augustine or the missionary zeal of Francis Xavier. Yet it will be sufficient. Because, as Saint Paul says, getting into heaven does not depend on "the one working or the one running but on God showing mercy."

The key to understanding this is the notion of quality, the inner and personal component of the material action, the disposition with which it is done, and the consciousness of acting in the name of Jesus. You don't have to be a millionaire to be a generous benefactor—merely one who gives "with a heart and a half," as the Irish are wont to say.

The trouble is that most of us underestimate the value of small actions and, instead, sit back to wait for the arrival of a great opportunity. (July 13, 2009.)

God, bounteous Father, you give to all without measure. Give us the grace to be generous givers despite the paucity of our means, so that when we give to others in the name of Jesus,

his abundance may compensate for our poverty and his love
embrace us both. We ask this in his name, Jesus Christ our
Lord. Amen.

September 19   ✠   *Questions*

Sometimes I think that the Scriptures are more significant for
the questions they pose than for the answers they give. There
are, for instance, more than two hundred questions in the Gospel tradition. The answers are not much use to us if we don't
have the questions, or if the questions come already packaged
with stale answers. With an unexpected question, we are forced
to consider our options. "Why spend your money on what is not
bread?" "What does it profit to gain the whole world and lose
one's life?" These are big questions because they concern the
ultimate issues of life, and they seem to intimate that we are too
concerned with everyday trivialities to consider them.

The gradual growing of wisdom within us is connected with
our willingness to confront these fundamental questions. Saint
Paul often reminded the early Christians to relinquish the aimless
life typical of pagans, with its emphasis on the present satisfaction of desires and its refusal to look beyond the horizons of space
and time. All of us have a yearning for a more abundant life, but
we need to know how to attain it. And we need a certain discipline of life that will keep us on the track and not allow us to
wander off, chasing butterflies.

It is by God's gift that we begin to be challenged by life's
questions. This is an effect of faith—the experience of a connectedness with a reality that is beyond both sense and intellect.
By whatever channel it enters our life, faith motivates us to search
for the ultimate meaning of our existence and to recognize and
embrace the glimmers of truth that come our way.

A second gift of God is the sacrament of the church. A sense
that we belong to the communion of believers, and so we do not
have to solve every single mystery ourselves. We can be content

knowing that there are limits to our understanding. It is enough to see that part of the whole truth that can be seen from where I am. I trust others to see more clearly what I cannot. (July 31, 2014.)

> O God, beyond all knowing, our hearts and minds are rest-less because they cannot rest fully in you. Help us to see what is necessary for us to find our way and to walk boldly, with confidence in those who are companions on the journey. We make this prayer through Christ our Lord. Amen.

September 20   ✝   **Ransom**

In the Gospel of Mark Jesus expresses his mission as being "to give his soul as a ransom for many." It is a familiar text, and because of that we often don't think very much about it. Yet, what does it mean?

In English, *giving one's life* means "to give up one's life," "to die." In that case the saying would refer especially to the final culmination of Jesus' life. We could, however, also translate it, in accordance with the similar usage in the Fourth Gospel, as "to risk one's life," as a shepherd does when he confronts the wolves threatening his sheep. But perhaps we can push the image a little further and translate it in terms of dedication: "to give oneself," or "to give all one's energy." Such a rendering bespeaks a certain intensity in giving.

But what does the word *ransom* mean in this context? To whom is it paid? God? The devil? Both options rest on fairly shaky theology. Perhaps the term is better defined not by the price paid but by its function, "to take the place of," or by its effect, "as a means of liberation."

The beneficiaries of this action are indicated by the phrase *for many*. This is not the same as we read later, "on behalf of many." The preposition used here is *anti*, the same one used in "An eye *for* an eye and a tooth *for* a tooth." It indicates a measured exchange. And, of course, *many* is not necessarily less than *all*; it simply indicates that a great number of people are involved.

Taken with the preceding text, this may be read thus: "The Son of Man came not to be served but to serve: *to serve generously in place of the many* [who are unwilling to serve.]" Thus, following Philippians 2, the service that Jesus offers is an act of self-emptying that is the ultimate gift of self; in some way he is our representative; his service is an exemplar and perhaps even a substitute for ours.

And we are called to follow. Jesus was not merely being philosophical in describing his mission thus; he was also setting out what is involved if we are to be his disciples. We also are called to serve generously in place of the many who are unwilling to serve. (March 4, 2015.)

> *Lord Jesus Christ, you are the way that leads to eternal life. Help us to walk in your footsteps, wholeheartedly committing ourselves to a ministry of service for the sake of those whom you have destined to be saved by the knowledge of the truth. For you are our Lord for ever and ever. Amen.*

September 21 ✠ *Realism*

A quality that is not always appreciated in biographies of saints is that most of them were very realistic and down-to-earth people. They were not dreamers. They were clear-sighted and practical people who had, by long practice, rid themselves of the delusions that, for the rest of us, cloud our judgments and bedevil our actions. They were people who saw a need and stepped in to remedy the situation.

Saints are realists about themselves. This means two things. Firstly, they do not expect of themselves more than what flesh and blood is able to deliver. We are not superheroes. We need to eat and drink and take our rest. We get tired and grumpy and sometimes disappointed. We are still a work in progress. Our outlook on life is limited, conditioned by family and education and culture. We belong to the little people. If we forget about these things we will be always pushing ourselves beyond healthy limits and end up self-destructing. Secondly, however, the saints recognized something more than our native weakness and limitation. They understood that we are called by God to greatness, and we are empowered to live up to that call.

Self-realism is the basis of a healthy acceptance of others. When our self-image is based on reality, we have no fear of what others may think of us and we have considerably less need for their adulation. This means that we are more likely to accept them as they are, a mixture of positive and negative qualities. Our first impulse is not to wish they were different, but to view them as being very like ourselves. On this basis, we can then choose to encourage what is good in them while protecting ourselves, as necessary, from the harmful effects of their limitations. We act, as God does, more in pity than in blame.

Realism in our approach to God means not only that we ourselves are prepared to stand in nakedness and truth before God, but that we are also fully prepared to embrace the reality of what God is. People who have twisted religious attitudes generally have a distorted image of God. The God of the Gospel is a God of infinite love and mercy, giving and forgiving, bearing and forbearing. Any other god is a fabrication of our own.

True religion is grounded in the reality of our self-acceptance, the reality of our acceptance of others, and in the reality of a God who stands above and beyond all human conceptions. That is religion in spirit and in truth. And it is very down-to-earth. (June 29, 1969.)

> *God of all times and seasons, teach us to approach you in humility and truth. Help us to accept our littleness before you and our dependence on your grace. Give us the boldness to accept reality and to rejoice in your plan to bring all things to completion. We ask this through Christ our Lord. Amen.*

September 22   ✠   **Reconciliation**

In the biblical story of Joseph, retold in the musical *Joseph and the Amazing Technicolor Dreamcoat*, there is an emotive scene in which the now all-powerful Joseph reveals himself to the nervous brothers who had sold him into slavery. It is easy to imagine an angry confrontation in which the wrathful Joseph takes revenge on those who betrayed him. Instead we have only tears of happiness and the reestablishment of good relations. For most of us, it would have been payback day. Here, however, all grievance is shunted aside in the joy of reunion and reconciliation.

It is important to keep in mind the emotional component of real reconciliation. It is not merely a legal device to end a long-standing wrangle, but the reuniting of hearts severed through previous hostile interaction. Reconciliation is not a denial of facts, nor is it the whitewashing of objective wrongness, nor the denial of the hurt experienced. Rather, it is the result of a deliberate choice to let go of the grievance that is a cause of pain to both parties. When real reconciliation occurs there is an outburst of relief on both sides, the upsurging of an affection that has been pushed down by concentrating too exclusively on the other's faults. There are no benefits to a state of nonreconciliation; all those involved are the worse off for it.

To be the active agent in advancing reconciliation demands a certain largeness of heart: the ability not to be stuck in the past, to get over unpleasant situations and move forward. It also demands a certain philosophical stance, a recognition that we are one, single human family, and that any action or inaction that creates or maintains division among us is a crime against humanity.

Having a heart possessed by a spirit of reconciliation is a vital precondition for moving more deeply into prayer. We cannot open ourselves to God when our attention is dissipated by ongoing wars with our neighbors. We who are so much in debt to God cannot afford to withhold from our neighbors the release they owe us. We must learn to forgive as we are forgiven, and even to be ready to leave our gifts lying by the altar while we go off to seek to restore lost peace. Perhaps the example of Joseph and his brothers will give us the courage sometimes to do so. (July 9, 2009.)

> *Lord Jesus Christ, you came to bring all humanity into unity, and you prayed for the coming of the day when all divisions would cease. Give us the will and the courage to be peacemakers in our community, to leave aside our own grievances, and to bring together those who have become estranged. For you are our Lord for ever and ever. Amen.*

September 23 ✠ **Redeeming the Times**

The phrase *redeeming the times*, from the fifth chapter of the Epistle to the Ephesians, is a clear pointer to a sometimes-forgotten aspect of our Christian discipleship. We are not only to take care that our personal behavior conforms to the standards of the Gospel and to make sure that we endeavor to see and serve Christ in our neighbor, but we are also called to contribute our portion to offsetting the evil that is so rampant in the world around us.

Redeeming the times in which we live calls us to go beyond passivity and to stop believing that our pessimistic complaining does any good. It means rolling up our sleeves and getting our hands dirty, as it were, by actively involving ourselves in making the world around us a better and godlier place. We can think globally, if we wish, but it is important that we act locally. We need to be sobered by the thought that sins of omission are the most common failings among those who are religious. We don't do many bad things, but, alas, we also don't do many of the good things that are possible for us.

Linus Pauling, the scientist who won the Nobel Prize twice, wrote an article about ethics in the 1960s. He had arrived at the conclusion that the most universal and most fundamental moral principle was what he termed "the minimization of suffering." Good people are those who are actively involved in reducing the suffering of others. Here, as elsewhere, "quantitative judgements don't apply." We do what is possible, even though it seems to have less-than-global consequences. We should never let the fact that we cannot improve everything serve as an excuse for doing nothing.

All of this seems to imply that each of us may have to develop a sense of global responsibility. Starting from where I am, I am responsible for making the world a better place. A more human place. A place more open to the divine. (November 4, 2011.)

> *Creator God, help us to become active workers in the task of restoring the world to the beauty intended by you in the act of creation. Help us to be a force for good in our own little world, tolerating its imperfections with patience and taking care to bear our part in redeeming the times. We ask this in the name of Jesus our Lord. Amen.*

September 24 ✠ *Reframing*

One of the perennial problems believers face is unanswered prayer. The New Testament is unequivocal in promising us that our prayers will be heard. And so we pray. And nothing happens. And then we doubt. No wonder the Epistle of Saint James describes the situation as being in two minds: we accept the promise, but we do not see the result.

Jesus encourages us to persevere in prayer even when it seems to yield no benefit. There are two different ways of taking this recommendation.

- The first is that portrayed in the parable of the woman grinding down the unrighteous judge. This is the path of attrition. Jesus is recommending that we do not let up; eventually something will happen. Foreigners are often puzzled by the game of cricket. A test match is played over five days, and there may well be long stretches in which nothing seems to happen. The challenge for both sides is to remain alert, because at one point an opening will occur and the whole course of the match may be changed. Prayer demands that sort of vigilance from us. There is no instant gratification, but if we persist and persist, something will almost inevitably happen.

• Another image may be found in an artillery bombardment. A battleship trying to sink an enemy cruiser will fire a round, note where it falls, and adjust and fire again. And adjust again and fire again, moving ever closer to the target until it strikes home. In our prayer, our first expression of a desire may not seem to make contact; it comes back to us. Perhaps we reexpress it and try again. And again. Finally, maybe after a considerable lapse of time, we say what we want to say in a way that reaches into the heart of God and is heard.

Prayer is necessarily a dialogue and not a monologue. When we begin to speak with God we may have only the foggiest idea of what it is for which we are really praying. Confronted with the absolute truthfulness of God, we feel obliged to shift our position a little, and so, gradually, we begin to send forth a more truthful prayer. Our needs are being reframed. We are beginning to see issues in a wider context. Prayer changes events less often than it changes us. No matter how hard we try, our faith doesn't move mountains. So, as the old story goes, "If the mountain won't come to Muhammad, then Muhammad will come to the mountain." In prayer we consent to be changed. (August 16, 1998.)

Lord Jesus Christ, you have commanded us to be bold and confident in our prayer. Help us to allow prayer to change us so that, by the light of the Holy Spirit, we begin to have a deeper and more intense awareness of where we stand in relation to God. For you are our Lord for ever and ever. Amen.

September 25 ✠ Rejection

Perhaps the most tragic line in the New Testament is found in the prologue to the Fourth Gospel. "He came unto his own, and his own received him not." This is an assertion borne out by the full narrative of Jesus' life. It was not only Nazareth that did not welcome him; he is rejected by crowds of his own compatriots. And it is delusional to think that we might have acted differently if we had been there.

Rejection is one of the things that we fear most. Perhaps we are scarred by youthful experiences of not being asked to dance or being the last one to be picked for a sports team. Human beings are, as Aristotle reminded us, social animals. We are happiest when we are in the midst of our friends and most anxious when we are separated from our familiar company. If heaven is ultimate communion, then we cannot bear to think of what its opposite may be.

All of us experience rejection in some slight form or another. We know that it paralyzes us, rendering difficult what should be within easy range of our capabilities. We commit many sins of omission through our fear of rejection, and sometimes we reject others simply to avoid being ourselves rejected. We thrive in an environment of acceptance, but, despite a show of bravado, we begin to wilt when we are subjected to general disapproval.

Jesus did not meet with universal acceptance—for the most part the commitment of his followers was tepid, transitory, and conditional. As Christians, we have to be prepared to keep soldiering on, without the benefit of mass approval. We are called to demonstrate that boldness that was typical of the apostles after the descent of the Holy Spirit. To recognize that whatever others think of us, God loves us dearly—whatever the ups and downs of our own response to that love. As Saint Paul reminds us, if God is for us, what does it matter if others are against us, since nothing can separate us from God's love in Christ Jesus? (January 7, 2010.)

Heavenly Father, you so loved the world that you gave us your only Son. Help us to receive him when he comes and to learn from him how to love and welcome others. Give us the strength to bear gracefully whatever reproaches may come our way. We ask this in the name of Jesus our Lord. Amen.

September 26 ✠ *Rejoice*

Jesus' wish for his disciples was that his joy would be in them. What this seems to indicate is that Jesus was a man who was patently joyful. Perhaps we are wrong to place too much emphasis on his being "a man of sorrows." It is far more likely that his public ministry—in contrast to that of John the Baptist—was characterized by joyfulness and freedom. No doubt it was this that attracted the crowds. You attract more flies with honey than with vinegar.

Perhaps we also insist too much on the onerousness of discipleship, notwithstanding Jesus' saying that his yoke was easy and his burden light. Fidelity to the Gospel is not a gloom-laden cloud that engulfs life and renders it unbearable. On the contrary, following the path of Jesus means walking in the light. It is a source of purity of heart, endowing us with a simplicity and transparency in which we may be more fully touched and transfigured by the outshining of God's presence in thousands of the events that bestrew our way through life.

One of the prime manifestations of the presence of the Holy Spirit is the deep sense of confidence and contentment that remains unshaken despite surface disappointments and troubles. This is not just a frothy lack of seriousness or a biochemical high, but something that rises from deep within. Joy is the result of the indwelling of the Holy Trinity in our hearts. As Léon Bloy wrote, "Joy is the most infallible sign of the presence of God."

Among many ancient Christian writers, sadness was regarded as a vice, and giving into it was seen as sinful. To be sad seemed to them an indication of a weakness of faith, hope, and love. How could a person who was accepted and loved by God have any cause to be gloomy? So we read of the apostles after their imprisonment and flogging, "They went forth rejoicing that they had been found worthy to suffer for the name of Christ."

This is not to deny that suffering remains in the world and that when it strikes us we are close to being overpowered by it.

Yet there is something deeper than the pain we feel; it is from this that we must draw our strength. "Rejoice always in the Lord. Again, I say, rejoice." (April 2, 2013.)

> *Creator God, you have made us to participate in your infi-*
> *nite joy, and despite the toil and persecution of this valley*
> *of tears, you inspire us with hope and confidence. Help us to*
> *rejoice always and to be bearers of your joy to all whom we*
> *encounter. We make this prayer in the name of Jesus our*
> *Lord. Amen.*

September 27 ✠ *Relax*

As an occasional celebrant at weddings, one of the things I have tried to communicate to the bride and groom, by word and by attitude, is that their wedding day is magic. "Relax and enjoy yourself. Whatever you do, you can't put a foot wrong." It is a privileged occasion and the focus for so much love and goodwill that is at other times present but submerged. It is not a royal occasion watched by millions; it is simply a gathering of friends who wish the couple well.

In the gospels Jesus presents the kingdom of God as a wedding feast—not as a funeral. There is no need for a sober code of conduct with a list of minute prescriptions to be followed. It is a privileged occasion in which we become ever more conscious of the abounding love of God and the goodwill of all. Nothing can be allowed to spoil this time of happiness.

Perhaps we are a bit slow in identifying anxiety as one of the major enemies of fervent Christian discipleship, notwithstanding the repeated admonitions in the New Testament to set aside all care. Jesus insists that we remember that our Father cares for us more than for the lovely lilies in the field or the beloved birds in the sky. Instead of having to listen to preachers exhorting us to try harder, perhaps we should be advised to try less. To yield control. To go with the flow. Yes, if we want to make real music we have to play the right notes, but, at a certain point, we have to allow the power of the music to take over and control what we do. There is spirit-content hidden behind the notes that is greater and more beautiful than we are, and under its impulsion, a more moving and powerful result will accrue. We have to step back and allow the transformation to occur.

We are empty vessels. By human labor, perhaps over many decades, we fill ourselves with water. But then the moment of a different encounter comes, and the water is transformed into wine—and not only *vin ordinaire*, but something spectacular. No wonder the wedding guests are so happy. (January 19, 1992.)

> *Father of All, you have invited us to join the eternal banquet to celebrate the marriage of heaven and earth. Free us from all hesitancy and care and allow us to luxuriate in the sunshine of your unconditional acceptance and love. We ask this through Christ our Lord. Amen.*

September 28   ✠   *Remain*

One of the most important words in the Fourth Gospel is *remain*. Used in various senses and, unfortunately, translated in various ways, the verb is found forty-one times in the Gospel of John and a further twenty-four in the Johannine epistles. Sometimes it is rendered as "abide," which has a loftier connotation; "remain" is more familiar because it keeps the everyday flavor of the original usage.

Writing perhaps a generation after the earliest gospel, the Fourth Evangelist has a mystical approach to discipleship. It is more than morality. Our following of Christ involves us in a deep interpersonal relationship with God: we remain in God; God remains in us. It is not, however, a static relationship. Our challenge is to keep on remaining and even to go deeper in remaining. Through all that befalls us, in good times as in bad, we are to bind ourselves ever closer to God. Through thanksgiving and praise when the sun shines; through heartfelt petition as the storm clouds gather. Nothing can separate us from the love of

God. Every situation can serve as an invitation to strengthen the bond that unites us.

Remaining in God is not something that we can manufacture for ourselves. It is necessary that we be reborn through the Spirit of God, elevated to the point where we become capable of receiving a new life that is beyond human capabilities. Beyond new birth, the Spirit remains with us as our Advocate, a friend at our side, making intercession for us and empowering us to live the kind of life to which we have been called.

There is another word used in the Fourth Gospel that describes an appropriate response to this gift of God: *remember.* We are often to call to mind the grace that has been given to us, to become conscious of its promptings, and to find new energy in following its guidance. "Forgetfulness is the death of the soul." The saints were those who lived mindful of this source of power within them and drew on it to enable them to live the heroic lives that we admire but fear to imitate. If only we knew the gift of God, we might be a bit bolder in taking a risk for the sake of the kingdom. At least sometimes. (April 29, 2014.)

Lord Jesus Christ, you have promised to remain with your church until the end of time. Help us to live more mindful of your presence within our hearts, and open our eyes to see your presence in all our brothers and sisters. For you are our Lord for ever and ever. Amen.

September 29   ✠   ***Remediation***

In any group, situations arise in which there is conflict among the members. Sometimes it is one against one; at other times it is several against several. The biggest mistake is to leave the task of reconciliation to those involved: either to let them slug it out among themselves or, by themselves, to find a way to restore harmony. Perhaps it is better to see such conflict as wounding the unity of the community, and therefore it is the group or family or community itself that must take steps actively to promote reconciliation.

Sometimes too much energy is expended on trying to establish the proportion of blame to be assigned on each side. This is a thankless task since it involves the impossibility of harmonizing contrary narratives that have already hardened into permanently adversarial form. And there is always the tendency to favor the side of the dispute that more closely approximates our own outlook.

It is also clear that harmony cannot be imposed from outside, since that will be perceived by one party or both as doing violence to their rights.

The remedy is simple but difficult. Both sides are to step back from the issues that divide them and to engage in the mental discipline of refusing to allow the dispute to enter their thoughts. Evagrius of Pontus notes that one of the greatest impediments to prayer is the memory of past wrongs suffered. Banishing the memory of something hurtful is not denial or repression, but the deliberate decision to walk away from an area of conflict to concentrate on other matters. Letting the body heal itself. Time often provides a remedy by setting matters back into proportion.

Bystanders can often act subtly as intermediaries, but there will be many hours of helplessness coming sometimes from the complexity of the situation and sometimes from simply sharing the acute pain of others. The important thing is not to appear to give total assent to the narrative that comes from either side. Often we would love to say, simply, "Get over it," but there is rarely an opportunity where such frankness can be fruitful.

We are all one body, and the success of our common enterprise, whatever it is, depends on maintaining a high level of trust and interdependence. The ultimate remedy for all contentiousness is simply the conscious strengthening of what binds us together and, perhaps, exploiting the moment when a breakthrough becomes possible. (September 7, 2008.)

> *Lord Jesus Christ, when two or three or more gather in your name, you are in our midst, but so is the burden of conflict. By your action in our midst bring us ever closer together, so that dissension and division may cease and we may come to*

experience together the peace of your kingdom. For you are
our Lord for ever and ever. Amen.

September 30 ✠ *Republican Virtue*

As the Roman Empire prospered and grew richer, many of its
citizens looked back in nostalgia to a time when the majority were
austere, self-forgetful, and hardworking—unlike the self-indulgent
idlers of their own day. They embraced the concept of "republican
virtue," even if they had no taste for living it. They were fond of
a story about Lucius Cincinnatus, who, after his retirement from
public life, was plowing a field on his farm when envoys were sent
requesting his aid in repelling the threat of imminent invasion.
He accepted, become dictator, ruled for sixteen days, defeated
the invader, and then returned to his plowing. However spurious
the details of the myth were, he was celebrated as the embodi-
ment of the national character: well-grounded, pragmatic, effective, sober. A safe pair of hands.

We have our myths also. They go in the opposite direction.
Often biographies of holy people are tinged with what we might
call a taste for celebrity sainthood. The ones who are held up for
our admiration and imitation are those who have lived fairly
spectacular lives. They were learned, eloquent, influential; they
had visions and worked miracles. They shone like the stars in the
vault of heaven. They were miles away from the daily grind that
is our field of battle.

We may ask, is there a place for hidden virtue? In response, we
might point to Jesus' observations about the Pharisees. Jesus insists that our good works—fasting, prayer, almsgiving—should be
done in secret, so that nobody else knows about them. Hiddenness
is the best friend of holiness. We may remember the Russian
tradition of the holy fool, saints who feigned craziness so that they
would not be admired. A bit extreme, but the point is well made.
We don't have to parade our virtues; if they are real they will
manifest themselves independent of our efforts at public relations.

Saint Joseph is a good example of "republican virtue," as he is presented in the infancy narratives. A good and faithful servant, a hardworking man who responded to the call, did what was asked of him, and then quietly slipped into the background. (March 19, 2012.)

> *Loving Father, help us to be untiring in doing good, according to the example of your Son. Open our eyes to see the needs that are all around us, and open our hearts to reach out to the needy in ways that are both self-forgetful and effective. We ask this through Christ our Lord. Amen.*

October 1 ✠ *Resistance*

Saint Paul makes the point that no external force can be a barrier between us and God; troubles, persecutions, principalities, and powers are all incapable of coming between us and God's mercy. They are all external influences.

The gospels confirm what our own experience makes us suspect, that what interferes with our relationship with God is not external but internal. It is our failure to respond to the call of God that serves as a barrier between us. God, of course, remains unchanged. We, however, are affected by the manner in which we give or refuse our consent to what God is asking of us.

What begins with reluctance soon moves into resistance and, if we are not careful, develops into rebellion. What was indifference at the beginning eventually develops into overt hostility. This is the tragedy relayed in the gospels. In the fullness of time, God so loved the world that he sent his only Son; he came unto his own but his own received him not. What began as indifference developed into a hostility that shouted out for his crucifixion. We may well puzzle about what it was in Jesus' teaching that caused such a storm of hatred that led to his horrifying death.

Whatever the immediate trigger to the demand for execution, I think that the beginning of the process must be seen as indifference, as nonacceptance, as a reluctance to be disturbed or challenged. Once a journey down this road began, ever stronger arguments had to be raised to support the choice until, eventually, the unthinkable becomes an option.

This slow erosion of integrity is a process from which none of us is immune. Once we begin to resist the truth in one small area, there is a tendency for the scope of resistance to be widened. The voice of conscience is muted, and our reason industriously manufactures a rationale for our conduct.

When we hear of genocidal actions in other times and other places, we think that we could not possibly allow ourselves to be implicated in them. Yet those involved were initially no worse than us. But one day a door opened before them, and they chose to pass through it. And without any alarm bells sounding, they went down that path and, in the process of persecuting others, destroyed themselves.

Rebellion is dramatic, but resistance is far subtler; at the heart of both is an unresponsiveness to conscience and an insensibility to the evidence that is staring in our faces. (October 29, 2009.)

Loving Father, open our hearts to receive your Word with respect and gratitude. Give us the humility to be guided by our conscience and the strength to continue the journey even when the road is rough. We make this prayer through Christ our Lord. Amen.

October 2   ✠   *Restoration*

In the Dark Ages before football, people used to entertain themselves by talking about theology. Vehemently. Like football talk, it was a binary process with no effort expended in reaching any accommodation with the opposing viewpoint. It was all or nothing: the losers were excommunicated, declared "anathema," cursed beyond redemption. To a simple soul like myself, it often seems that "orthodoxy" was more a matter of having the right politics than any special expertise in theology.

About three hundred years after his death, Origen of Alexandria was declared anathema by the Synod of Constantinople for his teaching on *apocatastasis*. Although it is used in Acts 3:21, this difficult term usually refers to a theory that the damned will be restored to God's favor at the end of time; in which case, their punishment is not everlasting. Even if we accept that such teaching is heretical, it is important to note that at the heart of every doctrine labeled as heresy there is a kernel of truth.

The so-called heretics argued that from God's standpoint, every divine action in the world of space and time has been directed to filling heaven. The cosmos exists precisely for the purpose of making sure that there are no empty places at the heavenly banquet. To teach that even some of the noble creatures whom God has created are languishing in eternal darkness is an affront to the merciful designs of the Creator. It is to infer that either God's wisdom was defective in creating them, or that God's power is defective in being unable to release them from torment, or that God's love is defective in not caring about their unspeakable suffering.

What would the Good Shepherd say to this? He left the ninety-nine in the desert to seek the lost sheep and restored it to the flock. I heard recently that at a Mother's Day dinner it was the family member who was absent who most occupied the minds of those present. The unspoken word often outweighs overt conversation. Can the saints truly experience unalloyed happiness if I am excluded? Is the love of Christ so impotent? Is heaven for some and hell for others?

Am I a heretic? Maybe. But if I am, it is because I take seriously the statement in the First Epistle to Timothy that it is God's will that all people be saved and come to the knowledge of the truth. Working out the mathematics of who will be saved and who will be damned is beyond me. But I believe that any solution that places limits on the boundless mercy of God must be wrong. "Our hearts may condemn us, but God is greater than our hearts. For God knows the whole story." (May 6, 2001.)

Merciful God, restorer and lover of innocence, look with pity on your sinful people. Help us to overcome our inherent weakness, and free us from the bonds of bad habit so that we may serve you in holiness and justice all the days of our life. We ask this through Jesus Christ our Lord. Amen.

October 3   ✠   **Resurrection**

The acid test of our faith is whether we believe in resurrection; in the first place, the resurrection of Christ, but also our own resurrection into eternal life. If asked, most of us would respond in a way similar to Martha's response when Jesus asked her the question just before he raised Lazarus. When Jesus asked, "Do you believe this?" she responded with a string of familiar formulae that attempted to conceal a lingering doubt. "The lady doth protest too much, methinks."

Cardinal Newman distinguished two kinds of assent: a notional assent and a real assent. A notional assent indicates merely that we do not consciously disbelieve something and, for the time being, are prepared to act as if it were true. A real assent, on the other hand, demands that what we believe has an integral part in our thinking and acting. A real assent is upbeat; it generates confidence, trust, optimism, and the like; it is not bedeviled by hesitancy.

We need to avoid the trap of reducing our Christian discipleship to mere morality or metaphysics. Christianity is more concerned with living than with thinking or acting. If we have a real faith in resurrection, then our evaluation of what happens in this life is necessarily modified. Perhaps we will learn to say with Saint Paul, "The slight momentary afflictions are preparing for us an eternal weight of glory." Believing in the resurrection may not lessen the pain, but it gives us the hope that there is something beyond the pain.

The basis of our faith in the resurrection is an experience of the immediacy of the spiritual world. We are more likely to believe that there is more to reality than meets the eye if we have been moved by something outside our normal range of experience. If something deep within us has been stirred into life. If grace has shot its laser beam into our center and called forth a joyous assent. The touch of God creates in us the realization that there is more to human life than this world dreams of. "Eye has not seen, nor ear heard, nor has it risen in the human heart to conceive, what God has prepared for those who love him." (July 17, 2014.)

> *Loving and all-powerful Father, you raised your Son from the dead, and you call us to follow him through death to eternal life. Strengthen our faith, support our hope, and inflame our love, so that we may go forward in boldness to the future you have prepared. And we ask this in the name of Jesus our Lord. Amen.*

October 4 ✠ *Revelation*

Jesus is presented in the gospels as something of a superhero: he goes about driving out demons, curing the sick, raising the dead, and walking on water, all the while teaching wisdom and welcoming strangers, the marginalized, the alienated, and those considered untouchable. In the well-known scene at Caesarea Philippi he commissions Simon Peter to continue this work.

This was surely a case of sending a boy to do a man's job. Peter was poorly equipped for the task. According to the Acts of the Apostles, he was illiterate. He seems to have been unable to comprehend the vast vision of Saint Paul. His character, as attested in the gospels, was weak, intemperate, and inconsistent.

It is not natural talent that qualifies Peter to continue Christ's work, and not his morality. What recommended him was the fact that he was open to receive a revelation from the Father and to act upon it. Elsewhere in the gospels Jesus exults in joy at the fact that the Father reveals the mysteries of the kingdom not to the wise and prudent, but to little ones. Those who, like Peter, do not belong to the great ones of the earth. As Jesus said elsewhere with obvious reference to the Pharisees, "That which is highly esteemed by human beings is an abomination to God."

Peter has a role in the dissemination of the Good News of the kingdom because he is in contact with the spiritual world. The mandate he receives is not a personal authority to be exercised at whim but an emptiness, an openness that leaves room for inspiration from above. In the Fourth Gospel Jesus often claims that the source of his authoritative teaching and of the signs he performed was his union with the Father. Jesus was the unimpeded channel by which more abundant life was given to us.

As with Peter, as with the other disciples to whom a similar mandate was given, so with us. We will do the work of God and further the kingdom to the extent that we open ourselves to the revelation reserved for little ones. (August 27, 2017.)

Heavenly Father, we thank you for revealing Christ your Son to us. Help us to receive this message with meekness and to allow it to shape our lives into the likeness of Christ. We ask this in the name of Jesus the Lord. Amen.

October 5   ✠   **Risk**

One of the things we may notice as we get older is that we become more risk-averse. We rely on our fund of knowledge and experience to deal with most situations that come our way. We are a little bit hesitant to try untested strategies because we can never be quite sure that they will produce the results we want. And then we wonder why our life seems to be getting stale.

The parable of the Talents is a reminder that the gifts of God are given to be used. They are not for the adornment of our self-image or for private entertainment; they are given to advance the coming of God's kingdom and to provide some common benefit. Most of us have talents that remain hidden. Shamefully so. Good health, material, mental, or emotional resources, strength of arm or character, together with all the various skills and capacities are given by God not to keep but to use. Not to bury but to invest. Not to hide under the bed but to shine forth from the mountaintop. To be shared with those who have less. To make the world a better place. Having talents places us under a serious obligation to use them.

It is hard to give due weight to sins of omission because usually we are guilty of them because the challenges they involve go unnoticed. We are busy doing something else, and they pass beneath our radar. This means that we have to make time to be proactive in our assessment of what good we might accomplish in our limited sphere of influence. Sins of omission are usually not so dramatic that they hit the headlines, but cumulatively they cause much damage. Remember the saying, "It is sufficient for evil to prosper that good people do nothing."

Like the wretch in the parable of the Talents, we are often fearful of the risks of pursuing imaginative courses of action. We are scared of making mistakes, forgetful that the one who never made a mistake never made anything. We dread criticism. We don't want to stand out from the crowd, not adverting to the fact that being middle-of-the-road is another word for mediocrity.

Our faith should embolden us, partly by opening our eyes to the needs around us and to the urgency of the call to do something. As Jesus said, "It is God's plan that I do the works of the One who sent me while it is yet day. For the night comes when no one can work." Last time I looked it was still day, so we still have time to act before the darkness looms. (November 18, 1984.)

Lord Jesus Christ, you call us all to work in your vineyard and to bring all people to salvation and the knowledge of the truth. Give us the energy to advance your kingdom as best we can, and instill in us the confidence that will not allow us to become discouraged. For you are our Lord for ever and ever. Amen.

October 6   ✠   *Road*

In 1987, after a fortnight spent visiting the ruins of twelfth-century Cistercian monasteries in Britain, I decided to take a cross-country route to Manchester Airport. With a road atlas on the seat beside me I tried to negotiate the twists, turns, and roundabouts as best I could, but I had no idea of where I really was. Being England, there was no sun from which to take guidance. Meanwhile, I was driving through endless farmlands with cows looking up at me in surprise as I sped past. I was on a middle-level road when, suddenly, a sign appeared in the sky. Well, not in the sky—on a post. It was a sign for the airport. Relief flooded me. Although I had another thirty miles to travel, I felt safe. I was on the right road.

Jesus tells us that he is the "way." The Greek word is more ordinarily translated "road." Far less abstract. All we have to do to arrive safely is to find the road that leads to our destination, stay on it, and keep driving. Well, Jesus is the road to eternal life. Remain with him (as a branch remains on the stock), and everything will be fine. Christ is our road; relax, do not be anxious. Even though, at the moment, you seem to be traveling through unfamiliar territory that does not seem to be leading you to where you want to go, relax. Remain on the road.

In a sense, once we are on the right road we have already arrived at our destination. As Jesus said, "Those who see me see the Father." We rejoice in the anticipation of our arrival, even though there is still a hard slog ahead.

A road is for traveling; there is no point in being on the road if we are standing still. I have to keep following the road, and that means two things. Firstly, I make Christ my traveling companion in all the changes and challenges that life brings me. Second, as we move together, I try to become more Christlike. Then I am no longer just on the road, I also am the road; and that helps others to find their eternal home. (May 22, 2011.)

Lord Jesus Christ, you are the road that leads to eternal life; you are the truth that guides us on our journey; you are the life that gives us energy to continue our pilgrimage. We thank you and praise you for ever and ever. Amen.

October 7 ✝ **Runaway Train**

The kingdom of heaven is like a runaway train. It is unstoppable. We use this imagery for situations in which something increases or develops very quickly and cannot be controlled. The kingdom of God is not a tentative enterprise; it is coming whether we like it or not.

The primitive version of the parable of the Sower in Mark's gospel makes the point clearly. In the process of sowing, three seeds are lost. Only three. One falls on the path, another on rocks, and a third among briars. The rest fall on good soil where they await the season for sprouting. The seed does not have to do anything; it simply sits in the soil and lets natural processes take effect. As another parable in Mark's gospel notes, growth occurs *automatically*—that is the Greek word the gospel uses. The eventual harvest is not only inevitable, it is superabundant. As the grain of mustard demonstrates, size doesn't matter when God is at work.

This truth was evident to Saint Paul, who exclaimed, "I planted. Apollos watered. But it is God who gave the increase." He took no pride in the spread of the Gospel; this was due to the intrinsic power and authority of the Good News. "It is not a matter of the one who runs or the one who works. It is God showing mercy."

The word of God proclaimed by Jesus has an authority that ultimately cannot be resisted. It causes reverberations in the human heart, even though there is often a time delay before these are recognized or acted upon. This means that it is incumbent on believers to be tireless in proclaiming the Good News, by word and example, in season and out of season. This remains true even when the proclamation seems unwelcome or provokes persecution. Within us the obligation of responding to the word is irresistible: like Jeremiah or Saint Paul, we may be led to exclaim, "Woe is me if I do not preach the Gospel!"

God's work continues. It is unstoppable. The kingdom is indeed like a runaway train bringing to all people the gifts that

Christ came to give: righteousness, peace, and joy in the Holy Spirit. (July 16, 2017.)

> *Loving Father, the Word that goes forth from your mouth does not return to you empty-handed. Help us to welcome this word with open hearts. Give us boldness to be fearless in making it known to all people. We ask this in the name of Jesus the Lord. Amen.*

October 8 ✝ *Safety Net*

Most of us are used to working with a safety net. We make some provision for situations to change or for things to go wrong. Then we won't be caught resourceless. We were a bit surprised when Jesus sent his untried disciples off on a mission of evangelization without taking precautions. It is as though he was saying to them, "You cannot do God's work if you insist on having a safety net."

We find this challenge an affront to our cherished human prudence. We much prefer the parables Jesus offered about calculating the odds before building a tower or going to war. To divest ourselves of the extra baggage we carry "just in case" is unthinkable. On this basis, I can imagine that Jesus might say to us, as he said to Simon Peter, "Your way of thinking is human and not divine."

So, the Gospel not only obliges us to a code of behavior that seems beyond our reach, but also asks us to let go of our human prudence and entrust everything to Providence. It is as though Jesus were continually saying to us, "Cast into the deep," or calling us, as he called Peter, to walk across the water.

Such apparent recklessness is not foolhardy, but is grounded on a solid trust in God's ways of dealing with us. By accepting the challenge, we transcend the limits imposed on us by all kinds of fear. We move to a different level of existence, in which constraining boundaries are ignored. By overriding our timidity we move into a zone of greater freedom; we feel more fully alive.

Think of the kind of trust exercised by skilled acrobats, hurling themselves into space and relying on the split-second timing of their partners to catch them—without a safety net. There is risk involved, but it is a calculated risk, based on an assessment of their catcher's abilities. So, is it risky to trust God, to respond to a summons, to accept a vocation, to take up a challenge? What happens if it goes sour? What happens if I have got it all wrong? Yes, there is a risk from the human side. But with God there is no deviation from what has been promised.

The Acts of the Apostles tells us that it was the Holy Spirit who endowed the apostles with the gift of boldness, delivering them from the secure stagnation of immovable complacency and sending them off to convert a hostile world. Maybe we should hope for that same gift, drawing us to participate in the adventure of God's kingdom—even though a safety net is not part of the bargain. (July 16, 2000.)

> *Lord Jesus Christ, you call us to go forth and proclaim the kingdom. Give us the courage to fearlessly step out from our familiar territory and expand our horizons. Inspire us with the confidence that your providence is guiding us and sustaining us in the work of bringing all people to salvation and to the knowledge of the truth. For you are our Lord for ever and ever. Amen.*

October 9 ✠ Salt

When Jesus tells his disciples that they are the "salt of the earth," the phrase usually passes without our noticing what a curious expression it is. What does it mean to be the "salt of the earth?"

We know that part of the quality of salt is to be unassuming. No normal person wants the flavor of salt to dominate their meal. The purpose of adding salt is not to superadd flavor, but to bring out the natural and inherent taste that is in the food. It is like cleaning a window so that you can look on the scenery with greater clarity. You don't want to see the window; you want to see the view. Salt encourages the latent flavor to come forth and delight us. But it is strictly a backroom operation; salt does its work and retires. That is why some of the classiest restaurants do not have salt on the table and, if a diner were to ask for some, they would risk a tirade from the chef.

The followers of Jesus are like salt because the religion they practice is meant to bring out the inherent, God-given qualities of life. It enhances fully human existence; it is not some kind of substitute for it. Christianity is meant to serve, not to tyrannize. This is a simple enough proposition, but somehow it often seems forgotten. Its modest role on the sidelines of society is left aside in an attempt to become the playground bully.

Nor should we worry that the church is becoming more like the "little flock" of which Jesus spoke. If it really lives up to the challenges posed by the gospels, it may well seem to be too hard for the many people who now populate the ecclesial margins. There is no reason to drop standards in an effort to accommodate the uncommitted. We should remember that Abram was able to bargain with God that Sodom would be saved if ten righteous persons could be found in it. As with salt, a small number of fervent souls is sufficient to change the quality of the whole.

Our task as believers is to maintain our saltiness; not to let ourselves succumb to the universal dumbing down of anything precious, but to glory in the distinctiveness of our vocation as followers of Jesus, seeing it as our way of contributing to the whole mass of humanity by somehow bringing to the fore its inherent truth and goodness. (June 8, 2010.)

> *Lord Jesus Christ, in calling us to follow you, you are offering us an opportunity to share in your mission of bringing the world to salvation. Help us to keep faith with you through the integrity of our lives and by the openness by which we reach out to others. For you are our Lord for ever and ever. Amen.*

October 10   ✠   *Salvation*

After Jesus' uncompromising demand that the rich man sell all his goods in order to become a disciple, the disciples wondered among themselves, "Who can be saved?" It sounds like other "Who can" questions that are usually rhetorical. Who can lose weight? Who can run a marathon? Who can learn a foreign language? The anticipated answer is "I can't."

To which our bridling response is often, like Barack Obama, "Yes we can." When I was a child, my mother used to insist that there was no such word as *can't*. We belong to a culture that believes, rather deludedly, that everything is possible to those who try.

In this case such optimism does not apply. The question is badly formulated. "Who can be saved?" Salvation is not an action that we do, like running a marathon. Salvation is a matter of receiving something from someone else. The form of the verb *to be saved* is passive, not active. Salvation depends on the saver (or Savior) and not on the saved. God is the agent of salvation; it is what God does to us and for us because nothing is impossible with God.

On one occasion, I was at the beach and I saw a man floundering in the surf. The lifesavers (as we call them in Australia) fetched him out and deposited him on the beach like a stranded whale, whereat he spewed forth a vast amount of water and lay there panting. After a few minutes he got up, dusted the sand off his chest, and walked straight back into the surf, crying out over his shoulder, "I was all right, damn you."

The point of the story is that we don't appreciate being saved. It is a humiliation. The glory goes to the one who saves us; being saved makes us look like dummies. It is not so hard to be saved. All it takes is the capacity to get our lives into an unredeemable mess. Then salvation is possible. Of course, we furiously resist, but God is stronger than we are and, with a mighty arm and an outstretched hand, knocks us out and carries us off into safety. (February 27, 2012.)

Lord God, with you nothing is impossible. Break down our resistance to your love and lead us forth into the freedom that belongs to your children. We ask this in the name of Jesus our Lord. Amen.

October 11   ✠   *Sartre*

Jean-Paul Sartre is known for his saying "Hell is other people," often interpreted far beyond the writer's intent. I would like to offer two alternative riffs on this saying: "Without God, other people are hell" and "With God, other people are heaven." The sentiment Sartre expressed points to the ultimate destination at which atheism eventually arrives. A world without God is not heaven; it is closer to hell. Aleksandr Solzhenitsyn, after reviewing all the horrors committed in the twentieth century, summarized his judgment in the words of a Russian folk saying, "Men have forgotten God. That's why all this has happened."

This is not to say that believers never commit atrocities, nor that unbelievers are never capable of finding happiness together. It is to affirm that life becomes impoverished when God is banished, despite fevered protestations of the contrary. To deny God involves denying that part of humanity which comes alive only when touched by God. It is largely to eliminate the spiritual and contemplative dimension of human life and to operate out of a very diminished humanity. There are good atheists and bad believers, but it is easier to be good if you have faith in God. I have often wondered whether people who stop coming to church regularly, thereafter consider themselves better people for it. Some insist that it has made no difference to their lives, but I wonder what others who know them would say.

In the 1970s many tried to establish alternative communities on a purely secular basis. Almost none of them survived. The sociologist who founded the nearby Moora community said, in retrospect, that if he were doing it again, he would set up a religious community, so that there would be a vision that transcended the people who constituted it. Without God, other people can be hell.

In the Nicene Creed we profess our faith in the "communion of saints." This means that we affirm our belonging to the universal assembly of God's people. In a sense, we are saying that we are already in heaven—except we don't realize it fully. In the presence of God, other people are heaven. No doubt this is why medieval monks spoke of the monastery as a "cloistral paradise." Insofar as our lives are lived in the presence of God, other people become for us a source of strength, consolation, and delight. That is a long way from hell. (November 1, 2002.)

> *Lord God, source and origin of all that is good, help us to live together as members of your family, caring for one another, bearing one another's burdens, making peace before the sun sets, and learning to grow in love. We ask this through Christ our Lord. Amen.*

October 12 ✠ *Scandal*

How distressing it is to live at a time when the scandal of sexual abuse within the Catholic Church has become public knowledge. Each of us would, no doubt, choose different words to describe our reaction: confusion, hurt, shame, anger, a sense of betrayal, broken trust, disenchantment, sadness. Or all of the above. We are shocked at the extent of sexual misconduct, especially with underage persons, at the failure to deal with it resolutely, at the dishonesty involved in covering it up going all the way to the top, and at the priority given to saving money over the pastoral care due to those broken by the crimes.

First of all, we have to roll with the punches and accept that there is truth in the allegations. The media coverage and public outrage are not merely the result of some anti-church conspiracy. The crimes happened. We may not permit ourselves the luxury of denial.

Secondly, we should thank God for these revelations. Society has played a prophetic role in our regard, forcing us to take measures to bring such crimes to an end, to repair our broken structures, and to engage in corporate repentance and reparation.

Thirdly, we, as members of the church, need to do whatever lies in our competence to improve matters; to try to make the church a safer and more transparent place. And we must insist that our leaders do better.

Fourthly, perhaps we need to change our image of the church, in the direction indicated both by the gospels and by Vatican II. Not as a wealthy political power broker, but as a community of believers who are, in humility and poverty, committed to doing good and minimizing evil.

Fifthly, the challenge involved in cleansing the church involves a reemphasis on spiritual activities and, especially, a recommitment to prayer and intercession—not least on behalf of those who have been the victims of past evil. This summons to prayer includes all us. If we prayed more, perhaps the world would be a better and a safer place. (June 16, 2002.)

> *God, all-powerful and all-merciful, cleanse your church of all that is an affront to your goodness and does harm to people. Teach us to lament the past and mend our ways. Help us to become known for innocence and honesty and kindness. We ask this through Christ our Lord. Amen.*

October 13 ✠ *Schism*

In 1997, in the course of filming *Air Force One*, the actor Harrison Ford was permitted to spend a day in the Clinton White House as a fly on the wall, to observe how a president performs his task. His conclusion was that the president acts normally, but you can tell who is the boss by the way the people around him acted.

The same rule applies to our understanding of Jesus. We can get some sense of who he was by the impact he had on those around him. All the gospels tell us that the miracles wrought by Jesus often provoked wonder and awe and sometimes raised questions in the minds of those who observed them. The Fourth Gospel, written some sixty years after the events, notes that the actions of Jesus caused a division or schism among the people. Some were positively impressed, and some were antagonized.

Jesus himself declared that he had come to bring not peace but a sword of division, liable to tear families and nations apart. "It is for judgment that I have come into the world: to restore sight to the blind and to make blind those who see." The coming of Jesus provoked a crisis. There was no more chance of sitting on the fence and maintaining a noncommittal attitude to what was taking place. A decision had to be made. The double-minded had to make a choice. "He came unto his own and his own received him not." "This is the judgment: the light came into the world and people preferred darkness to light."

The coming of Jesus shone a spotlight on his contemporaries: their inner nature is revealed by the ways in which they responded to his presence. It is the same for us. In some way or other, the light has shone in our hearts and we have caught a glimpse of the spiritual world. And so we are plunged into a quandary. How we respond to that little illumination is an indicator of who and what we are. We are defined by how we respond to the outshining of light. Does it lead to faith, healing, and commitment? Or are we confined ever more tightly within our own little world of self, stubborn, hard of heart, and unwilling to change? We can't continue to sit on the fence. The hour of decision has arrived. (March 26, 2017.)

Lord Jesus Christ, you are the light that has shone in our darkness. Help us to respond positively to your presence in our lives so that, following you, we will not walk in darkness but have the light of life. For you are our Lord, for ever and ever. Amen.

October 14   ✠   *Seasons*

To a large extent our perceptions of our immediate environment are shaped by our instinctive understanding of seasonal variation. What would be considered an unseasonably warm day in winter would be perceived as a cool day in the height of summer. The arrival and departure of the seasons means that our experience of particular realities changes according to the season.

As the famous reading from the third chapter of Ecclesiastes reminds us, there is a season for everything under the sun. This is more than mere poetry; it is reality, and we had better get used to it. Everything changes. For us to keep growing we need to have something of an athletic disposition; we need to keep adapting to the changing world around us. It is easy to drown in nostalgia and spend our time lamenting the demise of the past. The past has passed, and we have to deal with the present.

It has been observed that most of the great heresies in the church have been conservative heresies. Wild-eyed revolutionaries never get much traction for their ideas, and any movement they start barely lasts their lifetime. On the other hand, the status quo has boundless sources of inertia; it is able to refuse the challenge of the new simply by insisting on the solutions proposed by a previous generation. One does not have to be very creative to stop things happening, just obstinate. By way of response, all of us need to insist that while being faithful to its tradition, the church is also called to respond to the signs of the times.

A similar situation can arise in individual lives; perhaps we know persons who simply cannot deal with unsolicited change. They keep doing the things that used to work, despite the increasing heaviness they experience in doing so and the lack of satisfactory results. Like Jerusalem of old, they failed to notice the time of their visitation.

There are seasons in our life. What was appropriate in youth may not be suitable for mellower years. If we are wise, we will not allow ourselves to adhere to attitudes and practices that have passed their use-by date. The providence of God continues to intervene in our lives, and willingly responding to its changing demands will fill us with energy and happiness. On the other hand if, like Howard Hughes, we immure ourselves in our penthouse to ensure that nothing around us changes, we will be dead long before our heart stops beating. (September 26, 2014.)

Lord God, gracious governor of all times and seasons, help us to respond to your action in our lives. Help us to recognize your hand in all that happens and teach us to understand that nothing can separate us from your love. We ask this through Christ our Lord. Amen.

October 15 ✛ *See More*

At a certain point to the north of Melbourne, the road ends in a T-junction. A choice has to be made whether to turn left or right. In the one direction is Seymour, in the other Kilmore. The decision that confronts us here mirrors one that we may face often in our lives: to see more or to kill more—to try to reach a deeper understanding of a situation or to reject, despise, or inflict violence on another. To see more is to kill less.

So much of our vocation as followers of Jesus involves seeing more than meets the eye. The portrayal of the Final Judgment in Matthew 25 narrates that those who are being judged were asking the puzzled question, "When did we see you?" It seems that the main quality that separates the sheep from the goats is their willingness to look beyond the obvious to see what is hidden beneath the surface. When we see the full picture, we tend to respond differently. The Gospel invites us to see Christ in multiple disguises.

It is the eye of faith that enables us to penetrate the layers of earth under which the treasure is hidden. It enables us to appreciate the true value of the pearl of great price. This means that we tend to evaluate issues according to standards that are different from those of secular society. The gift of faith is not merely believing certain truths; it is a subtle initiation into higher modes of prudence and discernment and wisdom. It gradually brings about a change in the way we view life and in how we live it.

Our faith-fueled perceptiveness derives from our easy familiarity with the spiritual world; it comes from our daily contact with God in prayer. When prayer is part of our life, it becomes easier to sense the hand of God in what otherwise may seem to be meaningless happenings. Stop praying, and life begins to fall apart. (July 25, 1999.)

*Loving Father, open the eyes of our heart to see beyond and
beneath ordinary things. Help us to perceive your presence
in our brothers and sisters who cry out to us in their need.
Strengthen our wills to seek the realities that surpass human
understanding. We ask this through Jesus Christ our Lord.
Amen.*

October 16 ✠ *Self-Doubt*

People are sometimes surprised when I recommend taking regular
doses of self-doubt. In our feel-good culture, anything that compromises our sense of self-worth is avoided. We want people to
have a positive opinion about themselves, seeing it as the springboard from which laudable actions stem. Yet self-approval that
is dependent on not looking too closely at our attitudes and
behavior is on very shaky ground. Refusing to examine all the
data about ourselves seems already to indicate our fear that the
outcome of the investigation will not be to our liking. Our self-
acceptance is all a sham.

There is a world of difference between the two men who went
to pray in the temple. The Pharisee was in full spate of self-
congratulation concerning his acts of righteousness. The tax collector was conscious only of the mess he had made of his life.
Both stand before God. The tax collector stands in truth. The
Pharisee is deluded. The prayer of the Pharisee went no further
than himself. The tax collector's cry for mercy effected a full
repair of his relationship with God. Wouldn't it be an act of
charity if we could tap the Pharisee on the shoulder and give him
a few question marks to sprinkle on his litany of self-approved
virtues? A little self-doubt would go a long way.

There are probably people around who consider that we or I
could do with a bit of self-doubt. They notice that we are far too
sure of ourselves, and, as a result, we overlook some areas of our
life that cry out for attention. The businessperson who neglects
their family, the policeman who takes bribes, the politician who

indiscriminately toes the party line—don't they all maintain a façade of righteousness that they themselves soon begin to accept as true? Some may well believe that they are victims to the point that their actions are exempt from scrutiny and, so, never confront their own possible complicity. Wouldn't it be a kindness to hold up a mirror and ask them to look more closely? Wouldn't a little hesitation be salutary for domineering bosses who take for granted that their cowed workers enjoy being bullied?

I can think of lots of others who would profit from self-doubt. That probably indicates that a little of the same would do me no harm as well. If I can get to the point of admitting my limitations and my failures to myself and to God, then, as the tax collector found out, it may have positive consequences in all areas of my life. (March 3, 2015.)

> *God of truth, the hearts of all people are naked and unveiled in your sight. Help us to stand before you in honesty, admitting our failures and asking for mercy. Help us also to avoid holding others to standards that we ourselves cannot meet. We ask this in the name of Jesus our Lord. Amen.*

October 17 ✠ *Separation*

In the Old Testament, as also among the rabbis and at Qumran, holiness was usually understood as expressed by separation from ordinary, everyday, use. The vessels that were used in the sanctuary could not also be devoted to profane use. The sanctuary itself, the holy of holies, was concealed from public view by a veil. Israel was considered a holy nation because it stood apart from the pagan peoples surrounding it. The priests and Levites were distinct from the other tribes. There was much fuss about clean and unclean foods and vessels, and various rites of purification were regarded as obligatory. The whole culture of Old Testament religion was permeated by the idea of holiness as separation from what was profane. Even God's act of creation is described in the first chapter of Genesis as an act of separation between light and darkness, and between upper waters and lower waters, and boundaries and walls were set in place to maintain the division.

To be inside the dividing wall was to be good. What was outside was not worthy of consideration. The peoples who did not belong to the holy people were regarded as unholy. They could be plundered, enslaved, and killed without scruple. Wiping them off the face of the earth was considered as doing a service to God. The ultimate expression of this attitude was the act of placing a city or a people "under the ban." This involved a sacred obligation to completely eliminate those so cursed, without exception. To break the ban and to try and save something from utter destruction was a criminal offense before God.

The Greek word for what does not belong to the sphere of the sacred was *koinos*; it was common or profane. It is interesting that one of the ideals for holiness that we find in the New Testament is *koinonia*: commonness, communion, community. The task of the church is seen as the propagation of this communion far and wide. It is precisely its mission to break down the walls of separation and extend this communion until it reaches the ends of the earth and the end of the ages. The missionary task of the church is one of ingathering so that, eventually, all may come to salvation and to the knowledge of the truth, so that they may be of one heart and one mind. The walls of separation are to be definitively dismantled. (May 22, 2007.)

> *Creator God, you have made us to be one people, bearing your image and stamped with your likeness. Break down the walls of division that we have built, and open our hearts and our homes to offer hospitality to all, after the manner of your Son, who welcomed even those whom others held at a distance. We ask this in the name of Jesus Christ our Lord. Amen.*

October 18 ✝ *Service*

The teaching of Jesus about the exercise of authority is unambiguous. It is to be a matter not of domination but of service.

This is a very challenging idea, since our understanding of how authority works is shaped by the secular environment in which we have been reared. The person in authority is, first of all, the boss. The rest of us are obliged to do what the boss wants, in small matters as well as in those that are more important. As a result, bosses get what they want and enjoy high status; we do what we are told and keep to our proper place.

It is very easy to superimpose the rhetoric of service on this secular model of authority. In part, this is because most of us have never had servants. And we certainly haven't had slaves over whom we exercise the power of life and death. And so, those in authority redefine *service* in a manner that suits their preferred style of acting. For the rest of us, it is very hard to see that servants should signify their status by gold and jewelry and sumptuous garments—to say nothing of palaces and limousines. Such symbols of worldly status are in stark opposition to the precepts of the Gospel.

I would have thought that the ideal servant would be one who is generous and self-forgetful in giving; humble and gracious in receiving. A servant is one who is ready to stand on the side, awaiting a summons to serve. A first-class server is attentive, watching and listening, ready to act when someone is in need of their help. Helping because of others' need, not because of their own need to do so or to be seen to do so.

The servant-disciple is not like the Pharisee who puts loads on others' backs and does not lift a finger to help them. I am truly a servant if by my intervention the lives of others are made easier. As a result of my action, the other should walk away happier.

Sometimes the service that needs to be rendered is the offering of advice or correction. My first abbot used to insist that this will work only if persons in authority have a solid history of genuine concern for the welfare of the other. A word to the wise suggesting a change will probably find a welcome only if, over time, it has been preceded by ten words of affirmation and encouragement and love. (February 19, 2008.)

Lord Jesus Christ, you came not to be served but to serve and to give your life as a ransom for many. Help us to be infused by your spirit of humility and love so that we place ourselves and our resources at the service of all who need our help. For you are our Lord for ever and ever. Amen.

October 19 ✠ *Shame*

In the immediate aftermath of the liberation of France at the end of World War II, in a time that should have been euphoric, women who had been forced into collaboration were publicly shamed. Led through the streets with shaven heads, they were reviled and spat upon. This notwithstanding the fact that few in the jeering crowd had, in those very difficult times, conducted themselves in a manner beyond reproach.

It is wonderful to have sinners with whom we can compare ourselves favorably. This is why tabloid newspapers and cheap journalism thrive on exposing the sins of others—especially the failings of those who seem richer, more powerful, or more popular than their readers. In some way, condemning others is a means of avoiding confrontation with our own darkness.

When confronted with the woman caught in adultery, Jesus does not approve or condone her actions; he bypasses the question of her guilt with the simple admonition, "Do not condemn." I must keep remembering that there is One who judges and it is not I. The measure I use on others is the same as that which will be applied to me.

There is an ancient story about a monk found guilty of fornication. The following Sunday the priest revealed his sin and excommunicated him, declaring, "There is no place in this church for sinners." As the poor monk shuffled out, a holy and wise senior rose to his feet and followed him, muttering, "If there is no place for sinners, there is no place for me."

The reason we deny our common humanity and want to put others to shame is that we think that by shaming them we exculpate ourselves. We would do much better to concentrate on examining our own consciences and, with a view to obtaining mercy for our own transgressions, embark on a course of showing mercy to others in thought, and word, and deed. If we slow down our precipitate urge to judge others, we may begin to see things differently. It often happens that the merciful eye perceives the fuller truth of the situation that is hidden from those who rush to hasty condemnations. (April 1, 2001.)

> *Merciful Lord, you alone are holy. Help us to become so aware of our own need for mercy that we freely offer it to others. Teach us to be slow to judge others and even slower to condemn, knowing that all of us alike will soon stand before the judgment seat of God. For you are our Lord for ever and ever. Amen.*

October 20 ✠ *Shepherds*

Shepherds and sheep have an enviable reputation in the Bible. Sheep are seen as mild animals, and lambs are proposed as spotless white symbols of innocence. Shepherds, for their part, are wise, diligent, and caring. The reality is somewhat different. Sheep are often stupid. In Jesus' time, shepherds were often viewed with suspicion at the local level because their nomadic ways made them uncontrollable; they were at best nuisances, at worst criminals.

We find that Jesus was among those who idealized shepherds; it is clear that no real shepherd would leave the remainder of the flock unprotected while he went off in search of the stupid stray. It is not a commercially viable proposition to risk the whole flock for a single sheep. Furthermore, even if we accept the image, we have to note that carrying the strayed sheep back to the flock on his own shoulders was not a sign of affection: it was the most efficient way of rejoining the flock. Jesus used this impossible image to portray the extravagant and effective love that God has for all. God will seek out the lost and bring them back.

The Fourth Evangelist pushes the image further. He notes that there is a deep interpersonal connection between the shepherd and the sheep; he knows them, and they recognize and respond to his voice. Christ as shepherd is not merely one who exercises external control over the flock, but one who has a deep understanding of each of those entrusted to his care. He knew what was in their hearts—a proposition often illustrated in the stories of the Gospel tradition. Jesus leads his flock through connaturality—we follow him because he is one of us, like us in all things except sin.

But there is more—an even wilder assertion. So greatly does this shepherd care about the sheep that he is prepared to die in their place. No ordinary shepherd would willingly do this. We have passed beyond human affairs into a totally different world of values. The extravagance of divine love is such that surpasses our understanding. "Understand the love God has for us in that Christ died for us while we were still sinners." Divine love far exceeds anything we call by that name: it is proactive, unconditional, intense, and all-embracing. We can catch only glimmers of its total extent. (April 26, 2014.)

> *Loving Father, shepherd of our souls, help us to hear your voice and to recognize it as guiding us to a more abundant life. In life and in death, may we never separate ourselves from your love. We ask this in the name of Jesus our Lord. Amen.*

October 21 ✠ *Shield*

In the Psalms God is described many times as a shield. The *magen* was a circular shield carried on the left arm, leaving the right free to hold a sword. The basic idea in applying this image to God was to affirm that although we are surrounded by enemies, the Lord interposes himself between us and them to ward off any attacks that might cause us harm. There are other defensive metaphors applied to God in the Psalms. God is a stronghold, a rock, a refuge.

If the spiritual life is seen as a combat against the forces of evil—and sometimes it certainly feels like that—then we cannot rely on our own strength alone. We need a superior source of protection. We may not be willing to accept this, wanting to stand on our own two feet. In such a case, it is only when we are gravely wounded by an overpowering attack that we begin to see the need to invoke the protection of God.

Sometimes this involves a kind of foolhardiness in rejecting all other forms of self-protection. When Jesus sent the Twelve out to proclaim the kingdom, he expected them to be almost naked. No extra clothes, no money, no food, no plans. They were to rely for board and lodging on whatever the providence of God would provide. Some of the saints have interpreted this injunction literally. Most of us probably don't rise to such heights. But all of us need to be confident that the kindly providence of God will be our shield against whatever could cause us irreversible damage—physical, moral, or spiritual.

The Twelve were sent forth in an upbeat manner; when they returned, they were exuberant in describing the wonders that God had wrought through their agency. Their experience grounds a certain confidence in what Jesus later promised, that they would perform deeds even more spectacular than what he himself had accomplished.

The price of such a happy outcome is the willingness to yield control. To let things happen. Not to work according to a master plan, but to respond to the call of each moment. To perceive Providence in everyday circumstances and not to postpone action until some apocalyptic event lands on our doorstep.

If God is our shield, then we are protected. If we are protected, then we can act with boldness, confident that all things work together unto good for those who love God. (September 24, 2014.)

Lord God, you are a shield that protects all who take refuge in you. Give us boldness as we go out to proclaim the Good News of your kingdom, knowing that in all things we are the conquerors because you have loved us. We make this prayer in the name of Jesus the Lord. Amen.

October 22   ⊹   **Shortcuts**

We are all devoted to finding shortcuts in any journey we make or in any process in which we are involved. Our focus is always on arriving at our destination or getting the job finished. Time is of the essence. We do not always appreciate that moving forward at a more leisurely pace often means that we do things better or derive much more pleasure from the journey we have undertaken.

Being so fixated on finishing often means that we pay slight attention to what happens after the beginning and before the end. The long middle stage. Instead of practicing mindfulness and cherishing every moment, we rush past at high speed, failing to be moved by anything in the ever-changing landscape. We submit our environment to control by refusing to take any note of it; that way it cannot influence us, either to comfort or to challenge. It is always "Full steam ahead!"

We receive the content of our faith as a finished product of nearly twenty centuries of development. It is all neatly packaged and tied with a ribbon. We are not always aware of the conflicts and struggles that contributed to what we have received. It was only because people asked questions that answers were sought and eventually found. In a sense, the questions were more important than the answers. And not all the answers provide a response to every aspect of the questions. There are still unresolved difficulties. Perhaps we think that, in some way, we ourselves can avoid all the searching and doubting that contributed to the formulation and growth of official doctrine.

In living our faith we must expect also to go through the agonies of question and answer before we arrive at a definitive stance. It is unrealistic to expect that somehow we will be exempt from doubts, difficulties, dilemmas, and darkness, or that in some way we will be protected from compromises and backsliding. There are no shortcuts in the spiritual life. If we are to receive mercy, we must first discover our need for mercy and recognize how much we have in common with the rest of humanity—even those we esteem to be less worthy than ourselves.

Salvation is a great benefit, but we cannot be saved unless we first get our lives into a mess—or, rather, we cannot feel our need for salvation until we recognize that our lives really are a mess. There are no shortcuts. (April 18, 2004.)

Loving Father, you call us to yourself, despite our hesitancy and our many failings. Give us the courage to believe what you have promised and so to go through life confident that we are always loved by you, no matter how often we have wandered from the way you have set before us. We make this prayer in the name of Jesus our Lord. Amen.

October 23 ✠ *Silence*

There is an interesting scene in the gospels where, after the Twelve had completed their first experience of evangelization, Jesus settles them down and says, "Come away and rest a while." He calls them into the desert to be still. To get away from the tumult of activity, to recollect, to gather their thoughts and process their experience.

It is not a suggestion that we ourselves are likely to heed. Recently I have read several accounts written by brave adventurers who have put aside their electronic devices for an hour, a day, or even a week and been astonished to discover the richness of a life without incessant interruptions and noise. We have got to the point where a soundless world has practically ceased to exist, and we are the poorer for it.

The Venezuelan conductor of the Los Angeles Philharmonic, Gustavo Dudamel, insists that the silence of the audience is an essential part of an orchestral performance. It is not nothing. It adds something that is missing when the orchestra rehearses in an empty auditorium. When conducting he often reduces the volume so that those listening must strain to catch the music. The silence becomes almost audible. The audience is spellbound. This is not the silence of a stone, but a silence indicative of concentration, intensity, depth. It is like the silence to which the book of Revelation refers when it says, "There was silence in heaven for half an hour." To break that silence would be a profanation.

Silence, considered as the gift of interior recollection, is essential to Christian discipleship. Especially today, with the seemingly universal triumph of the banal and trivial. So many words, so few meanings! We need to hear the words Christ addresses to us: "Come away and rest a while. Make friends with your own inner reality. Free yourself from the tyranny of the obvious and grow in sensitivity to the unseen world of the Spirit."

Silence brings three benefits. Firstly, it makes us more aware of our inward enslavements and addictions and motivates us to free ourselves from their grasp. Secondly, by giving us an opportunity to consider, it helps us to choose the most life-giving path. Thirdly, it stirs up in us the energy to go beyond our comfort zone and venture into new territories. All of us need to recognize the value of silence and to take steps to provide ourselves with more opportunities to be quiet and still. Silence is a source of empowerment; without it we are lost. (Undated.)

Lord Jesus of Christ, Word spoken from the infinite silence of God, inflame our hearts with a desire to go deeper into the reality that you reveal. Give us the ability to sit in silence to await salvation from God, to be still and learn that God is God. For you are our Lord for ever and ever. Amen.

October 24   ✠   *Silly Sheep*

My sister Mary once said that, when she hears of the division between sheep and goats in the gospel of the Last Judgment, she would rather be a goat than a sheep. Anyone who has had close contact with ovine reality would know that sheep are not just woolly, they are downright stupid. That is why they need to be herded by dogs; they are not smart enough to cooperate with the shepherd on their own.

When Jesus described himself as a shepherd and his followers as sheep, he was not paying us a compliment. The crowds that came sheepishly to Jesus were bootless, with no idea of where they wanted to go or what they were supposed to be doing. Jesus saw this and set himself the task of instructing them. Maybe in the process of becoming more intelligent some of them might have made goats of themselves, as Simon Peter did when he tried to walk on water, but any spark of liveliness is better than remaining forever in their native dullness. Jesus did not hesitate to include stupidity among the resident vices that are a toxic presence in the human heart.

Even the disciples closest to Jesus were not immune from stupidity and recalcitrance, if we are to believe the Gospel of Mark. If we are honest, we might admit that there is something of the silly sheep in all of us. Once we recognize this, then perhaps we will be prepared to admit that we qualify for admission to the school of Christ. We need life-giving acceptance, support, guidance, discipline, and correction if we are to be kept moving along the road that leads to eternal life.

How does this work out in practice? It is simple. Don't be a goat and run off on your own. Allow yourself to accept the Lord's shepherding. Sometimes stop what you are doing. Come away into solitude. Rest. Breathe. Be conscious of the presence of Jesus. Listen to his word. Be formed and reformed according to his mind. Learn compassion with others, but also with yourself. (July 19, 2009.)

Jesus, Good Shepherd, without your guidance we will lose ourselves in the maze of life. May we welcome your word with great rejoicing and allow it to form us in your likeness so that we may come safely to the heavenly home that is prepared for us. For you are our Lord for ever and ever. Amen.

October 25   ✝   *Sin*

In our Sunday liturgy, the word *sin* seems to be used more often in the common texts than *God* or *Jesus*. This being the case, it is important that we have an accurate understanding of what the term implies. The danger is that we confuse psychology and theology. When the liturgy speaks of sin it is referring to the impaired state of our relationship with God. This is not to be identified with our feelings of guilt, failure, or low self-worth. Whether there is a basis in reality for these feelings may be a moot point, but they certainly cannot be taken as an indication of how things stand between us and God.

Saint Paul is quite blunt on this matter: "All have sinned and fallen short of God's glory." For the Christian, a sense of sin is not a matter of abasement, self-rejection, or self-hatred. Our tendency to view all issues in terms of morality makes us think that sinners are simply those who have behaved badly. But, in reality, a sense of sin is simply the result of looking in the mirror of life and saying, "I am not God." I am imperfect because I am a created being still in the process of growth. I am a sinner in that I fall short of what God intends me to become, sometimes through weakness or ignorance, but sometimes through willful resistance to God's plan. But the story has not ended yet.

Taking a developmental view of sin means that when we who may, perhaps, live relatively blameless lives profess ourselves to be sinners, we are not exaggerating our moral deficiencies, but simply affirming that we exist in a state of dependence on God's creative mercy. We find the courage to make this assertion because we have had some sort of direct experience of God's goodness and kindness and have come to the realization that although sinful behavior may distance us from God, it does not distance God from us. We are not surprised or depressed by our failures but see in them the occasion for a more complete reliance on the recuperative intervention of God. To say "I am a sinner" is simply to affirm that I depend totally on God for my ultimate salvation. (February 8, 1998.)

Loving Father, have mercy on us. We were created by you, redeemed by your Son, and sanctified by your Holy Spirit. Help us to rejoice in the gifts we have received and to look forward to their culmination in heaven. We ask this in the name of Jesus our Lord. Amen.

October 26 ✝ *Slippery Slope*

I suppose all of us, at some time or another, do something about which we feel ashamed. Eventually. If, after a passage of time, we throw off the cloak of denial and rationalization, we wonder how on earth we got ourselves into a particular situation. Though we often massage our memories to regard it as a "moment of weakness" or a "spur-of-the-moment impulse," usually this is not true. For every heinous crime there is a backstory. For every impetuous outburst there is a slow buildup of negative energies.

Just as the key element in our conversion is a change in our thinking, so the habitual content of our thinking bears a serious responsibility when we allow ourselves to be led off the right path. This is why the Desert Fathers, for example, placed such emphasis on remaining in charge of our thoughts and not allowing them to wander off at the behest of sub-personal tendencies within us. The most horrendous sins against humanity have their origin in thoughts. Thoughts that are allowed to grow into desires and thence into actions. Mental betrayal is the first step in the long road downward.

Contrary imaginations start the process of eroding our values long before we abandon those values or engage in actions contrary to them. In India I was once shown the overflow outlet of a water storage used to gather the huge monsoonal downpours. Below the spout was a stone on which the stream of water fell. In the middle of the stone was a hole. The rock had been worn away by years and years of overflowing water. It didn't happen in a day, or in any way it could be noticed. But slowly and inexorably, the water did its work.

In a pluralist society our dearest beliefs and values will be under constant attack, and even rock-solid commitment can be worn away by the constant flow of contrary propaganda. If we are to maintain the integrity of our faith, we need to seek a counterbalance. The more we are under threat, the more we need to maintain and even intensify our practice of prayer and reading and our involvement with the church. Perhaps we need to seek counsel in dealing with the particular issues that confront us. But it is not enough to drift along, thinking that everything will turn out all right in the end. This is a slippery slope; it is easy to go down, but very difficult to clamber up again. (October 6, 2002.)

> *Loving Father, as we journey to your heavenly kingdom, keep before us the words and example of your Son. Help us to cherish his teaching and follow his example so that we do not lose our way, and so that we can serve to support others. We ask this through Christ our Lord. Amen.*

October 27 ✛ **Slowness**

The slow-cooking movement began in Italy in the 1980s, associated with the name of Carlo Petrini. The ideal was to return to traditional and regional methods of preparing food and to offset the burgeoning influence of fast-food outlets and the reliance on microwaves and frozen food. In some ways, this contrarian movement can be seen as a symbol of what needs to be done if we are to retain our balance in a world of value creep, where we find ourselves accepting social beliefs and values without really subjecting them to critical examination.

When I began using a computer, also in the 1980s, I had to find other things to do while the computer clunked its way through the tasks I had assigned to it. Now I become stroppy if I have to wait more than a few seconds for anything. Speed seems to have become essential to us in all that we do. Whatever we want, we want it yesterday.

There is a value in taking things slowly. Especially in the Gospel of Mark, we see Jesus interposing a delay before he responds to a request. The effect of this is twofold. On the one hand, it gives time for the person asking for a miracle to consider what is happening. To enter more deeply into the full meaning of what is about take place. Secondly, this growth in awareness has the effect of enlarging our capacity to receive, to savor the gift more fully when it arrives.

In our life of prayer, we need to adapt ourselves to the slow rhythm that God prefers. Even though our needs are obvious and urgent, it is important for us to experience them in depth rather than wanting God to flick them away. More often what we are seeking from God is muddled with a variety of motivations and desires. We need to slow down so that we can sort through these, so that we arrive at some clarity about what is of the first importance. For this we can pray. And there is a good probability that our prayer will be heard. And our delight will be all the greater. (December 2, 2005.)

> *Loving God, teach us to pace ourselves according to the rhythms of your will. Help us to understand the needs that drive us to prayer and to rid ourselves of mixed motivations, so that we may wait in patience for the time of your visitation. We ask this through Christ our Lord. Amen.*

October 28 ✠ *Snapdragons*

For a time, when I was a small boy, I became obsessed with snapdragons. Eventually I decided to invest some of my fortune in growing them myself. I went to the local florist and bought a packet of seeds. All the way home I was excited by the brightly colored picture on the packet, but when eventually I tore it open I was disappointed to find only some weird, unprepossessing objects that had no relationship to the flowers. Assured that everything was OK, I planted them and watered them every day. After a week, nothing seemed to have happened, so I dug them up to check. I was right. Nothing had happened. That was the end of the snapdragon saga. I was deflated and disappointed. And that is why I have grown up bitter and twisted!

Seeds and flowers and growing things make great images for what happens in the spiritual life. Jesus the woodworker never spoke about growth in godliness in terms of planning and measuring and fitting things together. He preferred to point to the mysterious rhythms of growth typical of the plant world. The kingdom of heaven is like a seed growing secretly: it is not like the building of a skyscraper, reaching up into the heavens like the tower of Babel.

Similarly, the community of those who follow Christ is more like a vine than a business corporation. There are different elements, each with their own function: stock, trunk, branches, leaves, and, best of all, fruit. And there are seasons of growth. There is a time for wintering, a time for bursting back into life, a time for flowers and fruit, and a time to let go of the leaves and begin to wind down. All the seasons are important; each has a distinctive role to play. Our task is to remain with Christ through the changing seasons of our life, whatever be our present call and function. We do not have to understand what is happening except that, if it is happening, it is from God's hand.

To return to the snapdragons. Children don't understand patience or perseverance. Waiting is an abomination for them. They want immediate results. As they grow wiser, however, they will begin to recognize that we cannot impose our expectations on the mystery of life because life is even more complicated than growing snapdragons. But the end product is far more beautiful. (May 1, 1988.)

> *God of all growth, teach us to be patient while you work your wonders on us. May we not be discouraged by the slowness of the process or by the surprises it brings, but let us be full of confidence that all will be well. We ask this in the name of Jesus, your Son, our Lord. Amen.*

October 29 ✠ **Sowing and Reaping**

There is much pathos in the saying quoted by Jesus in the fourth chapter of John's gospel: "One person sows and another reaps." Although we know from experience that this is often true, so wedded are we to the linkage of cause and effect that we are affronted by it. We expect that the person who puts in the hard yards will be the one to enjoy the fruits of the labor. We are upset by the idea that we should be prepared to invest effort without ever seeing the results or winning the rewards.

Jesus is reminding us that in our work for the coming of God's kingdom it is necessary that we aim at arriving at purity of intention. That we are really working for the kingdom and not, in some devious way, for ourselves. This means going beyond self-interest and striving to achieve some degree of disinterestedness and detachment in serving God and in doing good for others. We are reminded of Charles de Foucauld, who seems to have had no impact in his lifetime and only posthumously began to exert influence. Likewise, however much we admire the tenacity of the martyrs, it is hard for us to believe that we will achieve more by dying than by living.

The way out of this impasse is to keep in mind that salvation is a collective exercise. We are distinct members of a single body. This means that we are part of a larger plan; our job is to do our bit, in the expectation that others are doing theirs. We sow, others reap. According to an old saying, "The blood of martyrs is the seed of Christians." Obviously, they are not around to take pride in the outcome.

We do not measure our efforts by their immediate result. We are called to have confidence in the providence of God that gives us a task to do. We do not have to reap the benefits; it is blessing enough for us to be privileged to share in the sowing. Besides, God is never outdone in generosity. (August 10, 2013.)

Loving Father, grant us the gift of generosity in our service of you and our neighbor. Help us to persevere in our sowing

and to rejoice in the fruits that others will share. We ask this
through Christ our Lord. Amen.

October 30   ✛   *Sponge-Listening*

At least since the time of Carl Rogers, listening has been understood to have an important role in human relations. He understood, as we will understand ourselves if we try it, that listening is a very demanding activity. Really listening, that is. Probably many of us have experienced fake listening. From woolgathering bureaucrats, for example, who can listen for hours without taking anything they hear to heart. They absorb it like a sponge, but it has no impact on them because they have taken a preferential option for not rocking the boat. Doing nothing is always safer.

Jesus admits that sometimes it seems that sponge-listening is the way God responds to our prayers, even in the most urgent circumstances. God seems unmoved. This despite the fact that Jesus taught that God's benevolence extends to both the good and the wicked, that we should come before God boldly, freely asking for our needs, and that God specializes in doing the impossible. How does it happen, then, that when we pray there is no result?

There are three truths we should recognize about prayer. Prayer *never* changes God; God remains ever infinitely benevolent in our regard. Prayer *sometimes* changes events; if you pray often for particular things, you will notice that "coincidences" happen more frequently than you might expect. Prayer *always* changes us. Sometimes we are energized to remedy matters ourselves. Sometimes we are inspired to ask for help. Sometimes we learn to redefine the situation. Sometimes we learn patience. Sometimes we learn to endure. We may not always recognize at the moment that our prayer has been answered, but often—even always—in retrospect, we will come to the conclusion that God has heard our prayer. It may take years or decades before we arrive at this point.

God is not a sponge-listener. The challenge for us is not to abandon our prayer in disgust. Not to give up on prayer. Not to give up on God. From eternity God sees the whole of time in an instant; what we think is good for us now may not stand up to scrutiny in a wider context. Jesus tells us to be certain that God will act in response to our prayer. How and when is not for us to determine; God will act when and how it profits us most. (October 17, 2004.)

> *Lord Jesus Christ, teach us to pray. Help us to grow in confidence that our Father always hears our prayers and responds to them. Teach us how to be patient while God's loving plan unfolds in our lives. May we never lose hope in the proactive mercy of God. For you are our Lord for ever and ever. Amen.*

October 31 ✠ *Standover*

Have you ever noticed that sometimes, when reading a familiar text, a single word lights up and does a somersault before your eyes? Something to which you have never previously adverted. Recently I had this kind of experience reading the narrative about the hospitality offered by Martha and Mary to the itinerant Jesus.

As you will remember, Martha interrupts her labors to approach Jesus and complain. The Greek verb is rarely translated with its full force, perhaps because it is shocking. It says, with a note of abruptness, that Martha "stood over" Jesus (the aorist participle *epistasa*.) This verb usually has a threatening connotation similar to the English word *standover*. Its meaning is given in a dictionary as "using intimidation or threat of force to coerce others into submission or compliance." As in "standover tactics." It seems that Martha, the mistress of the house, felt herself to be the superior and wanted to assert her authority. The incident was less about the division of labor than about the exercise of control.

It is significant that, in the Gospel of Luke, the noun related to this verb is reserved exclusively for Jesus. Six times he is named as the *epistata*, the one with authority over demons, over sickness, over the disciples. Martha is not so much complaining about housework as asserting that in her own house she is the boss. Her will must be done.

A zeal for control is almost always accompanied by inner disturbance. It is quite the opposite of the spirit of the Sermon on the Mount, in which God's concern for even the least of creatures is celebrated. Seeking to control involves snatching the duty of care out of God's hands and, thereby, allowing oneself to be torn apart by what is, after all, none of one's business. Inappropriate care is likened to disordered desire in that it can strangle the growth of God's word within us and weigh down the heart. To the extent that we are determined to control things ourselves, our submission to God lags, and, gradually, our life falls apart.

Mary's receptive and contemplative attitude, sitting at the feet of Jesus, is the opposite of wanting to be in control. The contemplative soul does not dictate terms but trusts in Providence. Such persons open the heart of their soul to receive the word and bear abundant fruit in due season. Do we imitate Martha or Mary? The choice is ours. (July 18, 2004.)

> *Creating and sustaining God, your loving concern embraces all that is. Help us to be solicitous in the things for which we are responsible while leaving to your providence what is outside our sphere of influence. Teach us how to yield control. We ask this through Christ our Lord. Amen.*

November 1   ✠   **Stephen**

In the stylized account of Saint Stephen's martyrdom given in the Acts of the Apostles, we see him presented as following in the footsteps of Jesus. He accepted his death in a spirit of child-like meekness, even to the point of forgiving his murderers and interceding for them. This notwithstanding the fact that stoning is a particularly barbaric form of execution. Every rock that is hurled inflicts a different pain as it finds its target, and meanwhile, the hate-filled faces of those standing around are perfectly visible to the victim. Death comes slowly, and the fury of the crowd will not fade until life has been fully extinguished.

We may well ask how it was that Stephen was able to maintain his equanimity in the face of such hostility. The text suggests how this came about. Stephen "was filled with the Holy Spirit and, looking up to heaven, saw God's glory and Jesus standing at God's right hand." Filled with joy and hope at such a vision, he was able to regard the horrific suffering inflicted on him as a "slight momentary affliction," in no way comparable to what awaited him on the other side of death. He endured, as the author of the Epistle to the Hebrews wrote of Moses, "as if seeing the unseen."

There is a lesson for us here. In life and in death it is the intensity of our contact with the invisible world of the spirit that will give us the fortitude to be patient amid the inevitable trials that will come our way. We will probably not have to endure anything like the suffering inflicted on Stephen and the other martyrs, but we will certainly have to go through hard times before we enter God's eternal kingdom. How we handle these will depend on the extent to which heartfelt prayer has become a part of our lives. Not just the spontaneous prayer that comes to us when troubles strike, but the dogged daily prayer by which we slowly open our lives to God. Fidelity to regular prayer is when we build up our capacity to maintain our course, even in times of contradiction and persecution. "We have seen his glory," writes Saint John, and we are prepared to endure much in order to share in it more fully. (December 26, 2001.)

Lord Jesus Christ, help us to follow your example of making time to spend in solitary prayer and deep communion with God. May our prayer become a shaping force in our lives so that we are not defeated by difficulties but remain constant in the sure and certain hope of your protection. For you are our Lord for ever and ever. Amen.

November 2 ✠ *Stirrer*

Many of the ancient Latin collects that we still use in the liturgy used verbs inviting God to be bestirred or asking that we also be stirred. It is as though we are asking for God to rock our boat, to rattle our cage, to shake us out of our complacency. We don't always remember that the effect of God's interventions in human history is usually to challenge the status quo. God's call is to change.

One way of looking at the saints is to see them as stirrers. Take Saint John the Baptist. The whole world was abuzz at his birth; crowds flocked to see him and listen to his doom-laden words. This was no soothing purveyor of pious platitudes. He was a fanatic, holding up a mirror to the compromises that bedeviled his listeners' lives and shattering the defensive walls with which the good people were surrounding themselves. His message was a call to change: radical, deep-seated, all-embracing change. And eventually he paid the price.

I don't suppose I would dare to pray, "O God, send a stirrer into my life to make me uncomfortable." I don't want to be confronted by my hidden compromises, my rationalizations, my wishy-washy half-heartedness. I am too scared to pray, "Bestir yourself, O God: send someone to summon the tempest, to wake me up so eventually I may be motivated to reduce the level of inconsistency in my daily life." Oh no! I need to acknowledge that the peace that Christ comes to bring is not, as Dom Helder Camara noted, the peace of a stagnant swamp, unaware of its own decay. It is the peace that flows from the pursuit of goodness and the embrace of wholeness. It is a peace that requires effort—and most of us have to be stirred if we are to rise from our slumber to move toward it.

Like John the Baptist, the saints are stirrers; their role in Christ's church is to keep us from the deadly sleep of complacency and motivate us not only to look forward to the coming of the kingdom but to work hard to welcome it in our own lives and in our own environment. (December 9, 2007.)

Lord God, stir up your power and come to help us. See our
weakness and blindness, and send us help to strengthen our
arms and open our eyes so that we may serve you in holiness
and justice all the days of our life. We ask this in the name
of Jesus our Lord. Amen.

November 3   ✝   **Stop**

I had a friend who used to say occasionally, "Don't just do some-thing: stand there." I suppose it was a reaction to our belief that there is always something that we can do to improve a situation. Perhaps in it there is also the hint that "they also serve who only stand and wait," as John Milton once wrote in Sonnet 19. Our culture greatly exalts activity over passivity and receptivity. In so doing it is propagating an activist view of human life that risks having nothing to say about the role of receiving and suffering. This despite the fact that we realize that a person's true character is often more amply revealed in bearing hardship than in trium-phant achievements.

We tend to believe that doing anything is better than doing nothing—even if it is the matter of doing the wrong thing. Phy-sicians may inflict unnecessary surgery on those with one foot over the threshold of death simply because their compassion won't allow them to do nothing. Doing something for the sake of doing something is scarcely a reasonable choice if there is no positive outcome.

Jesus warns us quite clearly, "Do not work for the food that perishes, but for that which remains for eternal life." There is no benefit in investing a lot of energy in projects that will not yield proportionate results. "Why spend your money on what is not bread?" "Do not go on living the aimless kind of life that pagans live." "Seek God's kingdom first, and everything else will be given to you in addition." "It is not a matter of one who runs or one who works but of God showing mercy."

Maybe this seems to us too risky an approach. We tend to take for granted that everything we want to achieve in life has to be self-generated. If you want to get ahead, you have to work for it, invest time and energy in it, make the most of your opportunities. God's kingdom is not governed by such rules; everything is, to our way of thinking, topsy-turvy. The first are last, the lowly are exalted, the one who works least gets equal pay. There is no advantage in sweating under self-imposed obligations. What we are called to do is to open our hearts to the life-giving and energizing onrush of God's mercy, to be still and learn that God is God. To us also Jesus says, "If only you knew the gift of God." (August 2, 2009.)

> *Loving Father, whose nature it is to give without restriction, help us to step aside and allow you to act. Give us the grace to pause and reflect and the wisdom to see your providence at work in everything that happens. We make this prayer in the name of Jesus our Lord. Amen.*

November 4 ✠ **Submarine**

I was born in a submarine, and have spent my whole life within its confines. Happily. It is a very large submarine, and there is an abundance of variety; activities, relationships, entertainments— bread and circuses. They tell me that outside the submarine there is a wide world of wonders beyond anything I have experienced, but that is only hearsay. For the moment I have plenty to keep me occupied.

This world of space and time seems vast, and beyond it the boundless universe is yet more immense. Yet beyond the spatial and temporal sphere there exists another universe. Not a parallel universe, but one that surrounds and upholds the world we live in. Our world seems to be self-sustaining, yet we have no idea of why the world of space and time exists or by what energy it has evolved to become what it is today. The greatest defect in our knowledge is that we cannot grasp how what is seen relates to what is unseen.

Because of this we claim an autonomy for our world, and this is our greatest sin and our greatest ignorance. Like the submarine, the world may seem to provide everything we need for life and happiness, but, like the submarine, the world did not make itself and exists only through the grace and favor of realities outside itself.

Our real and substantial happiness can come only by living in harmony with the unseen spiritual world. How do we accomplish this? By recognizing our dependence on realities beyond our understanding and building into our personal philosophy a space to be filled with the infinite mystery that surpasses understanding. Our only appropriate response to the absolute is to withdraw from the bread and circuses and to leave ourselves open to receive the self-revelation of the eternal God.

God has spoken to our race in varied ways at different times and, most of all, through sending the Son of his love. Jesus remains with us, as he promised. Present to us, if we have a care to turn our attention to him. In most lives there are moments of revelation, intense experiences that open before us a new range of possibilities. It is as though God has chosen to visit his people, to open our eyes to the greater mystery that surrounds us and sustains us. Our role is to respond appropriately to this revelation. (August 6, 2017.)

> *Creator God, you have made us for yourself, and our hearts are restless until they make their home in you. Help us to seek you more diligently, to welcome you more warmly, and to love you more intensely. We ask this through Christ our Lord. Amen.*

November 5 ✠ *Subtlety*

An interest in and, eventually, a commitment to religion is grounded on a response to data that is not universally perceived. Otherwise everyone would be religious. Speaking about the existence of God, Saint Thomas Aquinas taught that it was eminently knowable, but he added the qualification, only by those who are wise.

This reminds us of the time when God appeared to Elijah, not in the earthquake or the storm but in the faint rustle of a gentle breeze. Most of us would be more likely to respond to the God of thunder and lightning, as on Mount Sinai, but God's preference seems to be to enter into our lives in a much subtler manner.

This means that if God is to become part of our inner landscape, we need to develop skills of interior silence. We need to take the opportunity to step back from the marketplace, to turn off the various electronic devices that keep us entertained, and to take a little time apart. The English philosopher Alfred North Whitehead once wrote that "religion is solitariness; and if you are never solitary, you are never religious" (*Religion in the Making*).

To make contact with the spiritual world it is necessary, as Jesus taught us, to go into an inner chamber and close the door. The brain cannot generate sufficient sensitivity while it is occupied with all kinds of alternative attractions. We need to learn physical stillness and interior quiet. Both pose a strong challenge. When we attempt to sit still, an irresistible restlessness invades us and we want to go somewhere else. As soon as we try to settle into a welcoming quiet, a riot of contradictory images and emotions infiltrates our mind. To achieve quiet we need first to engage in active resistance against unseemly intrusions.

Yet those who seek will find. It will not be in high drama and excitement but in the muted tones typical of Christ's life here below. He will come to us as one who lived a life that was ordinary, obscure, and laborious; unless we are sufficiently disengaged to recognize him in these conditions, we will surely miss his arrival. (January 20, 1991.)

Lord Jesus Christ, you come to us as one who is meek and humble of heart. Help us to recognize your presence in the most unlikely circumstances and give us the strength to welcome you with joy and generous self-giving. For you are our Lord for ever and ever. Amen.

November 6 ✠ ***Sub Tuum***

In 1937 the John Rylands Library in Manchester published a fragment of a papyrus that had originated in Egypt and was dated about the year 250 AD. On it was written the earliest known prayer to Mary, addressed here as *Theotokos*, "the one who gave birth to God" or "Mother of God." The full text of the prayer could be reliably reconstructed because it is well attested in Greek, Coptic, and Latin versions. The full text of this ancient prayer is, "We fly to your protection, O holy *Theotokos*. Despise not our prayers in our necessities, but deliver us from all dangers, O glorious and blessed ever-virgin."

This papyrus prayer, known in Latin as the *Sub tuum*, probably originated in Alexandria during the Valerian or Decian persecutions, but its use has continued in the churches of both East and West, even to the present. For example, in the wake of the Reformation and beset by civil and sectarian strife, the Cistercian general chapter of 1533 prescribed the daily singing of this antiphon—a practice that continued for more than four hundred years.

Today the church is again in a state of crisis, though not so much from overt persecution or from cataclysmic divisions. The church has been wounded by its own scandals: sexual abuse and its concealment, financial mismanagement, complicity in corruption, and inept governance. There is discord between so-called conservative and progressive elements. We are suffering massive hemorrhaging of membership due to disedification, the influence of secularism, and the indifference generated by increasing affluence. And it seems that the visible institution has missed the bus on many moral issues dear to our contemporaries.

While we are obliged to do whatever is within our competence to lighten these liabilities, we should never underestimate the importance of praying for the radical reform of the church. And if we are at a loss about how to do this, perhaps we can learn from the example of our forebears in the faith for 1,800 years and pray to Mary, Help of Christians, to deliver us from the dangers that threaten us as a church, which make it more difficult for us to be true servants of the kingdom of God. (May 24, 2013.)

Lord Jesus Christ, look upon your church beset by so many evils and, by the intercession of Mary, Mother of the church, strengthen the forces of renewal and enable us to live our lives worthy of the vocation to which we have been called. For you are our Lord for ever and ever. Amen.

November 7   ✠   *Subtraction*

When we think of a king, we think of a human being plus—plus riches, status, power, respect—one who has acquired all that is highly esteemed in this world. This is why the image of Jesus as king is liable to lead us astray. He himself taught that what is highly esteemed among human beings is an abomination before God. Therefore, we have to remind ourselves, as he said to Pilate, that his kingship is not of this world. Jesus became king not by addition but by subtraction. He emptied himself. He is king because he passed beyond earthly bonds; he was free of whatever would hold him captive by its charm.

Jesus was supremely free; he was a king because of his total and radical detachment, which was itself made possible only by his total and radical attachment to a higher reality—the will and plan of his Father. Because he wanted nothing that he did not have, Jesus was not drawn to anything that could deflect his will from the work that his Father had sent him to accomplish.

The court of Christ the King is not to be found in royal palaces and in the penthouses of tycoons. He himself tells us that if we wish to serve him, we do so by attending to the needs of the least likely: the homeless, the poor, those deprived of liberty, those rejected and despised by all. We do not have to climb the highest echelons of society to find our King; he is to be found and loved and served among those who seem to be the least deserving of our attention: those whom we might consider as the undeserving poor.

If we desire nothing on earth, we have everything we want. We are free. We may as well be kings and queens. To the extent that we can disentangle ourselves from enslaving cupidity we are free to be filled with Christ. We are ready to receive the gift of a more abundant life. And, if that is not enough, it is Christ's promise that we shall also reign with him forever. (November 20, 2011.)

> *Lord Jesus Christ, your kingdom belongs to the poor and lowly. Help us to serve you by our willingness to be counted among the little ones of God's faithful people, who honor you more with heart and hand than by word alone. For you are our Lord for ever and ever. Amen.*

November 8 ☩ *Suffering*

The Fourth Gospel has fewer miracle stories than the other gospels, but the evangelist takes more care in providing a fuller context for the narratives. He does this with a view to offering a more complete explanation of the work that Christ did among the people of his time and continues to do today.

The story of the man born blind, told in Chapter 9, is more than an account of a miraculous cure. The bodily blindness of the man is understood as a metaphor for a more universal state: a lack of enlightenment (both intellectual and moral), interior darkness, hopelessness, obstinacy, being shackled to the past, unhappiness. To a greater or lesser degree, the blind man represents us all.

The disciples ask why this suffering should be inflicted on us. Jesus' answer may puzzle us. We suffer so that we may have the joyous experience of being delivered from that suffering—so that God's gracious works may become manifest. This is also the lesson of the book of Job. Pain is inseparable from human existence: it is the most universal of all human experiences. If suffering has a meaning, it is because it leads us to a place to which otherwise we would not go—to a recognition of our finite being, to becoming conscious that there is innate in us a hope that transcends evidence, to a sense of dependence on God, and, eventually, to the affirmation that all things work together for good for those who love God.

Suffering is part of the divine pedagogy; it breaks the shell of self and teaches us to reach out beyond ourselves in hope—sometimes in desperate hope—to other people and to God. Sometimes only an earthquake can knock down the walls within which we have immured ourselves, and God in his mercy allows that earthquake to do its work. Thanks to it we discover the superabundance of love that, all the while, was waiting for us behind the wall. It is a hard lesson, but it is the only way that we will be brought to our senses. (March 14, 1999.)

> *Jesus, bringer of wine when the vessel is empty, fill our void.*
> *Restorer of strength to crippled limbs, end our immobility.*
> *Provider of bread to the spiritually hungry, feed us with*
>   *yourself.*
> *Bearer of Light to a darkened world, enlighten our blindness.*
> *Outshining of love to our indifference, fill our hearts.*
> *Liberator of those in bondage, set us free.*
> *Jesus our way and our truth, lead us to eternal life. Amen.*

November 9 ✚ *T-Shirt*

I like to think that, as Christ accompanies each one of us on our journey, he is wearing a T-shirt. Emblazoned on its front is the slogan "I'm with stupid," with an arrow pointing in our direction. There is no reason to be insulted. There is plenty of evidence to support the assertion: our darkness of mind, our weakness of will, and our occasional flashes of real nastiness taken together seem to indicate that we qualify for the title. Oddly, Christ is not repelled by our obvious limitations.

The important word on the T-shirt is not *stupid*, it is *with*. Jesus comes to us as Immanuel: God-with-us. He is like us in all things except sin. We have come to accept the reality of such solidarity without too much surprise, but it was shocking for Jesus' own contemporaries. God coming among us was not expected to do ordinary things such as eating and drinking, sleeping, meeting people, making friends, going to weddings. There is, however, something even more shocking. He participated in a ritual for the cleansing of sins. That is what John's baptism was. Saint Mark's gospel is perfectly clear on this point. Jesus pushed solidarity to the point where he took on himself the sins of humanity; he did not hesitate to identify with our sinful race.

You know better than I that if you consent to be the guarantor of another person's loan, then if that person defaults, you become responsible for the whole debt. So, in a way, our sins are attached to Jesus' account. As Saint Paul writes, "The sinless one became sin for our sake."

Jesus is eternally conjoined with us sinners, just as he associated himself with persons of insalubrious reputation during his time on earth. He has joined us on our journey. And he invites us to join him as he makes his way back to the Father.

When our life's journey ends we must make the great transition to eternal life. As we approach the pearly gates, Jesus comes up to walk beside us again, as he did with the disciples of Emmaus. And he is wearing a different T-shirt. This time it reads, "Stupid is with me." And so we pass through unchallenged into eternal life. (January 9, 2011.)

Lord Jesus Christ, friend of sinners, travel with us on our journey through life. Lighten our labors by the joy of your presence, and help us to overcome the many difficulties that beset us on the way. For you are our Lord for ever and ever. Amen.

November 10 ✛ **Talents**

It is happy accident that, since the fifteenth century, the English word *talent* has meant "giftedness" or "skill." In the ancient world it was a measure for precious metals such as gold or silver.

Whether George Bernard Shaw was correct in saying that a talent was sufficient to buy a racehorse, it certainly represented a considerable sum.

The parable of the Talents makes the point that each of us is richly talented, though in different degrees. Just as it does not make much difference whether you have one billion dollars in the bank or five billion, so the value of our particular talents cannot be assessed by comparing them with what others have received. They have a unique and intrinsic value in themselves, and they form part of a total reality in which different forms of giftedness cohere to produce a wonderful and many-colored result. We are part of Christ's Body; in that body, each member has different gifts and different functions, but all jointly contribute to the glory of the whole.

In the parable, the servant who fails to make use of the gifts given is cast into exterior darkness. Perhaps this is our most significant sin: not to make use of the gifts we have received in order to produce a good result, not just for ourselves but for all. Why do we fail to use our gifts? I think it is not usually out of perversity or passive aggression. Sometimes it is because we fail to recognize them and develop them. Equally often it is out of timidity or a lack of appropriate boldness.

It is the role of the Christian community to recognize the giftedness of its members, to provide scope for its exercise, to aid its development, and to ensure that it operates in harmony. If this happens, then the world will be a better place and the gifts of God will not be allowed to lie idle. (November 14, 1993.)

Creator God, you have endowed each one of us with unique talents and possibilities. Give us the strength to use these gifts to develop ourselves, to serve the community in which we live, and to give glory to you, the source of all giftedness. We ask this through Christ our Lord. Amen.

November 11   ✠   **Temple Tax**

In the early 1970s I was at Mass in a parish church in the Netherlands. At that time the parish collected a "pew fee" from anyone who wanted to sit down. The seats were not for the riffraff, despite the fact that the church was nearly empty. In a splendid display of passive aggression, those who paid for the privilege did so with the smallest coin in circulation, worth scarcely more than nothing and which I saw nowhere else. The resentment and scorn of the dwindling number who still came to Mass was evident. If it was their church, why did they have to pay to sit down?

A similar objection is evident in Jesus' response to the collector of the temple tax. For Jesus, the temple was intended to be a house of prayer for all the nations, his Father's house. Why should the children have to pay? In fact, the temple offerings had been hijacked by an upper-class clique and were used as an income stream to support their better-than-average lifestyle. We also may wonder whether it is right for working-class people in faraway Galilee to be obliged to contribute.

Jesus pays, but he does so in a manner that indicates his scorn. His prophetic gesture of finding the shekel in the fish's mouth expresses his detachment from the wheeling and dealing that characterized the temple authorities of his day. Later he will confirm this stance by driving all the hucksters from the temple precincts. For the moment, he is prepared to work a miracle and, thereby, to drop a bomb—using "salvific surprise" as a technique to start a process of reflection that might eventually lead to conversion.

In our own time, also, many sincere and serious believers have trouble in the "pray-obey-pay" model of church membership. Firstly, they are looking for a church that invites and values a broad spectrum of participation. Secondly, they are looking for a church that understands and responds to the religious experience that has led believers to seek a more fervent discipleship. Thirdly, they may well have some doubts about the corporatization of the church, turning it into a big business, requiring serious fund-raising, and, perhaps, forgetting about the poor. Temple taxes and pew fees are really telling people that they do not belong. (August 11, 2014.)

> *Lord Jesus Christ, you built your church on the faith of or-dinary men and women and instructed them to become de-tached from the wealth and privilege of this world. Teach us to seek first the kingdom of God, confident that all other necessary benefits will be given us as well. For you are our Lord for ever and ever. Amen.*

November 12 ✝ ***Temptation***

An ancient translation of Job 7:1 much quoted in subsequent discourse reads, "Is not the life of the human on earth a temptation?" Far from being an occasional intrusion on a normally serene life, temptation is the state in which we all live. As rational beings we have the power of choice. At each moment we can choose how to respond to the particularities of our situation. We are more human if we make many choices; we are less human if we stand back and allow things to happen without any intervention of our will. We become passive, like debris carried along by the tide of time.

Temptation is useful because it forces me to choose between two options. The quality of my humanity depends on whether the choices I make are predominantly good or bad. My response to temptation reveals what I am. Instead of seeing temptation as an affliction, perhaps I should welcome it as an opportunity to reassert the overriding values that I seek to embody in my life.

My best friend in time of temptation is a lively conscience. Seen by many as the voice of God, conscience helps us to throw off the wet blanket of habitual rationalization to see issues as they really are. To discern the difference between good and evil. If our conscience is disabled, we are in a helpless situation. We lack the capacity to see the moral consequences of our actions and, after repeated acts and many denials, slowly sink into a state of sin in which we no longer know or care about the difference between right and wrong.

Temptation is a wake-up call. Not only is it an invitation to take a stand on our values, it is often a potent reminder of the weakness of our will and the wobbliness of our virtue. Frequent temptation forces us to cry out frequently to God for help and forgiveness. So, maybe, it is not such a bad thing. (February 10, 2008.)

> *Father in heaven, lead us not into temptation that we cannot resist. Forgive us our sins, deliver us from evil, and foster in us a confidence in the help of your ever-present grace. We ask this through Christ our Lord. Amen.*

November 13 ✠ **Theophany**

The history of salvation, as it is presented to us in the Bible, is punctuated by moments of theophany—that is, when God makes an appearance in human history. The unforeseen intervention of God has the effect of alerting key figures to the existence of a world beyond space and time and the demands that this makes on how we conduct ourselves. The appearance of God demands a recalibration of our vision of the ultimate goal and meaning of human existence.

God appears to Abraham, Isaac, and Jacob to call them forth to claim ownership of the Promised Land. God calls Moses to lead their descendants from the darkness of slavery into freedom. God enters the lives of Isaiah, Jeremiah, Jonah, and the other prophets to give them the mission of calling the people back from sin and error into a more liberating life of fidelity. And, in the fullness of time, God so loved the world that he sent his Son, to be for us the way that leads to a more abundant life.

And still the flashes of light continue. The three apostles gaze awestruck at the transfigured Jesus at the summit of Tabor. Mary Magdalen comes running with the news that Christ has risen from the dead. Saul of Tarsus is blinded by a sunburst on the road to Damascus, and his life is changed forever.

God appears to human beings, not as entertainment to satisfy their curiosity, not usually simply to comfort and console, but mostly to send them on a mission that would further the purpose of bringing all to the saving knowledge of the truth, long hidden from ages past and now revealed.

In our own small way, this happens also to us. Our capacity to accept the norms of Christian behavior depends on our ongoing contact with the spiritual world and with God. Once this connectivity is diminished, our energy for living as Christians is diminished. It is worth our while to stay tuned and maintain our sensitivity to the stirrings of the Spirit in our heart, since these may well be the beginnings of something greatly desirable in our lives. (July 20, 2016.)

Lord God, in times past you spoke to our ancestors in varied ways, but now you continue to speak to us through your Holy Spirit. Open our hearts to receive your words of comfort and guidance and strength. We ask this through Christ our Lord. Amen.

November 14 ✠ *Thoughts*

For most of us, the Ten Commandments, especially if interpreted broadly, are a bit of a stretch. Usually we can keep within the boundaries they demarcate, but it requires effort. We are conscious that there are tendencies within us that, even if they are not expressed in action, draw us in the direction of violence, lust, and theft. It takes a definite decision on our part not to follow down the track they indicate.

Jesus taught that the Ten Commandments were to be not the point of arrival, toward which we journey, but the point of departure. Discipleship begins with the keeping of the commandments and proceeds from there. This is clear in the case of the rich man who had observed all the legal requirements "from his youth," but fell short when it came to the extra demands that Jesus makes on those who want the full package.

It is not enough to avoid actions that defile us or injure our neighbor; we are instructed to avoid even the thoughts that are generated by the negative energies within us. Lustful imaginations, dreams of violent retribution, and seething resentments may not be obvious to the superficial observer, but this does not prevent their inflicting damage on the one who allows them entry into the mind. These thoughts seem so slight. They can scarcely be considered as overt rebellion against God, since they enter uninvited. Yet our allowing them even temporary residence in our hearts can lead to the mental betrayal of all we hold dear. It is this slight turning away from the good, which is so small as to be scarcely noticeable, that may well be the beginning of a much greater infidelity farther down the track.

Jesus calls us to a discipleship of mind and heart as well as a discipleship of action. It is best to start early: to be vigilant concerning the first beginnings. Saint Teresa of Avila notes that it is easier to uproot a weed when it is small; if we wait for it to grow, we will have much more trouble. As the Desert Fathers taught, watch your thoughts and your actions will look after themselves. (March 10, 2017.)

> *Creator God, all that you have made is good. Help us to fully attach ourselves to the good things that come from your hand that we may never succumb to thoughts or inclinations that harm us or injure our neighbor. We make this prayer through Christ our Lord. Amen.*

November 15 ✠ *Tigers*

I have read that tigers, when hunting their prey, emit two kinds of sound. Audible to all is their growling, which is a celebration of the meal they are about to enjoy. But that is merely window dressing. The other sound has a crucial role in the process of catching their prey. At about twenty kilohertz it cannot be heard, and yet it performs the function of paralyzing and petrifying their targets so that they cannot move—like a rabbit marooned in the headlights. And so, dinner is served.

The word of God is like a tiger. It operates on two levels. On the first is its patent content. The narrative of the life of Jesus, the exhortations of Saint Paul, the prophetic oracles of Jeremiah. These may ring a bell in our hearts and cause an echo that helps us to sort things out in our life. But God's word operates at another level as well. At this level, there is no overt content to stimulate our mind. It is subliminal. The significance at this level is not the content of the communication between us and God, but the fact that we are in communication. Our opening the Bible is an act of opening ourselves to God, and before we have read a single word, the relationship has been re-actualized.

Our heartfelt reading of or listening to God's word demonstrates that we are on speaking terms with God. Notwithstanding the many breaches in the relationship and the ongoing threats, we are still able to stand before the Lord and open our hearts and lives to comfort and challenge. In the phrase wrongly attributed to Winston Churchill, "Jaw-jaw is better than war-war." Even though we may be in a state of overt rebellion against God, the fact that we have enough confidence in divine mercy to come before God in a spirit of listening attention means that the door to repentance and full reconciliation has not yet been slammed in our face.

Marshall McLuhan's maxim, "The medium is the message," is relevant here. By giving our attention to the ongoing conversation between ourselves and God, we are allowing God fuller access to our lives. Who knows what the outcome will be?

"Do not be mournful. Do not weep. The joy of the Lord is your stronghold." This day the word is being fulfilled, even as you listen. (Undated.)

Loving Father, you speak to us at different times and by different means. Help us to listen more carefully to your words, for they are our guide to eternal life. Give us boldness in

*responding to your call and in expressing our needs to you
in hope and confidence. We ask this through Christ our Lord.
Amen.*

November 16   ✜   *Tipping Point*

A tipping point is a moment when a relatively small event can
precipitate major change. A climber's stumble can dislodge a
boulder and cause an avalanche. The straw that breaks the camel's back. The factors that coalesce to create the perfect storm.

We find many instances of the tipping point in the gospel narratives. We see this particularly in the stories in which Jesus calls.
Especially in the Gospel of Mark, the word *immediately* appears.
Jesus calls, and *immediately* the one called rises and follows. This
seems to indicate that Jesus judged the window of opportunity
well, and it also demonstrates what is said in various places in
the Gospel tradition, that Jesus was a man with an incisive perception of what was transpiring in the human heart. It was this
quality that enabled him to bypass what may otherwise have been
negative appearances. Among those he called were tax collectors,
ignorant fishermen, and women of dubious reputation. The professionally righteous he mostly did not call; he categorized them
as "whitened sepulchres," bright and shiny on the outside, while
within was death and the smell of corruption.

But the call of Jesus is not magic. The rich man went away
sadder when he found Jesus' demands to be so radical, as did the
man who had first to bury his father. And Judas Iscariot did not
long remain spellbound. Jesus wept over Jerusalem precisely
because its people did not recognize the hour of its visitation.
And then the moment passed.

Even at a favorable time, the call of Jesus demands a stretch.
We must give our free assent to the summons, and though compliance is possible, it always asks of us a little more than we intended giving. We rarely say no. We more usually procrastinate.
The effect of this is that when urgency is lost, the fragrance of

grace evaporates and soon all is forgotten. We have not recognized the hour of our visitation, and trying to reconstruct it afterward never works.

The moral of the story is the familiar verse of the psalm: "If today you hear God's voice, harden not your hearts." God's providence is signposting the way to a more abundant life by so many small events in daily life. If we make a habit of responding to them, we may discover that they are propelling us much farther than we anticipated. And that is a cause for rejoicing. (June 8, 2008.)

> *Lord God of all creation, in all that happens you call to us and guide us along the path to more abundant life. Make us responsive to your call and bold in following your lead so that your plan of salvation may be accomplished on the earth. We ask this in the name of Jesus our Lord. Amen.*

November 17 ✠ ***Tongue***

One of my brothers, as a small boy, went through a brief phase of sticking his tongue out at people and asking, "Is my tongue dirty?" Without recommending that level of hypochondria, it is perhaps an aspect of human behavior that is worth investigating because it is from the abundance of the heart that the mouth speaks.

That is probably bad news for most of us. Often what we say reveals elements of our inner life of which we are unaware. It has often been noticed that people who invest a lot of energy in virtuous living often compensate by being careless about what comes out of their mouth. If our conduct is blameless, then our inherent malice has to find some other medium by which to express itself. Religious people often try to coat their nasty speech with a patina of piety, but the venom is still there.

In the first place, malice is directed to third parties. Obvious examples of this are gossip, slander, and detraction, where we inform others of matters that will lead them to think less highly of our victim. If we are especially self-righteous, we might try to disguise our ill will. "I am worried about John: his drinking/anger/envy/laziness seems to be getting worse. Why, only yesterday, this is what happened." And so we have a pretext for bad-mouthing poor John while feeling entirely blameless.

At other times our tongue becomes our weapon of choice to attack others, sometimes overtly, sometimes more subtly. We rebuke those who displease us, insult them, humiliate them in front of others, threaten them with even greater penalties. And then we sail off, serene in the assurance of our own innocence.

We can also use our tongue to engage in a campaign of self-promotion, tirelessly celebrating our achievements and exaggerating our successes. I suspect that nearly everything we say comes packaged with a meta-message intended to vaunt our superiority. No wonder Saint James seems to think that if we can get our tongues under control we are already perfect.

Since subtraction is difficult, why not try addition? We can start using our tongue to do good. We can lubricate social life by the exchange of the common civilities. We can preempt disputes by freely admitting our errors. We can encourage others and make their lives a little happier. And we can stretch ourselves by being dedicated to saying, "Thank you." By such means the tongue becomes a friend of integrity, not its enemy. (February 26, 1995.)

> *Lord Jesus Christ, teach us to put a guard over our mouth so that what comes forth from it does no harm to our neighbors but, instead, encourages and supports them in goodness and truth. For you are our Lord for ever and ever. Amen.*

November 18   ✠   *Torah*

Today we will have an examination on Hebrew. Question 1: Please translate the following Hebrew word: *torah*. If you answered that *torah* means "law," then you fail. You have plenty of company, but that does not dilute the inadequacy of this answer. A recent Jewish commentary on the Psalms habitually translates *torah* as "teaching." The fundamental meaning relates to instruction or direction and, when applied to God, revelation. The emphasis is on the enlightenment that we receive from God, not on the idea of an enforceable law. The heart of Old Testament religion was communicated when God spoke to Moses face-to-face; his efforts to transcribe the practical consequences of this revelation on tablets of stone were entirely secondary.

The Septuagint translation of the Hebrew Scriptures into Greek from about the third century before Christ translated the word as *nomos*, which does mean "law." This coincided with the rise of the petty legalism associated with rabbinic Judaism. As a result, revelation came to be identified with its practical demands, and God came to be seen both as lawgiver and judge. The Latin use of the harsh-sounding monosyllable *lex* added to the process of hardening.

It is God's self-revelation that is the beginning of real religion. This is something that lifts humankind beyond its limited vision of right and wrong. The revelation of God relativizes every human norm and rule. Nothing can be the same again. But, as is clear from the Psalms, this revelation is not a burden but a source of joy and happiness. "Blessed are those who walk in the *torah* of the Lord." It is good news. It is the beginning of a pathway to a more abundant life. The commandments are like safety rails along the roadside. They are meant to prevent us from wandering off the track into the dangerous thickets that surround it. Commandments are secondary. Revelation is what matters most.

The way of *torah* was the way of Jesus—the ultimate self-revelation of God. He came among us to proclaim the Good News of the kingdom, not a new set of regulations. To follow his teaching is to walk the way of the Beatitudes that will lead us to a more abundant life. This attitude was reflected in Saint Paul's emphasis that what matters before God is mostly our faith. Observing the precepts of a written code is, at best, secondary. (December 17, 2006.)

O Wisdom, you come forth from the mouth of the Most High.
You fill the universe and hold all things together, strongly and

sweetly. *Oh, come to teach us the way to truth, to a more abundant life, to true happiness. Teach us to rejoice always. For you are our Lord for ever and ever. Amen.*

November 19 ✝ **Touch**

Saint Mark's gospel manifests an interest in the mechanics of healing. When Jesus cures someone it is usually by touch. He sees a person who is afflicted and makes contact with them by reaching out and touching them. This is particularly dramatic in the case of lepers, who were condemned to live in isolation; the law forbade touching them, believing "uncleanness" to be contagious.

Jesus is presented to us as the hand God reaches out to sinners, spanning the gap between us and God and offering us the promise of a more abundant life. Perhaps we can visualize Michelangelo's painting in the Sistine Chapel—the Creator's outstretched finger communicates life to humanity. By God's gift we are made alive.

This is also our mission: to bridge the gap, to come closer. The opposite is to stand aloof, to remain at a distance, to pass by on the other side of the road and deliberately fail to see the wounded man pleading for help. We do this by declassifying him as our neighbor. The first stage of every war is this assertion that others are not like us; we do not belong together. By demonizing others we create enemies, and once this is done, we do not need to justify our hostility. They are enemies. They are aliens. We owe them nothing. They no longer qualify for our fellow-feeling or compassion. They are untouchable, and so we need to build walls to maintain our separation from them.

Jesus brought a different message. In his imaging of the Final Judgment he calls us to a hands-on benevolence that changes a stranger into a neighbor, to forgive our erring brother or sister seventy-seven times, and to embrace our enemy with the arms of prayer. By such means we come out of the cold and go inside, where all alike are feasting together. (February 16, 2003.)

Loving Father, help us to tear down the walls of indifference,
fear, and hostility that separate us from one another. Help
us to live in solidarity in the world which you have created
for us. We ask this through Christ our Lord. Amen.

November 20 ✠ **Transcendence**

At the heart of every culture there is an attraction to the spiritual
world, a fascination with the secret, unseen heart of reality. This
is why the most cherished artefacts of a culture carry some sort
of intimation of something more than can be seen or heard or
handled. A great painting has many more layers of meaning than
a simple photograph. A great piece of music causes thunderous
reverberations in the depths of our being. The gift of the artist
is the ability to inject spiritual content into the material fabric
of matter and sound. Permeating the visible world of space and
time and the everyday events that occur there is what Aboriginal
Australians understand as Dreamtime. Our human integrity demands that, even while pursuing our mundane lives, we maintain
contact with this hidden source of energy and wisdom.

What is true of cultures is true also of persons. There is a deep
spiritual reality underlying what can be seen on the surface.
Mostly its presence is unregarded. But, from time to time, we
become conscious of a feeling that there is more to life than what
presents itself to our casual gaze. We become aware of a mysterious yearning that surpasses the desires we have for the various
items that we hope to acquire. There is a space within us that
these baubles cannot fill. To turn our back on these intuitions will
lead us into the denial of an important facet of our humanity—
our openness to the spiritual world.

There sleeps within us all a wild desire that is dissatisfied with
the tidy life that our ego and the expectations of others have
imposed upon us. This was surely one of the recurrent themes in
the novels of Hermann Hesse, which were so popular in the 1960s
and 1970s. We have to throw off the constraining bonds of con-

ventional identity and embark on a pursuit of authenticity and genuine fulfillment. Whether such a radical revolution is required of us all may be questionable, but some steps need to be made toward a greater appreciation of the truth that we will become fully alive and fully human only to the extent that we go beyond the needs and demands of the ego. We all need to come to a self-giving love that takes its quality from beyond the frontier of self-hood and is, in fact, modeled on that infinite life in whose image and by whose abundance we were created. (August 29, 1993.)

> *O God beyond all our imagining, lead us forth from the confinement of human thought and expectation to that dreamtime that knows no restriction. Help us to yearn for that which no ear has heard, nor eye seen, nor human heart imagined. Lead us to that which you have prepared for those who love you. We ask this through Christ our Lord. Amen.*

November 21 ✠ *Treasure*

The parable of the Treasure Hidden in a Field can be read in less than a minute. Jesus gives us a simple image that highlights certain aspects of God's manner of dealing with us. For all its brevity, there is much in this little story that is worth pondering.

The first thing to notice is the notion of gratuity. All is grace. All is free. Stumbling across buried treasure is sheer accident; we cannot plan it. Unlike the woman searching diligently for a lost coin, this discovery is not a matter of a systematic search undertaken using all the latest gadgets. It is a completely unexpected surprise. A eureka moment. So also is our first glimpse of God's kingdom. All true religion is a response to God's self-revelation—in creation, in other people, in the Word, in inner experience. Religion is not a self-made activity; it is response. God first loved us, and it is in our perception of that love that we are compelled to begin to walk by a different path.

The second insight that the parable reveals is that the discovery of the treasure is a source of joy. Our whole attitude to life is changed; the world seems like a different place. To many people religion seems like a dreary thing, a wet blanket that dulls their innate liveliness and condemns them to a less-than-happy existence. The parable says something different. The revelation of God brings joy and energy. It tends to make us see things differently and, as a consequence, act differently.

The third point that the parable makes is that the enthusiasm of the discovery generates a willingness to take whatever steps are necessary in order to acquire the treasure that we have merely glimpsed. We sell everything to buy the field in which the treasure is hidden. Whatever loss we sustain is nothing compared to the profit received in acquiring the field. The parable insists on this. It does not say that someone sold everything, bought a field, looked for treasure, and eventually found it. No. First the treasure was found. After that nothing else mattered except to acquire the treasure. This is the pearl of great price, compared with which everything else seems of considerably less value. (July 27, 2014.)

> *Loving Father, in revealing yourself to us you have given us a glimpse of what we desire more than anything else. Give us the courage to be guided by our desire, so that with joy we may abandon all to find the All. We make this prayer in the name of Jesus our Lord. Amen.*

November 22   ✝   *Tribalism*

I was raised a tribal Catholic, and I am grateful for that. I grew up accepting that Catholicism, with all its pomps and works, was the default form of Christianity and, practically speaking, the only certain way of arriving at heaven. There was a strong sense of the difference between "us" and "them," with the unspoken implication that "our" way was the right way. This certainty gave a sense that every piece of the jigsaw of life fitted together neatly, whether or not I understood the details.

The difficulty that arises with the idea of tribal Catholicism is that it is a contradiction in terms. *Catholic* means "all-embracing, all-inclusive." There are no outsiders. Tribalism, on the other hand, sets arbitrary boundaries that divide people from one another; it promotes the interplay of shared prejudices and fails to recognize the good qualities that are present outside the self-created frontiers. It is as though we judge people by the clothes they wear: if they wore no clothes, we would see only people who, although different, look remarkably alike.

There is a dirty secret in tribalism despite its feel-good propaganda. The boundaries on which it relies for its sense of well-being are based on fear, resentment, and envy. Maybe we are secretly afraid that others have seen some part of the truth that we may have missed. Perhaps we resent their freedom from the mass of obligations that membership in the tribe imposes. It may happen that we are drawn to envy because those outside seem to be having more fun than we allow ourselves. I suppose that if we make any progress in our experience of God, we will begin to have doubts about the inside-outside division. If God has no favorites, then that means that the demarcation lines that we have drawn are not visible from heaven.

If you read the New Testament you will discover that we are not the only ones caught in the trap of tribalism. It is not so easy to recognize that the God who is our God is also the God of those whom we piously reject. We have to change our way of thinking. Vatican II started the process, but we need to work on putting it into practice. We have to begin to think of a Christianity without frontiers: *Christianisme sans frontières.* (September 28, 2003.)

> *Creator God, it is your will that all people be saved and come to the knowledge of the truth. Open our eyes to perceive your providence at work in every corner of the globe, leading all toward that abundance of life which Jesus, your Son, came to earth to give. Help us to see your merciful designs more clearly. We ask this through Christ our Lord. Amen.*

November 23   ✠   *Trinity*

Nowadays I find that I have to be very careful when I commit a crime. Apparently, we are always dropping off hairs and other assorted body parts that can be scooped up and analyzed by forensic experts. Each of these bits is stamped with my unique genetic signature, my DNA; from it I can be identified as the perpetrator of the act, and I'm gone. Even the least scientific among us know a little about DNA; we know that it is a unique identifier, and we know that it contains the key to understanding many of our most intimate characteristics—if only we have the ability to read it.

Suppose I were to ask about the DNA of God. Of course, I am speaking in images. What is the signature characteristic that is at the heart of everything God is and does? We have to rely on a very pale human word to describe it, but it is the best we can do. In fact, Saint John helps us out. He says, "God is love." A moment's thought is probably sufficient to convince us that in this case, "love" is no more than a shallow metaphor for the divine reality—it scarcely manages to embrace the totality of what human love involves.

Love seems to imply intimate and ultimately truthful giving and receiving between persons. This is the deepest truth of what is barely indicated by the doctrine of God as Trinity. In human love there are elements of generating, nurturing, enabling, forgiving, repairing, making happy, uniting, and many other positive interactions between people. In other words, love has a tendency to reach out and extend its influence, transforming anything it touches. One who falls in love discovers a winter's day suddenly transformed into spring.

What we are asked to believe is that God is not some cold metaphysical abstraction but a warm, exciting, dynamic conversation of shared life between persons. An eternal, self-sustaining exchange of love. Relationship is intrinsic to God. To be sure, we cannot, in this life, comprehend the reality of the inner life of the Trinity. That is testimony to the weakness of our intellects;

it does not impugn the reality of God. There is, however, a lesson we can take away from this dogma: if God is love, then the more loving we are, the more Godlike we are becoming. (May 26, 2002.)

Father, Son, and Holy Spirit, the source of all blessing, to you be honor and glory through all ages, now and forever. Amen.

November 24 ✢ *Trust*

One of the difficulties we face in reflecting on the parables Jesus told concerning the relationship of sheep and shepherd is that the image has become woolly and sentimentalized. The chapter needs to be read in the context of a rising tide of hostility following the curing of the blind man and the altercation that followed. Lurking in the background are the robbers and false shepherds whose concern is to exploit the sheep and against whom Jesus is directing his teaching.

The ultimate goal of shepherding is for the sheep to have safety from predators, freedom of movement, and good pasture. The success of the enterprise is to be measured in the sheep, not in the shepherd. The competent shepherd is one who leads his flock to a more abundant life; his own profit is secondary.

Applying the image to himself, Jesus asserts that he is the one who has the unique and exclusive possibility of leading his disciples to eternal life. There is no alternative. As far as his followers are concerned, they have unmediated access to their shepherd so that they can exist in a state of mutual recognition and trust. Trust is not as easy as it sounds. It almost always involves not knowing quite where we are being taken. It involves walking along paths that may be unfamiliar and seem to lead nowhere. The desire to arrive is expressed in our willingness to follow the guide.

To those who wish to apply for the position of shepherd of Christ's flock, Jesus clearly states the requirements. This is not a profit-making position. Those who get the job must be more concerned with benefitting the flock than simply being seen as leaders. They must take the trouble to know their sheep. To win trust they must give trust. If it comes to the crunch, they must be prepared to die for the sake of those in their care. Total trust needs to flow freely: from the Lord to the shepherds, from the shepherds to the sheep, from the sheep to the shepherds, from the shepherds to the Lord.

Meanwhile, Christ remains the chief Shepherd of his flock; those who are entrusted with the role represent Christ; they do not replace him. (April 13, 2008.)

Lord Jesus Christ, Shepherd of all who follow you, teach us to recognize your voice amid the clamor of our daily lives. Give us the openness to let your call echo in our hearts so that we may follow you, our way and our truth, into the glory of eternal life. For you are our Lord forever and ever. Amen.

November 25   ✠   **Truth**

Week by week we are admonished to upgrade our behavior. A worthy ambition, no doubt, but how do we achieve this goal? It seems to me that there are two ways to do this: the way of the law and the way of truth.

The way of the law demands self-control. We make rules for ourselves and rigidly adhere to proper standards so that we never deviate from the path of righteousness. These rules may derive from a written code of conduct compiled by somebody else, or they can be principles that we adopt for ourselves. Does the way of the law achieve its goal? The immediate answer is yes. On reflection, however, we need to qualify this; it works well for a while and only in designated areas. Often there are other zones of conduct that it fails to cover.

The way of the law has two liabilities. The first is that it tends to create a kind of hardness within us. Because we spend so much time and energy actively struggling against our own contrary inclinations, we tend to become a bit rigid in our conduct and severe in our judgment of others. Much of the joy goes out of life. Secondly, our efforts to push behavior in one direction tend to make the opposite direction more attractive until finally we are overpowered by temptation. We see this in literature with fallen clergymen—as in Somerset Maugham's *Rain* and William Golding's *Rites of Passage*.

The way of truth is much more effective. It summons us to integral self-knowledge: to see ourselves as we are, as we are called to be, and as one with others. This involves reducing the symptoms of untruthfulness, such as the denial of our fragility, the repression of our awareness of contrary tendencies, the refusal to accept full responsibility for our acts, the rejection of our solidarity with others, and forgetfulness of God. The truth to which Christ calls us involves the acceptance that we are called not to be perfect, unfailing, and blameless, but to be accepted, forgiven, and loved. By a God who transcends human rules. (September 1, 1991.)

> *God of mercy and compassion, teach us to entrust ourselves to your parental care. Help us to accept ourselves in all our frailty and to base all our confidence on your power to bring to perfection what you have created. We ask this through Christ our Lord. Amen.*

November 26   ✟   **Two Legs**

The disciple's life with Jesus is contained in a simple phrase with two elements: "Come after me." The two legs by which the disciple fulfills that command are being active and being guided. By the first disciples bestir themselves to start moving; by the second they commit to following not their own plans but the mission entrusted to them by Jesus.

The *activity* to which disciples are called can be qualified by a large variety of words: generosity, relinquishment, movement, boldness, energy, idealism, constancy, perseverance. These are outcomes that require a definite and sometimes heroic act of the will. They do not happen automatically. They are the heartfelt response to the call of Jesus that brings about a change in our way of thinking and changes the way we evaluate issues and, so, generates a change of behavior.

There is, however, a danger that unrestrained action might transform itself into a species of fanaticism. The work in which we engage is not our own; we are participating in the work of Jesus, the shape of which will not always be clear to us. So, *guidance* is necessary. There is always the possibility that Jesus will say to us, as he said to Simon Peter, "Your way of thinking is only human; it is not from God." A disciple is a lifelong learner, always in a state of formation under a Master. On the one hand, this involves taking care to hear the words of the Instructor and receiving them reverently and humbly. Allowing oneself to be instructed. On the other, it is a matter of being part of a community of disciples, picking up from others what one has failed to catch.

If I find myself stopped on the road, or sliding backward, or sinking under the waves of sub-personal forces, I check these two legs.

Have I ceased moving, overcome by inertia? Is there resistance to inner or outer change? Have I allowed myself to become idle, self-indulgent, or a professional procrastinator?

Alternatively, have I lost direction? Am I too afraid or too ashamed to ask for help? Too self-preoccupied to care? Have I allowed my individualistic needs to drive me off course?

Jesus calls us to come after him, not to stay as we are but, by his grace, to become what he is. (January 27, 2002.)

Lord Jesus Christ, you call us to follow along the way you walked. Give us the courage to respond to your summons, the generosity to invest our energies in proclaiming your kingdom, and the perseverance to remain with you even when life seems very difficult. For you are our Lord for ever and ever. Amen.

November 27 ✝ **Uglification**

This is a word I came across recently. The sound of the word is almost as unpleasant as the reality it describes. It refers to the process by which we justify treating others badly. We reduce them to their least pleasant attribute; we dehumanize them. If you think about it, every war begins with a propaganda blitz on enemies, their tainted history, their present crimes, their inhumanity. They are "them" and not "us." This gives a spurious sense of legitimacy to whatever horrors we choose to inflict upon them. They deserve it.

Meanwhile, back at the ranch, we love our families; we cherish our acquaintances and are good to the strangers who qualify for our acceptance. We go to church and listen to the gospel telling us to love our neighbor and nod our heads in solemn agreement. We are too humble to describe ourselves as blameless, but, in reality, we think there is little for which we could be reproached.

Certainly, love is a reality in our life. The problem is that we have set boundaries around our love. Perhaps we are more aware of those we have excluded than of those whom we accept. That is why so much of our conversation concerns the failing of others. We reject so many people without the benefit of a fair trial, but solely on the basis of tribal prejudices and hasty impressions.

It was this situation that drew from Jesus the parable of the Good Samaritan. We have to allow our humanity to go out from itself to meet the humanity of others, uninhibited by unflattering labels. Even our enemies. Here is an example. In November 1941, in all the confusion of the desert war in North Africa, German general Erwin Rommel unexpectedly came across a New Zealand field hospital full of wounded enemy combatants. He greeted patients and staff courteously, bulked out their failing supplies, and passed on, leaving them in peace. To see our common humanity in the most unlikely people and then to express our solidarity by action is to make everyone our neighbor. As Jesus said to the expert in the law who had posed the question, "Go and do likewise." (September 3, 2002.)

Heavenly Father, you have commanded us to love without restriction. Send into our hearts your Spirit of love so that,

*day by day and hour by hour, we may pull down the walls
that separate us from those who are different and recognize
in them our common humanity. And we ask this through
Christ our Lord. Amen.*

November 28   ✠   *Unblocking*

We all know the right answer to the question the Pharisee asked
Jesus about the greatest of the commandments. Jesus' answer
surprised no one, since the rabbis were saying the same thing.
We certainly hear about it often enough. I am often amazed at
just how banal, boring, and repetitive some preachers can make
any discussion of the topic.

My first question is this: How can you have a commandment
to love? The law concerns itself with external acts. We must pay
taxes; we are not obliged to like it. We must avoid racial vilifica-
tion, but the law cannot compel us to have respect for others.
Children must eat parsnips and brussels sprouts; it is useless for
parents to command them to enjoy doing so.

We get around this by affirming that love is an act of the will,
not mere sentiment. We must grin and bear it. This is to sidestep
the issue. Jesus commands us to love our neighbors, not just to
do the right thing by them. We are commanded to enter into
that zone where love is given and received, experienced, and
expressed. This is certainly a challenge, but how can it be an
obligation?

If we go to the First Epistle of Saint John we find an insistence
that the "new commandment" is not new. It is ancient. It preexists human choice because it is an imperative of human nature.
Expressions of love are aroused naturally whenever we encounter something good. Unless there is an obstruction, blockage, or
interference with that natural movement.

The practical consequence of the commandment to love is an
obligation to identify, acknowledge, and neutralize whatever
stands in the way of this natural impulse. Love is of our nature.

Not to love is unnatural. If we remove the blockages, the way to love lies open.

What are the obstacles we need to tackle? First is the blindness that does not permit us to see the goodness in others. Second is selfishness; this makes us hold ourselves back or treat others badly so that things will turn out exactly as we wish. The third is more mysterious. It is envy, the evil eye that sometimes makes people perversely want to destroy what is good, beautiful, or successful.

We are commanded to remove these obstacles, to unblock our natural affective tendencies. If we do this, we will find that a deep and sincere love follows without much drama. (October 25, 2008.)

> *Lord Jesus, in commanding us to love, you are inviting us to follow in your footsteps. "Give us what you command and command whatever you will." For you are our Lord for ever and ever. Amen.*

November 29   ✠   *Uncompromising*

Saint Paul seems not to have been averse to making uncompromising statements. One of his most challenging declarations is found in the First Epistle to the Corinthians: "If for this life only we have hope in Christ Jesus, then, of all people, are we the most to be pitied." This sentence affirms that the meaning of Christian discipleship cannot be found without reference to the future life. It is only our participation in the life of heaven that will enable us to make any sense of what we are now experiencing.

If Paul were around today, he would be taunting the purveyors of the "prosperity gospel" for their nearsightedness. Jesus certainly promised a hundredfold in this life (though not without persecutions), but these present blessings are only a sample or a down payment of what is to come. The ultimate rewards of the kingdom transcend all experience and are far beyond what the human heart can envisage. They are more than we can understand or describe. They cannot be reduced to enhancements of our existence in time, no more than the Gospel can be reduced to morality or a system of metaphysics.

It takes a bit of courage to affirm an afterlife; we cannot prove it, and the pictures of it that are in the popular imagination are farcical—white gowns, halos, and harps. Even for many righteous people who are regular churchgoers, there is a tendency to wall off any belief in the afterlife and confine their attention to trying to live a good life in the present. Sometimes it seems bad manners to mention a future life, even at a funeral. And there is not much of a market for sermons that point to a future judgment and thence to a division between sheep and goats.

Saint Paul is saying that Christianity is meaningless if there is nothing beyond the grave. Discipleship involves effort, sacrifice, hardship, renunciation. All this is accepted in the hope that things will change when the new era dawns. Because we seek the things that are above, we are better able to tolerate bad things here below. Our definitive salvation is not something that has been already achieved. It is to be hoped for. We are not to be pitied because we have the promise of Christ that a place has been prepared for us in our Father's house. Even on the bleakest days, when it is hard to get out of bed, we have something to look forward to, ultimately, if not immediately. (February 22, 1971.)

Lord Jesus Christ, you have promised eternal life to those who follow you. Give us the courage to believe in your promises and the confidence to endure whatever suffering comes our way, knowing that nothing can separate us from your love and concern. For you are our Lord for ever and ever. Amen.

November 30 ✠ *Uncovering*

Perhaps you know the old joke about the politician who receives a telegram with a simple message: "All is known." He leaves town on the next train. Most of us would want to do the same. We do not want our real secrets revealed to the whole world. Curiously, Jesus approaches such exposure from a different angle. He says, "Fear not . . . all will be revealed." For Jesus the Last Judgment will be primarily an act of mercy, an act of salvation, in which the children of God are called into their eternal inheritance.

In this judgment the whole story will be revealed, and not only individual moments. It will be more than a matter of examining in isolation every thought, word, or action against the law of God; it includes comprehending how these actions came about—not just the actual event, but the long buildup and the inner forces that made the event likely. Christ is our advocate, as Saint John says, our defense attorney and not our prosecutor. The evangelist continues, "Even though our hearts condemn us, God is greater than our hearts, for God knows everything." As the psalm sings, "God knows of what we are made; God remembers that we are dust."

It is sometimes hard for us to get our heads around the idea that God's mercy far exceeds the extent of human malice. This is an instance of the law of divine superabundance. Sin is horrible. The wonder of God's love is that it not only negates sin and its effect but also replaces it with forgiveness so complete that sin disappears. "If you were to mark our guilt, Lord, who would stand?" The abolition of sin is God's professional hallmark. This is why Jesus keeps telling us, in the Sermon on the Mount, to leave aside all anxiety. God cares for us.

The Gospel is good news. Let nothing disturb us. But perhaps we need to remember that is good news not only for us but for all. If we are happy to escape a quick judgment, maybe we should repay the favor by being a little slower to condemn others, who are no less weak or misguided than ourselves. (June 20, 1993.)

Loving Father, your care for all your children is without limits. Teach us to have confidence in your loving concern so that we may image your generosity to us in the way we treat others. We ask this through Christ our Lord. Amen.

December 1 ✠ *Unity*

Jesus' final discourse during the Last Supper, as given in the Fourth Gospel, manifests a strong emphasis on unity. Reading it, we are quickly made conscious that, although we proclaim in the Creed that the church is one, there is much disunity among Christians. This is patently true of the state of relationships between various ecclesial bodies, but it is also true on a more local level, within families and communities. Such disunity is the source of dysfunctionality and malaise, and it needs to be addressed. Yet it soon becomes obvious that it is not easy to reunite what has been divided.

Most people who have been called to arbitrate a situation of conflict come to the conclusion that neither side is blameless. The responsibility for the quarrel is not always symmetrical; often more fuel is added to the fire from one side than from the other. The fact remains, however, that just as it takes two to tango, it takes two to have a fight. So long as we remain fixated on identifying which party is the culprit, we have little hope of moving toward a reconciliation.

What most of us don't stop to consider is that in most cases of social division the root cause is a fundamental division within the persons involved. We cannot achieve perfect unity with others when we (and they) are divided within ourselves. The way to unity is the way of personal integrity. It is easier to come together when our words truly represent what we think and feel and hold dear, and when our works are in harmony with what we say. So much interference to relationships comes about because of a lack of transparency; we don't do as we say, and we don't say as we really think.

If we really want to reduce the comparison, competition, polarization, and war on which our society seems to be built, then our first step must be to be faithful to our own nature and calling. To be true to ourselves. Remaining faithful to the word of Christ—becoming more Christlike—will almost certainly put us beyond fair criticism. It will attract and not repel. In our own

small way, we advance the unity for which Christ prayed.
(May 22, 2012.)

> *Lord Jesus Christ, you prayed that those who followed you
> would be one in heart and mind. Grant us the grace to elimi-
> nate within ourselves what threatens our relationship with
> others so that we serve the process of healing that you began
> in your days on earth. For you are our Lord for ever and
> ever. Amen.*

December 2 ✠ *Universality*

We often try to paper over our defects by giving them a different
name. A nation ruled by a dictator calls itself "democratic." Factory-
baked cakes are labeled "homemade." A conservative political party
adopts the title "liberal." And we are continually renaming the
smallest room in the house to avoid referring to its function.

Is it the same with the "catholic" church? Is the name reflective of the reality or an effort to disguise it? *Catholic* means
universal, all-inclusive, nonexclusive. We accept this in theory,
but we are constantly tempted to restrict the broadness it implies. It may well be that the church has an open-door policy and
any may enter, but, in practice, entry is controlled by keen-eyed
bouncers. We want the membership of the church to be good,
and we think that we can achieve this by excluding those whom
we consider unworthy.

In rejecting others we are really rejecting ourselves. It is well-
known that what we find especially abhorrent in other people is
usually indicative of our own unrecognized vicious tendencies.
The reason I despise an angry person is because inwardly I myself
am seething with rage. If I demand a high standard of conduct
for admission to the kingdom, I will soon find myself dubious
about my own worthiness.

The catholicity of the church has its foundation in the unconditional nature of God's love. The door to salvation is open because this is what God wills, not because of any quality in us.

Acceptance into God's kingdom is not dependent on my approval; it is the result of God's invitation. The New Testament insists that God's will is that all are to be saved and come to the knowledge of the truth. This includes pagans, tax collectors, and sinners, and there seems to be a preference for those on the margins of society. Entry into heaven—unlike the Melbourne Club—is not restricted to the rich and influential.

All are called. All make the journey in their own unique way. All have the opportunity to share in the banquet of divine being. This is the heart of the Good News. This is what makes Christ's church "catholic." (January 2, 1994.)

> *Father of us all, you so loved the world that you sent your only Son to seek out the wandering and lost. Help us to accept everyone and to be active in welcoming all people to share with us the more abundant life your Son has brought. We ask this in the name of Jesus our Lord. Amen.*

December 3 ✠ *Unknowing*

One of the qualities that sets us apart from monkeys is the fact that we often ask the question, "Why?" Little children pose this question often. We know when we don't know something, and sometimes we know that we don't know. I don't know what tomorrow's weather will be, for example. Especially in Melbourne. We are often restless when we don't know something that we think we should, and we feel good when we discover the answer to our question.

It doesn't take long to figure out that the world is bigger than my brain. There are plenty of things that I don't understand. The fact that I don't understand something does not mean that it is not a reality. I don't understand how cars work, but I drive them. I don't understand electricity, but I use it just about every hour of every day. I don't understand the science behind vaccination, but all my life I have willingly lined up for any injection that was available.

If I accept this, then I can hardly be surprised if my knowledge of God is not comprehensive—even though I have degrees in theology. God's dealings with humanity don't always make sense to me, but that is due to a defect on my part and not to any fault on God's. Sometimes God's choices seem strange to me, but I am scarcely an expert. "How odd of God to choose the Jews," went the saying attributed to William Norman Ewer. Why not the Hittites? Answer: I don't know. Why did God choose such losers to be his apostles and the foundation of his church? Same answer. Which means that I am not competent to make judgments on the options that God takes.

I am like a passenger on the train of history. I am not the driver. I am not the controller. I am being carried along with many others to my destination, thanks to the cooperation of many unseen hands. All I have to do is to stay on the train. Yes, I do sometimes have an active role to play, but usually it is relatively minor.

As Christians, we are called on to accept the reality of an unseen world that surrounds us and permeates every element of our existence. We operate by faith and not by sight. Yes, our comprehension is far from complete, and we would be incompetent to argue for its validity. But what we have is an inner assurance of the reality of the invisible universe. What we experience bathes our unknowing in a warm glow of hope that is not full daylight, but yet is far from darkness. (June 12, 2005.)

Creator and sustainer God, help us to trust in your merciful providence to bring us to eternal life, even though we must journey through many changes and reversals of fortune. Give us the buoyancy to remain afloat even while the storms rage around us. We ask this in the name of Jesus our Lord. Amen.

December 4   ✠   *Unprofitable Servants*

Jesus' injunction to his disciples to regard themselves as "unprofitable servants" is one of those passages in the Gospel tradition that shows a certain pungency in the way Jesus dealt with his immediate followers. They were not to get above themselves. They were merely the interface between God and those whom they were called to serve; the good that was done was done by God.

Most of us are hungry for appreciation, affirmation, and even adulation. We want our efforts to be recognized and our successes crowned. Almost inevitably we feel envious of those who are the recipients of honors. If they are regarded as superior persons, then that makes us inferior. It is only very reluctantly that we go to take the last place.

"Who is greater," Jesus asks the Twelve at the Last Supper, "the one serving the meal or the one sitting at table? Yet, here am I among you as one who serves." In the upside-down system of values that Jesus promulgates, it is the invisible, self-effacing servant who is regarded as more important than the pontificating lord.

In some of the Father Brown stories by G. K. Chesterton, the villain is someone who seems invisible: a postman or a waiter or some other menial functionary. Everyone saw him, but none of them could describe him. His personality was subsumed by his function. He was simply one among many unimportant people, indistinguishable from the rest.

Jesus asks his disciples to have this kind of transparency as an ideal. They are not on an ego trip; they are there to proclaim the kingdom. Like them, we are called to efface ourselves and allow the Good News to speak for itself—which it does with power beyond anything we could accomplish. We may encounter complex situations that far exceed any skills we have to deal with them; instead of being discouraged and withdrawing, we should seek ways in which to commend to God what we cannot resolve. To step back, as it were, and allow God to act directly. With a bit of practice we may learn to glory in our infirmity, and then the power of Christ will be active through us. (November 14, 2017.)

Lord Jesus, you call those who follow you to a life of service.
Give us the boldness to be ministers of your word and your
compassion to an unbelieving world, and help us to recognize

our limits and so to make room for your all-surpassing power.
For you are our Lord for ever and ever. Amen.

December 5 ✠ **Unveiling**

God is unveiled before human eyes in many and varied ways. Each of us receives the revelation in a very particular form that is unique to ourselves. We are probably familiar with the theme in Jesus' teaching that, in the matter of revelation, it is the poor, the simple, the lowly, and the childlike who have priority. The rich and the powerful are sent away empty. "That which is highly esteemed by people is an abomination before God."

Perhaps we need to see this matter from another angle. It may well be true that those who receive the revelation of God become thereby humble and childlike. Having been exposed to the fearsome fascination of the infinite God, they cannot see themselves as anything but poor and simple souls. To catch sight of something inestimably greater than ourselves immediately returns our self-esteem to reality. In my own little pond I may be a big fish, but if I move out into the ocean I soon recognize that I am no more than a minnow.

Catching sight of God is life-giving. We may feel smaller because of it, but the experience itself fills us with wonderment and love. We become enthusiastic, desiring to be irradiated yet more by this attractive outflow of goodness. It is this experience of something of the reality of the spiritual world that starts us off on our journey toward God. The Latin translation of the story of Jacob's struggle with the angel ends with the joyous outburst, "I have seen the Lord face to face and my soul has been saved."

If it happens that we begin to doubt that we are worthy of even a faint shadow of such a vision, what can we do about it? Perhaps if we make ourselves less, if we empty our lives to make room for God, then it will be possible for us to be filled with light. In some way the face of God will be unveiled before us, and our souls will be saved. (July 15, 2009.)

Lord God, you have revealed yourself to us in many and varied ways. Open our eyes so that we may gaze with wonderment on your hidden presence in our midst, and give us the grace to live more conscious of your all-surrounding love. We ask this in the name of Jesus our Lord. Amen.

December 6   ✠   *Unworthiness*

If Queen Elizabeth were to visit our town, whom would she meet? No doubt our local celebrities: fat-bellied aldermen and their hangers-on. The rest of us would be kept behind barriers, permitted only to gawk. And any person considered particularly undesirable would be kept out of the way for the duration of the visit.

If Christ were to visit our town, whom would he meet? The same spotty elite? No, he seems not much interested in these people. He comes by bus instead of in a Rolls Royce with police escort, and he doesn't turn up where the ninety-nine are waiting with the brass band. Instead he goes off in search of the one who was excluded, saying, "I was sent to the lost sheep." He greets such a person warmly, and together they go off for a drink and a meal, while the band plays on and all the dignitaries are shuffling their feet and anxiously scanning the horizon for signs of his arrival.

The people with whom Jesus prefers to spend time are certainly exclusive—but that is because honesty and integrity and lack of humbug are so rare. He does not much associate with the privileged, the rich, and the socially superior—those with class. If they want to join his circle they are welcome, but it means a step down, not a step up. It means mingling with tax collectors, such as Zacchaeus, and those formerly demon-possessed, such as Mary Magdalen. It means risking contagion from lepers and standing beside the disenfranchised. It means hearing Jesus say, "That which is highly esteemed by human beings is an abomination before God." It means adopting a different philosophy of life, renouncing ambition and dependence on wealth and privilege. It means passing through the eye of a needle and becoming like little children. A real change of heart and self-understanding.

If we can learn to repeat the words of the centurion in the gospel with real sincerity, then Jesus will probably want to seek us out. He came to make contact with the unworthy. Curiously, we make ourselves worthy by professing our unworthiness. This is why before we come to Holy Communion the church puts in our mouths the words, "Lord, I am not worthy." And the Lord responds to such an admission, "These are my kind of people." (August 8, 1982.)

> *Lord Jesus Christ, you came as a physician not to the healthy but to those burdened with illness and infirmity. Give us confidence to approach you even though we feel unworthy. Give us the boldness to kneel before you and say, "Lord help me." For you are our Lord, for ever and ever. Amen.*

December 7   ✝   **Us and Them**

One of the more remarkable aspects of Jesus' earthly career was his willingness to break bread with those generally regarded as disreputable. In this way he can be seen to have been the champion of the marginalized. But we should not forget that, on occasion, he also dined with Pharisees. This duality is a frustration if we are the sort of people who like to have everything clearly defined and set in concrete. Jesus moved between both extremes of contemporary society.

The lesson we can learn from this broad conviviality is that perhaps we need to stop dividing the world between "us" and "them." So many of our activities—politics, sports, even religion—seek to retain the adherence of their members by inculcating a strong sense of "us" in opposition to "them." We thank God that we are not like the rest of humanity, and they thank God that they are not like us. There are so many ways of dividing humanity: race, religion, age, gender, wealth, and a thousand more. We cultivate our identity by a process of exclusion and by a kind of competitiveness aimed at demonstrating that our loyalties are absolutely undivided.

As a result, we live in a world of walls and our sense of well-being depends on the continuance of these solid means of division. We see them as protection from invading hordes of barbarians waiting to encroach upon our sacred space, as if we were the Roman Empire in the final stages of its terminal decline. But they are merely material embodiments of our own inner fears.

Perhaps we need to follow the example of Jesus and break down a few walls and learn to live as good neighbors. We can't hope to set the world on fire with our zeal for more commonality, but we can begin to take a few steps in our own immediate situation. One of the best beginnings to building bridges is conversation. Just as we know that when acquaintances fall out a great gulf of silence grows up between them, so we can narrow the gulf between "us" and "them" by exchanging a few words and permitting ourselves to discover that others are not so different. The simplest conversation establishes contact that, if it is allowed to grow, will transform the "them" into "us." (March 4, 2017.)

Lord Jesus Christ, friend of all, you came to bring together a divided people and to teach us to live in solidarity and peace. Help us to reach out to those near who are strangers, to extend the hand of friendship and support, and thus to find in them those with whom we hope to share eternal life. For you are our Lord for ever and ever. Amen.

December 8 ✝ *Vanity*

"Vanity of vanities and all is vanity." These memorable opening words of the biblical book of Qoheleth have many echoes in the thoughts of philosophers, but, for the most part, we don't pay them much attention. In the midst of life they seem pessimistic. We prefer to look on the bright side. Yet as we get older this sentiment seems to make more and more sense. So many matters

that we once considered as vitally important now seem little
more than frivolous. The changing fortunes of football teams may
once have dictated how we felt about life; now we are somewhat
free of that. Whatever residual interest we retain tends not to
spark huge emotions.

We live in a world in which delusional expectations are rou-
tinely promoted by politicians, advertisers, and well-meaning
purveyors of new trends. A change in toothpaste will not win
you new friends, nor is the consumption of frothy beverages liable to lead you to a more abundant life. This means that if we
accept these false-friend promises, we are prone to be hit by
eventual disappointment and frustration. This is a lesson of life
that we will all learn eventually.

In 1799 a Lutheran theologian, Friedrich Schleiermacher, proposed that the essential core of religion was a sense of absolute
dependence on God. "Dependence?" you say. "How can that be
a good thing?" Strangely enough, it is. Depending on God alone
makes us independent of everything else. It frees us from all the
false dependencies that threaten to enslave us. "Put no trust in
princes," says the psalmist, "in mere mortals in whom there is
no help."

When Qoheleth talks about the essential emptiness of things
and their incapacity to satisfy our deepest yearnings, he is thinking particularly of the tyranny of nostalgia about the past and
dreaming about the future. His remedy for the kind of existential
dread he describes is to live in the present. To stop complaining
and enjoy what you have. "Eat, drink and enjoy your work. . . .
This comes from God." Make the most of what you have. Otherwise you are just chasing the wind. You will never catch it, and
you will end up exhausted. (September 25, 2014.)

*Creator God, you have implanted in our hearts a desire for
you that nothing else will satisfy. Help us to see the good
things of this world as gifts of your love and to use them as
stepping stones by which we lift ourselves up toward you. We*

*ask you this in the name of your Son, whom you have given
us as the way to eternal life, now and forever. Amen.*

December 9 ✠ *Variety*

There is a kind of subsidiary message in the story of Mary and
Martha: it is possible to welcome Christ in different ways. Both
workers and entertainers are necessary if we are to offer hospitality; we expect both food and conversation. One without the other
would probably leave us wondering whether we were really welcome.

That qualitative differences exist among people cannot be
disputed. We each have our own temperament and history; we
each have different skills and opportunities. By nature and grace
we are distinctive. It is unreasonable to expect everyone to be
willing and able to do every task with a similar degree of ease.
One may whip up a soufflé without a shudder, yet crash to earth
at the prospect of speaking in public. Another may have boundless patience with a demented grandmother, but be unable to fill
in a tax form correctly.

If we were all the same, the total level of competence in any
group would be reduced. If we were all the same, the skill of the
group would be identical to any one member. On the other hand,
because we are all different, when people get together they enjoy
a much wider range of competencies than any one person within
the group. Difference is enriching.

When I become irritated by another's lack of competence and
willingness, I am unfair to that person, who undoubtedly has
skills that I lack. There may, however, be darker motivations at
play. By underlining another's defects I may be hoping to offset
the many superior qualities that person possesses because these
threaten my own fragile sense of self-worth. Especially when
criticism is chronic and carping, I am probably giving way to
competitiveness and envy. Fearful of being weighed on the scale
and found wanting, I try to influence the outcome with a little

negativity. I need to explore the origins of any gratuitous judgment I make about another. Being different from me is not necessarily a bad thing.

If I were secure in who and what I am, I would be content in any situation. I would contribute a measure of harmony to any group of which I am a member. I would have the gift to acknowledge the fine qualities of others, to praise and celebrate them, knowing that what belongs to one ultimately contributes to the well-being of all. (July 19, 1992.)

> *Creator God, you have made us all in your image and likeness, and you have given each of us the mission to embody a different aspect of your glory. Help us to be confident in what you have given us and respectful of what you have given to others, so that we may live in peace and support one another by cooperation and patience. We ask this in the name of Jesus our Lord. Amen.*

December 10   ✝   *Vianney*

Saint John Vianney, the Curé of Ars, is a good reminder that none of us enjoys every possible gift of talent. When we talk about the saints, it is easy to imagine that they excel in every field of human endeavor, or at least in those that are worth valuing. Surely it is unfair to criticize Mother Teresa of Calcutta for her poor tennis, or John XXIII for his clumsy dancing, or Teresa of Avila for her ignorance of Hebrew. It may well be true that these saints had these defects, but these deficiencies do not detract from their essential goodness and holiness. The ample rotundity of Saint Thomas Aquinas may have led to an impaired athleticism, but it did not inhibit the workings of his brilliant intellect.

To most of his contemporaries, John Vianney must have appeared like a poor goose indeed. His skills seemed so limited that he was lucky to be accepted for ordination, and afterward he was sent to a parish where his ineptitude did not matter, so uninterested in religion were the people of the locality. Strangely,

Vianney was the right man for the job. His lack of learned eloquence was counterbalanced by a disciplined lifestyle, a willingness to walk miles to reach the abandoned, and his immense
patience in listening to people. Estranged Catholics came to him
from miles around because they found in him someone who was
prepared to listen to their stories and to respond to them with
God's own mercy and compassion. A thousand well-preached
sermons would never have achieved half of what his uncompromising kindness brought about.

Perhaps it is time to rid ourselves of the delusion that absolute
perfection is worth pursuing. In the lives of all of us there are
chapters of failure and infidelity. More often than not these are
the times in which we learn something. In God's providence, the
lessons we learn in such circumstances often equip us with the
competencies we need to help others in trouble. Human life is
very complicated; if we remove the blemishes, we may find that
there is nothing left. (August 4, 2015.)

> *God of infinite perfection, teach us to be content with the*
> *limitations of nature and grace in which we live. Help us to*
> *understand that your grace accomplishes what we cannot*
> *and your mercy provides a remedy for our failures. We ask*
> *this through Christ our Lord. Amen.*

December 11   ✝   *Violence*

Pope Benedict recently got himself into a bit of trouble when,
speaking at Regensburg, he suggested that maybe violence has
been inherent in Islam from the very beginning. He has since
spent a certain amount of time backpedaling on that particular
statement. I imagine the point that he was trying to make was
that despite many, many failures in its history, there is in Christianity—even in residual Christianity—an ideal of nonviolence.
This involves embracing the ideal of loving one's enemies, being
prepared to offer forgiveness freely, and renouncing all claims to
vengeance. This is a difficult ideal to propose, and it is not sur-

prising that there have been countless and scandalous failures. But failure does not make nonviolence less of an ideal, toward which we are all exhorted to progress.

During its long history, the church has often grappled with the morality of warfare. To what lengths may a government go to protect its population from external violence? How preemptive may its defensive actions be? How total may be the destruction wreaked on those who violate its security? And if we want to debate history, we can ask how blameless were the Crusaders who killed and maimed and ravaged under papal sanction, all the while bearing the sign of the cross on their tunics?

It is interesting to confront such questions, but it is more important that we narrow our perspective to look at the role violence may play in our own lives. Do we use violence as a means of getting our own way? It does not have to be physical violence: we can inflict mental or emotional blackmail on others through shouting and bad language, by tantrums and passive aggression, through withdrawing our support and walking out and slamming the door. Violence has many forms, some of which are not always recognized as violence by the perpetrator but are felt as such by the victim. This is especially true in cases of sexual abuse. There is much violence around us, and if we are not careful, we will begin to mimic such behavior as a means of getting what we want.

A nonviolent world is greatly to be desired, but we can make a start by looking at our own immediate environment and asking ourselves whether we could not improve matters by being gentler, less assertive, and more respectful of the right of others to be themselves. (February 19, 2007.)

Lord Jesus Christ, meek and humble of heart, teach us the way of nonviolence. Help us to see in those we meet brothers and sisters worthy of our respect. Give us the self-discipline to restrain our violent tendencies and to do all that we can to become real peacemakers in our own environment. For you are our Lord for ever and ever. Amen.

December 12 ✝ *Visibility*

Telescopes for the viewing of stars are usually located on moun-taintops or in deserts because too much light makes the stars more difficult to see. That's why we can't stargaze during the day. When we see more, we see less.

The New Testament seems to understand this principle. There is a contrast between faith and sight, between seen and unseen, visible and invisible. Blessed are they who do not see and yet believe.

The mystery to which we give the name "Ascension" indicates a change in the visibility of Christ, not in his presence. After the Ascension, the only means by which the disciples could make contact with their risen Lord was by faith: sight, hearing, and touch all fell away. The contact was achieved not at the level of feeling but at the deepest level of our being, the level of spirit.

Faith is not diminished by lack of sight; it demands it. It is not second best because it does not see with bodily eyes. Visions and apparitions are strictly for amateurs; for professional believers, there is only the luminous twilight of faith. We worship in spirit and in truth beyond and beneath the conscious agitation of this-worldly processes. That is why Jesus said, "It is better for you that I go."

By the mystery of the Ascension Christ's presence is no longer localized, as it was when he trod the dusty roads of first-century Palestine. He is no longer restricted to a single point in the spa-tiotemporal continuum. The risen and ascended Christ is with us in his humanity wherever we are. "I am with you always," he said. The mystery of the Ascension is a celebration of presence, not absence.

The darkness that makes the light more visible is designed to help us to "seek the things that are above." If we try to convert the community of Christ's disciples into some kind of this-worldly organization, with this-worldly ambitions, and using this-worldly means, the danger is that we will lose sight of that for which we are really looking. That is why Jesus praised poverty and powerlessness and warned us to expect persecution.

No wonder some of Christ's most fervent disciples sought mountaintops and deserts. They recognized that where there is too much light, we can't see the stars. (May 15, 2010.)

Lord God, Loving Father, strengthen our faith in your Son so that our hearts may be fixed on things above. And, in our dealings with things of this world, help us to bring some of what we receive from our prayer into the lives of others. We ask this in the name of Jesus our Lord. Amen.

December 13 ✠ **Waiting**

We live in a world which does not like to wait. Instant gratification is the norm, and we are finding it more and more objectionable to endure even a short delay. Inevitably, the expectation of a rapid response infiltrates our spiritual life and our prayer. We want things to happen quickly.

If we are halfway wise, however, we probably realize that some things take time to reach their full development. Rome was not built in a day, and any worthwhile art or craft takes years to master. Unless we plan on dying young, it will be many years—even decades—before our spiritual life begins to manifest the degree of intensity for which we hope. God's work in us proceeds at its own pace; it has to operate on several levels simultaneously, and the transformation it seeks to accomplish is so radical that there are many other issues that must be faced before it can flower.

In the beginning there were often strong feelings of devotion and sudden spurts of generosity. As the years pass and spiritual values begin to take root in our everyday behavior, the rate of progress declines. It may well seem to us that nothing much is happening. We may think we are stagnating. Yet, in an undramatic way, God is still at work. What is asked of us is the patience to remain with the process.

The years of waiting bring about changes in us; above all, they teach us to be less impatient for tangible results. We may become gradually aware that our desire for God is growing and becoming more focused. That we have a broader perspective on life and are less disturbed by daily trifles. Meanwhile, the seed of God's planting is sprouting within us. Even though we cannot control or accelerate its growth, it is daily stretching forth to its season of fruitfulness. This is why Jesus tells his disciples to learn the art of waiting—you will see yet greater things. (May 17, 2012.)

Lord Jesus Christ, help us to relinquish control over spiritual lives so that you may work more freely within us. Keep us patient with our own obvious imperfection until that day when your work is complete and your glory shines forth. For you are our Lord, for ever and ever. Amen.

December 14 ✝ *Wakefulness*

As a student in Belgium I worked in the parish at NATO headquarters. I still have a plaque in my office bearing the NATO crest and its motto, *Vigilia pretium libertatis.* That is bad Latin for "Vigilance is the price of freedom." This means that freedom is not free; it costs. Proactive effort is required to be safe. This is also the theme of the gospels that are read as Ordinary Time morphs into Advent: stay awake.

Evangelical wakefulness is not like a man sitting on the front veranda with a shotgun on his knees, awaiting the arrival of the burglar, while intruders enter through the back door and ransack the house. True vigilance is not passively waiting for something to happen, but actively seeking a closer perception of reality.

Jesus warned us not to think that the coming of the kingdom would be an external event. He told us to ignore false messiahs, false prophets, and lunatics of every stripe who would announce that the end was near. The kingdom of God, he said, is very close; it is among you, it is within you. The kingdom is not an external spectacle but God acting within us to bring goodness and peace and joy in the Holy Spirit.

We are to go inside. If we do not know what is happening within, then we will be forever slaves to subconscious tendencies and urges. Unless we develop a good measure of spiritual literacy we will be strangers to our inner world, unable to life mindfully, attentively, wakefully. To a disciple who asked the way of salvation Abba Pambo replied: Find your heart and you will be saved.

Within we will find both challenge and strengthening to enable us to go beyond social conditioning and media brainwashing to become more aware of the beliefs and values by which we live. This will help us to understand why we do what we do. It frees us from the enslavement that follows mindless living. We begin to enjoy the freedom of the children of God by entering our inner space . . . often.

When we go within we find ourselves because we also find God. We discover a deep hopefulness within, a confidence that comes from looking forward to eternal life. A hope that fills us with joy and also gives us patience and endurance and resilience when hard times arrive. (December 3, 2017.)

Lord Jesus Christ, help us to remain vigilant as we look forward to your manifestation in glory. Help us to overcome our tendencies to mindless living, and do not allow us to become forgetful of your lovingkindness. For you are our Lord for ever and ever. Amen.

December 15 ✠ *Walk on Water*

A confrere on a solitary, early morning walk through downtown Kalamazoo was surprised to hear a mysterious voice saying, "Walk on water." It was not an angelic command, as he first suspected, but a recorded voice telling him it was now OK for pedestrians to cross Water Street.

Simon Peter heard these words from the mouth of Jesus. He tried, and he failed because his faith was defective. We should take warning from this because, in a sense, this is what Jesus is saying to us every day. "Walk on water. Do the impossible." How we respond to this summons will indicate at what depth our faith operates. The church teaches that all that Christ had by nature,

Christians also have, but by grace. And Jesus himself told the apostles that they would do greater things than he himself had accomplished. Knowing this, are we ready to walk on water?

If we look at the New Testament we will find that there are impossible commands awaiting us. "Be perfect *as* your heavenly Father is perfect." "Forgive us *as* we forgive." "Love one another *as* I have loved you." *As* is a small word, but it indicates an order of magnitude beyond our imagination and even further beyond our performance. And how many other admonitions there are that, although not completely impossible, are unlikely to be within our reach anytime soon.

If we believe that new life is given to those who are "in Christ," then we have to make a leap of faith and act *as if* these impossible commands were everyday tasks for us. With even a minuscule amount of faith, we will soon be moving mountains without even raising a sweat. Or perhaps not. It may well be that, like Simon Peter, when we try to walk on water we do it badly and begin to drown. This is not such a bad thing because in such an outcome we can cry with the apostle, "Lord, save me for I am perishing." Our failure itself has had a good result; it has taught us to recognize our dependence on the Lord, and it has opened the door to a heartfelt prayer. If we hadn't taken the risk, we would not have failed; if we had not failed, we wouldn't have prayed. In such a way our spiritual life inches forward. (August 1, 2011.)

> *Lord Jesus Christ, give us faith as large as a grain of mustard so that we can move the mountains that obscure you from our sight. Teach us to walk on water so that we may continue your mission in the world, that all may be saved and come to the knowledge of the truth. For you are our Lord for ever and ever. Amen.*

December 16   ✠   *Walls*

When Pope Paul VI visited the Philippines, Imelda Marcos arranged for him to visit her hometown of Tacloban. As planning progressed, it became evident that there was a problem. The road connecting the airport to the center of the city ran through some of the worst slums in the island. Not the sort of thing you would want a distinguished visitor to see. Marcos's solution was to build a high wall along the side of the road, on the understanding that what you cannot see will not upset you.

This is a trick with which we may ourselves be familiar: to wall off from consciousness whatever might disturb us. Like the priest and the Levite in the story of the Good Samaritan, we cross to the other side of the road so that we can claim not to have seen the wounded traveler calling out for our help. And at the Last Judgment we will stretch out exculpatory hands and appeal to the Judge, "When did we see you in need?"

The wall blocks out challenges, but it also blocks the urgings of our conscience calling us to repentance. How unlike King David we are. When the prophet Nathan accused him of adultery and murder, he didn't seek refuge in phony explanations or excuses but said simply, "I have sinned." Most of us have not reached that level of honesty; we offer excuses, minimize the fault, distract attention, blame others, or attack the accuser. If all else fails we confess to the lesser evil: ignorance. "Nobody told me it was wrong," or "I didn't know the gun was loaded!"

As adults we remain responsible for the effects of our mindless living, for being unaware or thoughtless. If you are involved in a traffic accident due to inattention, it is no use saying to the police officer, "I had my eyes closed at the time" or "I was speaking on my phone." A chosen lack of awareness increases the level of fault. It is no excuse.

Walls that limit awareness separate us from life-giving challenges. They also prevent us from acknowledging our true guilt, asking pardon, and receiving the precious gift of mercy. They need to be demolished. (September 26, 2004.)

Lord Jesus Christ, you have taught us to live in the truth of love. Help us to recognize life-giving choices as they present themselves so that we may habitually choose what is good

*and reject what is evil. For you are our Lord for ever and
ever. Amen.*

December 17 ✠ **Wavering**

Saint Peter probably would have preferred not to respond to Jesus'
question, "Who do you say I am?" In such circumstances, it is
much easier to sit on the fence than to commit oneself to a definite answer. No doubt Peter himself was surprised by the profession of faith that came forth from his mouth. Expressing himself
with the first words that came to his lips, he bypassed his brain
and spoke straight from the heart. This Jesus recognized. Peter's
answer was not the considered response of human reasoning but
the spontaneous expression of what, all the while, he was learning
at the very center of his being. The Father had revealed the truth
to a little one; it was from the Spirit of God that he spoke. Hidden behind human words, a divine mystery was expressing itself.

Peter's bold statement was at odds with the life he lived and
the way he thought. It was a seed planted by God that had yet
to sprout and grow and bear fruit. It was a beginning. Meanwhile,
Peter had the humbling experience of discovering how little influence this gift had on the rest of his life. Like us, he soon discovered that even the most fervent beginning is often bedeviled by
distractions, deviations, dalliances, and even defeats.

Yet Peter's subsequent history shows us that he kept stumbling
forward until, at the end, he willingly embraced the cross he had
previously feared and fled. Peter would never have proposed
himself as a model of unwavering fidelity to those who came
after. All his life he seems to have wavered and wobbled. In the
end, however, his commitment to Jesus won through. Why?
Because, despite the instability of the disciple, Jesus remained
committed to him. Divine grace flourished in the fertile field of
Peter's weakness. (August 22, 1993.)

*Lord Jesus Christ, when you called Simon Peter you knew
that he was a person of many weaknesses, as we are. As you*

*supported him in his journey, remain also with us, and bring
us safely to that more abundant life which you have promised
to those who follow you. Hear us, for you are our Lord for
ever and ever. Amen.*

December 18 ✠ *Whole Story*

For most people, the prospect that everything is known and about
to be revealed would seem more like a threat than a promise. If
some exotic guru came to town who was able to read hearts, I
would probably buy a ticket to somewhere else. The fact of the
matter is that there is probably enough evidence to sink any of
us: youthful indiscretions, unguarded remarks, personal failures,
bad moods, and maybe moments of real nastiness. The last thing
that we want is to find all this on the front page of the newspaper.

I have often thought that it would be possible to produce two
distinct films of my life, one presenting me as a worthless scoundrel, the other advancing the case for my canonization. Both true.
The knack is in the editing. In my life—and I suspect in most
lives—there is abundant material to support both propositions
if presented selectively.

This means that if I, or anybody else for that matter, want to
make a judgment about the quality of my life as a whole, I have
to take the whole of the evidence into consideration. That is not
possible at this time because, last time I checked, I was still alive.
Snap assessments are habitually wrong. We need to delay a final
judgment until . . . the Final Judgment. Maybe it will be revealed
that those whom we demonize have played an important role in
the unrolling of the divine plan of salvation. We are not God. We
cannot tell the relative merits of individual lives.

There is an important text in the First Epistle of Saint John
that is worth remembering. "Even if our heart condemns us, God
is greater than our heart and knows everything." This seems to
suggest that God's judgment may be even more benign than that
of our own conscience. This is not to whitewash the evil we may

have done; it is merely to see it in the context of a lifetime's experience. This is God's specialty. We don't know enough to arrive at this point. That is why our negative judgments are so often unfair and unjust.

We can improve matters if we learn to postpone judgment until we have heard more of the story. We need the emptiness to listen to the whole story without letting our prejudices or our personal needs preempt the openness that allows the story to unfold. We will often find that there is more to a situation than we imagined. (June 22, 2008.)

> *Loving Father, you know of what we are made, and you love and accept us as we are. Help us to be gentle in our dealings with others, and teach us to withhold judgment until that glorious day when you come to judge the living and the dead. We ask this through Christ our Lord. Amen.*

December 19 ✠ **Widow's Mite**

If everyone in the country sent me one dollar, I would be a very rich man indeed. We sometimes forget that, more often than not, big things are simply an accumulation of little things. Little acorns into mighty oaks do grow! What happens for many of us is that we underestimate the small challenges that come our way and, instead, wait for something really big. When it does not materialize, we wonder why our lives seem to lack substance. On the other hand, we sometimes fail to realize that disasters are compounded because of a failure to do small things. We don't change the battery in the smoke detector, and so the house burns down. There are so many tragedies that could have been avoided by a small measure of foresight and appropriate preemptive action.

The gospel picture of the widow putting her last two coins into the temple treasury shows us that the size of the gift is measured more by subjective dispositions than by its monetary worth. The widow gave her all to God, her whole life. She could have kept back one of the coins for a rainy day, but she did not. She could have asked what difference this paltry donation would make when all the elite are giving from their abundance, but she did not. She gave simply, generously and without expecting any return.

A first lesson we can draw from this scene is that we should not underestimate the value of doing what we can, even if it seems of relatively little value. The giving is always more significant than the gift. A bunch of roses can be more valued than the gift of a racehorse, if it comes as a token of greater love. A second lesson is that we should not be afraid to give our all. The God who gives seed to the sower and bread for food will ensure that we are not left without resources.

The church is being strangled by minimalists: lawyers, accountants, and measurers of moral merit. Faith demands a certain boldness, a willingness to take risks without quibbling or compromise. If we seek first and foremost the kingdom of God, then we too will find that all other things will be given us in addition. (November 10, 1991.)

Loving Father, you care bounteously for all creation and repay those who leave all with a hundredfold in return. Help us to be generous in sharing what we have, recognizing that your gifts are intended for the benefit of all. We ask this through Christ our Lord. Amen.

December 20 ✠ **Windows**

The sixth chapter of Saint John's gospel runs to thirty column inches in the NRSV. It would have profited from the services of a good editor. It is incredibly rich in content, but there are so many diverse themes that readers may find themselves bedazzled. It really requires long hours of close reading, trying to keep all the different ideas together and allowing oneself to be stretched in the process.

In different ways throughout the chapter Jesus is presenting himself as the gift of the Father. In this gospel, the word *give* is often associated with God, as though it were an essential characteristic of the divine activity in the world. God gives. Above all, God so loves the world that he gives the Son. The effect of that giving is that we begin to share God's own life. Even as we continue to live and move in space and time, we are, in some incomprehensible way, already sharing in the eternal life of God.

For the evangelist, space and time exist within eternity, just as our Earth is only one small planet among millions of stars. We think much of what happens around us is of cosmic importance, even though it has little impact outside our own limited sphere of existence. As well might an ant think it can influence global events by what transpires within its own tiny colony. Yet Saint John sees time and eternity as interrelated. We are already living in eternity, except that we lack the capacity to perceive it. When we act under the influence of God, our actions have eternal significance. We are beginning to redeem time, repainting it, as it were, in the colors of eternity.

There are two windows in our world that enable a free flow between time and eternity. The first is personal faith, which allows us to see the world differently, to evaluate events differently, and to act in accordance with the model proposed by Jesus. It is by faith that we make personal contact with God in prayer and reinforce the bonds that maintain our connection. The second is by our participation in the life of the church and especially in the celebration of the Lord's Supper in memory of him. This takes us out of our narrow individualism and joins us in communion with the catholicity of God's people—the faithful of every age and in every continent who are with us, one heart and one soul. This is the celebration of the mystery where time and eternity overlap and intermingle. (August 17, 2003.)

Creator God, in you we live and move and have our being. Help us to become conscious of your presence in our daily lives and to live mindful that our days on earth are spent on a journey that will lead us to everlasting life. We make this prayer in the name of Jesus our Lord. Amen.

December 21 ✠ ***Winning Your Enemies***

The unity for which Christ prayed is a beautiful ideal, but it is not so easy to bring about on a practical level. Because each of us is unique, it is inevitable that there will be differences—and hence conflicts—among us. Every society has to devise strategies and tactics for dealing with internal division and resolving conflict. We might ask, How does the Christian community confront such issues?

When there are differences we often interpret them as constituting a win-lose situation. My efforts go toward ensuring that my claim to rightness is upheld and attacks against it are defeated. For me to feel that my grievance has been addressed, I need to see the other party proved wrong.

Jesus talks rather of winning your brother or sister. Not winning the argument. In the case of an objective wrong done to us—Jesus says, "If your brother or sister sins against you"—we are commanded to try to bring healing to the relationship on a one-to-one basis, perhaps explaining how we have been hurt without suggesting malign motivations or intentions. But as the first-century "Teaching of the Twelve Apostles" admonishes us, such an intervention must take place "in peace and not in anger." And Saint Benedict suggests that we take care to choose an appropriate time and place in which to make the approach. The relationship should be better after the intervention, not worse.

Whether the hurt is precipitate or long term, I must be prepared to let go of it. Sometimes people live for their grievances rather than with them; if the issue is solved, they fear that life will seem emptier. They have defined themselves by the hurts inflicted on them. We have to develop the adult capacity to tolerate those things that we cannot change, without losing our self-esteem. And if we really want things to get better, we should pray for peace, pray for our enemy, cast a sharper eye over our own lives to determine our contribution to the fray. And be prepared to give forgiveness at a discount. (September 8, 1996.)

Loving Father, forgive us our sins as we forgive those who sin against us. Help us to contribute to the unity for which Christ prayed so that where two or three gather in his name, he may be in our midst. We ask this in the name of Jesus our Lord. Amen.

December 22   ✠   With

One of the most important words in the Bible is *with*. Through all the changes of their tumultuous history, God's chosen people retained a sense that the Lord was with them. In the fullness of time God sent the Son to be our Immanuel—God-with-us. And Jesus himself repeats the promise to be with his followers in every age and in every place until the end of time.

The problem with this is that we are happy to have God at our side when things are going badly and we need some outside assistance, but when the sun shines and all our plans prosper, we turn our attention elsewhere. As one of our contemporaries remarked, "We have everything we want. We have no need of God." This is the exact opposite of what was said during the World War I: "There are no atheists in the trenches."

Many times in his writings Saint Augustine laments the fact that while God is always present to us, we are present to God only rarely. Our minds and hearts are elsewhere. We want to shake off any sense of dependence on God so that we can live what we believe to be an autonomous life.

God's presence to us in Christ is not a matter of surveillance— a permanent CCTV camera watching everything we do, with a view to catching us red-handed in the commission of a crime. Not so much watching us as watching out for us. Christ's presence with us is by way of accompaniment. Saint Bernard describes three ways by which Christ's presence forms around us. He is a dear friend, a wise counselor, and a strong helper. Christ is with us to give us a boost by his company, to support and console us. Christ is with us to be light for our conscience and a guide in times of confusion. Christ is with us to strengthen us by his grace to do that which otherwise seems impossible.

If Christ is with us, it makes sense for us to make the effort to be with him: to become aware of his presence as to seek his assistance in transcending our loneliness, our ignorance, and our weakness. To the extent that we open ourselves to his invisible action in our soul, our lives will become simpler, our hearts lighter, and our difficult times more bearable. (August 30, 2012.)

Lord Jesus Christ, dear friend, wise counselor, strong helper, remain with us as the evening of life approaches. Be our support and guide and consolation in all the challenges of life so that we may perform with willing heart the work you have assigned to each of us. For you are our Lord, for ever and ever. Amen.

December 23 ✝ **Withdrawal**

No matter how fervent we may consider ourselves, there is a precarious quality about the spiritual life that renders it prone to exhaustion. Romano Guardini once wrote, "Part of wisdom is to be careful of one's own wisdom. It is a virtue which is easily spoiled." There are periods in our life when everything seems to be going swimmingly and we find it difficult to restrain our admiration at our rapid progress. But, fortunately, these delusional intervals do not last long. Very soon we are back in the situation where the dogs of temptation are snapping at our heels and, even if we try to resist them, making our life miserable.

Mostly we are the source of our temptations. Sometimes this is because we have not recognized the full truth of our humanity: that we need to work hard to ensure that our worthy aspirations are not undermined by instinctual tendencies. Sometimes we are troubled because we have allowed ourselves to be invaded by toxic influences that create desires in us that are so strong that they seem to be needs. We cannot live without them. Thus, our noblest beliefs are often eroded by the sustained preaching of contrary values by the organs of social communication. Furthermore, our capacity to distinguish between what is true and what is false is often degraded by the excessive time we dedicate to entertainment. As Saint Bernard once remarked, an appetite for trivia involves turning our back on truth, and this leads to a decline in our capacity to discern. If you repeatedly use a chisel to open paint tins, it will lose its edge and no longer serve the purpose for which it was made.

The remedy is to withdraw, to spend some time apart, away from the shouting that aims to shape what we feel and how we think. To turn off the electronic devices and allow ourselves to experience a measure of solitude. This may seem threatening because we are exposed to unexpected data about ourselves, but such self-knowledge only brings us closer to the truth of our essential vulnerability. A good thing, if it makes us more careful. (February 26, 2012.)

Redeemer God, you formed your chosen people by leading them into the desert so that they could learn to depend on you alone. Help us to know our need for solitude and silence so that we might open ourselves more completely to your love. We ask this through Christ our Lord. Amen.

December 24 ✠ *Wrinkles*

Wrinkles come from a loss of flexibility. The skin gets old and tired and begins to sag. It is unable to keep up with the demand for constant change. It is the same for much-used wineskins. They are wrinkled, wizened, and withered, unable to cope with the outbursting vitality of the wine fermenting within. And so, calamity strikes and all is lost.

Perhaps the same is happening to me. I have become an old wineskin, set in my ways, fearful to accept new wine. Afraid that the energy of the new will burst me asunder. And so I remain empty. There is no wine to rejoice my heart. I am one of those of whom Mary said to Jesus, "They have no wine." A dry, weary land without moisture. The victim of life's journey, I was laid low and fell to the roadside, half-dead and hopeless. The priest and Levite pass by on the other side of the road, averting their gaze. No matter; they will join me soon enough.

Now I hear a call to look up and to lift up my heart, for a Good Samaritan approaches. He lifts me up from the dung heap and pours in oil with the wine. The oil of gladness to make the face shine, to soften the skin and make it smooth, bringing back the vigor and joy of youth. No longer wrinkled and fearful, I am ready to receive the new wine.

Our Good Samaritan exclaims, "Behold, I make all things new" and pours in the wine of the Spirit. The old age of sin is brought to nothing; my youth is renewed and my innocence restored. The new wine of Pentecost causes me to skip around like a young calf—even though it is only midmorning—and boisterously to proclaim the Good News to the world.

The spiritual world is marked by paradox. The humble are exalted, the hungry fed, and the rich and powerful dismissed and disgraced. Even though our visible body is aging day by day, our inward self keeps growing younger and stronger. By grace we find ourselves ever more willing to embrace the emerging new that God is accomplishing on earth, when the church will be seen as she really is, without spot or wrinkle. (February 27, 2000.)

Loving Father, we stand in need of two things. We ask that you heal our grumpy resistance to what is new and, at the same time, to flood our souls with a deep spirit of joy and celebration, so that we may proclaim to the world the wonders of your love. And we ask this in the name of Jesus our Lord. Amen.

December 25 ✠ *Wrong*

I think the world would be a better place if we could learn to repeat often what I may term "the magic mantra." Three words, easy to say but not heard so often. "I was wrong." It takes a certain measure of magnanimity to admit that I was in error or that I made a mistake. Perhaps my facts were wrong. Perhaps my opinion was unbalanced. Perhaps the way I expressed myself was hurtful. There are many ways in which a communication can go wrong, and I must accept responsibility for at least some of them.

When I engage in conversation, I am not only communicating information. For pure information, a person can consult reference books or take their chances on the internet. When I speak, more is happening than a transfer of data. If someone asks me the time of the next train to Tunbridge Wells, I don't just give a robotic recital of the facts. I communicate some emotion. I smile and answer courteously. Or I scowl and say, "Don't ask me, look at the timetable!" Almost everything we say comes packaged with emotion; it gives some indication of the state of the relationship.

It may well be that we always communicate correct facts, but sometimes the manner in which this is done requires us to undertake some repair work on the relationship. The first step toward this is learning to apologize and admit that we were, in some way, at fault. To build a bridge instead of a wall. To learn to go halfway and beyond to maintain contact.

The primitive Christian community strove to be of one heart and one mind. Yet the evidence that we have from the Acts of the Apostles shows that conflicts occurred then, just as they do now. This means that mechanisms of reconciliation had to be included in the dynamic of this common life: learning to live with differences, to let go of longstanding grievances, and to be proactive in moving toward forgiveness. That is probably the way ahead for us also. (September 5, 1999.)

Lord Jesus Christ, you have taught us to forgive those who offend us seventy-seven times and more. Give us a generosity of spirit that does not repay evil with evil but, instead, prays for those who now seem to be our enemies. For you are our Lord for ever and ever. Amen.

December 26 ✠ ***Wrong-Footed***

When I was a small boy at school, I was envious of the Emperor Constantine. Not so much because he ruled over a vast empire, but more because he had seemed to have the religious thing sewn up. This was my response to learning that he had put off his baptism until his deathbed. This delay meant that he had more elbow room during his life, avoided the necessity of confession, and still managed to sail serenely into paradise.

There is a lot of labor in being a Christian. We may think that the martyrs had it easy. Their moment of struggle was intense but relatively brief. Ours goes on and on and leaves no corner of our life untouched. We are sometimes acutely conscious of how much sacrifice is demanded of those who accept the invitation to follow Christ. At this point, however, we are in danger of taking on the role of the Pharisees, emphasizing what we do for God and wrongly thinking that our effort is what makes us commendable to God.

The opposite is true. God loved us first, before we had any chance of building up a high score of meritorious actions. Anything good we do comes from God; it is intended to be a demonstration of God's love for us, not a cause for blowing our own trumpet. If, however, we fall into the trap of self-satisfaction, God's love seeks to liberate us from our complacency by catching us wrong-footed, by allowing us to face a situation in which failure is inevitable. Not any minor sort of reversal, but failure in an area in which hitherto we had secretly been so proud. Such a disaster, however, is life-giving, if it teaches us that we too will have to rely on the indulgent mercy of God.

In heaven we will be surprised at how little of our goodness was due to ourselves and how much to God, usually working through others. We are more like Constantine than we assume. If, when we get to heaven, someone were to ask us how long we had to work in the vineyard to gain entry, we will probably say in all truthfulness, "Not long at all. I arrived at work well past the eleventh hour. I received from God much more than I deserved." (September 20, 1987.)

Loving Father, teach us to value your gifts to us above our own achievements. Help us to recognize that all that we have comes from your creative love, and all that happens comes from your fatherly concern. We ask this through Christ our Lord. Amen.

December 27   ✝   *X-Ray Vision*

It is becoming more common for airline passengers to be submitted to a body scanner before moving into the departure area. Passengers, if they are permitted to see anything, see only a cartoon image, but those observing behind the screen can penetrate the clothing and make sure that nothing is hidden underneath.

The Epistle to Hebrews tells us that God's word is like this. It is sharper than a double-edged sword, can penetrate right through to the division of soul and spirit, and is able to discern the quality of the desires and thoughts of the heart. Nothing can be hidden. All is naked and exposed. For most of us that is a bit threatening. We often like to play our cards close to the chest. We probably don't want others to know all that we know about ourselves, and we are even more reluctant to let them know what we don't know. I think that if somebody told me that there was a prophet who could read hearts, I would probably run a mile in the opposite direction.

Jesus himself knew the human heart. In the seventh chapter of Saint Mark's gospel he tells us what is inside: evil thoughts, fornications, thefts, murders, acts of greed, acts of malice. He also lists the vices from which these actions come: deceit, lewdness, envy, slander, arrogance, stupidity. Look at your neighbor. There may be no visible evidence of wrongdoing, but inside it may well be a different story. Look at yourself, and the same applies. Even if someone is able to say, "I am innocent of all these sins," that may be due to a lack of incentive or opportunity. And it is not necessarily a guarantee for the future.

Many of the saints enjoy a degree of x-ray vision similar to that evidenced by Jesus. Usually this is because they have first advanced far along the road of self-knowledge. Most of the vices preexist in the heart before they find external expression. They are inherent in human nature and, hence, universal. If you know yourself and your own vices, it is not so difficult to predict in what ways others will be tempted. There is no value in denial or repression. Rather, if we x-ray ourselves we will be able to uncover the unhealthy tendencies that influence the decisions we make. Then we can quarantine them or neutralize them, and then we will have the possibility of making better or more lifegiving choices. (August 30, 2009.)

Lord Jesus Christ, like us in all things but sin, you discern the workings of our inner self. Teach us to look within and to learn to live with the truth about ourselves so that we may always feel dependent on your mercy and willing to be indulgent toward others. For you are our Lord for ever and ever.

December 28 ✝ **Yes**

Saint Luke's account of the annunciation is more a tableau for our meditation than an historical account of a particular event. Despite the angelic apparition and the lofty language used, it is a simple story. Familiarity does not lessen the shock of what it narrates. God has made the whole plan of salvation dependent on the consent of one person: a young girl in a small village in an occupied country on the outskirts of empire. This girl has been given a veto on salvation history.

Saint Bernard dramatizes this moment with passionate artistry. Adam, Abraham, David, and all the great figures of the Old Testament are on the sidelines, breathlessly awaiting her response to the angel's summons. People of future generations stand in suspenseful silence to see which way the wind will blow. Here we have the cardinal point of cosmic history.

Mary's "Yes, let God do this" comes without any trace of presumption or elation. There seems to be no resistance or reserve. Just a simple yes. She describes herself as the Lord's slave-girl—the word *handmaid* softens the phrase that Saint Luke puts into her mouth—she is ready to do whatever is asked of her.

Jesus' conception is presented as the result of a total openness to God's saving will. Jesus' first moment of human existence is stamped with the word *yes*. "Here I am, I come to do your will." There was to be no "yes" and "no" in Jesus; he was to be all yes. He was God's "Amen" to Mary's assent, to the desire of all humanity, to the upsurging of all creation.

In the prayer for the feast of the Annunciation, we pray that we may become more like Jesus whom we acknowledge as our redeemer. This seems to imply that we are to become co-redeemers. How? By offering an unconditional yes to God and a determined no to unredeemed passions, prejudices, and our inherent nastiness. We do this in the awareness that each choice we make either advances the kingdom of God or resists it. Surprisingly, we also exercise a veto on God's plan of salvation—albeit a partial one. We can accept the mission entrusted to us, or we can turn aside; we can offer a cup of cold water to a thirsty throat or drink it ourselves. We are given the opportunity to add our "Amen" to the Good News; it is a chance too good to miss. (March 31, 2008.)

> *Loving Father, in many ways and at different times you call us, and you offer us the opportunity to share in your work of bringing all things to completion in Christ. Give us a generous heart to accept your summons and a humble willingness to devote ourselves entirely to your service. We ask this through Christ our Lord. Amen.*

December 29 ✟ *Yesterday's Troubles*

There is a plaintive song that I remember from my childhood, but have not been able to trace. It ran, "Yesterday's troubles are over and done. / Don't think of tomorrow, it hasn't begun." The last line contained the message "Making the most of each day." I don't know why I remember it, but it is good advice.

If getting older leads us to some kind of mellow wisdom, we begin to appreciate the relativity of all that happens to us and around us. So much of what we get het up about is of the most passing importance. In a week, a month, a year, it doesn't matter; we wonder why we were so upset. It is not that "life is mostly froth and bubble," or only the sum of "vanity of vanities"; life is very important, and the choices we make are of eternal significance. The danger is, however, that we become so obsessed with trifles that we fail to take a stand on the important issues with which we are confronted.

All of us make mistakes, some of them serious; mostly we carry on without looking back. This changes as life gets simpler, when we have fewer responsibilities and less to preoccupy us. We begin to revisit our past. At first there is a pleasant glow of nostalgia, but, slowly, we begin to remember the bad choices we made and the harmful behavior in which we indulged. It is as though we are being asked to settle accounts for actions long since passed. Sometimes shame or bitterness can spring up from nowhere and we begin to have doubts about the value of our past performance. We need to accept that this negativity is not only normal, it is profitable. It enlarges the scope of our self-knowledge and is a source of purification to the soul. It is usually a sign that grace is active.

If we are powerless to change the past, then we are, in a different way, unable to cope with the future before it arrives. Fearful projections about the future can prevent us from attending to the present. Without neglecting prudent foresight, we would do well to remember that just as we coped in the past, so we will survive whatever turns up on our doorstep.

Life is like a game of tennis. Stop reviewing the last ball. Stop trying to anticipate the next ball. Deal with the one that is coming straight at you. For the moment, it's the only one that matters. (August 23, 1998.)

*Creator God, Master of all our days, give us the wisdom to
take seriously the opportunities and challenge that we meet
today. Heal our wounded past. Give us courage to face whatever the future brings. And help us to discover in all that
happens the imprint of your loving concern. We ask this in
the name of Jesus our Lord. Amen.*

December 30   ✠   *You Are What You Eat*

This was the title of a series on BBC television based on a book
by Gillian McKeith. As it happens, it is good theology as well.
We become what we eat. When we receive the Body and Blood
of Christ sacramentally, we are engaging in a process of becoming
Christ, of being transformed into Christ and so capable of receiving the gift of eternal life.

This is a theme that recurs during the liturgy of the Christmas
season. The Word became human so that humans may become
divine. We might say that the ultimate purpose of the incarnation
is the divinization of humanity. This transformation is accomplished in all the elements of the liturgy, but especially when we
receive Holy Communion.

Since Vatican II the liturgy has been made more generally
accessible. Thanks be to God! The downside has been that there
has been a danger that when the liturgy became less mystifying,
we tended to reduce it to a series of human actions: gathering,
listening, contributing to the collection, praying, receiving communion. We tried to upgrade these as much as we could. In the
meantime, perhaps, we lost sight of the action of Christ in the
liturgy, accomplishing a work of sanctification far beyond any
human capability. There is something marvelous happening here
that surpasses human understanding. A mystery is being realized
in our midst.

In this mystery of faith we are in the process of being changed,
not dramatically, but in small increments throughout a lifetime.
In a wondrous exchange God's Son became human so that we

might become divine. Simultaneously, by eating Christ's Body we become Christ's Body, the Eucharistic community that is the church. Corporately we are Christ, individual members of his Body, called to belong together, to work together, and to create a unity. It is in the cohesion of all these different people who constitute Christ's Body that we are empowered to be living embodiments of the Gospel and channels of life and hope to all whom we encounter. We are called to be other Christs. (August 19, 2012.)

Lord Jesus Christ, you are the head of the body that is your church. Teach us how to contribute to the unity for which you prayed so that all may come to salvation and the knowledge of the truth. For you are our Lord forever. Amen.

December 31 ☩ *Zacchaeus*

Many of us don't have a clear idea of the emotional content of the term *tax collector* as it is used in the gospels. As a class these were unlovable men. They collaborated with the occupying Romans, they were extortioners, they were men of violence threatening those who could not meet their claims. Worst of all, they were rich, appropriate targets of envy for those with less. In general, good people shunned them. One of the surprises of the Gospel tradition is that it shows that Jesus seemed as happy to associate with them as he was with worthier people.

The story of Jesus' encounter with Zacchaeus is attractive because of all the colorful details that the evangelist included in his narrative. In Zacchaeus we get an idea of how grace works in our life. First of all, it inspires a thought that quickly transforms itself into a desire. He wants to see Jesus. Then comes the blockade of reason: that is not possible, you are too short. This is the usual form assumed by temptation at this stage. But Zacchaeus is not paralyzed by the difficulty; he acts. He runs ahead of the crowd. Then his imagination inspires some lateral thinking: "Climb a tree." And so the desired encounter takes place. But still grace works on. Meeting Jesus inspires him to change his life, to confess his sins, and to begin to do good.

The encounter with Zacchaeus inspired Jesus to set forth his mission statement: to seek out and save what was lost. Not to hobnob with the pious and respectable, but to build bridges to those who are apart, to preach the Good News to the disadvantaged. In clearly stating this sense of mission, Jesus is inviting us to join him in putting it into practice.

Our faith often inhabits a self-contained world. We are not so enthusiastic in reaching out to renegades and scoundrels but prefer to keep it to ourselves. Perhaps this is because we don't really appreciate what we have received. Usually, if we have good news, we want to share it. If somebody spills red wine on a tablecloth, everyone at the table is anxious to proclaim their particular good news of how to treat the stain. We can't hold it in. But we are rather reserved when it comes to stepping out of our routine to communicate to others the Good News by which we live. When a door opens, we should leap through. (November 4, 2007.)

> *Lord Jesus Christ, you came to call those who are weak and lost. Look on us with mercy and come to our aid. Strengthen our weakness, and guide our steps into paths that will lead us to a fuller life. And teach us to share what we have received with those who still stand in need. For you are our Lord for ever and ever. Amen.*